International Conference WWW/Internet 2019

Cagliari, Italy
7 - 9 November 2019

Editors:

Pedro Isaias
Luis Rodrigues

ISBN: 978-1-7138-0305-8

Printed from e-media with permission by:

Curran Associates, Inc.
57 Morehouse Lane
Red Hook, NY 12571

Some format issues inherent in the e-media version may also appear in this print version.

International Association for Development of the Information Society (IADIS)
Rua Sao Sebastiao Da Pedreira
No. 100, 30, 1050-209
Lisbon, Portugal

Phone: 351 21 3151373
Fax: 351 21 3151244

secretariat@iadis.org

Additional copies of this publication are available from:

Curran Associates, Inc.
57 Morehouse Lane
Red Hook, NY 12571 USA
Phone: 845-758-0400
Fax: 845-758-2633
Email: curran@proceedings.com
Web: www.proceedings.com

PROCEEDINGS OF THE 18th INTERNATIONAL CONFERENCE on WWW/INTERNET 2019

CAGLIARI, ITALY

NOVEMBER 7-9, 2019

Organised by

iadis

international association for development of the information society

Co-Organised by

As a member of Crossref (a non-profit membership organization for scholarly publishing working with the purpose to make content easy to find, link, cite and assess) each published paper in this book of proceedings will be allocated a DOI (Digital Object Identifier) number for its fast and easy citation and indexation.

Edited by Pedro Isaías

Associate Editor: Luís Rodrigues

TABLE OF CONTENTS

FULL PAPERS

SHORT PAPERS

POSTERS

DOCTORAL CONSORTIUM

FOREWORD

This book of proceedings contains the papers and posters of the 18th International Conference on WWW/Internet (ICWI 2019), held from 7 to 9 November 2019, organized by the International Association for Development of the Information Society (IADIS) and co-organised by University Degli Studi di Cagliari, Italy.

The WWW/Internet (ICWI) 2019 Conference aims to address the main issues of concern within WWW/Internet. WWW and Internet had a huge development in recent years. Aspects of concern are no longer just technical anymore but other aspects have arisen. This conference aims to cover both technological as well as non-technological issues related to these developments.

Submissions were accepted under the following main tracks and topics:

- Web 2.0
  - Collaborative Systems
  - Social Networks
  - Folksonomies
  - Enterprise Wikis and Blogging
  - Mashups and Web Programming
  - Tagging and User Rating Systems
  - Citizen Journalism

- Semantic Web and XML
  - Semantics Web Architectures
  - Semantic Web Middleware
  - Semantic Web Services
  - Semantic Web Agents
  - Ontologies
  - Applications of Semantic Web
  - Semantic Web Data Management
  - Information Retrieval in Semantic Web

- Applications and Uses
  - e-Learning
  - e-Commerce / e-Business
  - e-Government
  - e-Health
  - e-Procurement
  - e-Society
  - Digital Libraries
  - Web Services/SaaS
  - Application Interoperability
  - Web-based Multimedia Technologies

- Services, Architectures and Web Development
  - Wireless Web
  - Mobile Web
  - Cloud/Grid Computing
  - Web Metrics
  - Web Standards
  - Internet Architectures
  - Network Algorithms
  - Network Architectures
  - Network Computing
  - Network Management
  - Network Performance
  - Content Delivery Technologies
  - Protocols and Standards
  - Traffic Models

- Research Issues
  - Web Science
  - Digital Rights Management
  - Bioinformatics
  - Human Computer Interaction and Usability
  - Web Security and Privacy
  - Online Trust and Reputation Systems
  - Data Mining
  - Information Retrieval
  - Search Engine Optimization

This event received 103 submissions from more than 19 countries. Each submission has been anonymously reviewed by an average of four independent reviewers, to ensure the final high standard of the accepted submissions. The final result was the approval of 16 full papers, which means that the acceptance rate was 16%. A few more papers have been accepted as short and doctoral papers and posters/demonstrations. Best papers will be selected for publishing as extended versions in the IADIS International Journal on WWW/Internet (IJWI) (ISSN:1645-7641).

The conference, besides the papers' and posters' presentations, also features two keynote presentations from internationally distinguished researchers. We therefore would like to express our gratitude to our keynote speakers: Dr. Virginia Pilloni (Department of Electrical and Electronic Engineering, University of Cagliari, Italy) and Professor Luigi Atzori (Multimedia & Communication Lab (MC Lab) Head, University of Cagliari, Italy).

As we all know, organising these conferences requires the effort of many individuals. We would like to thank all members of the Program Committee for their hard work in reviewing and selecting the papers that appear in the proceedings.

We are especially grateful to the authors who submitted their papers to this conference and to the presenters who provided the substance of the meetings.

This Proceedings book contains a rich experience of the academic & research institutions and the industry on diverse themes related to the Internet and Web. We do hope that researchers, knowledge workers and innovators both in academia and the industry will find it a valuable reference material.

Last but not the least, we hope that everybody will have a good time in Cagliari, Italy and we invite all participants for the next year's edition of the International Conference on WWW/Internet.

Pedro Isaías, The University of New South Wales (UNSW Sydney), Australia
Conference & Program Chair

Cagliari, Italy
November 2019

PROGRAM COMMITTEE

CONFERENCE & PROGRAM CHAIR
Pedro Isaías, The University of New South Wales (UNSW Sydney), Australia

LOCAL CHAIR
Maria Lidia Mascia, University Degli Studi di Cagliari, Italy

COMMITTEE MEMBERS

Abdolhossein Sarrafzadeh, UNITEC New Zealand, New Zealand
Agostino Poggi, Università degli Studi di Parma, Italy
Alexander Troussov, Russian Academy of National Economy, Ireland
Amaury Trujillo, Iit-cnr, Italy
Andrea Kienle, University of Applied Sciences, Dortmund, Germany
Andreas Schrader, Insitute of Telematics, University of Luebeck, Germany
Anirban Kundu, Netaji Subhash Engineering College, India
Asadullah Shaikh, Najran University, Saudi Arabia
Chih-Cheng Hung, Kenneaaw State University, USA
Christos Bouras, University of Patras, Greece
Costas Yialouris, Agricultural University of Athens, Greece
Cristiano Costa, Universidade do Vale do Rio dos Sinos (Unisinos), Brazil
Daniel Cunliffe, University of South Wales, United Kingdom
Debajyoti Mukhopadhyay, NHITM of Mumbai University, India
Diana Andone, Politehnica University of Timisoara, Romania
Dickson Lukose, Personal, Australia
Dirk Bade, University of Hamburg, Germany
Dirk Thissen, Rwth Aachen, Germany
Elias Kirche, Florida Gulf Coast University, USA
Erick López Ornelas, Universidad Autónoma Metropolitana - Cuajimalpa, Mexico
Evangelos Sakkopoulos, University Of Patras, Greece
Fan Zhao, Florida Gulf Coast University, USA
Fuensanta Medina-Dominguez, Universidad Carlos III de Madrid, Spain
George Koutromanos, National and Kapodistrian University of Athens, Greece
Hector Migallon Gomis, University Miguel Hernandez, Spain
Hsiao Hsien-Sheng, National Taiwan Normal University, Taiwan
Isidoros Perikos, University of Patras, Greece
Ivanna Dronyuk, Lviv Polytechnic National University, Ukraine
James Thong, Hong Kong University of Science and Technology, Hong Kong
Janez Brank, Jozef Stefan Institute, Slovenia
Jörg Roth, Nuremberg Institute of Technology, Germany

KEYNOTE LECTURES

FORGET ABOUT THE BILL: IOT-BASED SOLUTIONS TOWARDS THE NET ZERO ENERGY BUILDING

Dr. Virginia Pilloni
Department of Electrical and Electronic Engineering,
University of Cagliari, Italy

Abstract

Smart Buildings Energy and Comfort Management Systems (BECM) are characterized by the presence of sensors, actuators and smart devices that give the opportunity to monitor and remotely control key equipment within buildings. In such an intelligent scenario, one of the major goals is to provide decision-support tools that enable users to make cost-effective decisions in terms of energy consumption. As a matter of fact, domestic electricity usage currently accounts for about 40% of the global energy consumption and contributes over 30% of total greenhouse gas (GHG) emissions. One of the main EU targets for 2050 is to achieve net-zero GHG emissions, which means transforming buildings and neighborhoods to develop net-zero energy districts. Nevertheless, user comfort is crucial when policies of Demand-Side Management (DSM) are put in place. Indeed, a system that optimizes energy consumption without considering user preferences and habits about appliance usage quickly leads to user disaffection from the system and abandonment of it.

The objective of this talk is to analyze the opportunities and challenges related to efficient management of energy within Smart Building and Smart Neighborhood scenarios. The talk will first introduce the technologies that can be used to address these challenges. It will later focus on the main approaches proposed by the literature for smart BECM. The talk will discuss how the analyzed approaches address the problem, and which constraints are considered in order to satisfy users' comfort requirements. Accordingly, the application of these approaches to some typical Smart Building scenarios will be investigated.

MONITORING PEOPLE MOBILITY IN SMART CITIES: APPLICATIONS AND TECHNOLOGIES

Professor Luigi Atzori
Multimedia & Communication Lab (MC Lab) Head,
University of Cagliari, Italy

Abstract

Understanding people mobility in urban areas is of key importance for the implementation of major city management tasks, such as: planning public transport services; overseeing security during big city events; and analysing the influence of public areas on city quality of life. This talk presents how the analysis of WiFi probes requests generated by mobile devices can contribute to build this understanding while preserving users privacy. Key mobility indicators can be extracted: crowd density per area of interest, people flows, recurrent mobility patterns, and mobility heat maps. These indicators are provided by the PmA solution developed by the MCLab, which has been tested in several real scenario, in the city of Turin, Alba and Cagliari.

FULL PAPERS

YOU'VE BEEN FRAMED! STUDYING PEOPLE CHOOSING OPTIONS

Mairéad Hogan and Chris Barry
NUI Galway
Galway, Ireland

ABSTRACT

This paper presents a research project that used eye tracking technology to study optionality within the online transactional process. The focus was on how micro-decisions can be framed: the option type; the impact of decision default values; and the types of decision constructs. It elaborates and improves on a pilot study that was used to test the experiment design. Prior research that identified problematic decision constructs informed the types of decisions studied. The main findings relate to participant task error rates.

KEYWORDS

Micro-Decision, Opt-in, Opt-out, Framing, Default Effect, Eye Tracking

1. INTRODUCTION

Opt-in rates on commercial websites are generally low, to the frustration of firms and marketeers. An opt-in is generally accepted as requiring express permission by an individual to allow the provision of some service or product, while an opt-out is where a course of action is pre-selected and the user must expressly deny that permission. The Cambridge Dictionary (Cambridge Dictionary, 2019) describes opt-in as "the fact of choosing to take part in an activity, arrangement, etc. rather than being forced to take part" . The same source describes an opt-out as "to choose not to be part of an activity or to stop being involved in it." Quick 'micro-decisions' are usually presented to users in the form of an opt-in or opt-out. Frustrated consumers have become accustomed to dealing with numerous opt-in and opt-out services and charges as they negotiate transactional processes. In a paper describing certain design practices in the low cost carrier (LCC) sector significant disquiet was expressed amongst consumers in respect of the number and ambiguous nature of a series opt-in and opt-out services, many unavoidable, once they had committed to purchasing a flight (Barry et al., 2011).

This paper describes a study of optionality focusing on how designers can frame decisions, the impact of default values, and the types of decision constructs. The analysis details the impact of each of these on errors in participant choice. Other aspects of the findings, such as cognitive load and gender effects, will be reported upon in later work. The findings reveal some exciting insights into the effect the presentation of choice by firms can have on consumer outcomes.

2. CHOICE AND OPTIONALITY

2.1 Choice Framing

The theory of rational choice, that has had such a tight hold over much research governing social and economic behaviour, has been questioned across a number of disciplines. Simon (1957) was among the first to signal its limitations by proposing the concept of 'bounded rationality'. Subsequently, Tversky and Kahneman (1981) theorised framed information could be encoded positively or negatively. Their research indicated the manner in which choice is framed to individuals significantly influences decision-making. They concluded the dependence of preferences on the formulation of decision problems constitutes a major concern for the theory of rational choice. Samuelson and Zeckhauser (1988) found decisions are often presented with 'influential labels', whereby there is nearly always one alternative that carries the label 'status quo'. In a series of experiments designed to test for status quo effects, they concluded decision-makers exhibited a significant choice bias towards the status quo. This also known as the default effect.

The default effect has been well documented (Johnson and Eagly, 1989; Ahmetoglu et al., 2010; Ploug et al., 2012; Anaraky et al., 2018). This is a phenomenon whereby the user is more likely to choose the default option when presented with a choice. In the case of opt-outs, this can result in users making an inadvertent purchase or accidently signing up to a mailing list. In the case of an opt-in, the default option is to decline to purchase or to sign up to a mailing list. While there is research recognising opt-out decisions can be problematic, with users often inadvertently making a purchase, or opting in to a mailing list (Bellman et al., 2001), there is little research on negative consequences of errors with opt-ins in the transactional process. In fact, opt-ins are generally seen as the more benign option, with the EU requiring the use of opt-ins for all distance purchasing European Union (2011).

2.2 Dimensions of Option Presentation

The presentation of options to consumers in contemporary B2C interactions is made up of a number of dimensions. Much of the research discussed earlier on framing largely related to a singular dimension, that of a polar decision, choosing one of two options. In the more sophisticated world of online consumerism, the presentation of choice and optionality can be greatly finessed. The presentation of an option may now have multiple, even layered, dimensions. Previous research (Hogan et al., 2014; Torres et al., 2014) determined options tend to be presented to the user in a variety of ways. Some options are straightforward with easy to understand defaults and choices, while other options are more complicated and require effort to decipher so as to identify the default and the action required to achieve the desired outcome. In addition, some options are simply presented to the consumer while others incorporate various levels of persuasion, presumably to encourage selection of the vendor's preferred outcome.

A desk analysis of 57 websites was conducted to determine the fundamental dimensions of option presentation for opt-out decision constructs in use in B2C websites. A total of 42 opt-outs were encountered across 17 of the websites examined. A number of dimensions were identified as contributing to option presentation: *control type* (e.g., checkbox, radio button or drop-down menu); *default value* (i.e., un-selected or pre-selected); *question or information framing* (i.e., acceptance, rejection or neutral language); *general purpose of the construct* (e.g., immediate revenue generation or permission to retain data); and *additional persuaders* (e.g., benefits of choosing the option or reassurance of privacy). In this study the default value and framing are the key variables examined. The work is restricted to checkboxes as these are the most commonly encountered control types for micro-decisions within the commercial transactional process.

2.3 Option Framing

Bellman et al. (2001) explored the impact of question framing on user decisions. In querying how consumers have unknowingly opted-in to something, they explored the tactics some firms employ to encourage consent. They identified different ways in which consent can be obtained and concluded there are consequential effects in how questions are presented to consumers. Indeed, by using the correct combination of question framing and default answers, firms 'can almost guarantee' consent. Lai and Hui (2006) also conducted research into the impact of question framing on user decisions. Their study indicates the manner in which the option is described, as well as the default option (i.e., checked or unchecked), has an impact on user choice. They found for opt-in decisions using checkboxes, users are more likely to accept an un-selected opt-in over a pre-selected opt-in. They suggest the positive language of acceptance is likely to influence the users' decision.

Question framing has also been shown to affect user choice (Tversky and Kahneman, 1981; Levin et al., 1998; Kuo et al., 2009; Anaraky et al., 2018), with positively framed messages more likely to result in the user opting in to the choice. However, most of the studies presented the choice to the user in a way that either emphasised the positive or negative consequences of accepting or rejecting the choice. Lai and Hui (2004) did examine the impact of acceptance and rejection framing as defined in this paper, along with the impact of the default value (either pre-selected or un-selected). They determined opt-ins were more likely to result in a positive selection when acceptance framing was coupled with an un-selected presentation. They identified no significant difference for opt-outs.

2.4 Using Opt-out Structures for Altruistic and Self-serving Outcomes

There have been cogent arguments for the use of opt-out structures to persuade or nudge people into making positive choices such as the consumption of better foods like whole wheat (Van Kleef et al., 2018), renewable energy (Momsen and Stoerk, 2014), organ donation (Johnson and Goldstein, 2003; Van Dalen and Henkens, 2014), climate change (Ebeling and Lotz, 2015), green environment (Schubert 2017), environmental conservation in hotels (Ebeling and Lotz, 2015), health surveys (Johnson et al., 2002) and retirement savings (Madrian and Shea, 2001; Beshears et al., 2009).

It has been observed that in recent years that some firms in particular sectors such as airlines, online car hire firms and comparison sites such as hotel reservations have been using design techniques that are not just unorthodox but of apparent deliberate design with a variety of self-serving ambitions. These include: making options unclear or ambiguous, leading consumers to make unnecessary choice; or deconstructing a final price with taxes, charges and items presented as options but which are, in fact, essential elements of the product or service (Barry et al., 2011; Barry et al., 2014).

3. RESEARCH APPROACH

As noted in Barry et al. (2016), eye tracking technology has been used extensively in web usability studies, alongside think-aloud techniques. This research project was conducted in two parts. In the first set of experiments on opt-out decision constructs, data was collected from 114 participants, 456 experiment trials and 23 Cued Retrospective Think-Aloud (RTA) sessions. The second set concerned opt-in decision constructs and collected data from 51 participants, 204 experiment trials and 12 Cued RTA sessions. The project was designed like this to control for construct type bias and potential confusion. This design was chosen from experiences with an earlier pilot study (Hogan et al., 2015). Thus statistical analysis was conducted, where relevant, on a between-subjects basis. The study was made up of three dimensions: an eye tracking experiment; self-assessment evaluations (subjective cognitive load); and Cued RTA sessions.

3.1 Eye Tracking Experiment

As the pilot study had highlighted the risks associated with the use of the eye tracking technology, significant effort was spent planning the experiments. Each of the variants of opt-out and opt-in decisions were examined: Un-selected Rejection Framing; Pre-selected Acceptance Framing; Pre-selected Rejection Framing; Pre-selected Neutral Framing; Un-Selected Acceptance Framing; and Un-Selected Neutral Framing (see Table 1).

Table 1. Decision constructs types

Construct Name	Construct Type	Default Value	Framing	Presented In
Un-Selected Rejection	USR	Un-selected	Rejection	Opt-in and Opt-out
Pre-Selected Acceptance	PSA	Pre-selected	Acceptance	Opt-in and Opt-out
Pre-Selected Rejection	PSR	Pre-selected	Rejection	Opt-out
Pre-Selected Neutral	PSN	Pre-selected	Neutral	Opt-out
Un-Selected Acceptance	USA	Un-selected	Acceptance	Opt-in
Un-Selected Neutral	USN	Un-selected	Neutral	Opt-in

The opt-out and opt-in decisions presented to participants were similar to real-world micro-decisions ordinarily facing users when engaged in a commercial transactional process on websites (Barry et al., 2014; Barry et al., 2016).

In each study, participants were presented with either four opt-in or four opt-out micro-decisions. Participants were told to buy the product in two instances and not to buy in the other two. For the opt-in decisions, the participant needed to take action to make a purchase. In the case of the opt-in, the default option was to decline the purchase. For opt-out decisions, the participant needed to take action to decline the purchase, with the default option being to purchase the item. The order of presentation of the four screens was randomized when presented to participants. The core webpage screen was a breakdown insurance product to which participants were asked if they require an enhanced monthly-costed, add-on feature. Each screen had a decision point with a checkbox beside it (see Table 2).

Table 2. Decision constructs presented to participants

Construct Type	Decision Construct
PSA – opt-out	☑ Rescue Plus includes free car hire and travel expenses. I want to purchase Rescue Plus.
PSN – opt-out	☑ Rescue Plus.
PSR – opt-out	☑ Rescue Plus includes free car hire and travel expenses. If you would rather not purchase Rescue Plus, please untick this box.
USR – opt-out	☐ Rescue Plus includes free car hire and travel expenses. If you would rather not purchase Rescue Plus, please tick this box.
USA – opt-in	☐ Rescue Plus includes free car hire and travel expenses. I want to purchase Rescue Plus.
USN – opt-in	☐ Rescue Plus.
USR – opt-in	☐ Rescue Plus includes free car hire and travel expenses. If you would rather not purchase Rescue Plus, please leave this box unticked.

4. EXPLORATORY ANALYSIS

Once the data was gathered, exploratory analysis was conducted. The main focus of this analysis was participant error rates. A participant is deemed to have made an error when they make a mistake in the decision they have been told to take. For example, when told to 'Buy Rescue Plus Insurance' by choosing to tick or untick a checkbox, they unknowingly take the incorrect action. The error rates for opt-in and opt-out constructs were compared and contrasted. Framing and default value were also examined.

4.1 Overall Error Rate

The first step in exploring our data was to examine the error rate for the different construct types.

Table 3. Error rate for opt-out constructs

Construct Type	Correct	Incorrect	Total
PSA	94 (82%)	20 (18%)	114
PSN	87 (76%)	27 (24%)	114
PSR	86 (75%)	28 (25%)	114
USR	72 (63%)	42 (37%)	114
Total	339 (74%)	117 (26%)	456

For opt-outs (see Table 3) the number of incorrect selections varied between the construct types, with PSA having the highest rate of correct selections and USR having the highest rate of incorrect selections. Overall, the rate of incorrect selections made by participants was quite high, ranging from 18% (PSA) to 37% (USR). Chi-square test was conducted to determine whether the relationship between construct type and error rate was significant. The test indicated significance (χ^2 (3, N=456) = 11.715, $p < 0.01$). However, the value for ϕ was 0.158, indicating the association was weak, only accounting for 2.5% of the variation.

Table 4. Error rate for opt-in constructs

Construct Type	Correct	Incorrect	Total
USN	43 (84%)	8 (16%)	51
USA	41 (80%)	10 (20%)	51
USR	36 (71%)	15 (29%)	51
PSA	25 (49%)	26 (51%)	51
Total	145 (71%)	59 (29%)	204

For opt-ins (see Table 4) the number of incorrect selections also varied between the construct types, with PSA having the highest rate of incorrect selections and USN having the highest rate of correct selections. Overall, the rate of incorrect selections made by participants was quite high, ranging from 16% (USN) to 51% (PSA). Chi-square test was conducted to determine if the relationship between construct type and error rate was significant. The test indicated significance (χ^2 (3, N=204) = 18.576, $p < 0.01$). However, the value for ϕ was 0.302, indicating the association was relatively weak, only accounting for 9.1% of the variation. The error rate for PSA was almost double that of the next highest, suggesting this construct was particularly problematic.

4.2 Opt-in Versus Opt-out Error Rate

As can be seen in Tables 3 and 4 above, the error rate was high for both opt-in and opt-out constructs, with 26% of decisions on opt-out constructs incorrect, and 29% of decisions on opt-in constructs incorrect. The variation in error rates is wider for opt-ins (16-51%) than for opt-outs (18-37%). The two opt-in constructs with the highest error rates (PSA and USR) are rarely encountered in practice (Barry et al., 2014), with most opt-ins encountered being the more straightforward USA or USN. This is perhaps due to the lack of benefit associated with misinterpretation of an opt-in. With the opt-outs, the USR has a considerably higher error rate than the other constructs. Again, this construct type is less frequently encountered than the others ((Barry et al., 2014; Barry et al., 2016). However, it is still encountered relatively frequently, particularly in sign-ups for mailing lists. The higher prevalence of this opt-out construct may be due to the perceived advantages to firms associated with users selecting the option, whether intentionally or erroneously.

The error rate for opt-in and opt-out were compared using Chi-square. Opt-in had 71% correct and 29% incorrect while opt-out had 74% correct and 26% incorrect. No significant difference was seen between the opt-in and opt-out constructs. As the USR for opt-out and the PSA for opt-in are rarely encountered, the error rates were compared for the more commonly encountered constructs. Again, there was no significant difference detected. Previous research (Bellman et al., 2001; Lai and Hui, 2006; Ahmetoglu et al., 2010) has reported increased likelihood of users signing up or purchasing when presented with an opt-out, rather than an opt-in, finding framing and default value to impact on user decisions. The findings in this study, do not support that premise (a similar result was found by Abbink and Hennig-Schmidt (2006)), perhaps because participants had pre-decided their desired outcome rather than being undecided.

4.3 The Effect of Default Action on Error Rate

The data was analyzed to determine whether the default action impacted on participants accuracy when making micro-decisions. For the opt-out constructs, the default action was to buy the add-on whereas for the opt-in constructs, the default action was to not buy the add-on. Chi-square was used to determine whether there was a significant difference in the error rate, depending on whether the participant's instruction was to choose the default action for the construct or to take action to change the default action. The analysis indicated no significant difference in error rates (χ^2 (1, N=204) = 0.024, p = 0.877 for opt-in and χ^2 (1, N=456) = 2.587, p = 0.108 for opt-out). This contradicts previous research indicating users tend to choose the default action when presented with a choice. However, in previous research (Johnson and Eagly, 1989; Ahmetoglu et al., 2010; Ploug et al., 2012; Anaraky et al., 2018) participants were allowed a free choice when presented with the options. The studies either examined rates of acceptance of the default action or presented the participants with a free choice. In this study, participants were told to buy or not buy so they had already made their decision regarding which action they would take. This suggests the default action only affects choice when the user has not already decided which action they wish to take. The default effect can be seen as an influencer for the undecided user, rather than a persuader for a change of mind.

4.4 The Effect of Construct Design on Error Rate

In this study the options were presented to participants using 3 different types of framing, as identified by the authors in previous research (Hogan et al., 2014). The frames (acceptance, rejection and neutral framing) are all commonly used in the presentation of micro-decisions on websites. Additionally, this study examines error rate when the user has pre-decided their course of action, rather than being undecided in their choice.

Lai and Hui (2004) suggest that the tick in a pre-selected checkbox can have an anchoring effect on users which results in amplification of the framing. Thus, a pre-selected checkbox with rejection framing acts as a negative anchor and is more likely to result in the user rejecting the option while a pre-selected checkbox with acceptance framing acts as a positive anchor and is more likely to result in the user accepting the option. If this were the case, one might see more errors for participants instructed to not buy than those instructed to buy for the PSA constructs and to see more errors for those instructed to buy than those instructed to not buy for PSR constructs. No significant difference was seen for either PSA or PSR when Chi-square tests were run. This suggests that while an anchoring effect may nudge a user towards a particular decision, it will not cause them to mistakenly choose an option if they have already decided.

4.5 The Effect of Framing on Error Rate

As default actions can impact on the users' selection, the framing of opt-in and opt-out constructs was examined separately as they have different default actions. As can be seen in Table 5, acceptance framing had the highest rate of correct selections, followed by neutral framing, with rejection framing having the highest rate of incorrect selections. A Chi-square test indicated that the framing had a significant effect on the error rate (χ^2 (2, N=456) = 7.209, p = 0.027). However, the value for ϕ was 0.126, indicating the association was weak, only accounting for 1.6% of the variation. Although the anchor effect did not have a significant effect on the error rate, the one un-selected construct type was eliminated from the test as it may have impacted on the result when coupled with framing. No significant difference was seen, suggesting that framing on its own does not impact on error rate for opt-out constructs.

Table 5. Error rate for opt-out constructs

Framing	Correct	Incorrect	Total
Acceptance	94 (82%)	20 (18%)	114
Neutral	87 (76%)	27 (24%)	114
Rejection	158 (69%)	70 (31%)	228
Total	339 (74%)	117 (26%)	456

The tests were repeated for opt-ins (see Table 6). When all constructs were considered, a significant difference was seen (χ^2 (2, N=204) = 6.637, p = 0.041). However, the value for ϕ was 0.177, a weak association, only accounting for 3.1% of the variation. The test was repeated using only the un-selected opt-ins. No significant difference was seen, suggesting framing on its own does not impact error rate for opt-in constructs.

Table 6. Error rate for opt-in constructs

Framing	Correct	Incorrect	Total
Acceptance	66 (65%)	36 (35%)	102
Neutral	43 (84%)	8 (16%)	51
Rejection	36 (71%)	15 (29%)	51
Total	145 (71%)	59 (29%)	204

5. CONCLUSIONS

This study set out to examine whether the design of the constructs used for micro-decisions in online, commercial transactions impacted on error rate when the user had already decided on the desired outcome. The study participants were told to either buy or not buy the product. The error rate was high for all construct types, although some were considerably higher than others. The error rates tended to be higher for less frequently encountered construct types than frequently encountered ones. The PSA for opt-in had an error rate (51%) of over three times the lowest error rate for opt-in (16% for USN), suggesting that this construct type was in some way misleading the participant. It is unusual to encounter a pre-selected opt-in on a website so the participants may have assumed a pre-selected checkbox was an opt-out. The difference in error rates for the opt-outs was not as extreme, perhaps because of the higher prevalence of all types of opt-outs on commercial websites. Despite the difference in error rates between opt-in and opt-out constructs, no significant difference was found in the error rates, suggesting users are no more likely to erroneously select an option on opt-out than on opt-in.

The default effect is a phenomenon whereby users, when presented with options, are more likely to accept the default option than change it. In previous literature, study participants were allowed a free choice. In this study, participants were told what decision to make when presented with the construct. If the default effect impacted the outcome, a higher error rate would be expected when the participant was required to change from the default action. No significant difference was seen between the error rates, suggesting the default effect does not apply when the user has already decided on the course of action they wish to take. Therefore, while it may influence the undecided user, it is unlikely to dissuade the decided user from their planned course of action.

The anchoring effect of a pre-selected checkbox has been shown previously to reinforce the framing of a construct, whereby acceptance framing is more likely to result in option acceptance and rejection framing is more likely to result in option rejection. It was posited that this results from more time spent contemplating the text presented to the user. In this study, no anchoring effect was apparent, likely because participants had pre-decided on the course of action and so, were less susceptible to the nudge power of checkbox pre-selection.

Once the default value of the decision construct was controlled, the framing of the construct did not have a significant effect on the error rate for either opt-in or opt-out. This contradicts previous research which states that acceptance framing is more likely to result in the user accepting the option offered while rejection framing is more likely to result in the user rejecting the option offered. Again, this is likely to be related to the fact the participants had pre-decided on the desired course of action.

This study has added to the body of knowledge on the use of opt-in and opt-out constructs on commercial websites. Previous research suggests designing constructs in a particular way can increase the number of users accepting or rejecting the option presented. This study suggests design is unlikely to change the user's mind if they have already decided on a course of action. Therefore, if a designer wishes to persuade an already decided user along a particular path, methods of persuasion beyond reliance on construct design need to be considered.

REFERENCES

Abbink, K. and Hennig-Schmidt, H., 2006. Neutral versus loaded instructions in a bribery experiment. *Experimental Economics*, Vol. 9, No. 2, pp. 103-121.

Ahmetoglu, G. et al, 2010. Pricing Practices: Their Effects on Consumer Behaviour and Welfare. Mountainview Learning. University College London.

Anaraky, A. et al, 2018. Reducing Default and Framing Effects in Privacy Decision-Making. *SIGHCI 2018 Proceedings*.

Barry, C. et al, 2011. Low-Cost Carriers and High-Tech Barriers - User Views on Questionable Web Design Practices in Ireland. *Irish Journal of Management*, Vol. 31, No. 1, pp. 43-58.

Barry, C. et al, Year. Perceptions of Low Cost Carriers' Compliance with EU Legislation on Optional Extras. *20th International Conference on Information Systems Development*, Edinburgh, Scotland.

Barry, C. et al, 2014. Confirming a Taxonomy of Decision Constructs in Business-to-Consumer Commercial Transactions. *23rd International Conference on Information Systems Development*, Varaždin, Croatia.

Barry, C. et al, 2014. Identifying essential and optional decision constructs in on-line transactional processes. *Information System Development: Improving Enterprise Communication*. M. J. Escalona, G. Aragón, H. Linger et al. New York, Springer.

Barry, C. et al, 2016. Framing or Gaming? Constructing a Study to Explore the Impact of Option Presentation on Consumers. *Information System Development: Transforming Healthcare Through Information Systems*, Springer International Publishing: 111-124.

Bellman, S. et al, 2001. On site: to opt-in or opt-out?: it depends on the question. *Communications of the ACM*, Vol. 44, No. 2, pp. 25-27.

Beshears, J. et al, 2009. The importance of default options for retirement saving outcomes: Evidence from the United States. *Social security policy in a changing environment*, University of Chicago Press: 167-195.

Cambridge Dictionary, 2019. Opt-in.

Ebeling, F. and Lotz, S., 2015. Domestic uptake of green energy promoted by opt-out tariffs. *Nature Climate Change*, Vol. 5, No., pp. 868.

European Union, 2011. Directive on Consumer Rights

Hogan, M. et al, 2014. Theorising and testing a taxonomy of decision constructs. *Journal of Customer Behaviour*, Vol. 13, No. 3, pp. 171-185.

Hogan, M. et al, 2015. An Eye Tracking Pilot Study on Optionality - Some Lessons Learned. *17th Irish Academy of Management Annual Conference*, Galway.

Johnson, B. T. and Eagly, A. H., 1989. Effects of involvement on persuasion: A meta-analysis. *Psychological Bulletin*, Vol. 106, No. 2, pp. 290-314.

Johnson, E. J. et al, 2002. Defaults, Framing and Privacy: Why Opting In-Opting Out1. *Marketing Letters*, Vol. 13, No. 1, pp. 5-15.

Johnson, E. J. and Goldstein, D. G., 2003. Do defaults save lives? *Science*, Vol. 302, No., pp. 1338-1339.

Kuo, F.-Y. et al, 2009. An exploratory study of cognitive effort involved in decision under Framing—an application of the eye-tracking technology. *Decision Support Systems*, Vol. 48, No. 1, pp. 81-91.

Lai, Y.-L. and Hui, K.-L., 2004. Luring the Prey: Attracting Online Consumer Participation through Choice Configurations. *American Market Association (AMA) Marketing and Public Policy Conference*, Washington D.C., USA.

Lai, Y.-L. and Hui, K.-L., Year. Internet opt-in and opt-out: investigating the roles of frames, defaults and privacy concerns. *Proceedings of the 2006 ACM SIGMIS CPR conference on computer personnel research: Forty four years of computer personnel research: achievements, challenges & the future*, Claremount, California, USA, ACM.

Levin, I. P. et al, 1998. All frames are not created equal: A typology and critical analysis of framing effects. *Organizational behavior and human decision processes*, Vol. 76, No. 2, pp. 149-188.

Madrian, B. C. and Shea, D. F., 2001. The Power of Suggestion: Inertia in 401 (k) Participation and Savings Behavior*. *The Quarterly journal of economics*, Vol. 116, No. 4, pp. 1149-1187.

Momsen, K. and Stoerk, T., 2014. From intention to action: Can nudges help consumers to choose renewable energy? *Energy Policy*, Vol. 74, No., pp. 376-382.

Ploug, T. et al, 2012. To nudge or not to nudge: cancer screening programmes and the limits of libertarian paternalism. *J Epidemiol Community Health*, Vol. 66, No. 12, pp. 1193-1196.

Samuelson, W. and Zeckhauser, R., 1988. Status quo bias in decision making. *Journal of risk and uncertainty*, Vol. 1, No. 1, pp. 7-59.

Simon, H. A., 1957. A Behavioral Model of Rational Choice. *Models of Man, Social and Rational: Mathematical Essays on Rational Human Behavior in a Social Setting*. New York, Wiley.

Torres, A. M. et al, 2014. The Identification of Decision Constructs used in Online Transactional Processes. *27th BLED eConference*.

Tversky, A. and Kahneman, D., 1981. The framing of decisions and the psychology of choice. *Science*, Vol. 211, No. 4481, pp. 453-458.

Van Dalen, H. P. and Henkens, K., 2014. Comparing the effects of defaults in organ donation systems. *Social science & medicine*, Vol. 106, No., pp. 137-142.

Van Kleef, E. et al, 2018. The effect of a default-based nudge on the choice of whole wheat bread. *Appetite*, Vol. 121, No., pp. 179-185.

CHARACTERIZATION OF SOCIABILITY ON ONLINE SOCIAL NETWORKS IN BRAZILIAN ELDERLY' PERSPECTIVE: A CASE STUDY ON FACEBOOK

Thiago Alexandre de Souza Silva, Natália Moreira de Paula, Glívia Angélica Rodrigues Barbosa, Ismael Santana Silva and Flávio Roberto dos Santos Coutinho
Centro Federal de Educação Tecnológica de Minas Gerais
Belo Horizonte, Brazil

ABSTRACT

This work aimed to characterize how online social networks support the sociability among elderly members of Brazil and to discuss the impact of this proposed sociability in the social interaction of these users. To achieve this goal, we conducted a case study on Facebook, which aimed to evaluate the sociability on this online social network in the perspectives of experts in HCI and elderly users view point. The results showed that the interface and interaction model of Facebook reflects on the experience of use and sociability of this members' group. As contributions, we present insights about the design and evaluation of social software more focused on the sociability of elderly users.

KEYWORDS

Online Social Networks, Elderly People, User Experience, Sociability, Facebook, Interface Evaluation

1. INTRODUCTION

An aging population brings challenges, such as keeping elderly people socially included, once the physical limitations due to age and changes in behavior may contribute to their social isolation (Braun, 2013). To minimize this isolation, there are initiatives that make use of Information and Communication Technologies (ICTs) to promote the social inclusion of this group of people (Chen and Schulz, 2016). For example, online social networks have features that facilitate the socialization of their users regardless of distance and time. Thus, when appropriate, these online networks can assist elderly people in interacting with their family, friends, other stakeholders, and keep them up-to-date on everyday issues. Thus, online social networks have resources that can help combat the social isolation of elderly people (Chen and Schulz, 2016).

However, the social inclusion of elderly population through online social networks may face difficulties (Chen and Schulz, 2016), once aspects that influence the use experience on such networks (e.g., communicability, usability, accessibility and sociability) may not be adequate to the specific needs of this group of users (Chen and Schulz, 2016). In other words, to enhance the quality of social interaction (i.e., sociability (Souza and Preece, 2004)) on social software to elderly people, it is necessary to adapt this kind of system in an inclusive way, taking into account the needs, constraints and visions of these users in relation to these platforms (Chen and Schulz, 2016) (Chen and Schulz, 2016). Therefore, it is necessary to conduct studies to investigate how online social networks have been supporting the interactions of elderly users, so that the demands of this group can be exposed and improvements can be discussed for that these networks become appropriate tools for the socialization of this group platforms (Chen and Schulz, 2016).

Motivated by this demand, the aim of this work is to evaluate and to characterize the sociability on online social networks from the perspective of Brazilian elderly users, through a case study on Facebook, the most used online social network in Brazil and in the world. To achieve the proposed goal, we investigated the following research question: *"Does the Facebook interface and interaction model support social interaction among elderly users?"*

The methodology to answer this question consisted in a three-step approach. Initially, we performed an evaluation from the perspective of Human-Computer Interaction (HCI) experts to analyze if the resources offered by Facebook are adequate to user experience (UX) (Nielsen and Budiu, 2015) and sociability guidelines (Souza and Preece, 2004). Subsequently, an evaluation from the perspective of elderly users was conducted with the purpose of analyzing the experience of use during the social interaction mediated by this system. Finally, we triangulated the evaluations' results and we discussed the impact of Facebook on the sociability of elderly people.

The main results allow a reflection about (1) how online social networks have been supporting the social interaction of elderly people and (2) the needs of this public in relation to this type of service. Thus, this research contributes to the HCI community may reflect about the importance of designing online social networks that enhance the satisfactory experience of elderly users, so as to stimulate the social inclusion of these users through this type of technological service (Chen and Schulz, 2016). In a complementary way, this work also reinforces the importance of sociability as a strategy to improve the user experience and social interaction on social software. Therefore, the findings presented here provide insights that are useful for designing and evaluating online social networks more focused on the sociability of elderly people in the future.

2. RELATED WORKS

In the literature, it is possible to find works such as those performed by Braun, 2013 and Bell et al., 2013, which aimed to characterize elderly people's perceptions in relation to online social networks, as well as the factors that encourage and discourage this group of users to use this type of online service. The research conducted by Bell et al., 2013 analyzed the opinions and perceptions of 142 North American elders and the work of Braun, 2013 was attended by 124 elderly people from Europe. Although these works were conducted in different regions, the results achieved were convergent and indicated that factors such as perception of utility and trust in the network contribute to elderly people begin to use online social networks. On the other hand, factors such as difficulties in interaction as well as social pressure negatively affect the use of this service by this public (Braun, 2013) (Bell et al., 2013). Thus, the papers discuss and present the demand for new research that: (1) characterize the needs of elderly people in relation to social software and (2) discuss how online social networks have been supporting the interaction of this group of users currently. According these researchers, from these investigate lines, it will be possible to implement improvements in these virtual environments directed to this public (Braun, 2013) (Bell et al., 2013).

Furthermore, Chen and Schulz, 2016 conducted a systematic review in the literature to characterize the effects that ICTs have on reducing the social isolation of elderly people. The review contemplated full articles related to the theme, published in English between 2002 and 2015. The proposed characterization made it possible to explain that, although they stand out as a valid alternative, ICTs do not always support the digital and social inclusion of old people adequately. The study also showed that barriers to this inclusion are associated with both social issues (e.g., resistance of elderly people to adopting technologies, family pressure), and difficulties with technology (e.g., complex functionalities and interfaces) (Chen and Schulz, 2016).

Given the results of this research, Chen and Schulz, 2016 suggest new studies: (1) to investigate and to discuss why current ICTs still present barriers for the interaction of elderly people, despite of their potential to the inclusion for this group of users, (2) to characterize which types of technologies can contribute to combat the social isolation of this group, and (3) to provide insights that contribute to the design and evaluation of ICTs that are more geared towards the social inclusion of elderly users (Chen and Schulz, 2016).

In this sense, the present work differs and complements previous research, since it seeks to evaluate and characterize the experience of use and sociability on online social networks from the perspective of Brazilian elderly users, through a case study on Facebook. Thus, the results of this work can contribute to the design of online social networks more focused on the use experience and sociability of elderly users (Braun, 2013).

3. ELDERLY SOCIABILITY ON FACEBOOK THROUGH EXPERTS' PERSPECTIVE

In the first step of our research, we performed an evaluation in the perspective of HCI experts to analyze whether the features offered by Facebook are adequate to UX guidelines (Nielsen and Budiu, 2015) and also sociability guidelines (Souza and Preece, 2004) available in literature, considering the profile of elderly users. We performed the proposed evaluation using the Heuristic Evaluation (HE) (Nielsen, 1994). The HE is an inspection method to evaluate interfaces and it is conducted by HCI experts, without the participation of users. During the evaluation following the steps of this method, the expert inspects the interface looking for potential problems which violate one or more guidelines (also called heuristics) that describe principles of quality of use (e.g., usability, UX, sociability). Subsequently, the identified problems are categorized according to their severity (i.e., catastrophic, large, small, cosmetic) taking into account the potential impact generated in user interaction (Nielsen, 1994).

As the set of guidelines to guide the HE can be modified or adapted according to the purpose of the inspection (Nielsen, 1994), to evaluate the appropriateness of Facebook's resources to the principles of UX and sociability in the context of interaction of elderly users, we conducted the HE using the UX guidelines presented by Nielsen and Budiu, 2015 and the sociability guidelines presented by Souza and Preece, 2004. These guidelines were adopted since user experience impacts on the quality of social interaction (i.e., sociability) mediated systems (Nielsen and Budiu, 2015)(Souza and Preece, 2004).

The guidelines of UX (Nielsen and Budiu, 2015) used were: UX1 - Contextualization for the user and adequacy to the resources; UX2 - Error handling and user assistance; UX3 - Clear, immediate and informative feedback; UX4 - Explain the interaction paths; UX5 - Alternatives in text; UX6 - Adaptable; UX7 - Perceptible; UX8 - Responsive design; UX9 - Navigable; UX10 - Readable; UX11 - Predictability and consistency; UX12 - Visibility and easy access to all existing information; UX13 - Minimizing user memory load; UX14 - Easy access to resources; UX15 - Help and documentation; UX16 - Good use of screen space; and UX17 - Encouraging interaction. On the other hand, the sociability guidelines (Souza and Preece, 2004) used were: S1 - Allowing people to develop their own identities online; S2 - Encourage empathy and trust among members; S3 - Encourage reciprocity; S4 - Maintain discussions on evidence and topics; S5 - Maintain different communication and interaction options; and S6 - Ensure protection and privacy.

We conducted the evaluation in the first half of January 2018 by two evaluators, with at least eight years' experience in the application of HE and by an Occupational Therapist specializing in the rehabilitation and inclusion of elderly people, with more than five years of experience in the area. The participation of this Occupational Therapist specialist contributed to that the HCI specialists could justify why the potential problems identified during the evaluation on Facebook could affect the quality of the social interaction of elderly users on this system.

During the evaluation, the experts considered eight distinct interaction scenarios on Facebook: (1) Create profile and provide basic information (i.e., name, work and education, residence, relationships, contacts, profile image); (2) Search by friends and send friend request; (3) Accept friend request; (4) Post content in a public and private way; (5) Posting content on a friend's wall; (6) Interact with posts from others in the news feed; (7) Chat through instant messages with friends; (8) Interacting in events; (9) Interact in groups and (10) Interact with notifications. The main results obtained in this step are presented below. After the inspection steps, the data collected by the experts were analyzed and consolidated so that it was possible to discuss the potential impacts of the features offered on Facebook in the experience of use and sociability.

3.1 Results

Through the evaluation, we identified 20 potential problems that violated at least one of the UX and sociability guidelines, which 60% were classified with severity 3 (i.e., large problem), 30% with severity 4 (i.e., catastrophic problem), and 10% with severity 2 (i.e., minor problems). Among the identified potential problems, it is possible to exemplify the difficulties of perceiving and accessing the options for editing and deleting a comment in a publication. As shown in Figure 1, the Facebook interface does not explicitly tell the user that a comment can be edited or deleted after submission. These options are hidden in the interface and, to view them, the user must hover the pointer to the right of the comment so that a button with the image of three dots (ellipsis points) appears. Thus, the way how Facebook provides the options for editing and deleting a comment may be a potential problem for senior users that can compromise the social interaction mediated by this online platform. Once, as the options are not explicitly on interface (i.e., they become visible only after dynamic interaction with the system), the user can make limited use or ignore the existence of these options.

As each identified potential problem may be associated with violation of one or more UX and sociability guidelines and the same guideline may be violated by different problems, to conduct the proposed analysis and to present the results in a consolidated manner, we verified how many guidelines were violated and how often these violations occurred in relation to the total number of problems. Figure 2 shows the consolidated results.

From the data presented in Figure 2, it was possible to observe that the guidelines "UX14 - Ease of access to functionalities", "UX4 - Explicit interaction paths" and "UX12 - Visibility and easy access to all existing information" were violated in, at least, 60% of the problems. In relation to guidelines specifically focused on promoting sociability and collaboration (e.g., S2 - Encouraging empathy and trust among members, S3 - Encouraging reciprocity and S6 - Ensuring protection and privacy), have been mapped to at least 20% potential identified problems.

Figure 1. Example of a problem on Facebook interface

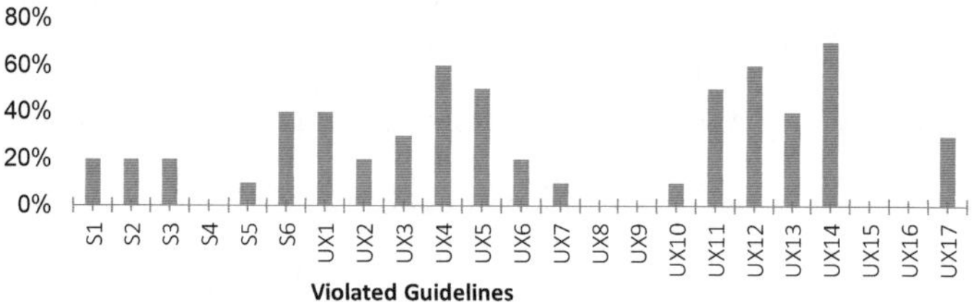

Figure 2. Frequency of violations of UX guidelines and Sociability on Facebook

Although the Facebook offers different resources to promote interaction among its members, considering the profile of elderly users, the violation of the guidelines mentioned above may impair the quality of elderly interaction. Once the Facebook does not explicit the possibilities of interaction in order to facilitate and stimulate the access and use by elderly people, this kind of user can ignore or make limited use of the offered resources. Consequently, Facebook may not be supporting social interaction of elderly users adequately through its interface (Braun, 2013) (Bell et al., 2013).

4. SOCIABILITY ON FACEBOOK THROUGH ELDERLY USERS' PERSPECTIVE

In order to investigate how elderly people have been using Facebook, as well as to characterize the perceptions and opinions of them regarding the interaction mediated by this social network, two evaluations were performed in this research: (1) Evaluation in Controlled Environment and (2) Survey with Facebook´ users. Next, we present these steps and the results.

4.1 Evaluation in Controlled Environment

We performed the evaluation in controlled environment in three stages: preparation, execution and analysis. All steps were conducted by two evaluators. During the preparation phase, we determined the objectives and tasks to be performed during the evaluation. In addition, the profile of the participants was defined, as well as the consent term. Finally, before the execution phase, a pilot test was conducted to verify that all the definitions and generated artifacts were adequate for the evaluation (Prates and Barbosa, 2003).

In the execution stage, the evaluations were performed with each selected participant. During this stage, the following steps were followed for each evaluation session: (1) receipt of the user, (2) presentation of evaluation objectives, (3) obtaining the participant's formal consent, (4) application of the pre-test, (5) observation of tasks performed by the user and (6) interview after test (Prates and Barbosa, 2003)

The following tasks were proposed to the participants: (T1) Create account in Facebook; (T2) Find friends through personal contacts; (T3) Configure profile; (T4) Send a message to friend; (T5) Delete friend; (T6) Post in timeline; (T7) Comment on post; (T8) Like Comment, (T9) Edit comment; (T10) Delete comment, and (T11) Access settings menu. During each assessment session, the evaluator noted and recorded: (1) the completion level of each task (i.e., completed without error, completed with error or not completed) and (2) questions and observations made by the participant during the tasks and the final interview.

In total, 17 evaluation sessions were held with different participants over 60 years of age. Among these participants, 60% declared to be identified with the female gender and 40% with the male gender. The 17 participants have been using Facebook for at least 6 months. In relation to the weekly frequency of use, all users declared to access the Facebook at least twice a week with the help of a relative. These 17 participants were selected using the saturation sampling technique (Marshall, 1996).

4.1.1 Results and Discussions

In relation to the execution of the tasks, the graph of Figure 3 shows the percentage of completion of each task by the participants. From these data, we can see that eight tasks (72%) were completed with error or were not completed by at least 40% (seven) of users. In addition, it is possible to highlight that the greatest difficulties of interaction focused on tasks related to creating an account (T1), finding friends (T2) and sending a message to a friend (T4).

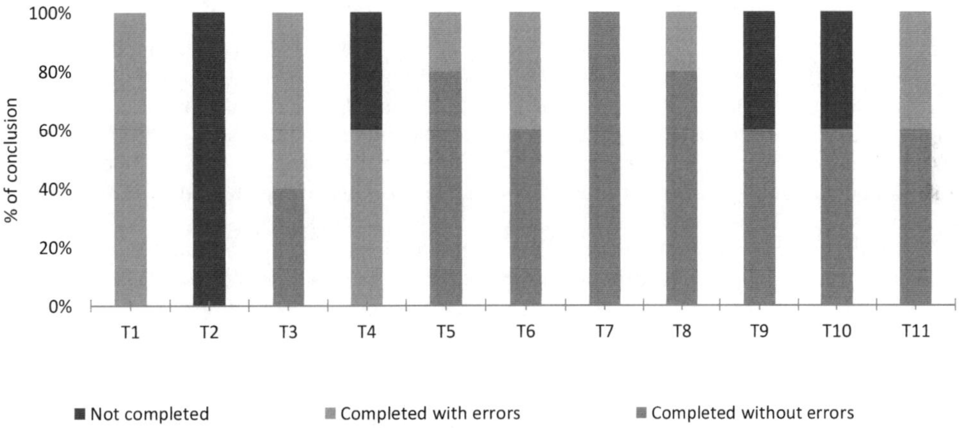

Figure 3. Percentage of completion of Tasks by Elderly Users

Regarding the task to locate and add personal contacts (T2), elderly participants could not locate and invite friends through the contacts registered in their personal emails. Participants in the evaluation sessions indicated that they did not perform this task because they did not understand whether the data requested by Facebook corresponded to (1) access information (i.e., login) of the email account or (2) Facebook itself or (3) because they hoped to find other ways to find friends on the network. To better understand these results, we asked to the participants about their experiences during the tasks execution. One participant P13 said: "*I did not execute the task because it must have an easier way to find my friends. I do not have email to locate anyone* "[P13].

Since all participants in this research already had a profile on Facebook, the difficulties and problems observed and reported by elderly people have caught the attention of the researchers. Moreover, the participants said that, in addition to the difficulties reported, there were other factors that contributed to the problems experienced during the execution of the tasks (e.g., difficulties to access the functionalities and information).

The results of the completion of the tasks (summarized in Figure 3) as well as the experience and perceptions report by senior people during the interview suggest that elderly users may encounter limitations to initiate the use of features offered by Facebook without the help of other people. These limitations may be associated with the potential problems identified by HCI specialists, especially those related to the difficulty of perception, recognition and use of available resources for interaction. Thus, the reported results suggest that the interface and interaction model of Facebook demands adaptations to enhance the sociability of old users.

4.2 Sociability Survey

The next step of this work was to analyze the perceptions and opinions of elderly users about the resources offered to stimulate social interaction on Facebook. To achieve this goal, an online questionnaire with seven questions was applied. The questions were grouped so that it was possible to identify: (1) the profile of the participants, (2) the participants' perceptions about Facebook's sociability features, and (3) suggestions to enhance the user experience and sociability in this social network. The questionnaire was publicly posted on Facebook on the researchers' personal page, as well as in Facebook communities focused on bringing together elderly people. The survey took place throughout the month of March 2018 and the four authors of this study analyzed the collected data.

The research involved the participation of 121 elderly people who access Facebook at least three times a week and use this service for at least one year. Regarding gender, 78% of elderly people were identified with the female gender and 22% with the male gender. The majority (56%) reported being in the age group between 60 and 65 years old, while 22% declared to be between 66 and 70 years old, 17% between 71 and 75 years old and 5% in the range between 76 and 80 years old. None of the participants claimed to be over 80 years old.

4.2.1 Users' Perceptions and Suggestions about the Sociability Features

Initially, the participants were asked to respond who was responsible for creating their personal accounts on Facebook. Among the participants, 50% of elderly users stated that friends and family were responsible for this task. On the other hand, 44% reported having created their own social network accounts and 6% of elderly people do not remember this information. These data converge with the data collected during the evaluation in controlled environment, once more than half of the participants in this phase also reported that family members created their accounts. These results point to a possible dependence experienced by elderly people during the process of account creation and initialization in the use of Facebook.

Regarding the motivations of using Facebook, the participants could indicate more than one reason. The collected data allowed us to identify that 83% of elderly people use Facebook to follow the content published on this platform and 78% access this online network to keep in touch with family and friends. In addition, 33% are on Facebook to keep old contacts, but also, make new friends, especially of other age groups.

Next, the participants were asked about: (1) what Facebook features they knew and (2) how often they use each known feature. The graph of Figure 4 summarizes the results obtained. It is possible to observe that at least 34% of participants stated that they did not know, did not use or rarely used all of the features present on Facebook to support social interaction. The limited knowledge and use of these features are an alert, since among these features unknown by elderly users, there are the resources that should be used to promote sociability, such as: (1) maintaining personal information in the profile, (2) find friends, and (3) share publications of interest.

Next, elderly people were asked to indicate suggestions that could contribute to improving the user experience and sociability on Facebook. Thematic analysis (Braun and Clarke, 2006) was used to identify and categorize the suggestions in participants' responses. The graph of Figure 5 summarizes the obtained results. As shown in Figure 5, all participants contributed with suggestions. Among the demands for improvements most cited by at least 70% of participants, it is possible to highlight: (1) "Ensure that error messages are easy to understand and help the user to take the correct action (suggested by 73%)"; (2) "Inform clearly what action is being taken by the user and the consequences of each action" (suggested by 77%); (3) "Facilitate listening and viewing content" (suggested by 70%), and (4) "Providing ways to help users navigate, find content" (suggested by 84%). In addition, it was possible to observe that most of the suggestions are related to: (1) ease of use, (2) feedback, (3) flexibility and (4) stimulation of social interaction in different ways.

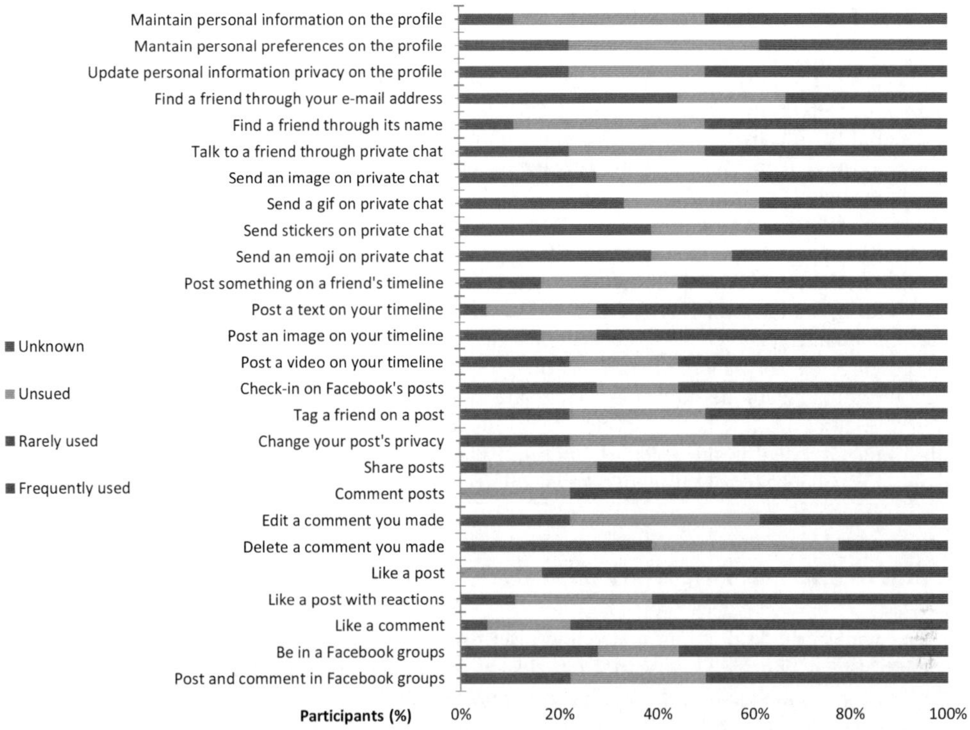

Figure 4. Sociability features of Facebook used by participants

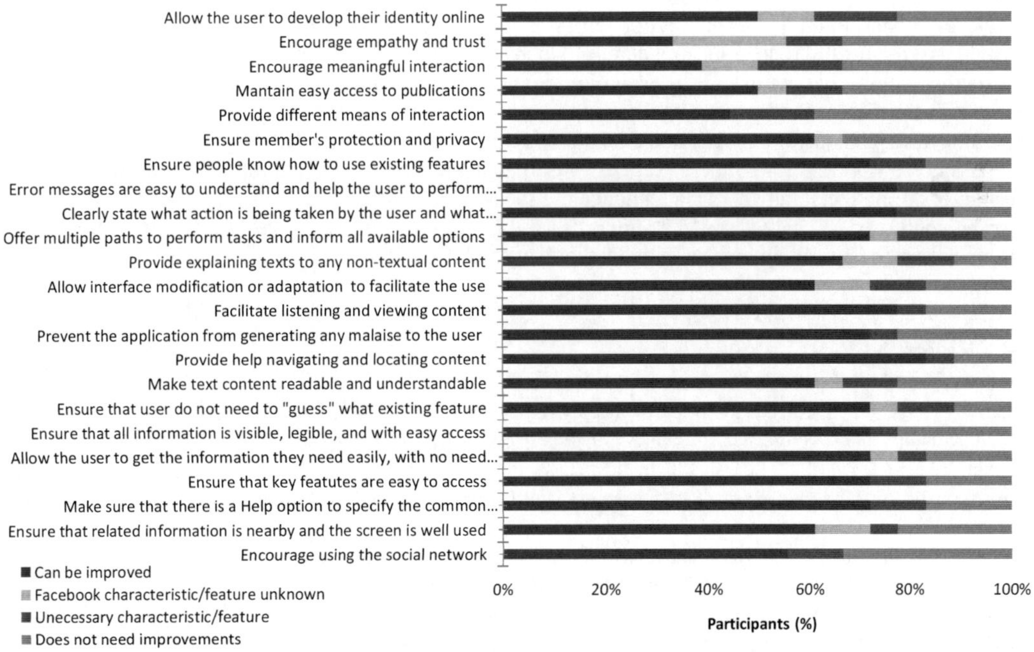

Figure 5. Sociability features of Facebook that, in the users' view point, can be improved

5. DISCUSSION OF RESULTS

In this research, we investigated whether: *"Does the interface and interaction model of Facebook support the social interaction between elderly users?"*. Initially, the results showed that Facebook offers features to support the sociability of its users, such as (1) sharing and viewing content and (2) diversified interaction with friends through posts, comments and chats. However, considering the profile and needs of elderly users, the HCI experts' evaluation showed that the Facebook violates some UX and sociability guidelines that seek to promote and stimulate social interaction on this type of platform. By violating these guidelines, Facebook may not adequately support the social interaction of senior people through its interface (Braun, 2013) (Bell et al., 2013).

Later, it was possible to show that elderly users may be facing difficulties to recognize and use the resources offered for social interaction on Facebook. For a significant number of participants, this system does not use interface and interaction elements consistent with their expectations and experiences. In addition, the discussed and presented results point to the fact that the problems reported by elderly people during the interaction often affect the autonomy of this audience when using Facebook. Aware of the limited use that has been made of the offered resources, both elderly participants of this research and the HCI specialists presented suggestions for improvements (listed in the graph of Figure 5) that could be incorporated into the interface and interaction model of Facebook so that this network can enhance the sociability of elderly people.

6. CONCLUSIONS AND FUTURE WORKS

Taken together, the findings presented and discussed in this paper advance the understandings about UX and sociability in online social networks for elderly public. Specifically, this study indicates how Facebook's interface and interaction model supports and limits sociability for users over 60 years old.

These results contribute to the HCI community may reflect about the importance of addressing the principles of UX and sociability on social software. This study also reinforces the importance of sociability as a strategy to improve the experience and social interaction of elderly people in online social networks. This is a relevant contribution, since elderly population is growing and they can find in social networks a favorable virtual environment to reduce social isolation (Chen and Schulz, 2016). Thus, this paper provides insights and recommendations that are useful for designing online social networks more focused on sociability of elderly people in the future. Furthermore, the adopted methodology might be reproduced in the evaluation of other social medias, considering the UX and social interaction of different interest groups (e.g., teenagers).

As future work, it is possible to suggest the implementation and evaluation of recommendations for the design of online social networks that enhance the social inclusion of elderly people. In addition, other surveys can be conducted to characterize the support of online social networks in the social interaction of different groups of users (e.g., adolescents and people with special needs).

REFERENCES

Bell, C., Fausset, C., Farmer, S., Nguyen, J., Harley, L. and Fain, W.B., 2013, May. Examining social media use among older adults. *In Proceedings of the 24th ACM conference on hypertext and social media* (p. 158-163).

Braun, V. and Clarke, V., 2006. Using thematic analysis in psychology. *Qualitative research in psychology*, p.77-101.

Braun, M.T., 2013. Obstacles to social networking website use among older adults. *In Computers in Human Behavior*, p.673-680.

Chen, Y.R.R. and Schulz, P.J., 2016. The effect of information communication technology interventions on reducing social isolation in elderly people: a systematic review. *In Journal of medical Internet research*, 18(1).

Marshall, M.N., 1996. *Sampling for qualitative research.* Family practice, 13(6), pp.522-526.

Nielsen, J., 1994. Usability inspection methods. *In CHI'94*, p. 413-414.

Nielsen, J. and Budiu, R. 2015. *User Experience for Mobile Applications and Websites*. In Design Guidelines, 506p.

Prates, R.O. and Barbosa, S.D.J., 2003. Avaliação de interfaces de usuário–conceitos e métodos. *In Jornada de Atualização em Informática do Congresso da Sociedade Brasileira de Computação* (Vol. 6, p. 28).

Souza, C.S. de and Preece, J., 2004. A framework for analyzing and understanding online communities. *In Interacting with computers*, 16(3), p.579-610.

B4HEALTH – AN ARCHITECTURE MODEL FOR PERSONAL HEALTH RECORDS WITH HL7 FHIR AND HYPERLEDGER FABRIC

Victor Giovanella Garcia, Alex Roehrs, Cristiano André da Costa,
Rodrigo da Rosa Righi, André Henrique Mayer, Rodolfo Stoffel Antunes
and Eduardo Souza dos Reis
Unisinos Software Innovation Laboratory - SOFTWARELAB / Universidade do Vale do Rio do Sinos - UNISINOS
Av. Unisinos, 950 - Bairro Cristo Rei - São Leopoldo/RS CEP: 93.022-750, Brazil

ABSTRACT

Health Institutions use the EHR (Electronic Health Record) for many years to register the patients' information electronically. On the other hand, this data is still in many different systems of the health institutions, which the patient interacted over life. During a medical appointment, one does not have a current view of the patient's health history. One of the goals of the PHR (Personal Health Record) concept is to obtain a unified view of the records scattered in various health organizations. Many experts now believe that blockchain technology allows storing a patient's pertinent medical information where needed, allowing both the patient and health care professionals to have access to up-to-date information. However, among the challenges to achieve the goal of an interoperable PHR model is the choice of a blockchain platform that supports the storage of this data in a secure, transparent, and decentralized manner. This article proposes an architecture model for health records based on blockchain. The main outcome is storing part of an electronic medical record in the proposed solution. It aims to process and store medical data, which comes from different health institutions safely inside the blockchain network. Then the EHR data is available to authorized stakeholders in a unique viewpoint through a decentralized blockchain application. After experimenting with two different blockchain frameworks, we decided to implement the prototype in a permissioned blockchain. We created and deployed a business network composed of two different organizations, which stored and shared EHR data among the network participants. Performance tests while retrieving EHR data from the blockchain showed an average response time in milliseconds of 201.08 with 500 users and 15,402.9 with 1000 users. Our proposed solution was able to address the main challenge faced by patients that have EHR data scattered in many distinct locations. The prototype supplies a unique view of this data where the participating organizations accessed the EHR data. However, a more robust hardware setup is necessary to test the blockchain solution in future works. Additionally, our intent is to focus on internal aspects of HIS, especially on how to convert the current EHR data from any health data standard to HL7 FHIR, as this would allow many different health institutions, which are using different data standards to take part in the network.

KEYWORDS

HER, PHR, Blockchain, Healthcare, HL7 FHIR

1. INTRODUCTION

According to Pons et al. (2016), the increase in Electronic Health Records (EHR) usage is generating new challenges and opportunities in the medical field, and increasing the use of digital content, both structured data as well as narrative text should offer many benefits. In addition to the original goal of improving clinical care through high quality documentation, EHR data can make contributions that are more significant to research and clinical workflows. In the health sector, although we live in the information age and there are already several systems that make the EHR of patients, the information is still spread in several systems of different institutions such as hospitals, ambulatories, clinics and doctors' offices. Authors in Fan et al (2018), believe the problem is that EHRs stay in a private database making patients leaving their data in various hospitals, this usually happens because life events take them from one hospital to another. Therefore, most patients lose access to past data even when it belongs to them. Moreover, according to Zhang et al (2018), it is essential to have secure and scalable data sharing for patients to receive effective treatment. During their lifetime, patients visit a variety of care provider's offices and to ensure these care providers have the most up to date information about their patients' health condition, they should be able to exchange information in timely and privacy-sensitive manner.

To solve the problem of information spread in different places, the author Roehrs et al proposed a Personal Health Record (PHR) model that aims to unify data from several sources. This model aims to provide patients with a unified view of their health records scattered in various locations. It also aims to make available to health professionals' access to updated patient data, even when changed in other health institutions with which the patient interacted. The OmniPHR model focuses on the distribution and interoperability of the PHR. The OmniPHR proposes a representation of the PHRs, organized hierarchically, encrypted, and distributed in chain databases in the network. These blocks can be in different healthcare organizations and even in a patient-managed repository. As OmniPHR's proposal is to promote an interoperable and distributed PHR architecture with security features for sensitive data, the authors found in the blockchain technology proper alternatives to compose the model's base architecture (ROEHRS et al, 2019).

There are some challenges faced by the OmniPHR model, such as the choice of the blockchain platform that will compose the model. Currently there are several blockchain platforms available in the market, among the main ones are Ethereum, Hyperledger Fabric, R3 String, Ripple and Quorum. Despite the popularization of the blockchain through Bitcoin, the behavior of a system that stores health data on a blockchain platform is not yet well known. It is unknown, which of the major platforms offer the best features to support the OmniPHR model, for the storage of health data. This work aims at creating a blockchain architecture model to store EHR data using a health data standard to support the OmniPHR model.

1.1 Scientific Contribution

There is a growing need for an interoperable health data system that supplies a common shared view of the essential data for a person and any healthcare professional involved in care, regardless of where the provider or the person is physically located, or the organization to which they belong. Too often, the people involved in the health process waste time by repeating information gathering, besides they lose critical information, or the patient provides it too late (AZARMA et al, 2017). The EHR may have scanned patient data, however getting this data from one clinician to another is still a major challenge, especially since patients often have multiple doctors requesting tests, prescribing medications, and supplying treatment. Many experts now believe that blockchain technology allows to store a patient's pertinent medical information where needed, as well as allowing patients to easily view their own medical histories. In addition, blockchain technology can also help with other aspects of health care, such as improving the application for insurance or other administrative processes within health networks, and health-related population data available to biomedical researchers (MERTZ, 2018).

This study aims to address the issues surrounding the creation of a blockchain-based health records architecture model. The research developed a blockchain model for the storage of a partial electronic medical record using the HL7 FHIR (Health Level Seven - Fast Healthcare Interoperability Resources) standard in Hyperledger Fabric. Besides the implementation the authors also executed some performance tests.

1.2 Research Question

The use of blockchain has an interesting potential for the storage of EHR because it offers a secure and distributed database that can run without a central authority or administrator. The blockchain has also gained interest as a platform to improve the authenticity and transparency of health data through many use cases, such as keeping permissions on EHR to simplify the processing of requests (ANGRAAL et al, 2017). For Dubovitskaya et al (2018), nowadays it is still a major challenge on keeping a patient's medical history with up to date information, because patients usually interact with many health organizations. Blockchain provides a unique opportunity to create secure and trustable health data management solution, for sharing important patient data between healthcare providers and researchers.

Although the use of the OmniPHR model can solve some of the problems faced by health organizations and their patients, it would still be necessary to choose a blockchain platform that best supports the implementation of the model. The currently available blockchain platforms are generic, being able to store any type of data, there is no specific platform for health data. With few studies involving the main available platforms, it is currently unclear which one offers the best features when it comes to storing health records that use health data standards such as HL7 FHIR. The B4Health is an implementation inspired in the OmniPHR model which aims at solving the challenges mentioned above.

1.3 Motivation

Health organizations implemented the EHR and it is routinely in use in most European countries. In addition to the use in patient care, these data have secondary use in analyzes, research, quality measurements, among others (RIKKA VUOKKO et al, 2017). As per Reisman (2017) interoperability itself is complex. The term refers to more than just the ability to exchange information. For two EHR systems to be truly interoperable, they must be able to exchange and use this information exchanged. For this to occur, the transmitted message must have standard coded data so that the receiving system can interpret it. However, the lack of standardized data is an issue that has plagued the United States health system for decades and now certainly limits the ability to electronically share patient data. For Zhang et al. (2018), to overcome such situation, it is necessary to have a standards-based architecture, which can integrate with existing HIS and related mobile applications to enable safe and scalable systems to improve decision support.

According to Mettler (2016), a constantly updated decentralized database has many advantages for the healthcare industry. These advantages become especially interesting when many different parties need to access the same information. Medical treatment processes, for example in care for the elderly or chronic diseases, are predestined fields of application, where Blockchain technology can create benefit. A variety of stakeholders (for example, general practitioners, specialist physicians, hospitals, therapists, etc.) and the amount of disruption in the media that disseminates the information involved during the treatment of a patient (e.g. change of media, multiple medical records, incompatible IT interfaces, etc.) can lead to lengthy, resource-intensive authentication and information processes for all medical stakeholders. Considering the potential of the blockchain for health data storage in a transparent, decentralized, and secure way, this project proposes the creation of a blockchain architecture model to store EHR, discovering its advantages and disadvantages, simulating the behavior of a real scenario.

1.4 Objective

The general goal is to develop a blockchain architecture model for storing part of an electronic medical record. For this, there are some specific goals, such as use the HL7 FHIR as the data standard for storing information on the blockchain platform. Store information about a patient's personal data that is on an electronic medical record that is using the HL7 FHIR standard. Compare the performance of the blockchain architecture model created with two other blockchain platforms, the consumption of hardware resources, analyze response time, and verify which platform had the least errors during the tests. Determine if the result obtained gives indications that these platforms would support the storage of data using the HL7 FHIR standard in a real scenario.

2. B4HEALTH

According to the main problem presented in this study, the EHR data needs to sit in a central repository ensuring both the security and confidentiality. To address this issue raised by the authors of the OmniPHR model, we proposed a blockchain architecture model for EHR storage called B4Health (Blockchain for Health). B4Health aims to solve the problem of scattered EHR data in many different systems of the health institutions with which the patient interacted throughout life. The authors also created it with the goal to serve as a blockchain model to support the OmniPHR as a repository to store the EHR data. Several health institutions, such as hospitals, clinics, doctor's offices, generate EHR data and feed the B4Health system with the information generated after each appointment. In B4Health, only healthcare professionals belonging to a health institution member of the network have access to patient data. The B4Health architecture is composed of several components, this section explains them in detail. In Figure 1, it is possible to have an overview of the system, where the different health institutions send the data safely, after it arrives in B4Health and the system treats and stores the EHR data. In the last step, the system enables both patients and health professionals, who have access to the shared EHR data to use it for helping in the patient treatment.

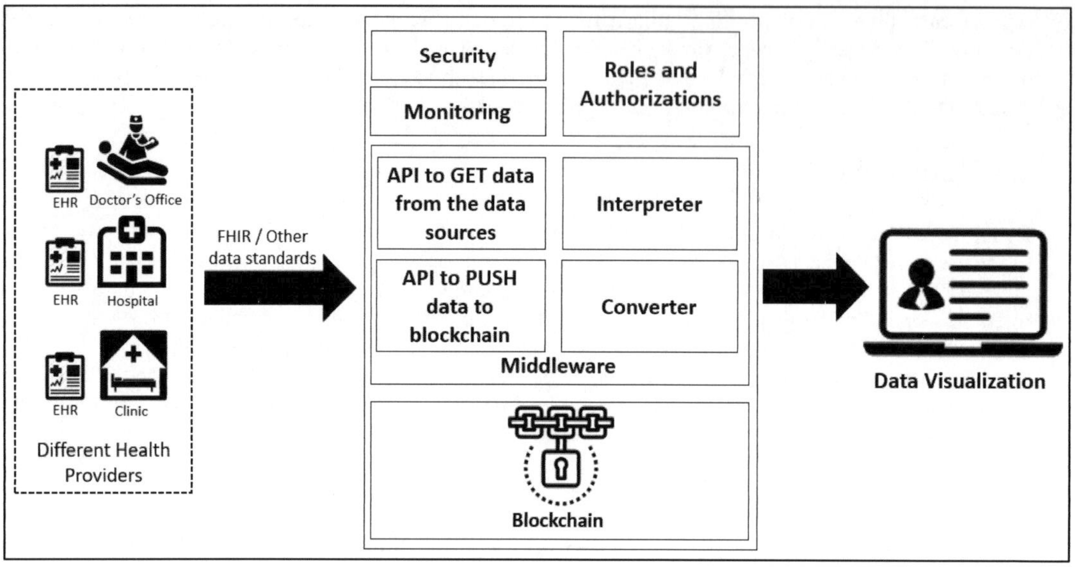

Figure 1. B4Health System Architecture

According to Roehrs et al (2017), safety is a key factor when dealing with health data. The security component is responsible for ensuring that the data leaves health care institutions and goes to B4Health, ensuring the confidentiality, privacy and integrity of the EHR. For this to be possible, we used encryption, digital certificates, and a mechanism for authentication of users who want to gain access to the information. Only health professionals authorized by the patient can access the data. For this, the authors created a structure with user roles. Each of these users has specific authorizations that differ them from one another. We created multiple roles with authorization objects tied to them. The patient can customize them to supply access to health professionals as needed and is able to fully control the access to their information available in B4Health. The monitoring component is for the user to monitor who has access to their data. Through this component, one knows who has permission to access the data. The patient can review a list of people who have access to the EHR data and decide whether to maintain or revoke the institutions' access to shared EHR data. The Data Management API handles fetching the data in the institutions' systems and stores it in B4Health. It authenticates with a user provided by the health institution to fetch the data through an exposed service.

The system encrypts the data before sending over the network or a VPN tunnel can be set up to ensure security between the senders and target system. The data converter is a key component when the system is dealing with data that does not follow the FHIR standard. The main role of the converter is to "translate" the EHR data that is using a different data standard (open or proprietary). This translation occurs automatically or with minimal user interaction. The converter is always looking to preserve the richness of the data. As many authors support the blockchain technology as a key solution for the future of EHR data sharing. We decided to experiment with the most known blockchains frameworks nowadays, Ethereum and Hyperledger Fabric. After exploring both frameworks, the authors started the prototype implementation using Hyperledger Fabric. The reasons that supported this decision are available in the Evaluation and Discussion section of this work. The patient and health professionals can access the EHR after the authentication with user/password and certificates occur. The health professional can access the patient data to which he or she has permission.

2.1 Results

The implementation started with the development environment provision, two virtual machines (VM) were setup with the operating system Ubuntu. The VMs had 2 CPUs Intel(R) Core (TM) i5-7300U CPU @ 2.60GHz and 4 GB of RAM each. The authors installed all requirements and dependencies along with the blockchain frameworks in each VM. As the next step, we started experimenting in each environment with two different blockchain frameworks, Ethereum and Hyperledger Fabric respectively. During this exploration phase, the goal was to become familiar with both frameworks and create a blockchain application capable of dealing with data from the ledger. The authors chose to start the prototype implementation in the Hyperledger Fabric framework, and to accelerate the development we used Hyperledger Composer, which is an open development toolset and framework that makes developing Hyperledger Fabric blockchain applications easier. A scenario of two hospitals exchanging patient EHR information in a private blockchain network was setup. To carry out such scenario, the blockchain network was comprised of two different organizations; each one had two peers, which were responsible to host the ledgers and chaincode. There was one certificate authority (CA) per organization in charge of distributing certificates to the involved actors. We deployed these components in one single host and implemented them as containers in a Docker runtime environment. After the blockchain network was setup, we modeled the B4Health business network and deployed it to the blockchain network.

The authors considered many aspects for the model evaluation. We started by researching and experimenting with different blockchain frameworks, then after many weeks of research and investigation we deployed the application to the chosen framework, deciding to implement the solution in a private blockchain. We used Apache JMeter to generate load against the Hyperledger Fabric blockchain network by simulating a real use case scenario where hundreds of users were accessing the application to retrieve patient EHR data that was already in the blockchain database. We manually loaded the EHR data to the blockchain prior to the tests. The authors configured Apache JMeter to send GET requests to the REST Server to retrieve information from the blockchain. Since the EHR data retrieval is the most common operation performed by the blockchain network participants, we collected and evaluated the performance of such operation. Each GET request retrieved 100 EHRs in text format, each received message body size was around 54557 bytes, while the number of sent bytes from JMeter was 129. JMeter generated load threads with a variety of users ranging from 50 to 1000. We used the following formula for data collection.

$$Average\ Latency\ time = \frac{SUM\ of\ latency\ time\ per\ GET\ request}{Total\ number\ of\ GET\ requests}$$

After we deployed the business network in the blockchain network, we tested it through a simulation of a real use case scenario. As there were two different organizations (Organization 1 and Organization 2), the examination began by adding members to the different organizations, these members received certificates to be able to access the business network through a REST server and perform actions with which they had permissions. Only authenticated members of the network could perform any EHR data manipulation. Considering the proposed scenario of this work, which was to create an application for patients to have a central point of access to their EHR information, in a real-life scenario the most common operations are data creation and data retrieval. For the prototype creation, the authors modeled partially the EHR asset with the Clinical Impression resource from HL7 FHIR standard, this resource is the outcome of the clinical assessment process.

Even though the prototype was running in a virtual machine with a few resources, the authors wanted to perform a stress test to understand the behavior under heavy load. We configured JMeter with 1500 users that executed GET requests for a period of 2 minutes. After the test began, the network stopped responding after 24 seconds, during which JMeter added around 12 users per second. While the network was still responding, the average response time per request was of 21,543.08 ms (milliseconds). When all the VM CPU resources were completely exhausted, the peers running in the Docker container environment stopped responding and went down.

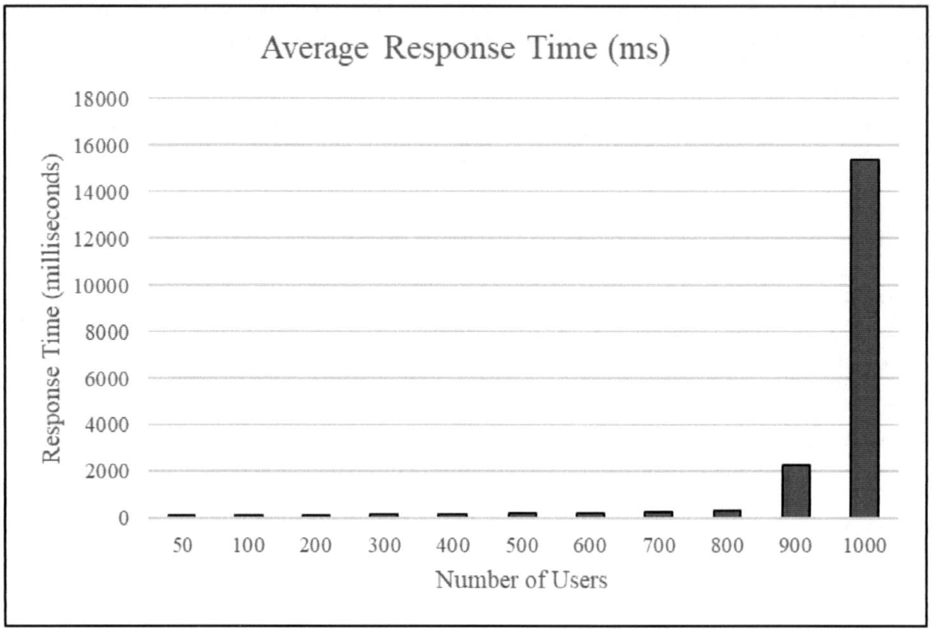

Figure 2. Average Response Time in Milliseconds

2.2 Discussion

Researches from around the world are working in many different projects regarding blockchain in the healthcare sector. For example, recently Chen et al (2019) proposed a blockchain-based encryption scheme for EHRs for different medical organizations and participating individuals (e.g. doctors, hospitals, medical labs, and insurance companies) to access EHRs stored in the blockchain with a higher level of trust. The authors found in the blockchain technology potential to share medical data safely, since EHR data leaking may result in compromising patient privacy. Alonso et al (2019) conducted a review of the existing research works in the literature, which conclude that the blockchain technology applied in eHealth finds new ways of sharing the distributed view of health data and promotes the advancement of precision medicine, improving health and preventing disease. His review of the research works shows that 5.56% of these works correspond to the year 2016, 22.22% to 2017 and 72.22% to 2018, which clearly tells that the research field interest on blockchain for healthcare is increasing over the past years.

After spending a couple of weeks experimenting with a simple setup of Ethereum and Hyperledger Fabric, we chose to continue with the prototype implementation using Hyperledger Fabric. The authors wanted to avoid the expenses related to Ethereum which has its own cryptocurrency, making mining a necessary requirement to run applications productively. On the other hand, Hyperledger Fabric is a private blockchain which does not require mining, it preserves the anonymity of users, making it impossible to verify the identity of account holders, and additionally it is an organization supported by more than 250 companies, including renowned key players from the global health sector industry.

Before starting the development of the blockchain application itself, we had to setup the blockchain network. The authors did not carry out the Hyperledger Fabric network setup easily, they had to learn about the infrastructure aspects of the blockchain network and its components. Fortunately, the Hyperledger Fabric has a wide documentation around the framework and an active online community to support its users. Most of the issues found during the infrastructure setup were about the installation and the network startup. Although the infrastructure setup was challenging, the blockchain application development using Hyperledger Composer framework helped to speed up the development related activities. It allowed to rapidly develop the B4Health use case and deployed the blockchain solution to the blockchain network. The authors chose the tests presented before because of the similarities with typical activities from daily operations executed in health institutions, but they executed them considering the specific use case scenario covered by this work. For example, when someone goes to a medical appointment, usually the doctor asks the person to describe the health history. However, in a scenario where there is a unique viewpoint of patient's EHR data, the doctor would retrieve the EHR history from the system, therefore there would be a lot of parallel reading requests happening. Similarly, after the medical appointment was over, when necessary the doctor creates new EHR records, therefore operations such as EHR update and deletion are not so common in this scenario.

Despite executing performance tests with up to 1000 users, it is worth to mention that the dataset used during those tests was small when compared with real productive scenarios of big health institutions. It is also fair to mention that we performed the tests using a small virtualized server with both organizations. Differently, in a real scenario each organization would use a separate server with much more hardware resources. The authors deployed the blockchain network to a virtualized server, the results collected with Apache JMeter showed an average response time of 336.95 milliseconds when retrieving 100 EHR assets with 800 users in a period of 2 minutes. The average response time showed a net time free of network time, that the application requires retrieving 100 EHRs in a single GET request. The authors believe that it is possible to improve those times, because considering a real use case scenario the end-user may filter by a specific period. Therefore, the system needs to retrieve less data from the ledger, saving both time and hardware resources.

When the CPU consumption reached around 80% of the total capacity, the average response time increased drastically by 45 times. This happened when performing the tests with 1000 users. Another unwanted behavior observed was when the CPU resources were completely exhausted while testing with 1500 users, the peers went down and the blockchain application stopped working completely. In a real use case scenario, the systems administrators could adopt prevention mechanisms to avoid such undesired situation and they could for sure size the blockchain hardware to supply the real network needs. The study had some limitations regarding the proposed architecture model and the tests.

The authors' first proposal was to collect the EHR data from the different health providers with their own built API. Once the data arrived in the B4Health system, the converter component converted from any data standard into FHIR. However, we did not implement this scenario as mentioned in the beginning of this section and because this work did not cover the internal HIS aspects, the interoperability aspects with other data standards were also not part of this work. Additionally, since all the involved components were in the same virtual server, it was not possible to test the solution's scalability due to this hardware restriction.

3. CONCLUSION

In this study, we presented a blockchain architecture model for electronic health records named B4Health. The institutions have been using the EHR to register the patients' information electronically for many years, however this precious data is in many different systems, creating data silos that make the patient care process less efficient. Many institutions implemented these existing HIS systems using different data standards, making it difficult or not possible to exchange information between them. Motivated to overcome such situation, the authors proposed an architecture model for health records based on blockchain. The main outcome was storing part of an electronic medical record in the developed solution, making it possible to have the EHR data available to authorized stakeholders in a unique viewpoint through a decentralized blockchain application.

Since there are many different available blockchain frameworks, the right choice of the platform is a key factor upon the success of any such solution. That was the reason we explored the two major blockchain frameworks available nowadays, Ethereum and Hyperledger Fabric. The model proposed an architecture for patients to have a unique view of their EHR data dispersed in countless systems. However, we still must confirm many other HIS aspects and business requirements not covered here. For example, due to the test limitations regarding dataset size and hardware resources, it is hard to affirm that the proposed model would be able to massively scale to become a national health network.

The authors must submit the prototype through a very robust performance test in the future. We must also cover another key topic in future studies, the interoperability between B4Health and the already existing HIS solutions. As future work, it is important to discover how to embed intelligence into the converter component, so it could convert EHR data stored in a different data standard to HL7 FHIR automatically without losing the data semantics. After going through this exploratory research, it was possible to prove that the blockchain technology has indeed the potential to address the major challenge concerning EHR data scattered in many locations. The authors were able to show using the framework Hyperledger Fabric that by resolving the open challenges mentioned above, all the different parties that need to access the same information in the patient care can benefit from the benefit created by blockchain. One can achieve this goal by working in close collaboration with already existing HIS solutions, as they are the main data source needed by any health care blockchain based solution like B4Health.

ACKNOWLEDGEMENT

The authors would like to thank the Coordenação de Aperfeiçoamento de Pessoal de Nível Superior - Brasil (CAPES) and Brazilian National Council for Scientific and Technological Development (CNPq) for supporting this work.

REFERENCES

Alonso S. G. et al, 2019. Proposing New Blockchain Challenges in eHealth. *Journal of Medical Systems*, pp 43-64.

Angraal, S. et al, 2017. Blockchain Technology Applications in Health Care. *Circulation: Cardiovascular Quality and Outcomes*, Vol. 10, No. 9, pp 253-265.

Azarma M. et al, 2017. Breaking the Healthcare Interoperability Barrier by Empowering and Engaging Actors in the Healthcare System. *Procedia Computer Science*, Vol. 113, pp 326-333.

Chen L. et al, 2019. Blockchain based searchable encryption for electronic health record sharing. *Future Generation Computer Systems*, Vol. 95, pp 420-429.

Dubovitskaya, A. et al, 2017. Secure and Trustable Electronic Medical Records Sharing using Blockchain. *AMIA Annual Symposium Proceedings*, pp 650-659.

Fan K. et al, 2018. Efficient and Secure Medical Data Sharing Via Blockchain. *Journal of Medical Systems*, Vol. 42, pp 136.

Mertz L, 2018. (Block) Chain Reaction: A Blockchain Revolution Sweeps into Health Care, Offering the Possibility for a Much-Needed Data Solution. *IEEE Journals & Magazines*, Vol. 9, no 3, pp 4-7.

Metler, M. 2016. Blockchain technology in healthcare: The revolution starts here. *2016 IEEE 18th International Conference on e-Health Networking, Applications and Services (Healthcom)*. Munich, Germany, pp. 1-3.

Pons E. et al 2016. Natural Language Processing in Radiology: A Systematic Review. *RSNA Radiology*, Vol. 279, pp 329-343.

Reisman M. et al 2017. EHRs: The Challenge of Making Electronic Data Usable and Interoperable. *Pharmacy and Therapeutics*, Vol. 42, no 9, pp 572-575.

Roehrs A. et al 2019. Analyzing the performance of a blockchain-based personal health record implementation. *Journal of Biomedical Informatics,* Vol. 92.

Roehrs A. et al 2017. Personal Health Records: A Systematic Literature Review. *Journal of Medical Internet Research,* Vol. 19, e13.

Roehrs A. et al 2017. OmniPHR: A distributed architecture model to integrate personal health records. *Journal of Biomedical Informatics,* Vol. 71, pp 70-81.

Vuokko R. et al 2017. Results of a systematic literature review from the perspective of secondary use of patient data. *International Journal of Medical Informatics,* Vol. 97, pp 293-303.

Zhang P. et al 2018. FHIRChain: Applying Blockchain to Securely and Scalably Share Clinical Data. *Computational and Structural Biotechnology Journal,* Vol. 16, pp 1-23.

IMPLEMENTATION OF A WEB-BASED AUDIENCE RESPONSE SYSTEM AS MICROSERVICE APPLICATION VS. MONOLITHIC APPLICATION

Iris Braun, Manuel Hoffmann and Robert Mörseburg
Faculty of Computer Science, Technische Universität Dresden, 01062 Dresden, Germany

ABSTRACT

Microservice architectures became very popular in the last years. These small services can be developed, tested and deployed more easily than a single complex monolith. Another aspect which favors microservice architectures is their vast horizontal scalability under high load. But it is often overlooked if their performance is really superior compared to monolithic applications. We investigated test strategies on microservices and defined performance metrics in order to compare the performance of a web-based test application implemented as a monolith as well as a microservices re-implementation. The goal is to decide whether the effort was worth to re-implement our audience response system as microservices or not.

KEYWORDS

Microservices, Monolith, Performance, Tests, ARS

1. INTRODUCTION

The amount of software systems using microservice architectures is constantly increasing. With the concept of microservices, the separation of functional units is further driven to the point where each component becomes an independent service. This is mostly motivated by developer comfort. Smaller and simpler units can be developed, tested and deployed more easily compared to a single complex monolith. Different components of a service can be developed by separate teams. Each team can choose a development style, programming language and technology stack which fits their needs best. Bugs in one part of the application can be fixed faster by updating only the affected services and new features can be introduced smoothly without the need to change other code.

Another aspect which favors microservice architectures is their vast horizontal scalability. While a monolithic application can only be replicated as a whole and with possible side effects on consistency, microservices are a lot easier to scale. If they are properly designed, new instances of a service simply handle part of the requests made to this service. It is usually designed to handle many concurrent requests and operates better under heavy load than a single service. With small and independent services, the application's parts which experience the highest loads can be scaled separately from the lesser utilized parts. This reduces overall infrastructure costs compared to replicating the monolithic application. Maintainability and scalability were consistently ranked as the most important motivations for migration of monolithic applications to microservices [Taibi *et al.* 2017].

However, these advantages come at a cost: To ensure service interoperability their public interfaces need to be defined and documented prior to development. Additional tests for each service as well as for service-to-service communications are required. For the application as a whole, one needs to decide whether the frontend is aware of the different microservices and calls them separately or if it operates against a common backend. In the latter case, a new layer is introduced into the backend which is responsible for accepting and routing traffic to the different services. This is commonly called an *API gateway* and can additionally operate as a load balancer for the individual service instances. Furthermore, to handle complex requests that involve operations on multiple services, a communication overhead is introduced between the separate service instances which doesn't exist in a monolithic application. Virtualization and containerization make the service deployment easier but introduce some overhead themselves.

In this paper we investigate performance testing strategies for microservices: First, we develop a test concept including different scenarios using single and multiple services. Then, we derive concrete test cases for our exemplary application under test – Auditorium Mobile Classroom Service (AMCS) – which is a web-based audience response system. Audience Response Systems (ARS) aim at enhancing the interactivity and quality of lectures by providing feedback to the students and the lecturer. They address problems like the lack of interactivity in huge university classes and facilitates learning in terms of an active, constructive and highly individual process. With AMCS the lecturer is able to construct learning questions, surveys and messages for distinctive students in the lecture [Kapp *et al.* 2014]. These interventions are delivered to the students during the session according to defined rules.

By using AMCS in huge university settings we recognized some performance lacks. Especially at the beginning of the lecture when all students login or register simultaneously or when answering the learning questions the performance breaks down. We made some further investigations to find the causes of this performance problems and identified the backend operations with multiple database interactions. That's why we decided to re-implement the backend as microservice application to separate the functionality into small services which can be scaled up when the system overloads.

We started with surveying open source load and performance testing tools. After detailed comparison of the features we chose one tool and implemented the different test scenarios. Then, we measured our application's performance using both the monolithic and the microservice backend. We compare and discuss the results in chapter 5. Our paper ends with a summary and outlook on further investigations.

2. CONCEPTS OF TESTING THE PERFORMANCE OF MICROSERVICES

We first explain the different scenarios how we tested our application. The overall goal is to load test as many facets as possible to create a full-blown picture of the application. This includes different configurations of nodes involved and their interconnection speed, different number of services and varying request loads.

a) Number of Services

The important thing to remember is that a microservice architecture appears as single interface to the end-user. However, it is possible that in one API request multiple services are involved in generating the response. Therefore, we categorized the test cases by number of services involved.

- *Single Service*: The single service scenario establishes the reference benchmark for response times. With one request we measure the round-trip-time from sending to receiving on client side. This is the minimal time needed for any request against the application under test.
- *Multiple Services*: To handle more complex requests, multiple services are involved into response generation. Thus we expect higher response times which include the duration of service-to-service communication. The performance then depends on the number of services, their corresponding IO operations and computing effort.

b) Varying Requests

To investigate the application's behaviour under different workloads it is necessary to vary the number of requests sent in a given period. We can distinguish between sending requests synchronously and concurrently which simulates the amount of users using the system under test in parallel.

c) Physical Distribution

We believe in a higher latency when all nodes are in different network domains. That is why we first test the services only deployed to a single host and after that they get deployed on multiple hosts, first all connected to the same network cluster and then to different clusters.

- *Single Host:* When deploying all services on one host the latency should be minimal because the services communicate via virtual networks. This is very fast.
- *Multiple Hosts:* In real applications the containers will be distributed over multiple machines to increase reliability and robustness. It makes a difference whether the containers are placed in one physical location or different ones.

- *Single Cluster:* Within the multiple host - single cluster scenario all services are distributed over multiple hosts which are placed in one physical location belonging to one data center. This means that all hosts have a high bandwith connection, the resulting latency in service-to-service communication should be really low.
- *Multiple Clusters:* This scenario consists of multiple services on different hosts distributed over different cloud platform providers all over the world. It is highly scalable and reliable and not dependent on one single provider. This results in higher latency and additional effort to manage vendor specific infrastructure.

3. APPLYING TESTING CONCEPTS IN THE PROJECT

3.1 Architecture of the Test Applications

3.1.1 Frontend

We used the frontend of the monolithic application to test both backend implementations. It is a standalone JavaScript Single-Page-App (*AngularJS*) running on *nginx* web server communicating with the REST interface of the backend. It can easily be configured to work with both backends. Only the backend's address needed to be changed because our microservice implementation was build with the same public API as the pre-existing backend. Once the app was configured it could be packed and delivered by a separate *nginx* webserver which we ran inside our cluster.

3.1.2 Backend

***a) Monolithic application*:** The monolithic application predates our microservice implementation and was used by us as it is. The backend is written in *Ruby* and uses a *Postgres* database. It serves all features to the clients via a REST API, because there also exist native apps for *Android* and *iOS*. All parts run as a single instance on the same virtual machine.
***b) Microservice application*:** Our microservice implementation is written in Java and uses the Spring Cloud software stack. MongoDB document stores are used for persistence. The complete application architecture is shown in Figure 1.

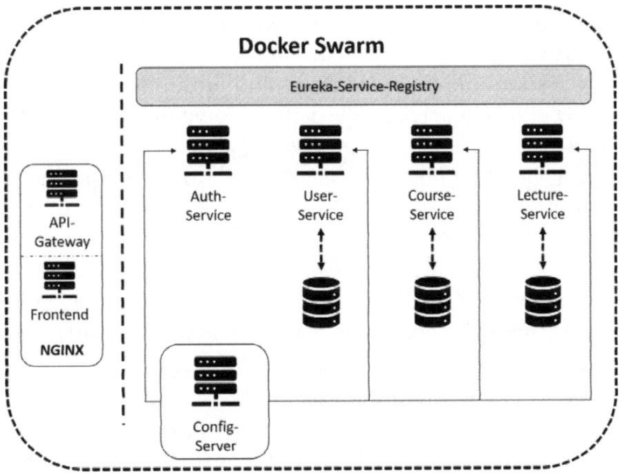

Figure 1. Architecture of the AMCS microservice application

Our microservices are deployed on three virtual machines. Two of them are located on the same host system. To simplify the deployment we decided to fully containerize our application using *Docker*. Furthermore, we used Docker's own cluster management engine, the *swarm mode* [Dockers2019]. To share the service images across all nodes in our cluster we had to provide a custom docker registry as a service.

Spring Cloud comes with a great set of tools to implement a microservice application: It includes *Eureka*, a service registry which we used for routing and service discovery. The service-to-service communication is handled by *Feign* clients, which use *Ribbon* as a client-side load-balancer. We already ran a *nginx* webserver to provide our frontend. It seemed only natural to include the routing functionality for the backend requests in it. Additionally, the *nginx* configuration is very well documented and there were resources available explaining its use as an API gateway [Crilly2018].

3.2 Concrete Test Plans

We already introduced in chapter 2 the concept of different parameters we could test. The next step shown here implements a concrete test plan. In Table I each specific test is described by a scenario name, the involved services, the kind of database access and how the load in terms of how many users accessing the application is distributed over time. The different user load distributions we have chosen are described next:

1) 100 users try to execute the given test in parallel
2) 100 users get ramped up from 0 within 10 s and execute the given scenario
3) 10 users per second over 60 s start executing a test

Each of the tests runs in three configurations:

• The first configuration uses the monolithic application for the performance tests.

• The second one runs all microservices with their databases on two machines which are placed in the same computing center hosted by the same provider. That means low latency for all service-to-service and service-to-database calls.

• The third configuration includes placing the databases on a different machine than the microservices. The database machine is hosted by a different provider whose data center is located in another region.

Table 1. Concrete Test Setup

Test plan No.	Service scenario name	Involved services	Database access	Distribution of user load
01	Login with registration	Auth-S., User-S., Course-S., Lecture-S.	Read and write access	(1), (2), (3)
02	Login without registration	Auth-S., User-S., Course-S., Lecture-S.	Read access	(1), (2), (3)
03	Enroll into one course	Auth-S., User-S., Course-S., Lecture-S.	Read and write access	(1), (2), (3)
04	Get lectures	Lecture- Service	Read access	(1), (2), (3)

3.3 Expected Behaviour

This section is for pre-evaluation of the results before running the tests. Usually there is a gap between the imagination how the measurements will look like and how they are in reality. We expect a difference between tests which require only read access to the database and those which also need write access. For that reason test plan 01 should be slower than test plan 02. They are doing exactly the same excluding the injection of new users into the database. Test 04 will need a significant amount of time too because of its database writes. Test 04 should be the fastest. It does not write anything into database and performs no service-to-service communication.

a) **Configuration dependency:** All tests which will run in the first configuration where the microservices and the databases are placed on two machines within the same computing center are expected to have a better overall performance. Database access needs more time then default inter-service communication. This leads to the expectation that a storage which is not in the same place then the services (configuration two) has longer response times. All in all every test runs in the second composition should take more time than its equivalent from the first one. In the microservice implementation there is an overhead because of service-to-service calls. The observation here should be that only test four takes a similar time compared to the monolithic application. In all other tests the monolith should be faster.

b) **Load dependency:** Another important factor is load distribution. Within the first load scenario both architectures should have poor performance. They use the same reverse-proxy which has to handle all requests at once. Only after passing this bottleneck the microservices will be slower again because they are in a virtual docker network. This network is flooded by the incoming requests itself and additional by all service-to-service communication. The second and third load distribution scenarios are expected to perform nearly similar within the first ten seconds. After this scenario 02 stops requesting so the application can deal with the remaining execution where scenario 03 continuously fires up requests. We are not sure how both applications handle the permanent load but we hope that microservices will perform better here because the execution is distributed over the different services and must not be handled by one application.

4. IMPLEMENTING THE TEST CONCEPTS WITH GATLING

Before we implemented our concrete concepts, we had to decide for one load testing tool. We reviewed scientific sources [Leverger2017, Suominen2017] as well as practical guides [Lönn2017, Toledo2017] combined with our experience to find the best suited performance testing application. We decided to use *Gatling.io* for our performance test implementation. The decision is based on multiple factors. We wanted to use a new and modern tool. That said, *Apache JMeter* is not fulfilling our requirements. We then read some comparisons of performance testing tools in general and some only comparing *Gatling.io* and *Artillery.io*. Gatling.io was mentioned as more stable and adding less measurement error because of its implementation in *Scala* where Artillery.io could probably add more inaccuracy to the results. We also reviewed the available tutorials and official documentations. Gatling.io provided much more information and starting guides. The last point for our comparison was the extensibility of the provided DSL. Where Gatling.io tests can be completely written in the programming language Scala, Artillery.io tests can be provided by YAML configuration files or in JavaScript.

We started with the implementation of our tests by recording all sequences that should be tested. Recording here refers to just click through the website and also enter data, e.g. names or course pins, within a special browser mode which saves all input data into an HTTP-Archive (HAR). In the next step this archive was imported into Gatling.io. The tool then converted these data into its Domain Specific Language (DSL). The generated code needed a refactoring and some additions. We separated the single steps which we want to reuse, like login, logout or enroll. Furthermore, that separation enabled us to drive different test cases by combining the single steps in different orders and execute them in so called scenarios.

Because we want to test thousands of different users interacting with the application, a user feeder was implemented. This feeder dynamically insert data into a given template. The template here is the JSON string that is sent to login a user and the inserted data are numbered usernames and passwords. To authenticate requests the application uses *JSON Web Tokens*. These tokens are generated when a user gets logged in for the first time and is stored at the client side. With each request a token has to be sent otherwise the request will not be executed due to authorization errors. For our performance tests we needed to extract this token from the login response and store it for each user so that the next request of this user is executed with the correct token to ensure that not only one user executes one request multiple times.

Our tests should apply different user loads in order to observe potential bottlenecks. Gatling.io provides various workloads [Gatling2019]. We used the possibilities of executing a bunch of users at once, ramping up users distributed over a given duration and requesting with a constant amount of users per second for a given duration. Finally, we need to test our microservice application and also the monolithic reference application.

5. EVALUATION

In the following we will present the test results in the different test scenarios described in chapter 2.

5.1 Test Plan 1: Register and Login a New User

This is one of the challenging scenarios. It involves a service-to-service request when the *authentication service* queries the *user service* if the new user is already registered. Then, another POST request is issued to register the user, this involves a database write operation. Finally, a token is generated and returned.

1) Load distribution 1: 100 users at once: Sending all user login requests at once puts the server under a very high load. The monolithic application is able to respond to nearly all requests (94%) successfully with a mean response time of 2031 ms. We believe that this relatively high response time is caused by the sequential execution of database writes, forcing late-arriving requests to wait until the first requests are completed.

The microservice application shows different results: In both cases, with the database running in the same or an external cluster, all login requests fail. Investigating this failure further showed that all data inserts were performed in the database but its response time exceeded the timeout limitations set by the Spring components in their default configuration. In our opinion, the performance might be improved by experimenting with configuration settings and service replications. This is beyond the scope of this paper.

2) Load distribution 2: Increasing user count: In this scenario the number of concurrent user registrations is smaller than in the previous one because the number of users increases over a period of 10 s from 0 to 100. This means that some users are already logged in when new users try to register and the overall database load is less than with 100 users at once.

The monolithic application serves all requests successfully and within a mean response time of 126 ms. This is more than sixteen times faster than in the previous load distribution scenario. The microservice application on the other hand is still struggling with the database timeouts. But due to the smaller number of parallel requests, more return successfully: With the database running in the same cluster we observe that 8% of the requests succeed, with an externally running database 28% of the requests succeed. This implies that the higher latency of an external database is far less significant than the configuration restrictions.

3) Load distribution 3: Constant user load: As in the increasing load scenario, the monolith is able to process all requests quickly. Once again, the mean response time is very low at 111 ms.

With an internal database 2% of the requests sent to the microservice application return with success. The percentage improves to 74% when an external database is used. We believe the reason for this behavior is the overall limited computing power and memory consumption of the cluster. With the database instance running in the cluster the available resources are further diminished.

5.2 Test Plan 2: Login an Existing User

In this scenario the user is already registered and only a read operation is performed on the database. The credentials are compared and a token is generated and returned.

1) LD1: The monolithic application shows similar behavior as in the first test plan with a request success rate of 93% and a mean response time of 1276 ms. Database reads are faster than writes and can be performed in parallel explaining the overall faster response. This leads to the conclusion that the database is not the limiting part of the system which seems to be the application server. In the setting using a database inside the same cluster all requests are successful. The mean response time is 2837 ms. With an external database we achieved a 93% success rate and an equal response time. While here the microservice application needs more than twice the time of the monolith we think that in more advanced use cases or under higher loads replicating some of the services might improve the performance and ultimately outperform the monolithic design.

2) LD2: In this scenario all requests in both the monolithic and microservice application are successful. Differences arise once again in the response time: As expected, the monolith responds the fastest with 67 ms, the external database requires 805 ms and the internal database configuration is the slowest with 2673 ms.

3) LD3: Compared to the scenario which includes database writes the systems perform better in this one. Nearly all requests in each configuration were successful. Only the external database showed a 4% failure rate due to the timeouts. The mean response times differ vastly: The monolith only requires 68 ms. The microservice architecture needs 3223 ms with the external and 4535 ms with the internal database.

5.3 Test Plan 3: Enroll into a Course

In this scenario existing users are logged-in. Afterwards, each of them enrolls into the same course.

1) LD1: When this scenario is run against the monolithic application 5% of all requests fail. Whereas in both microservice configurations all calls are successful. The mean response time with the microservice application and an external database is 1819 ms and with the internal database 2124ms. This is significantly slower than the monolith with 912 ms. We conclude that the microservice application has a higher success rate because the overall load of this scenario is spread between different services. They can be run on different nodes in the cluster. Therefore, the individual workload for services and databases, e.g. the authentication service and user database for login and the course service and database for enrollment, is smaller compared to the monolith where a single application and database handles each request.

2) LD2: In this scenario the number of parallel users is constantly increasing but the average request rate is lower than before. Hence, all application configurations can handle it without failing. Once again the monolith is the fastest with a mean response time of 61 ms. The microservice system with an external database requires 789 ms and with an internal database 1360 ms.

3) LD3: This load distribution is very similar to the previous one in terms of the monolith's behavior. It handles all request successfully in a mean time of 81 ms. The microservice application is noticeably slower in both configurations (external database: 4251ms, internal database: 5460 ms).

5.4 Test Plan 4: Get Lectures

Finally we measured the performance of a single service request. We chose the "*Get lectures*" operation which only requires a single database lookup. Because this is such a simple request all systems are able to respond successfully under every user load scenario. We found that the time needed to create a response by the microservice architecture is independent from the database's location. In each scenario the monolith was about twice as fast as both microservice configurations. They still responded within 200 ms.

5.5 Manifestation of the Evaluation Results

In order to verify the previous results we decided to run some more test scenarios. We chose the third user load distribution with a constant amount of users per second because we found this to be very realistic in our use case. Furthermore, we increased the number of concurrent user requests to 20 users per second as it resembles the situation at the beginning of a lecture with a lot of students best. With the monolithic application we observed a higher number of long-running requests than before. 60% of requests took longer than 1200 ms, 23% of requests failed entirely. The mean response time of all successful requests was 1809 ms. The response time distribution can be seen in Figure 2.

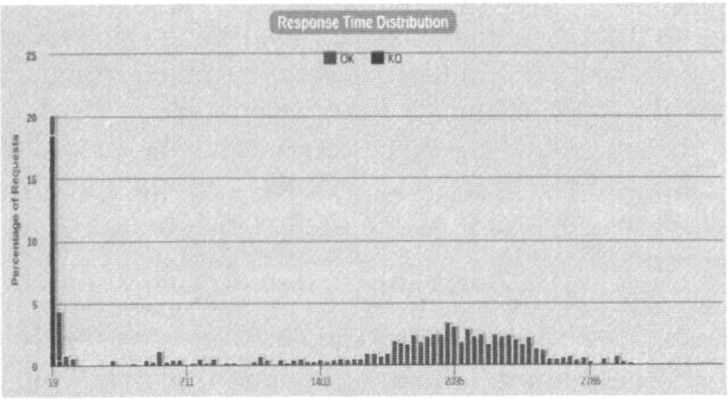

Figure 2. Response time distribution of the monolithic application

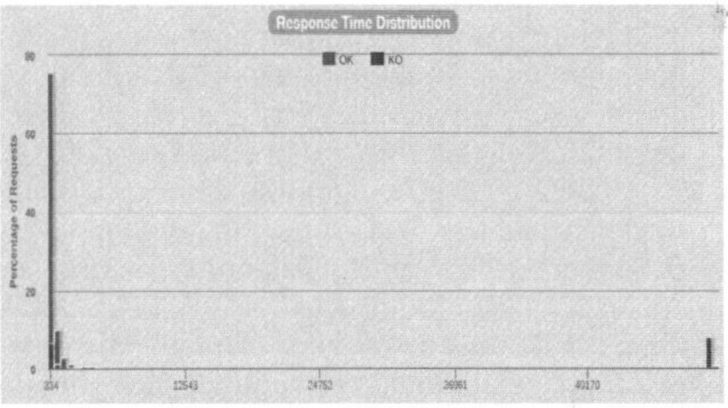

Figure 3. Response time distribution of the microservice application

The number of active users increases because the application is unable to process the incoming requests in time. Backed by these results we tried to employ the advantages of the microservice architecture. We replicated two services for this scenario, the user and authentication service, to allow the application to handle the increased load. We found that with this configuration the microservice application performed better than the monolith. Only 14% of requests failed, 19% took longer than 1200 ms and the mean response time of the successful requests was 429 ms. The response time distribution can be seen in Figure 3.

After finishing and evaluating all test results there are some main takeaways: While we tested the microservice application with different database setups we found that the location of the database has no impact on the overall application performance. Therefore, the deployment of the database can be adjusted to the individual circumstances and capacities. One major drawback of the microservice architecture is the communication overhead between different services. It is clearly visible that the number of services involved in the processing of a single request is proportional to the delay of its response.

In all of the previously tested scenarios the monolith responded faster than the microservice architecture. As we expected there is a limit to the number of concurrent users the monolith is able to serve. If there are more user calls the monolith's performance breaks down. This is the point where more replicas in the microservice system are able to adapt better to the high load factor.

6. CONCLUSION AND FUTURE WORK

To conclude, both monolithic and microservice applications have strengths and weaknesses. We found that for small user loads of up to 10 users per second the monolith was the better choice because it had a higher success rate and shorter response times. If the user load increases the microservice architecture performs better because of its ability to distribute load between different replicas. Contrary to our starting hypothesis the database was not the bottleneck and its deployment does not have much of an influence on overall performance. As expected the inter-service communication overhead is the main problem of the microservice application.

Therefore, it is not always beneficial to choose a microservice approach which is also the outcome of the performance measurements done in [Ueda *et al.*2016]. If the goal is to refactor an existing monolithic application, detailed performance monitoring is required to find potential bottlenecks and attack surfaces for improvement. There won't be a performance gain simply by splitting the application into different services. For larger projects which see a lot of user traffic the microservice architecture can improve overall performance. The monolithic system is both physically and financially limited in its scalability, whereas the microservice application is able to replicate individual services as required to adapt to varying loads. This can be done dynamically as well as cost efficient. While microservices offer a lot of developer comfort by decoupling the individual teams a special focus needs to be put on API design. We found that having a single service for each domain class is not the preferable approach as it increases communication overhead. One should rather design the services following either segmentation in the internal business logic or external usage patterns. This requires more effort by the developer but improves performance.

From a technical perspective we hold the opinion that the Spring ecosystem is not ideal for developing microservice applications. It was indeed very easy to get started because it had all the batteries included for setting up a basic application structure. But once we decided to go deeper it became clear that the documentation is lacking and the configuration is ambiguous. Furthermore, choosing Spring binds you to the Java ecosystem for almost every part of your application. It adds components like load balancing and service discovery to the individual services without explicit declaration from the developer. In our mind this is contradictory to the microservice approach of technologically independent development teams. We prefer to keep the services as lean and "micro" as possible, simply reduced to the application logic they're encapsulating. Any configuration and infrastructure provisioning should be left to external tools. In our microservice implementation we started by using Spring's own components but switched to use external tools like docker, the swarm load balancer and nginx as an API gateway.

Finally, it is important to stress that our findings are solely valid for the examined ARS prototype. We do not want to condemn microservices in general. As this is a very new and constantly developing field further research in efficient components and their performance measurement as well as in optimization techniques is required [Heinrich *et al.*2017].

REFERENCES

Crilly, L. 2018. *Deploying NGINX Plus as an API gateway, Part 1.* URL: https://www.nginx.com/blog/deploying-nginx-plus-as-an-api-gateway-part-1/.

Docker Docs. 2019. *Swarm mode overview.* URL: https://docs.docker.com/engine/swarm/.

Gatling.io. 2019. *Simulation setup.* URL: https://gatling.io/docs/3.0/general/simulation_setup/.

Heinrich, R. et al., 2017. Performance Engineering for Microservices: Research Challenges and Directions. *Proceedings of the 8th ACM/SPEC on International Conference on Performance Engineering Companion. ICPE '17 Companion.* L'Aquila, Italy, pp. 223–226.

Leverger, C., 2017. *Load testing fundamentals.* URL: http://colinleverger.fr/assets/projects/load_testing_fundamentals.pdf

Lönn, R., 2017. *Open Source Load Testing Tool Review.* URL: https://blog.loadimpact.com/open-source-load-testing-tool-review.

Kapp, F., Braun, I., Körndle, H., Schill, A., 2014. Metacognitive Support in University Lectures Provided via Mobile Devices. *Proceedings of the 6th International Conference on Computer Supported Education (CSEdu).* Barcelona, Spain.

Suominen, T., *Performance Testing REST APIs.* 2017. URL: https://www.theseus.fi/bitstream/handle/10024/140116/Suominen_Tero.pdf.

Taibi, D., Lenarduzzi, V., Pahl, C., 2017. Processes, motivations, and issues for migrating to micro-services architectures: An empirical investigation. *Proceedings of IEEE Cloud Computing 4.5*, Honolulu, USA, pp. 22–32.

Toledo, F. 2017. *Gatling vs. JMeter.* URL: https://dzone.com/articles/gatling-vs-jmeter.

Ueda, T., Nakaike, T., Ohara, M., 2016. Workload characterization for microservices. *Proceedings of 2016 IEEE International Symposium on Workload Characterization (IISWC).* Rhode Island, USA, pp. 1–10.

WHY AND HOW TO CAPTURE THE SEMANTICS OF WEB USER INTERFACES

Claudia Steinberger and Joachim Frießer
Department of Applied Informatics, Universität Klagenfurt
Universitätsstraße 65-67, 9020 Klagenfurt, Austria

ABSTRACT

Structured data on the Web has become very important over the last few years. Schema.org has proven to be the most recognized vocabulary for structuring data on the Web. However, most annotations using Schema.org's vocabulary describe exclusively content on websites. Today, these structured content data are mainly consumed by search engines to automatically browse websites with high speed and accuracy and to take over search efforts for humans. Annotated web user interfaces can hardly be found on websites or applications. Schema.org's offered vocabulary to describe actions in a structured way plays a minor role on websites or applications and is mainly applied on rich emails. Also most structured data tools and platforms do not support the annotation of actions triggered via the user interface of a website or application. In this paper we motivate the importance of a semantic description of web user interfaces and present possible application areas to consume these structured data. Thereon, we investigate the suitability of Schema.org for the semantic enrichment of web user interfaces. Since there are hundreds of classes and properties in Schema.org, we present a conceptual model of Schema.org classes and properties suitable to annotate user interfaces of websites or applications. We also show to what extent interactive elements on HTML5 websites or applications can be automatically mapped to these model elements. As a proof of concept we introduce *Schemator*, our WYSIWYG tool to support the semantic enrichment process of web user interfaces. *Schemator* is not only a comfortable structured data tool but acts also as a SAAS platform to store and manage structured web interface data separated from the underlying websites and applications.

KEYWORDS

Semantic Web, Web User Interface, Schema.org, Structured Data

1. INTRODUCTION

Today the challenge in designing websites lies on structured, high quality data. During the last decade amazing progress has been made in enriching data in the Web with semantic data that provides a machine-readable "meaning" of information and is layered over the information that is provided for people.

To structure data on the web, many vocabularies have been developed (Vandenbussche 2017) but Schema.org has proven to be the most widely acknowledged one (Mika 2015) (Guha et al. 2016). The big search engine providers have been the main promoters of Schema.org and semantic data enrichment of data in the Web. They developed a vocabulary [1] which is compact and easy to use to describe "things" on the Web and to make them interoperable and machine read- and understandable. Today structured data is consumed by search engine bots to correctly classify and interpret website content. It is used to feed their knowledge graphs (Paulheim 2017) and to provide better search results on end user requests. Better positions and representations in organic search results, knowledge cards or widespread online map services in turn motivate website designers and operators to provide structured data on their websites. Today over 10 million websites use Schema.org to markup some of their content. Compared to websites with a rather static set of pages that offer viewers with content details, interactive web applications, where user engagement is higher and dynamic content and actions predominate, structured data is behind.

This paper describes why and how to semantically enrich user interfaces of websites or applications beyond content and individual actionable elements. What would a machine-readable 'meaning' of website or application user interface elements and thus the understanding of their features enable? Structured user

[1] https://schema.org/docs/schemas.html

interface data could be used e.g. for the conversational handling of websites or applications using intelligent personal assistants or chatbots, for workflow management or to search the Web for special features. Structured user interface data could also be used by intelligent assistance systems as a means to guide a user through an application (Steinberger, Michael 2019).

In this paper we investigate the suitability of Schema.org to semantically enrich websites or application user interface elements. As there exist hundreds of classes and properties in Schema.org we present a conceptual model of appropriate Schema.org classes and properties to annotate interaction elements. We also show how interactive elements on HTML5 websites or applications can be automatically scanned and mapped to this model elements. As a proof of concept we introduce *Schemator*, our WYSIWYG tool to support the semantic enrichment process of web user interfaces. *Schemator* is not only a comfortable structured data tool but acts also as a SAAS platform to store and manage structured web interface data separated from the underlying websites and applications.

This paper is structured as follows: Chapter 2 presents application scenarios of structured data in the Web today focusing on the Schema.org vocabulary. Chapter 3 deals with the elements and relations of a web user interface, its semantics we intent to make machine-readable and how to describe them using Schema.org. We present a conceptual model of the necessary Schema.org excerpt and present an approach to map interactive HTML-constructs on websites to target classes of this model. Chapter 4 introduces the *Schemator*, a tool we built to evaluate our approach. *Schemator* supports the semantic user interface enrichment process as a SaaS and offers a WYSIWYG interface loading the web site or application under annotation. Chapter 5 summarizes our findings and gives an outlook to identified further research challenges.

2. STRUCTURED DATA ON THE WEB - PRODUCERS AND CONSUMERS

In recent years, amazing advances have been made in enriching data on the Web with semantic data that provide a machine-readable "meaning" of information. The number one consumer of structured data on the Web are machines, not humans. A human user never sees structured text on a web page, but e.g. web-bots or other "intelligent agents" do. Therefore, semantic interoperability and the exchange of data with an unambiguous meaning plays a major role in the Semantic Web.

Schema.org has proven to be the most acknowledged vocabulary to structure data on the Web. Schema.org is a collaborative community project promoted by the big search engine providers with the mission to create and maintain a vocabulary for structured data used on webpages, in email messages, and beyond. Schema.org can be encoded in RDFa, Microdata or JSON-LD and interpreted and individually used by any tool or service that receives the structured data (Mika 2015).

Today, structured data are mainly consumed by search engines to automatically browse websites with high speed and accuracy and to take over search efforts for humans. The annotation with structured data increases the chance of a website to appear as a rich result, for example a rich snippet, a featured snippet or quick answer. Rich results are in turn also often used as the sources for answers in voice search. As a result, Schema.org structured data are mainly produced and provided on websites in the context of semantic search engine optimization (Henry 2018) for content types with mostly direct or indirect commercial relevance like products, places, events, books, videos, films, persons, organizations and more.

Although most uses of the Schema.org vocabulary explain "things", there exist elements on websites and applications that are not content, but ways to take action. Schema.org also offers a vocabulary to describe actions in a structured way, simply called *Actions*. But structured action data can hardly be found on websites or applications. As Schema.org has grown, it offers various mechanisms for community extension as a way of adding more detailed descriptive vocabulary that builds on the Schema.org core. Nevertheless, the most extensions deal with content (Hepp 2015) (Barker et al. 2016) too, although some try to use and extend the vocabulary e.g. to annotate HTTP APIs to enable the automation of service calls (Simsek et al. 2018).

Annotating data for web content is complicated and costly but website designers and operators have been motivated in return for better search engine ranking and results. Producing structured data web designers have to deal with the vocabulary to use, how to simply create the desired annotations and how to represent, to store and to publish them. The demand for tools to produce structured data has grown. There exist a lot of annotation tools and plugins with different levels of automation. Most of them are not widely used because they are embedded in a CMS that enforces access rights to the CMS backend and usually only support certain

Schema.org classes. Some tools are strictly decoupled from the underlying website and generate and store annotations separated from the content. But the complexity of the offered vocabulary combined with missing WYSIWYG functionality often overburden the average producer of structured data. To counteract this (Khalili, Auer 2013) (Kärle et al. 2017) have worked on solutions for the creation, publication and distribution of semantic annotations of content in an easier and more intuitive way.

Besides search engines, knowledge graphs and knowledge vaults are one of the major consumers of structured data. Knowledge vaults are typically large scale knowledge bases that collect and express their data using a shared semantic vocabulary. Some are open for all to use and can be queried using an API. Their main goal is to store millions of entities and reliable, associated facts about those entities. Some of the more prominent players in development include Google Knowledge Graph and Knowledge Vault, Bing's Satori, DBPedia or Wikidata (Paulheim 2017) (Färber et al. 2018). Google uses its knowledge graph e.g. to generate knowledge cards shown in the search console.

Also other intelligent agents started to consume Schema.org annotations. The Schema.org markup "Speakable"[2] for instance enables language assistants to reproduce the contents of a website linguistically on demand. Annotations of content and actions in emails can help them to stand out from the rest in the inbox, be consumed to enable the user to call go-to actions very easily (e.g. order an item, check in a flight, reset password) or to summarize and to highlight key information in the inbox app. Also intelligent personal assistants start to support voice-activated actions based on annotated emails.

To the best of our knowledge, there is no approach to semantically enrich the user interface of a website or application. The machine-readable 'meaning' of all relevant website or application interactive elements and thus the understanding of its user interface functionality enables new possibilities for intelligent agents. Let's think, for example, on conversational handlings of websites and applications using intelligent personal assistants or chatbots, web application workflow management agents, online help agents, the interoperability of web applications with intelligent assistance systems (Steinberger, Michael 2018) or the possibility to search web sites and applications for certain functions.

With our approach we want to semi automatically generate, validate, store and publish semantic annotations beyond content and individual go-to action elements with the primary focus on the user interface of websites or applications. Our approach aims to create an open knowledge base that can be read and edited in the crowd, separating structured user interface data from the underlying websites and applications.

In the following we investigate how to semantically describe a web user interface with Schema.org and how to scan and map HTML5 interaction elements to our conceptual model of selected Schema.org classes. With *Schemator* we present a web application whose main purpose is to make the annotations of website or application functionality easy and intuitive. But *Schemator* is not only a platform for generation, editing and storage of annotations but also to validate and publish them. By this way *Schemator* offers a free and open knowledge base of structured user interface data collected in the crowd, separating structured user interface data from the websites they describe.

3. SEMANTIC DESCRIPTION OF WEB USER INTERFACES

Before we take a closer look at the *Schemator platform*, we present our research process on the semantic description of web user interfaces with structured data (see figure 1): First in (I), we selected typical website or application use cases like the homepage of our University, a well-known online shop and an online banking application. Based on these use cases, we identified and categorized those user interactions that we wanted to consume later in conversations with intelligent personal assistants, chatbots or intelligent assistance systems (Michael et al. 2018)(Steinberger, Michael 2018).

[2] https://schema.org/speakable

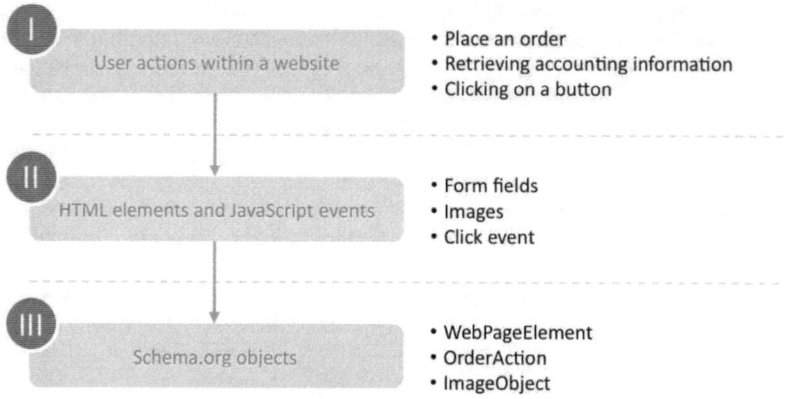

Figure 1. Step-by-step process for creation of the semantic user interface data following (Frießer 2019)

Thus, not every clickable HTML element on a website or application has been relevant for us. Fortunately, some of the big companies like Apple, Google, Mozilla and Microsoft have been working on the development of the HTML living standard (WHATWG). A concept named "inertness" was introduced there: If an element is identified as *inert*, the user agent (e.g. the browser) hast to ignore this element for user interaction (e.g. text search or selection). So we could identify a number of interactive HTML elements focusing only those covering at least an activation behavior as specified in (WHATWG): "*change*", "*click*", "*contextmenu*", "*dblclick*", "*mouseup*", "*pointerup*", "*reset*", "*submit*" and "*touchend*" (Frießer 2019).

The next challenge was to semantically describe the interaction elements found with the vocabulary of Schema.org. Schema.org covers a large catalog of classes and properties, but only a small part of the language is necessary to describe the identified interaction elements. Based on our use cases we developed in (III) a conceptual model of the Schema.org classes for that purpose. Figure 2 shows our target structured data vocabulary for the web user interface description:

A website or application can be described by using the class *WebApplication*. Every single page of a web application is characterized by the class *WebPage* that obtains respectively persist of multiple instances of the class *WebPageElement*. They are all subtypes of CreativeWork and therefore inherit properties such as name or description. *MediaObjects* and the more specific types *AudioObject*, *VideoObject* and *ImageObject* can be linked by applying the property *associatedMedia*. Every associated *WebPageElement* has a *potentialAction* property that is a *result* to another *WebPage* or *Action*. Finally a certain way for navigating through the different web pages may described as a *BreadCrumbList*.

What triggers the interaction with a *WebPageElement* can be described using the property *hasPotentialAction* referencing an *Action*. Each Action has a *name*, a *description* and a *result*. Latter is of type *CreativeObject* (and thus e.g. again a *WebPage*). Several specific *Action* types like *AchieveAction*, *SearchAction*, *CreateAction* and more are predefined in Schema.org (Steinberger, Michael 2019).

Our goal was to create structured user interface data according to this Schema.org excerpt model. Figure 3 shows a simplified example of the JSON-LD description of the launch site of Amazon.com (seen with Google SD-Tool)[3]. To create this kind of structured data, we wanted to map HTML user interface elements as automatically as possible to the selected Schema.org classes and properties. Thus, in (II) we investigated the HTML elements and Javascript events on our use case websites or applications in more detail. What semantic information about an identified user interface element can be retrieved from the document object model (DOM)?

[3] https://search.google.com/structured-data/testing-tool

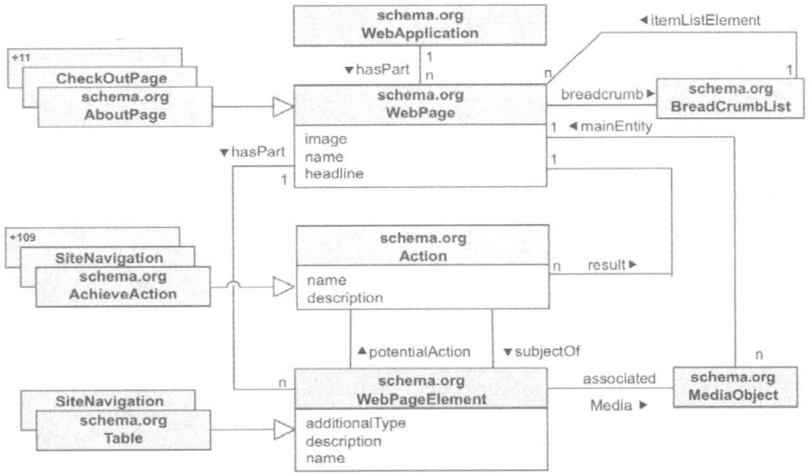

Figure 2. Conceptual model of Schema.org excerpt necessary for user interface description (Frießer 2019)

Figure 3. Structured user interface data of the launch site of Amazon.com seen with Google SD-Tool

Our investigations showed that the required semantic user interaction data could not be reliably and completely extracted from the identified HTML elements on the websites or applications (Frießer 2019). Some naming conventions have been specified in the semantics section of (WHATWG), which state that the name of a HTML tags can have a certain meaning and a clue for the purpose, e.g. the "*addr*" tag is used for an address. But such conventions are not reliably adhered to. Even the label or rather a text can be a hint for the functionality of e.g. button, but if an icon is used, a machine won't be able to guess or "see" what the purpose of the control is.

However, the knowledge gained about which interactive controls are associated with an event is sufficient for an initial draft of a website's structured user interface data, which must then be manually checked and supplemented. The next chapter takes a closer look onto the tool support for a semi-automatic semantic description of web user interfaces and defines the user roles and the architecture of our *Schemator* platform.

4. SCHEMATOR: STRUCTURED USER INTERFACE DATA MANAGEMENT PLATFORM

Schemator is a WYSIWYG tool to support the semantic enrichment process of web user interfaces. *Schemator* is not only a comfortable semi-automatic structured data tool but acts also as a SAAS platform to store and manage structured web interface data separated from the underlying websites and applications. Figure 4 shows the roles that users can assume working with *Schemator*: (1) *Tagger*, (2) *Content Admin*, (3) *Data Consumer* and (4) *Model Designer*.

The (1) *Tagger's* main task is to register and to annotate the user interface of websites or applications with *Schemator* and to produce structured user interface data in a semi-automatic this way: With his knowledge of the functionality of a particular website or application and the way a user typically performs certain tasks there, the *Tagger* creates structured data semi-automatically in a WYSIWYG mode and stores it on the platform. After a desired website has been selected or registered, he can view the website in "browser mode" superimposed into *Schemator* in a WYSIWYG representation. To edit existing or add new semantics to the depicted website or application, the *Tagger* can switch from "browser mode" to "annotate mode" (see figure 5). Interactive elements and their properties are displayed now in the *element catalog* on the left side of the user interface. By clicking on an element on the left, *Schemator* highlights the control (e.g. an input field or a button) and scrolls it into the *Tagger's* view if necessary. Now the *Tagger* is able to focus the interactive element and to edit the corresponding structured data. An advantage of using *Schemator* is that the *Tagger* does not need to have any previous knowledge of Schema.org. The input fields are dynamically generated based on the Schema.org excerpt model, as shown in figure 2.

To prevent villains from abusing the platform, the (2) *Content Admin* validates annotations, grants or denies user rights or bans unwanted websites. The (3) *Data Consumer* consumes structured data for further purposes in form of JSON-LD documents. In fact, the structured data can be also embedded as an external link target of a script tag. Finally the role of the (4) *Model Designer* is to define/edit the model of the Schema.org vocabulary that is supported by *Schemator* (at the moment the excerpt in figure 2 is supported). That means, *Schemator* is flexibly customizable this way.

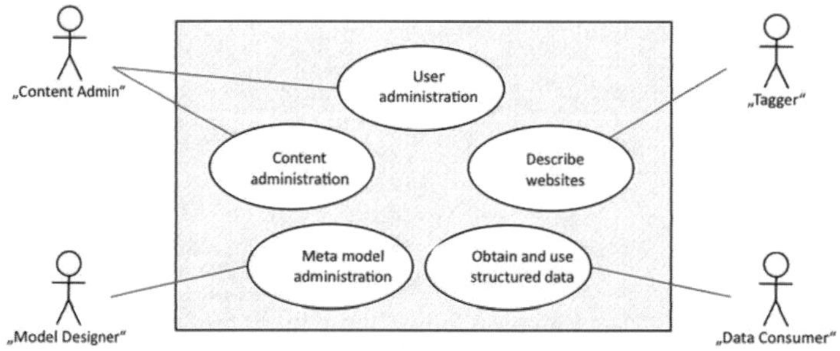

Figure 4. Use case diagram of the *Schemator* platform

The prototype of *Schemator* was implemented as a web application in the context of a master thesis at the Universität Klagenfurt and covers the main functionality for the "Tagger" and the "Data Consumer" roles (Frießer 2019). *Schemator* consists of a client and a server component. As figure 6 shows, due to security reasons the user agent does not directly interact with a website or application under consideration. The server component additionally acts like an "in between web proxy".

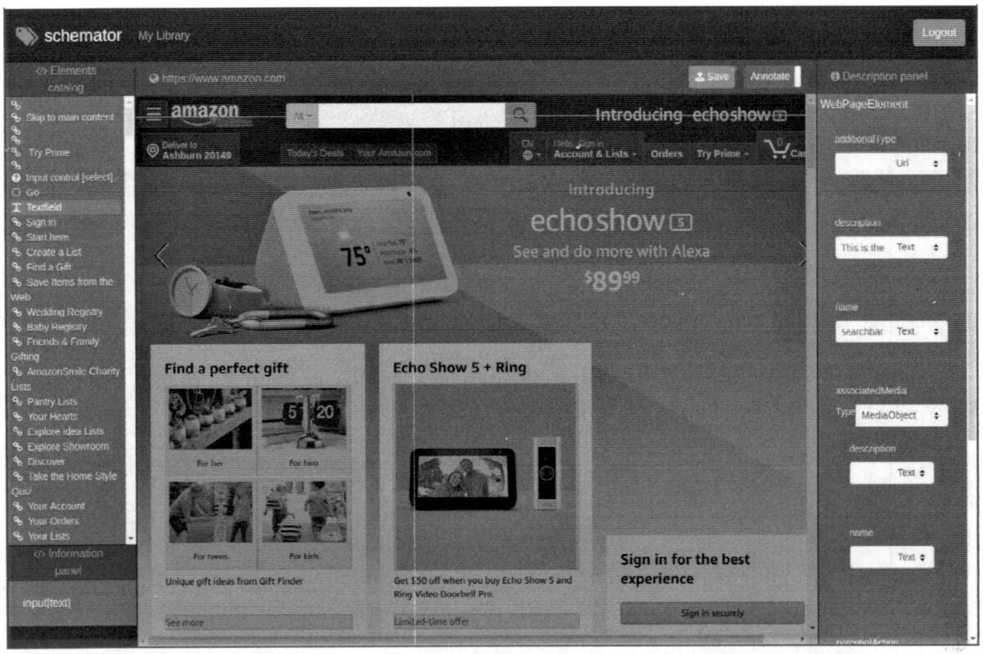

Figure 5. User interface of *Schemator* showing Amazon.com in the “annotate” mode

The *Content Checker* scans the website or application and only if it considered as safe, than *Schemator* acts like a real webserver proxy and saves the downloaded files in the *Web Cache Storage*. *Schemator's* main data representation and interchange format is JSON-LD, even for the representation of the Schema.org excerpt model as presented in chapter three. Because of the strong use of JSON-LD, MongoDB[4], a document-driven database, is used for persistent data management in the server component. The task of the client component of the schema is to recognize the potential "tag-worthy" interactive elements of the website.

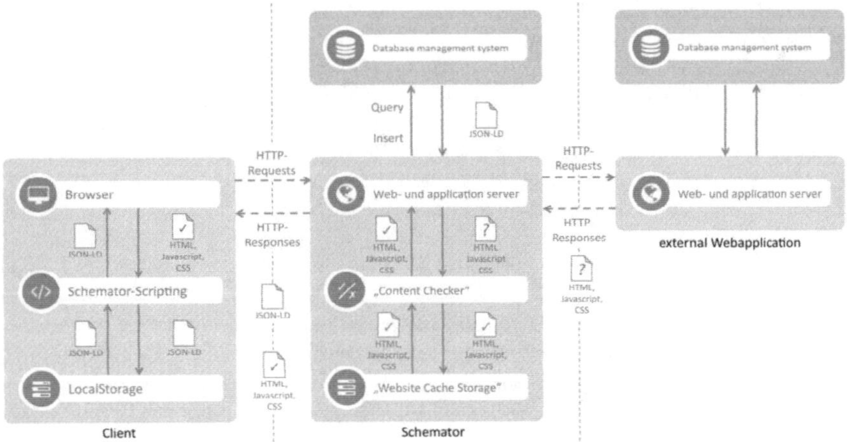

Figure 6. System architecture of the *Schemator* following (Frießer 19)

Some common frameworks like *Bootstrap* and *jQuery*[5] are used for the user interface and business logic, the latter framework is mainly responsible for the interactive control detection. Finally the *LocalStorage* as defined in (WHATWG) is used to temporary save valuable information of already annotated items. This architecture allows a disaster recovery of the data if the browser crashes during the tagging process.

[4] https://www.mongodb.com/
[5] https://getbootstrap.com/; https://jquery.com/

5. CONCLUSION AND OUTLOOK

In this paper we motivated the importance of structured user interface data and showed that the Schema.org vocabulary is suited also to semantically enrich the user interface of websites or applications. We presented a conceptual model of appropriate Schema.org concepts to annotate interaction elements and showed possibilities and limits to map interactive HTML5 elements to this Schema.org model elements.

As a proof of concept we presented *Schemator*, our WYSIWYG tool to support the semantic enrichment process of web user interfaces. The existing version of the *Schemator* does not yet fulfill all use cases shown in figure 4, but it covers the core functionality. The tagging process works and the resulting JSON-LD can be consumed by intelligent agents. *Schemator* is not only a comfortable structured data tool but also serves as a SAAS platform to store and manage structured web interface data separated from the underlying websites and applications.

In future we will continue developing the next version, collect structured user interface data of selected websites and applications and evaluate the *Schemator*. We will also work on the integration of *Schemator* into our active assisted living projects (Steinberger, Michael 2019).

REFERENCES

Barker, P., & Campbell, L. M. (2016). Technology Strategies for Open Educational Resource Dissemination. In P. Blessinger, & B. T. J., *Open Education: International Perspectives in Higher Education* (pp. 51-70). doi:10.11647/OBP.0103.03.

Färber, M., Bartscherer, F., Menne, C., & Rettinger, A. (2018). *Linked data quality of dbpedia, freebase, opencyc, wikidata, and yago*. Semantic Web, 9(1), 77-129.

Frießer, J. (2019). *Semantische Aufbereitung von Benutzeroberflächen von Webapplikationen für die aktive Assistenz mit HMBS*, diploma thesis, to be published in July2019.

Guha, R. V., Brickley, D., & Macbeth, S. (2016). *Schema. org: evolution of structured data on the web*. Communications of the ACM, 59(2), 44-51.

Hepp, M. (2015, June). *The web of data for e-commerce: Schema. org and GoodRelations for researchers and* practitioners. In International Conference on Web Engineering (pp. 723-727). Springer, Cham.

Kärle, E., Şimşek, U., & Fensel, D. (2017). *semantify. it, a Platform for Creation, Publication and Distribution of Semantic Annotations.* arXiv preprint arXiv:1706.10067.

Khalili, A., & Auer, S. (2013, October). *Wysiwym authoring of structured content based on schema.org*. In International Conference on Web Information Systems Engineering (pp. 425-438). Springer, Berlin, Heidelberg.

Michael, J., Steinberger, C., Shekhovtsov, V. A., Al Machot, F., Ranasinghe, S., & Morak, G. (2018). *The HBMS story*. Enterp. Model. Inf. Syst. Arch, *13*, 345-370.

Mika, P. (2015). *On Schema.org and why it matters for the web*. IEEE Internet Computing, 19(4), 52-55.

Paulheim, H. (2017). *Knowledge graph refinement: A survey of approaches and evaluation methods*. Semantic web, 8(3), 489-508.

Şimşek, U., Kärle, E., & Fensel, D. (2018). *Machine readable web apis with schema.org action annotations.* Procedia Computer Science, 137, 255-261.

Steinberger, C., & Michael, J. (2018). *Towards cognitive assisted living 3.0*. In 2018 IEEE International Conference on Pervasive Computing and Communications Workshops (PerCom Workshops) (pp. 687-692). IEEE.

Steinberger, C.,Michael J. (2019). *Using Semantic Markup to Boost Context Awareness for Assistive Systems* in Feng Chen, Rebaca I. García-Betances, María Fernanda Cabrera-Umpiérrez, Liming Chen, Chris Nugent: Smart Assisted Living, (to be published in October 2019).

Vandenbussche, P. Y., Atemezing, G. A., Poveda-Villalón, M., & Vatant, B. (2017). *Linked Open Vocabularies (LOV): a gateway to reusable semantic vocabularies on the Web.* Semantic Web, 8(3), 437-452.

WHATWG. https://whatwg.org/, retrieved on 2019/05/24

ARCHITECTURES FOR DELIVERING PROACTIVE NETWORK SERVICES IN DIVERSE BUSINESS ENVIRONMENTS

Don Allen
Ph.D.
Cisco Systems, Inc.
14765 Pristine Drive, Colorado Springs, CO 80921, USA

ABSTRACT

The introduction and adoption of cloud-based, as-a-service capabilities have had a dramatic impact on the network service management capabilities and the software architectures required to address the varied deployment requirements of customers. Historically customers were constrained, by cost, regulations, or technology, on how they designed and deployed their networks. In those environments customers deployed network management systems to manage the operations of their IT capabilities composed of vendor and opensource software. These systems were typically reserved for business-critical systems and had an operating cost above and beyond those of the business systems themselves. These support systems initially provided basic monitoring and alerting and over time expanded to include high value services such as security checks, compliance checks, policy management, and health monitoring. Over the previous decade there has been a move to migrate not only business capabilities but also the associated support systems into the cloud to reduce both software and administrative costs. This migration has not been ubiquitous across all industries due to regulatory, compliance, and security concerns as well as the nature of the company's inherent business. This has driven the need for network service management companies to develop architectures that adapt to these new deployment models. This paper identifies 4 canonical service deployment architectures under development to address the diversity of on premise, cloud, in-a-box, and hybrid business system deployment models.

KEYWORDS

Network Management, Architectures, Services, Software

1. INTRODUCTION

There have been several changes in the network management industry that are forcing new architectures to be considered, designed, and deployed. Network management systems are overlays on top of operating networks that are designed to ensure the availability of the network. Ensuring availability takes many forms; identifying potential vulnerabilities, misconfigurations, hardware failures, performance issues, predictions of future issues, etc. The availability and adoption of cloud-based as-a-service capabilities, the increased scrutiny on network security, company and individual data privacy, and managing overall risk have resulted in a diverse set of customer network architectures. It is not uncommon to see multiple network architectures deployed within a single, moderate size customer. Designers of network services that overlay or integrate into this application architectures have had to establish new engagement architectures when considering how to support the evolving landscape. Historically, network management systems have employed a central controller, deployed on customer premise, which utilized secure shell remote connections to a network element or a network element to controller push model, to obtain information from the network element. The central controller processed the data and would raise an alarm, send a notification, or provide some visualization of the data to an operator. As more and more network elements become more full-fledged software applications, opening remotely callable APIs, the network products are becoming more "open" and management agents deployed on those elements more capable. This presents a challenge to network management tool developers to utilize these newfound capabilities in ways that the support customer deployment constraints/requirements, interoperability, and DevOps.

The rapid expansion of internet access and use over the last decade has placed a significant burden on companies serving the larger markets (such as Facebook, Google, Amazon, etc.). In these web-scale companies the traditional network monitoring tools that raise alarms requiring human response are too expensive and slow to address the expectations of the customers using the provided services. These web-scale companies have moved to a highly homogenous network, compute, and storage environment and have had some success in developing autonomous, self -healing systems with automated remediation of some machine detected problems. Facebook has developed Facebook Auto Remediation (FBAR) service (Komorn, 2011), LinkedIn has developed Nurse (Sherwin, 2015), Google has developed several tools based on their Site Reliability Engineering principles with the goal of maintaining an always on/almost always on set of services. These capabilities all have a common core requirement in order to be able to provide automatous network management – homogeneity across their systems. This homogeneity keeps costs low, allows the reuse of automation across multiple "products", and target specific skills and knowledge needed to operate their systems. As the benefits of these types of systems have become more widely known across the industry, non-web-scale companies have become to request/demand comparable capabilities from their technology vendors. The net-scale inhouse management architects are typically composed 3 components; 1) Monitor, 2) Analyze, and 3) Act and focus on address operational issues with the service. The monitor component looks for events, analyze judges where the issue is "real", and if so tell the act component to perform some operation (such as restarting, adding, or removing a service component.

Cisco Systems, Inc. is a $50B company with hundreds of thousands of customers and over 60,000 partners. Cisco developers and supports networking, wireless and mobility, security, collaboration, data center, and internet of things products to customers across all business segments; financial, manufacturing, service provider, government, etc. Customers are looking to Cisco to develop network management solutions that will deliver the autonomous detection and remediation capabilities seen in the web-scale companies' implementations.

This paper will provide an overview of the capabilities that need to be deployed in a services-focused management framework across heterogeneous customer engagements and introduces four customer engagement architectures that are being used in the design of network service management software within Cisco Services to support the changing customer network deployments.

2. SERVICE NETWORK MANAGEMENT FUNCTIONAL CAPABILITIES

The business of providing network services to deployed environments has traditionally been focused on providing break-fix support, software upgrades, and professionals services (mostly providing expertise to customers for whatever they are willing to pay for within required margins). As networks have become more complex and expansive, new service-oriented capabilities have begun to be developed to reduce some of the growing complexity and to automate the more redundant, human intensive tasks and offload those to machines. To discuss automation in the context of architecture, it is relevant to describe the functional capabilities that must be addressed in those architectures.

A complete functional view of a network management architecture would require a considerable amount of space and is not required for this discussion. For descriptive purposes this paper will consider what constitutes the "back bone" capabilities required to overlay network management services on an operational network. This are represented in Figure 1 and described in the following section.

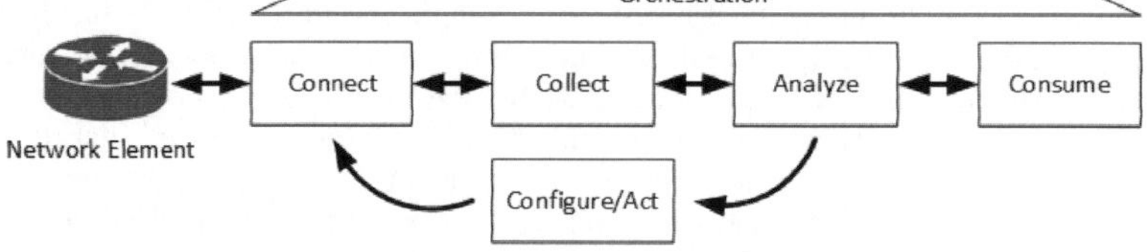

Figure 1. Backbone service management capabilities

2.1 Network Element

For the purposes of the discussion in this paper a network element is any network device (physical or virtual) or any application providing a service that requires the network to function. Examples of a device are a switch, router, server, firewall, etc. and networked service would be a call manager, media server, identity service, etc.

2.2 Connect

To collect data from and change the configuration of a network element some type of connection to the network element must exist. In network service management a connection has historically be in the form of a remote ssh to a device or via SNMP. Over the past several years network hardware and software vendors have been introducing software agents into the network element operating systems or application programmable interfaces (APIs) to access and operate on network elements remotely. The current environments mirror a bit the systems administration environment in the late 1980's and 1990's (Nwana, 1996). Network element connectivity can be managed directly through a connection to between the network element and a cloud API or through a product or service management controller (see Figure 2). Access to and management of the connectivity can be at the network element or controller level, increasing the flexibility required in service management architectures and the complexity to software lifecycle of those architectures.

2.3 Collect

There are two types of data available from a network element that need to be collected to support different types of analysis; in-motion and at-rest. In-motion data is the data that represents the operation of the services provided by the network element (e.g., packet flow, response time, syslog events, etc.) and the context in which that network element is operating (e.g., CPU or memory utilization, temperature, fan speed, etc.). At-rest data refers to the configuration of a network element such as which features are turned on and how those features are configured for use. Typically, at-rest data changes are infrequent and so have different collection, change tracking, transport, storage, and analysis requirements. At-at rest data for large, multi-component devices, and network wide solutions can be substantive in size (e.g. in the hundreds of megabytes).

The data available requirements to support the application of AI/ML and the response time required to maintain system availability are driving the need to place more analysis on the network element and to only collect the minimum data needed. Data collection requirements to support the different types of automation management must be aggregated and reconciled across the different consuming functions to minimize the network element resources used to gather and then transmit the data.

Data security, industry and government compliance, privacy issues, and transmission costs are all factors that impact what data is collected and where it is stored, the form it is stored in (anonymized or raw), and who can access it. Much of the network data needed to be collected for analysis contain potential negative business impact should a breach occur, and so customers are very protective of this data.

2.4 Analyze

As noted early, there are a multitude of services that can be delivered to support the continued operation and availability of network systems and these services are difficult at times to separate. In Gartner's Magic Quadrant for Network Performance Monitoring and Diagnostics (Ganguli and Corbett, 2019) the authors identify three primary focus areas of network performance monitoring and diagnostics tools; 1) digital experience monitoring, 2) networked application monitoring, and 3) network component interactions where each of their performance areas would provide analysis looking at real-time, historical, and predictive analysis. The focus areas combined with the type of analysis perform present a diverse set of requirements when it comes to collecting, aggregating, analyzing, and presenting results across a diverse set of network elements.

A discussion on network analysis would not be complete without some mention of the impact of Artificial Intelligence (AI) and Machine Learning (ML) on the future of network management. The opportunities for the application of AI/ML are quite broad while at the same time quite challenging. Developing ML base models to support predictive analysis require large training data sets, the more complex the environment the more data is required. The larger the training data the greater the computation power required to develop the base models and test them. The cost and uniqueness of the resources required preclude many businesses from having them available to them on prem and many network management vendors are beginning to offer cloud-based analysis capabilities (e.g., Cisco DNAC).

Analysis of network element data should be performed closer to the element itself to avoid the resources needed to transmit it. Pushing the data to the cloud uses network capacity as well transmitting a lot of data which in the end has operational value since it is typically "normal".

2.5 Consume

The need to make a change on a network element to remediate a detected issue requires components who have the proper access to a device and the appropriate permissions to execute the requisite actions. Historically few network element changes have been permitted by customers due to the potential impact on network or networked application availability due the inability of such changes to adequately address the complexity of the and interdependencies among network element. The use of command line interface to make configuration changes have been problematic in the past; the introduction of Netconf and Yang-based management capabilities with APIs have improved on previous states and have promise to automate a greater number of situations where automated issue resolution can be applied.

2.6 Orchestration

The overall control of the different network management capabilities across the network elements in a customer deployment is complex, requiring the coordination of distributed activities at the different deployment "layers". The orchestration capabilities required in a network management system start at the network element layer in monitoring and maintain the connection to a network element and end at the management of a configuration change to "like" devices across a multi-site network. There are no systems today capable of addressing the breadth of change, across the diversity of network elements, and perform that at the scale required for enterprise and service provider networks.

2.7 Configure/Act

The modification of a network element in response to a changing operations need (e.g., initial configuration, configuration change, on element data collection) requires the ability to make changes to the device configuration or to change the operational state of the device (e.g., start, stop, restart, etc.). Changes to a device can be made by a human or a management component and can be made through a remote command line interface (CLI) interaction or through an API (e.g., REST API, etc.).

3. DEPLOYMENT ENVIRONMENT

Customer networks have and continue to evolve from complete on-premise deployments where network management capabilities were bolted onto existing networks to the deployment of network elements that have been instrumented to integrate with either on premise or cloud-based management capabilities. The old deployments architectures have been supplanted by the introduction of as-a-service capabilities deployed in multi-cloud, private cloud, hybrid cloud, and hybrid (cloud and on-premise) architectures (Froehlich, 2018). The market has also seen an increase in the resources available on network elements to deliver the capabilities that previously had to be deployed on the network management controllers. Network management capabilities can now be found in the cloud, on controllers, and even on the network elements themselves. This section will describe the potential targets for deploying network service management capabilities identified in Figure 2.

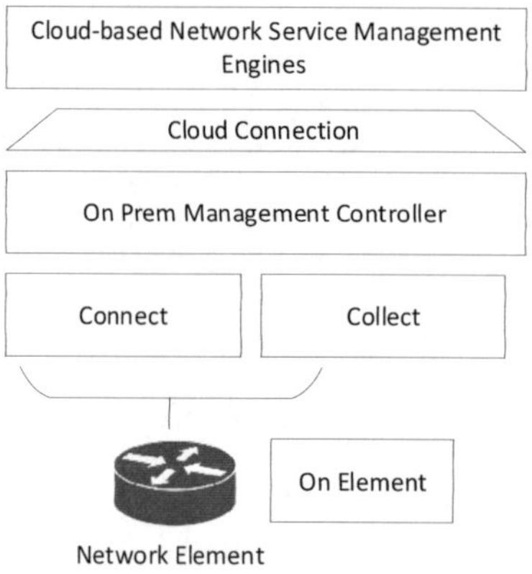

Figure 2. Deployment targets

3.1 On Element

Network devices (e.g., routers, switches, wireless access points, security devices) and networked solutions (e.g., call managers, collaboration suites, calendaring solutions) are providing additional resources to enable management services to be deployed and operated. These resources are limited and therefore are typically allocated to supporting data collection, simple analysis (e.g., parsing or RegEx execution), and temporary storage. Large devices have the potential to allocate more resources to network management activities, however their allocation and use could reduce the capacity of the device. Network device operating systems and application operating systems may include their own network management capabilities that can be accessed by management controllers via APIs which both reduces the amount of software that must be developed by the network management vendor and restricts what a vendor can do with a network element.

3.2 On-Prem Management Controller

On-prem management controllers can take many forms but all are common in their aggregation of network elements into a single management space. There management controllers access multiple network elements to collect, analyze, share results, and configure elements. On-premise management controllers can operate independently from the cloud with tightly controlled cloud access, or in a model where some capabilities are executed on prem and others in the cloud. On-prem management controllers can communicate with each other such as a network management controller utilizing another controller to collect network element data, analyze the data, and pass the results back to that initial controller to consume. Customers have demanded more integration among on-prem controllers as well as with existing in-inhouse develop capabilities because of the cost associated with connecting network elements to the management controllers.

3.3 Cloud-Based Service Management Engines

Network management capabilities are moving to the cloud in the form of Software-as-a-Service (SaaS) following the model utilized by Google Apps, ServiceNow, and DropBox and also utilizing Platform-as-a-Service (PaaS) provided by Amazon Web Services, Microsoft Azure, and Google Cloud Services. Network elements can be connected to these cloud-based capabilities either directly or through On-Prem Management Controllers and the "back-bone" capabilities consolidated in the cloud or distributed across the cloud, the on-prem management controller, and on the element.

A cloud-based service management system must expose the capabilities it provides via a set of APIs and provide highly secure protection of any customer data retained on that service. Network management services are dependent on the data from network elements deployed within a customer network, as well as those in cloud SaaS and PaaS deployments.

4. ENGAGEMENT ARCHITECTURES

Customer network architectures are unique to a customer. Small commercial customers tend to have very similar architectures with minor variations while large enterprise and service provider networks tend to be quite varied and distinct. In addition, larger company network architectures cannot be easily characterized as a "single" deployment architecture, typically there are multiple business-solution specific architectures within the larger company network architecture, each managed by a separate organization. Network management solutions providers must develop their capabilities to accommodate the variability and complexity of these environments. The single monolithic and highly integrated software architecture must migrate to one that maintains an internal operating structure but can be loosely coupled to all the other capabilities distribute across devices, on prem controllers, cloud providers and the network management controller. When designing functional architectures to address the different deployment models thinking in terms of everything needs to connect to everything and be deployable everywhere presents a huge hurdle to designing and implementing these systems. The development of different canonical engagement architectures that represent the different customer deployment models have enabled our organization to begin to design network management software to address the deployment variability and the needs of customer across our addressable markets.

Four engagement architectures have been used, three which could be considered truly canonical (Cloud Centric, Entrenched Keep, and In-a-Box) and the Hybrid-Hybrid that is more representative of what a medium to large company deployment might look like.

4.1 Cloud Centric Architecture

The cloud centric architecture addresses customers who have heavily invested in automating their network and application infrastructure. They want to use APIs to access network management capabilities in the cloud. These customers are heavily invested in their internal purpose-built systems and are willing to further invest in external professional services or self-invest in integrating with new capabilities. Some customers in this space will not allow vendor specific software in their infrastructure while at the same time they want to leverage the unique value that a vendor solution can bring to their operations.

Large and mid-size managed service partners fall into this bucket since they have historically heavily invested in systems to improve their efficiency in managing lots of customers. Customer expectation is that cloud services will comply with data sovereignty and protection governance based on the source location of the data and be able to audit it.

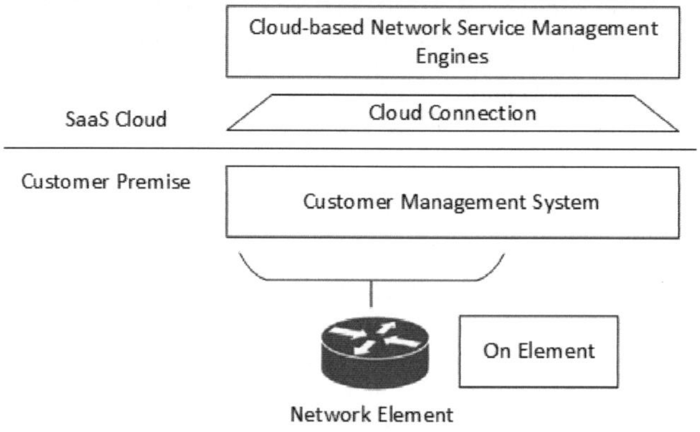

Figure 3. Cloud centric architecture

The Cloud Centric architecture (Figure 3) requires a customer to manage all network element connectivity, data collection, and configuration changes either through the customer's internal management system or connecting the device directly to the cloud-based service management engines. The cloud-based management engines expose APIs that identify the data to be collected, to receive the collected data, results, and remediations. As noted, this deployment model requires the customer to invest in the integration of their systems to the exposed management services giving the customer complete control over the software deployed in their environment and to leverage their investment in their internal systems.

4.2 Entrenched Keep Architecture

Customers who are very concerned about control and security because of industry/governmental oversight, potential negative impact to reputation due to a breach, or corporate fear associated with adopting new technologies. These customers do not want to send data over the internet and some do not maintain active connection to the internet. They are concerned with the potential impact of automation on the stability of their systems and want control over how a vendor capability is deployed. Customers understand that their requirements are not common and tend to over invest in custom work to address their unique requirements. Deploying vendor specific capabilities are the norm and integration across vendor solutions is expected.

Customers may use Cloud services to deploy business applications, but they maintain control of these systems, limiting their use to PaaS capabilities. Little to no information from the customer's network is sent to the cloud. On-premise controllers can use modern platform-as-a-service technologies but operate in a closed, cloud disconnected fashion. To deploy network management capabilities via an on-premise management controller the entire set of "back-bone" capabilities must be deployed and managed on the customer premise (see Figure 4).

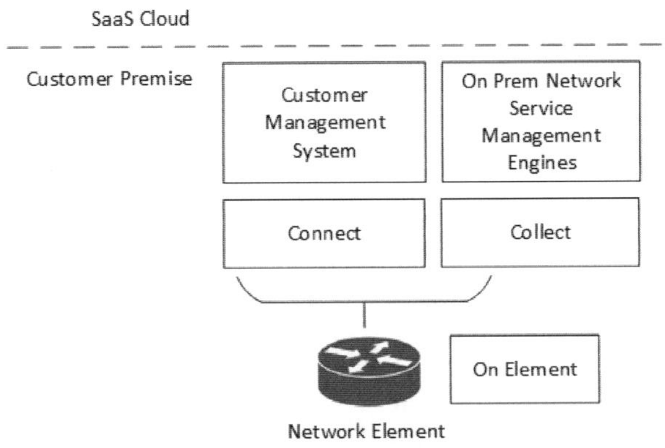

Figure 4. Entrenched keep architecture

4.3 In-a-Box Architecture

The In-a-Box architecture addresses the needs of most small and medium sized customers. These customers want to reap the full benefits of all the network management capabilities with minimal cost and minimal impact on their network operations. There expectations are that a network management capability can be quickly installed, value obtain with little effort, and that value can be increased as a function of the effort they invest in integrating it into their existing systems. They expect capabilities to be easily integrated into their existing products from the same vendor and with "popular" industry capabilities, either open-source of 3rd party pay-for capabilities available as cloud-based SaaS.

Customers expect incremental improvements to a capability and non-impactful upgrades and some may allow auto upgrades if there is a demonstrated track record for continued operation. These customers accept on premise or cloud-based capabilities based on where they are in their adoption of cloud-based services.

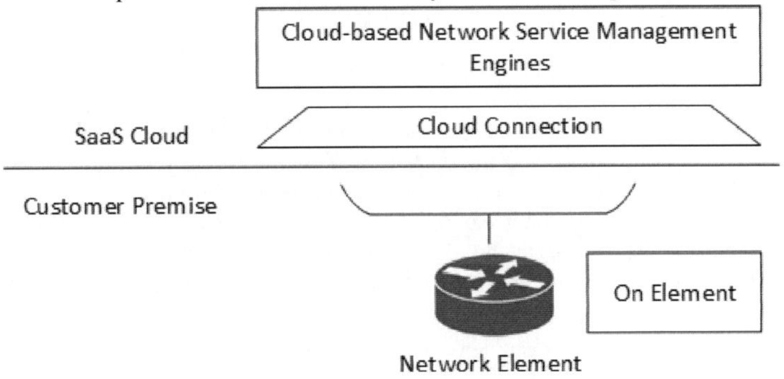

Figure 5. In-a-box architecture

The In-a-Box architecture represented in Figure 5 deploys the network management services as a cloud-based service. Customer configure access to devices via the network management interfaces and those services can connect to the device via the internet, collect data, analyze it, present the results via a web-based user interface, and make configuration changes directly to the device. Cloud managed on prem devices have been increasing as customers look to network element vendors to take on more of the routine management of their devices. Historically in-a-box solutions were targeted at consumers or small business, however there has been an increase in the use of these architectures in components at the edge of the networks in order to reduce the operational costs required to maintain them (such as wireless access points). Automated software updates, preconfigured feature configurations, etc. are minimal requirements for in-a-box network elements.

4.4 Hybrid-Hybrid Architecture

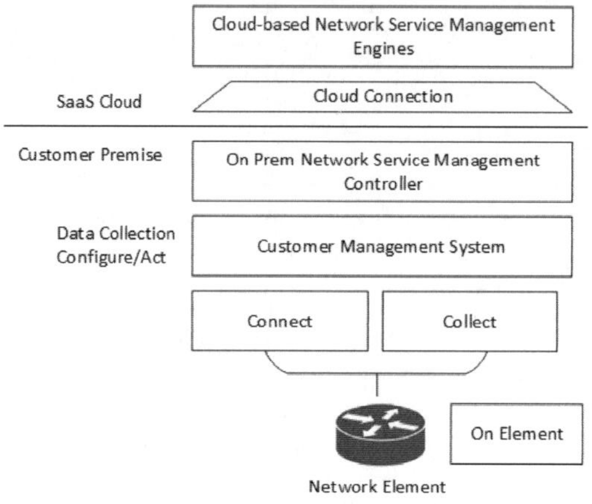

Figure 6. Hybrid-hybrid architecture

The Hybrid-Hybrid architecture conveys the need to support the deployment of different capabilities and specific features within a capability to different component. Large enterprise customers, particularly those who have a heavy cloud or internal system focus express a desire to have an on-premise network management component. This component would provide a control and communication consolidation function. This would allow to have a single point to manage access to a device and to connect those devices to the cloud-based network service management capabilities.

The hybrid-hybrid architecture in Figure 6 is an example of how backbone network service management capabilities might be distributed to the cloud, on-premise controller, and to the network element.

5. CONCLUSION

The introduction and adoption of cloud-based as-a-service capabilities have had a dramatic impact on the network architectures employed by customers and require changes to the architectures used by network management service providers to support them. Movement to these less expensive alternatives from historical customer network architectures is forcing network service management provides to reconsider how the design and build their software architectures to address the different customer architectures emerging. The next generation network service management capabilities must become more service/microservice based and fit with architectures that allow them to be deployed on network elements, on-premise network service management controllers, and accessed via API available in cloud-based network service management as-a-Service.

REFERENCES

Beyer, B. et al, 2016. *Site Reliability Engineering: How Google Runs Production Systems.* O'Reilly Media, Sebastopol, USA.

Bisordi, S. 2015. "Scaling the collection of self-service metrics [Online]". Available at https://engineering.linkedin.com/metrics/scaling-collection-self-service-metrics (Accessed June 5, 2019).

Froehlich, A. 2018. "Network Monitoring in the Cloud: 3 Options [Online]". Available at https://www.networkcomputing.com/networking/network-monitoring-cloud-3-options (Accessed 27 May 2019).

Ganguli, S and Corbett, T. 2019. Magic Quadrant for Network Performance Monitoring and Diagnostics [Online]" Available at https://www.gartner.com/doc/reprints?id=1-67RDTEE&ct=190211&st=sb (Accessed 15 May 2019).

Komorn, R. 2011. "Making Facebook self-healing: Automating proactive rack maintenance [Online]". Available at https://code.fb.com/production-engineering/making-facebook-self-healing-automating-proactive-rack-maintenance/ (Accessed 1 April 2019).

Nwana, H. S. 1996. "Software agents: an overview," *The Knowledge Engineering Review*. Cambridge University Press, 11(3), pp. 205–244.

Sherwin, B. (2015) "Introducing Nurse: Auto-Remediation at LinkedIn [Online]". Available at Introducing Nurse: Auto-Remediation at LinkedIn (Accessed 1 April 2019).

THE APPLICATION OF RECOMMENDER SYSTEMS TO DATA-DRIVEN DIGITAL MEMORY

Tingyu Luo and Miguel Baptista Nunes
Sun Yat-Sen University
Guangzhou, Guang Dong, China

ABSTRACT

Data-driven digital memory applications lack predefined navigation paths and strict hierarchical structures. They are based on large collections of memory items that can become overwhelming to users. Recommender systems can improve user experience through the proposal of personalized relevant items. However, very little academic literature has been dedicated to discussing this type of filtering of digital memory resources and the provision of customized contents to active users. In this paper, an architecture of a hybrid enhanced recommender (HER) system, which integrates collaborative filtering and content based filtering techniques and resolves most of the weaknesses of the individual approaches. This architecture also proposes an ontology to build semantic user profiles and represent memory items to mitigate the lack of semantics of traditional content-based method. Through combining those techniques, this architecture has the potential to cope with data sparsity problems, avoid overspecialization issues and partially resolve cold start problems.

KEYWORDS

Digital Memory, Recommender Systems, Content-Based Filtering, Collaborative Filtering, Ontology

1. INTRODUCTION

With the expansion of globalization, the preservation of cultural identity and diversity have become a pivotal issue. The United Nations Educational, Scientific and Cultural Organization (UNESCO) keeps adding cultural heritage sites into the list of World Cultural Heritage. Different countries and local governments are publishing policies and strategies to support cultural preservation projects, whilst organizations such as museums and libraries are encouraged to apply advanced technology to protect and popularize traditional cultures and academic researchers are inspired to do delve in this field. In China and following this trend, the archival academic community has been actively engaging with the concept of "Digital Memory" (Feng, 2012). This type of digital application aims to create internet-based digital resource warehouses based on digital archival resources containing a wide variety of memory media documents in the form of text, pictures, audio, video and others. In China, digital memory applications focus on all aspects of tangible and intangible heritage, history and culture as well as Chinese daily life endeavors, social life and notable events.

This area of research has recently grown both in interest and funding, notably in China, and many publications have emerged in the field of digital humanities focusing on the development of applications that collect and present digital cultural resources online (Luo *et al.*, 2018). This development is partly due to an increasing valuation of cultural identities in a progressive globalized and integrative society and to the increasing number of digital resources emerging on the web and social networks. The key problems in harnessing this increasing amount of diverse and heterogeneous resources are related with organization, namely classification, content generation and presentation. The most common used organization method is classification, such as topical classification, hierarchical classification, classification based on geographic location or event timelines. This resource organization then enables digital memory content generation model as well as user centered presentation designs. Luo and Nunes (2018) identified three ways of generating contents for digital memory applications: data-driven, hierarchical and pre-determined path. Pre-determined content generation model is widely used in story telling projects, in which resources are organized according to pre-defined lenses, aims and navigational paths. This is a "one size fits all" type of application providing fixed paths and fixed layout of resources. Hierarchical models are organized according to pre-defined hierarchical classifications. Criteria such as, events, time periods, geographical locations, memorable themes, timelines and specific institutions are often used to aggregate resources. However, this linear classification based on limited feature or events often ignores the value of semantic relationship between different resources and therefore affects the retrieval efficiency. Furthermore, the hierarchy-based content generation model prevents effective customization of the digital resources according to user's needs and preferences and limits user experience. Data-driven content generation model resolves this problem by combining dynamic collection of user's preference data with the semantic characteristics of resource items.

This last generation of digital memory application relies heavily upon recommender systems and provides a dynamic bridge between resources and users. According to Isinkaye et al., (2015), recommender systems are a form of information filtering systems that solve the problem of information overload by filtering vital information fragments out of large amounts of dynamically generated information according to user's preferences, interests, or observed behaviors. This type of systems has been widely used in fields such as e-commerce (Linden et al., 2003), book recommendation (Rana & Jain, 2012), movie recommendation (Ha et al., 2012), etc. Digital memory data-driven generation models use recommender systems basic theory to enable users to deal with digital memory resources overload. However, there are very different approaches and techniques developed according to different theoretical perspectives, purposes and intended outcomes. Therefore when discussing data-driven digital media there are several potential alternative design architectures that can be considered.

This paper identifies the main-stream recommender filtering techniques and discusses their respective characteristics, features and affordances. The paper then discusses their applicability to digital memory and discusses the relative merits of the different recommendation methods in relation to their capability to deal with digital memory resources as well as user's behaviors and needs. The paper then concludes by proposing a specific architecture for this type of digital application.

2. LITERATURE REVIEW

2.1 Studies on Digital Memory

Generally speaking, digital memory study involves disciplines such as psychology, sociology, computer science, history, communication, archival science and culture study (Shao, 2014). Memory can be classified into cultural memory, historical memory, individual memory, collective memory, social memory, media memory and digital memory according to the different lenses used by the different disciplinary perspectives. From a thorough analysis of extant literature, the studies addressing digital memory can be classified into 7 aspects:

a. The application of digital records/memory. Researches published on the topic of the application of digital records/memory are mostly about the use of digital records such as social media (Sternfeld, 2011), digital archives (MÜLLER, 2017), online communities in different disciplines' study: history (Milligan, 2012; Chassanoff, 2018), media archaeology (Fyfe, 2016), memory study (Henninger & Scifleet, 2016), disaster study (Su & Gibson, 2016);

b. The development of digital memory tools, applications or platforms. Researches about building online digital memory platform involves different topics, some are event-driven, some are people-driven, some focus on interface design, organizing resources or information retrieval, for example: Vicente-Hernández et al (2011), Gulotta et al. (2014), Roiu (2017). In China, digital memory related researches are more focused in this area, including the general discussion of applications' architecture, the technologies which can be applied in terms of protecting culture heritage.

c. The implications of digital memory. Including the implications of the growing impact of information technology, globalization, digitalization on digital memory (Mitra, 2005), (Oiarzabal, 2014). The implications of the increasing number of digital memory platforms and born-digital records on resources curation (Gulotta et al., 2014), humanities (Kunt et al., 2017), history (Slumkoski et al., 2008), policies (Mitchell, n.d.).

d. Strategies, policies, rights and legislation for digital memory. Such as the exploration of strategies implemented to manage electronic resources (Feng & Zhang, 2010), the protection of privacy (Majovski, 2012), the policies and practices that facilitating corporations (Chigariro, 2014).

e. Relevant technologies and approaches. Research in this category normally involves the study of specific technology which contributes to the development of digital memory or memory institutions, such as Khan et al. (2009), Seifi (2011), Dobbins et al. (2013) and the study of approaches which improves information management Samiee et al. (2012) and Convery (2011).

f. Factors that affect the development of digital memory, including cultural, political, social and ethical issues Boamah et al (2016) and Glanville (2010).

g. Publications about practical projects and practices.

However, not much literature has been dedicated to discuss data-driven digital memory and the corresponding filtering of digital memory resources through recommender system.

2.2 Studies on Recommender System

Recommender systems deal with the problem of information overload by providing users with personalized, exclusive content according to their specific and identifiable interests (Konstan & Riedl, 2012). Studies on recommender systems can be classified into the study of recommendation filtering techniques, the study on how to evaluate recommender systems and the application of recommender systems in different fields. Recently, different approaches have been developed to build recommender systems commonly divided into collaborative filtering, content-based filtering and hybrid filtering (Isinkaye et al., 2015).

Collaborative filtering is the most mature and widely used technique, it recommends items either by identifying other users with similar rating of interest in different items or by identifying similar items through different user's rating on items. One of the earliest examples of collaborative filtering uses a user-item rating matrix to recommend items to the active user. GroupLens is a classic example of a news recommender system applying memory-based collaborative filtering technique and help users to locate their preferred articles (Resnick et al., 1994). Another common example of collaborative filtering technique is model-based and applies instead machine learning algorithms as proposed by Breese et al. (1998) and Nathanson et al. (2007). Typical successful applications of applied collaborative filtering techniques include the pioneer book recommender systems by Amazon (Ziegler, 2005) and the very early email-based music recommender system Ringo (Chen, 2008).

Content-based filtering techniques are originated from information retrieval theories. The aim of content-based filtering technique is matching items' features to users' preferences, without comparing different users' preferences. One of the basic principles behind this technique is calculating similarity between current item and items which user liked before. Predictions are made based on information of the active user and ignore contributions from other users or items (Celma and Serra, 2008). The core concept behind content-based filtering method is similarity calculation. Music, movies and non-textual items are often filtered through keyword represented contents similarity using Dice Index (Jannach, 2010). Text-based items are often filtered through Cosine Similarity. Other approaches use clustering techniques, such as Billsus et al.(2000), who has applied Nearest Neighbor to find items that match user's short term preference. Manning (2010) has compared the effectiveness of different machine learning information retrieval methods such as SVM, Naive-Bayes, Racchio that are eminently suited to be used in content-based filtering techniques. The use of artificial intelligence (AI) methods in this type of filtering has also been extensively studied. One the earliest pioneers in this area - Pazzani (1999) - proposed an intelligent agent that attempted to predict user web page preference by using a naive Bayesian classifier. With the arrival of the Big Data era, Rao (2012) has presented research on how to apply keyword-based content filtering method in distributed system.

Although collaborative filtering and content-based filtering techniques are widely adopted both in academia and industry, several limitations of these methods have been identified (Adomavicius and Tuzhilin, 2005). Collaborative filtering methods have been found to present problems such as: cold-start; sparsity and scalability. On the other hand, content analysis methods of the present problems of overspecialization and cold-start.

As a result, hybrid filtering which combines two or more filtering techniques are proposed to improve the quality of recommendation. The rationale of the combination is to maximize the merits and minimize the weaknesses of the individual recommender method. Hybrid algorithms commonly use both items' attributes and the ratings of users, some also incorporate additional external information and knowledge sources into the recommender processes. Jannach et al. (2010) have categorized hybrid strategies into: integrated mixing, parallel mixing and linear mixing. Integrated mixing such as hybrid feature combination often integrates data used in different techniques and then apply this data into selected filtering technique. For instance, Basu (1998) has combined a form of collaborative preference feature with content catalog to determine peers in the same community. Parallel mixing, often runs different recommender techniques at same time and adopt a strategy to combine the result from those subsystems. A common example of parallel mixing is weighted hybrid, where the prediction score results from the calculation of the weighted average of predicted values from different recommendation techniques. Linear mixing approaches, such as switching and cascade hybrid often employ different recommender techniques sequentially. Tran (2000) presents an example where he developed an architecture of a hybrid recommender system which can switch filtering techniques according to user's behavior and rating data.

Although this paper focus on the recommender system architecture, it should be acknowledged that research on recommender systems also addresses many other aspects, such as design of the interface; human-computer interactions; holistic evaluation of the system.

3. CRITICAL ANALYSIS ON RECOMMENDATION FILTERING TECHNIQUES FOR DIGITAL MEMORY

As stated above, this paper aims to discuss the applicability of recommender systems to digital memory and discuss the relative merits of the different recommendation methods in relation to their capability to deal with digital memory resources and user's needs. Since, recommendation filtering technique are the core component of recommender systems this critical analysis evaluates the three main types of recommender systems filtering techniques identified above against their potential in the specific context of digital memory. Furthermore, as discussed in the introduction, this paper specifically focusses on data-driven digital memory applications that most benefit for recommender systems. In data-driven digital memory the repository of memory items (data) can be (driven) retrieved, analyzed, manipulated and represented according to user's expectations, culture, and social anticipations as well as personal perspectives (Luo and Nunes, 2018). The recommender systems can therefore be the drivers of the memory representation being dynamically offered to the active user.

3.1 Collaborative Filtering and Digital Memory

According to Halbwachs (1992), the continuous necessity for extracting and preserving collective memory for social use and keep group consciousness and identity is the main reason for the need for digital memory applications. The intention is therefore that this collective memory can be revisited and experienced by current generations and left as an inheritance for future ones. A person may have agency in several social networks each of these exhibiting a specific group identity, thus recognizing users characteristics is pivotal in recommending memory resources. Collaborative filtering is a domain independent technique which predicts preferences of an active user based on other users' similar interests and choices. This makes it imminently suitable to be used in digital memory applications. Furthermore, collaborative filtering techniques do not give recommendations directly base on explicit statements of user's social network members, but people who give same ratings on different contents potentially indicate their similar identity. This is extremely useful in eliminating any bias or prejudiced profiling.

For instance, an item matrix can be developed to store user's rating on each item – a user-item matrix – and then Pearson correlation or cosine correlation can be used to calculate similarity between different users. Based on this similarity, a cluster of candidate of users can be selected that is estimated to be similar to the current active user and then used to predict which items the current user may be interested in. Alternatively, collaborative filtering methods can also use model-based techniques to develop a classifier or cluster to predict weather a given user will like a certain item or not. The model can be constructed using machine learning and data mining techniques such as decision trees, clustering algorithms, neural network and regression analysis. After the model is built, the system can then automatically make predictions based on user's rating and give recommendations.

However, there are some limitations of collaborative filtering techniques as mentioned in literature review. One of the most significant problems is cold-start, which characterizes the phenomena emerging from the lack of data necessary for similarity calculations related to new users that just started to browse the system or new items that have just been added. As for digital memory applications, it is impossible to have all required data in the system on users and items, when the system is initially built. Furthermore, in data-driven digital media new users and items will be continuously added, so when applying collaborative filtering techniques the system must routinely solve cold-start problems both for new users and new items. Another problem with collaborative filtering in data-driven digital media is data sparsity. For a digital memory application which may have thousands items, it is unlikely that users are able to browse through all of those items one by one and give ratings on each of them. Normally users will only rate a small set, so the user-item matrix may become a sparse matrix. If the data is too sparse, it will affect the quality of recommendation as it is hard to find neighbors.

In conclusion, although collaborative filtering technique is good in recommending digital memory resources, due to the nature of collective memory building and the need to for the rating of items, problems of cold-start and sparsity may hinder the efficiency and efficacy of the recommending process.

3.2 Content-based Filtering and Digital Memory

Content-based filtering technique is a domain related method in which the recommendation is heavily reliant on the characterization of items, as for text-based contents, features can be computed automatically so it is widely used in recommending news, web pages and publications. In digital memory applications using content-based recommender system, items and user profiles are both represented through feature-based vectors. For text-based items, features are automatically selected through TF-IDF – an acronym for "term frequency–inverse document frequency", which is a statistic that is intended to reflect how important a feature is to an item in a dataset (Jannach et al., 2010). For none text-based items, such as videos and images, resources can be annotated by metadata that describe accurately their main attributes. Once the feature-based vectors is computed for all items, similarity between user profile and items is then calculated through cosine correlation.

As content-based filtering techniques also rely on user's past data, it cannot avoid the problem of user cold-start. However, it can solve item cold-start problem and the data sparsity problem through exploiting content information. In addition, this filtering technique is more sensitive to the changes of user's preference, it can give timely recommendation based on user's current preference. The disadvantage of content-based filtering technique is that the recommendation is heavily reliant on descriptions of items. However, in order to better manage, preserve and retrieve digital memory resources, every item has to be coded according to predefined meta-data and stored in XML or RDF format. So, what is perceived as a disadvantage in other contexts, proves to be a benefit when applying content-based filtering techniques to recommend digital memory resources. However, this type of filtering approach may result in overspecialization and lack of serendipity. Overspecialization refers to the problem that users are restricted to getting recommendations similar to items already defined in their profiles (Zhang and Vijay, 2002). Lack of serendipity is closely related to overspecialization, it could even be seen as a consequence this problem, in the sense that it prevents the finding of unexpected or unintended items that could have been found through browsing for instance (Foster and Ford, 2003). Another shortage of content-based techniques is the concentration on simplistic user recommendations and meta-data ignores quality aspects on the item. For example, a digital memory item maybe recommended to a user just because that same user liked items in the same topic as before. In this case, there is not quality control over the items being proposed; only similarity measures.

Knowing what affect user's needs on particular domain is pivotal to content-based filtering technique since we need to decide what features should be included to describe available items. As a result, to implement content-based filtering techniques, the first step is to understand user's information needs related to particular digital memory resources, and then organize items according to these needs. In data-driven digital memory recommender systems, both user profiles and memory contents are represented using the same feature vector space. After that, similarity between users' profile and each item can be calculated and contents, which do not match with user's interest, would be filtered out by setting an appropriate threshold.

In conclusion, due to the rich meta-data description of digital memory resources, content-based filtering techniques can be used in recommending digital memory resources, and this technique successfully avoids the disadvantages of collaborative filtering techniques, such as data sparsity and item cold-start problems. However, due to overspecialization and considering only the preferences of one individual user, it is hard to give recommendations that enable serendipity discovery and good quality assurance.

3.3 Hybrid Filtering Techniques and Digital Memory

As mentioned before, hybrid filtering techniques are developed to try to resolve limitations of applying single filtering methods. Table 1 contrasts the collaborative filtering approaches and content-based approaches, identifying the advantages and disadvantages of each in digital memory resources recommendation. The third row suggests what might be achieved in an ideal hybrid which combines the two techniques. In more recent years, increasing number of researchers are exploring how to incorporate additional side information and external knowledge resources into the content-based recommendation process to improve its shortages (Lops et al., 2019.). One of the widely adopted approach to access external knowledge is linked open data as proposed by (Di et al., 2012) and (Musto et al., 2017). Melville et al. (2002) also discussed how to improve data sparsity problem of collaborative filtering through content-boosted method.

As the result of the previous critical analysis and discussion the final section of this paper proposes an enhanced integrated mixing hybrid recommender system that maximizes the combined effects of the individual techniques in digital memory. This architecture is enhanced because it includes a pre-profiling component to resolve the cold-start problem and also adopts a domain ontology to solve the overspecialization problem of content-based filtering technique.

Table 1. Comparison between collaborative filtering techniques and content-based techniques

Technique	Advantages	Disadvantages
Collaborative Filtering	A. Using the concept of social group to give recommendation which is essential to social memory. B. Personalized recommendation.	E. Data sparsity. F. Cold-start (user and item).
Content-based Filtering	C. Sensitive to short-term variance. D. No ramp-up required.	F. Cold-start (user) G. Overspecialization.
Ideal Hybrid	Maintains: A, B,C,D Resolves: E, F(item cold start resolves)	F(user cold start not resolved)
External Knowledge	Maintains: A, B,C,D Resolves: E and G	F(user cold start not resolved)

4. A THEORETICAL PROPOSAL OF AN ARCHITECTURE FOR AN ONTOLOGY-BASED HYBRID ENHANCED RECOMMENDER SYSTEM FOR DIGITAL MEMORY APPLICATIONS

Figure 1 shows this research's proposal for an architecture of a Hybrid Enhanced Recommender (HER) system. This architecture consists of 7 components: the Interactive Interface Agent (IIA), the Pre-Profiling module, the Collaborative Filtering Engine (CFE), the Content-based Engine (CBE), Database of User's Rating, Digital Memory Items Database.

The main job of IIA is to interact with users in different situations such as guiding users through registration and login, getting user's feedback for each recommended item, view and change of user's interest profiles.

As discussed in section 3.2, the item cold-start problem is successfully resolved through applying content-based method, but the user cold-start problem still remain. This architecture proposes a pre-profiling module to deal with this problem. If a new user registers, the interface will guide the user to rate a group of representative items and few other random items, these ratings are then passed to database of user's rating and are used to learn their profile.

The goal of CFE is to find similar user of the active user and extract terms of their preferred contents and pass this result to CBE. It first receives user's login information from the IIA and query the database of user's rating to get the ratings on items of that user, the ratings on items of other users. Then, the CFE finds the neighbors of the active user through calculating the similarity scores between that user and other users. User profile is then represented by top N features which reflect the preference of its neighbors and are extracted from the items which they liked before.

The purpose of CBE is to recommend items that best represent the group's preference to which the active user is assigned to. To mitigate the lack of semantics and overspecialization issues of the traditional content-based method, a subject ontology was adopted to represent and integrate the features of digital memory items and user profiles. The idea is to use a semantic network and a spreading activation strategy to infer features of items the user may be interested in. The CBE then matches the semantic user profile against semantic item representations and produces a ranked list of potentially interesting items. The list will then be presented to the user though the IIA, so that the active user can view and rate items. The CBE also modifies the user's interest profile after receive user's rating on recommended items.

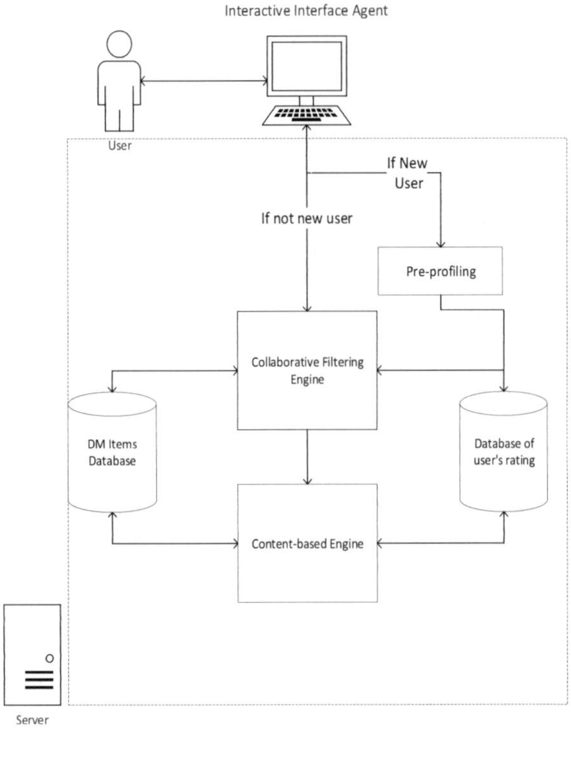

Figure 1. Architecture for integrating Collaborative filtering and Content-based filtering techniques

5. CONCLUSION

Based on a critical analysis of different information filtering techniques against the nature of digital memory, this paper proposes an architecture for a hybrid enhanced recommender (HER) system. It is expected that this HER architecture will increase satisfaction and boost user experience of data-driven digital memory applications by providing digital memory resources based on user's preference data. This architecture integrates collaborative filtering and content-based filtering techniques in order to resolve individual weaknesses of these filtering techniques. In addition, it proposes the application of subject ontologies to build up semantic user profile and item representations. Such a hybrid recommender system will have all the advantages of both techniques, namely applying the concept of social group to give recommendations which are essential in socially constructed memory; giving personalized recommendations; exhibit sensitivity to short-term variance; and no ramp-up issues. Additionally, it uses a pre-profiling component to avoid a problem common to both individual techniques: user cold start problem.

REFERENCES

Adomavicius, G., & Tuzhilin, A. 2005. Personalization technologies: A process oriented perspective. *Communications of the ACM*, Vol.48. No.10, pp. 83–90.

Basu, C., et al. 1998. Recommendation as classification: Using social and content-based information in recommendation. *AAAI Technical Report WS-98-08*, pp. 714-720.

Billsus D, et al. 2000. A learning agent for wireless news access. In *Proceedings of the 5th International Conference on Intelligent User Interfaces*, New Orleans, USA, pp. 33-36.

Boamah, E. et al. 2016. Cultural, social and political factors influencing the adoption of Digital Preservation Management in Ghana. *Innovation : Journal of Appropriate Librarianship and Information Work in Southern Africa*, Vol.53, pp. 6–20.

Breese, J. S. et al. 1998. Empirical analysis of predictive algorithms for collaborative filtering. In Proceedings of the Fourteenth conference on Uncertainty in artificial intelligence. Madison, USA, pp. 43-52.

Celma, Ò., & Serra, X. 2008. FOAFing the music: Bridging the semantic gap in music recommendation. W*eb Semantics: Science, Services and Agents on the World Wide Web*, Vol.6, No.4, pp. 250-256.

Chen, L. S. et al. 2008. Developing recommender systems with the consideration of product profitability for sellers. *Information Sciences*, Vol.178, No.4, pp.1032-1048.

Chassanoff, A. M. 2018. Historians' Experiences Using Digitized Archival Photographs as Evidence. *The American Archivist*, Vol.81, No.1, pp. 135–164.

Chigariro, D. 2014. Collaboration in the management and preservation of audio-visual archives: a case study of the National Archives of Zimbabwe. *Doctoral dissertation*, University of Western Cape.

Convery, N. 2011. Information management, records management, knowledge management: The place of archives in a digital age. In *The future of archives and recordkeeping: A reader*. pp. 190–212.

Di Noia, T et al. 2012. Linked open data to support content-based recommender systems. In *Proceedings of the 8th International Conference on Semantic Systems*. New York, USA, pp. 1-8.

Dobbins, C. et al., 2013. Exploiting linked data to create rich human digital memories. *Computer Communications*, Vol. 36. No.15–16, pp. 1639–1656.

Foster, A and Ford, N. 2003 Serendipity and information seeking: an empirical study. *Journal of Documentation*, Vol. 59 Issue: 3, pp. 321-340

Isinkaye, F., Folajimi, Y., & Ojokoh, B. 2015. Recommendation systems: Principles, methods and evaluation. *Egyptian Informatics Journal*, Vol.16, No.3, pp. 261-273.

Müller, K. 2017. Between Lived and Archived Memory: How Digital Archives Can Tell History. Retrieved June 17, 2018, from http://www.redalyc.org/html/550/55051207002/

Nathanson, T. et al. 2007. Eigentaste 5.0: constant-time adaptability in a recommender system using item clustering. In *Proceedings of the 2007 ACM conference on Recommender Systems*, Minneapolis, USA, pp.149-152.

Konstan, J. A., & Riedl, J. 2012. Recommender systems: from algorithms to user experience. *User Modeling and User-Adapted Interaction*, Vol. 22, No.1-2, pp.101-123.

Oiarzabal, P. J. 2014. Migrant Memories in the Ephemeral Digital Age: The Case of the Basque Institutional Diaspora in North America. *Identity Palimpsests: Archiving Ethnicity in the US and Canada*, Vol. 297, No.314, pp. 297– 314.

Pazzani, M. J. 1999. A framework for collaborative, content-based and demographic filtering. *Artificial Intelligence Review*, Vol.13, pp.393-408.

Feng, H. L, & Zhang, N. (2010). Developing a National Strategy for Electronic Records Management (ERM) for China: Key Features IQ: *The RIM Quarterly*. Vol.26, No.1, pp. 35–37.

Feng, H. L. 2012. 档案记忆观、资源观与"中国记忆"数字资源建设. *档案学通讯*, Vol.3, pp 4-8.

Fyfe, P. 2016. An Archaeology of Victorian Newspapers. Victorian Periodicals Review, Vol.49, No.4, pp. 546–577.

Glanville, L. (2010). Web archiving: Ethical and legal issues affecting programmes in Australia and the Netherlands. *Australian Library Journal*, Vol.59, N0.3. pp. 128–134.

Gulotta, R. et al. 2014. Legacy in the Age of the Internet: Reflections on How Interactive Systems Shape How We Are Remembered. In *Proceedings of the 2014 Conference on Designing Interactive Systems*. Vancouver, Canada. pp. 975–984.

Ha, I., Oh, K. J., Hong, M. D., & Jo, G. S. 2012, November. Social filtering using social relationship for movie recommendation. In *Proceedings of the International Conference on Computational Collective Intelligence*. Berlin, Germany. pp. 395-404.

Halbwachs, M. 1992. *On collective memory*. University of Chicago Press.

Henninger, M., & Scifleet, P. (2016). How are the new documents of social networks shaping our cultural memory. *Journal of Documentation*, Vol.72, No.2, pp. 277–298.

Jannach D. et al. 2010. *Recommender systems: an introduction*. Cambridge University Press. Cambridge, England.

Khan, H., et al., 2009. *The International Journal of Digital Curation*, Vol.4, No.3. pp. 209–221.

Kunt, G., Székely, J., & Vajda, J. (2017). Making (DIS)Connections: An Interplay Between Material and Virtual Memories of The Holocaust in Budapest. Retrieved from http://www.lidemesta.cz/assets/media/files/19-2017-2/Kunt.pdf

Linden, G., Smith, B., & York, J. 2003. Amazon.com recommendations: Item-to-item collaborative filtering. *IEEE Internet computing*. Vol.1, pp76-80.

Lops, P et al. 2019. Trends in content-based recommendation. *User Modeling and User-Adapted Interaction*, Vol.29. No.2. pp.239-249.

Luo, T. Y. et al., 2018. Establishing a digital memory application model from an information science perspective: A systematic literature review. In *Proceedings of the 11th International Conference on ICT, Society, and Human Beings 2018*, Madrid, Spain.

Luo, T.Y., & Nunes, M. 2018. Conceptual Integration of Archives, Data, Information and Information Technology for Digital Memory Applications: The CMDMA Model. In *Proceedings of 2018 the European Association for Digital Humanities Conference*. Galway, Ireland.

Majovski, K. 2012. Data Expiration, Let the User Decide: Proposed Legislation for Online User- Generated Content. *University of San Francisco Law Review*, Vol. 47, pp. 807–838.

Manning, C. et al. 2010. Introduction to information retrieval. Cambridge University Press. Cambridge, England.

Melville, et al. 2002. Content-boosted collaborative filtering for improved recommendations. In *Proceedings of the 20th Conference on Innovative Applications of Artificial Intelligence*, Vol.23, pp.187-192.

Milligan, I. 2012. Mining the 'Internet Graveyard': Rethinking the Historians' Toolkit. *Journal of the Canadian Historical Association*, Vol. 23, No.2. pp. 21

Mitchell, C. L. Informationalism and Katrina, Analyzing How Digitalization Affects Policy Making. Retrieved from http://citeseerx.ist.psu.edu/viewdoc/download?doi=10.1.1.539.912&rep=rep1&type=pdf

Mitra, A. 2005. Digital Memory. *Journal of Information, Communication and Ethics in Society Kybernetes*, Vol.12, pp. 3–13.

Musto, C. et al. 2017. Semantics-aware Recommender Systems exploiting Linked Open Data and graph-based features. *Knowledge-Based Systems*, Vol.136, pp.1-14.

Rao W et al. 2012. Move: A large scale keyword-based content filtering and dissemination system. *IEEE 32nd International Conference on Distributed Computing Systems*; Macau, China. pp. 445-454.

Rana, C., & Jain, S. K. 2012. Building a Book Recommender system using time based content filtering. *WSEAS Transactions on Computers*, Vol.11, No.2, pp 2224-2872.

Resnick, P. et al. 1994. GroupLens: an open architecture for collaborative filtering of netnews. *Proceedings of the 1994 ACM conference on Computer supported cooperative work.* Chapel Hill, USA, pp. 175-186.

Roiu, C. I. 2017. The Challenge of Multiple Identities – Multi-ethnicity in Genealogy, Local History and Regional Memory – Challenges and Opportunities for Libraries and Other Memory Institutions. *In Proceedings of the IFLA 2017 Satellite Meeting on Genealogy and Local History*, Martynas Mažvydas National Library of Lithuania, Vilnius, Lithuania, pp. 1–10.

Samiee, M., et al. 2012. Proposing a paradigm for the management of digital images of the NLAI(National Archive of Iran) according to the Open Archival Information System(OAIS) Reference Model. In *Proceeding of the Archiving Conference, Archiving 2012 Final Program and* Proceedings. Vol. 2012, No. 1. pp. 153-158.

Seifi, L. 2011. Digitization and digital preservation of manuscripts and access in organization of Libraries, Museums and Documents Centre of Astan Quds Razavi Library in IRAN: A case study.

Shao, P. 2014. 媒介作为人类记忆的研究-以媒介记忆理论为视角. Doctoral dissertation, 浙江大学.

Slumkoski, C., et al., 2008. History on the Internet: The Atlantic Canada Portal. *Journal of History on the Atlantic Region*, Vol. 48, No.1, pp. 132–55.

Sternfeld, J. 2011. Archival Theory and Digital Historiography: Selection, Search, and Metadata as Archival Processes for Assessing Historical Contextualization. *The American Archivist*, Vol.74, pp 544–575.

Su, C., & Gibson, P. L. 2016. Digitizing the Memorial: Institutional and Vernacular Remembrances of the Taiwanese 921 Earthquake and Typhoon Morakot. In A. Hajek, C. Lohmeier, & C. Pentzold (Eds.), *Memory in a Mediated World*. Palgrave Macmillan. pp. 74–89.

Tran, T., & Cohen, R. 2000. Hybrid recommender systems for electronic commerce. In *Proceedings of the Workshop on Knowledge-Based Electronic Markets*, AAAI Press. University of Waterloo, Ontario, Canada Vol. 40. pp. 78-84

Vicente-Hernández, L. et al., 2011. The Almirall Project: a portal of 19th century culture and thinking. In *Proceeding of the IFLA Satellite Conference: A Bridge to Knowledge for Sustainable Development*. La Havana, Cuba.

Zhang, T. and Vijay, S. 2002 Recommender systems using linear classifiers. *Journal of Machine Learning Research*; Vol. 2, pp. 313 - 34.

Ziegler, C. N., et al. 2005. Improving recommendation lists through topic diversification. In *Proceedings of the 14th International Conference on World Wide Web*. Seoul, Korea. pp. 22-32.

LOYALTY PROGRAMS IN TOURISM – HOW INFLUENCERS AND COMMUNITIES CHANGE WORD-OF-MOUTH MARKETING

Jacqueline Fäs[1] and Darius Zumstein[2]
[1]*Lucerne University of Applied Sciences, Zentralstrasse 9, 6002 Lucerne, Switzerland*
[2]*Zurich University of Applied Sciences, Stadthausstrasse 14, 8400 Winterthur, Switzerland*

ABSTRACT

Conventional loyalty programs in the hotel industry often are outdated and should adapt to the digital age. This research shows that common loyalty programs have negative connotations, because hotel guests are inundated with them and the immediate benefits are not noticeable from the customers' point of view. A sustainable loyalty program ideally offers playful incentives so that guests do not lose interest in it. Research found that many guests like to be part of an exclusive online community, where loyalty programs should be based on. Building a community, it is important that all stakeholders can derive added value and do not feel exploited. Moreover, empirical results show that hotel guests expect personalized incentives and offers. To provide these, tourism companies should cooperate with third-party partners. Communities on digital platforms like Instagram or Facebook can generate new guests by word of mouth, short eWOM. Experiences show that recommendations are made when expectations are exceeded: To increase this effect, incentives are still seen to be meaningful, but the nature and (digital) communication channels are changing. Social incentives, such as exclusive events, services or personal guest care, are clearly preferred instead of monetary incentives. It is also human interaction that binds guests to a hotel, which cannot be compensated by monetary incentives only. When guests are individually and immediately rewarded and when their expectations are met, word-of-mouth on social media lead to new customers. Moreover, research indicates that guests often act as micro-influencers on social media and ratings platforms. If they are convinced and find "instagrammable moments", they intrinsically report about a hotel and their services on social media. To recommend a hotel to friends, most guests do not expect anything in return, because they want to be credible and authentic.

KEYWORDS

Loyalty Programs, E-Tourism, Influencer Marketing, Online Marketing, Community Marketing, Hospitality

1. INTRODUCTION

A *loyalty program* aims to bind customers to a company and retain them for the long term. To achieve this, they must offer the company a certain (monetary) incentive to participate. Important is that the customer feels a sense of appreciation (Lewis 2004, p. 286). Loyalty programs are also widespread in the hotel industry. These offer the possibility to treat the customer individually according to his value for the company (Peppers & Rogers 2004, p. 22).

Research showed that economic incentives, especially in hotels, often lead to a new booking because people are afraid that they otherwise might lose their reward. However, a real connection with the hotel could be proven especially with *social incentives* (Melancon et al. 2011, p. 343f).

In addition, *social media and influencer marketing* have seldom been integrated into loyalty programs so far. Influencers, in particular, can no longer be neglected as a new instrument of the marketing mix. Especially among younger target groups, *YouTuber and Instagrammer* are authentic opinion leaders. In social media like Instagram, Twitter and YouTube, influencers now have more reach than conventional media (Kohn 2016, p. 52). There is no doubt that social media are responsible for a brand and its loyalty (Oracle 2018, p. 7).

The Swiss SV Hotel AG is aware of this problem and would therefore like to use its own hotel brand «Stay KooooK» to launch a new kind of loyalty program. The new hotel brand «Stay KooooK» aims to combine the best out of Airbnb, Hotel, Microliving and Hostel. The idea of this new concept is to convince customers with a place where you feel like home without missing any advantages a hotel would offer.

This paper therefore clarifies the following main **research question**: *What kind of loyalty program hotels like «Stay KooooK» can launch to maximize the loyalty of its guests?* Since the main research question is complex, the research project was divided it into following seven sub research questions:

1. When is a hotel guest called loyal?
2. What are satisfied guests willing to invest in a hotel brand like «Stay KooooK»?
3. What motivates hotel guests to recommend the brand?
4. What would hotels, such as the SV Hotel group, invest in loyalty programs and loyal guests?
5. What do guests expect from a modern hotel for their loyalty?
6. What have be considered when implementing a contemporary loyalty program?
7. How can the loyalty program be used for social media marketing and customer acquisition?

In order to answer these research questions, first current literature was analysed. This secondary research of the project showed that the topics of *long-term stays and digital loyalty programs in the hotel industry* are rather unexplored fields of research. To close this gap, eleven guideline-based interviews were conducted in spring 2019. The **second chapter** shows the results from primary and secondary research. The **third chapter** discusses the synthesis of these results before the **fourth chapter** ends up with a conclusion and an outlook.

2. DIGITAL LOYALTY PROGRAMS IN THE HOTEL INDUSTRY

The underlying research project followed a *qualitative research* approach. In fact, little research on long-term travellers and the possibility of new loyalty programs was carried out in the hotel industry. For this purpose, an *inductive, explorative cross-sectional study* was conducted. This included eleven guideline-supported interviews, which were evaluated by topic for each interview group. The respondents consisted of two female and two male hotel guests, three internal experts from SV Hotel group and four external, neutral experts from the hotel industry and social media marketing. In order to compare the results on an aggregated, general level, the transcribed results were summarised in text form as individual case analyses.

2.1 Basics of Digital Marketing in the Hotel Industry

The literature research has shown that the topics relevant to the present work were mainly discussed in the English literature. Various general studies on customer retention and loyalty were analyzed. However, the research concentrates primarily on loyalty programs with an ecological and social incentive for customers.

New research results on loyalty programs show that *non-monetary incentives* have to be taken into account (Fehr & Falk 2002, p. 688). *Social incentives*, such as belonging to a community or signalling a social status, are just as attractive as monetary ones (Fehr & Falk 2002, p. 706). The issue of so called *instant rewards* is also gaining in importance and is seen as necessary to gaining attention and trust in today's fast-paced world (Tahal 2014, p. 7). *Word-of-mouth* (WOM) and customers' recommendation of a product or service still is regarded as the highest sign of customer loyalty (Ryue & Feick 2017, p. 84).

Furthermore, literature shows that approaches of gamification are changing user behaviour (Thorpe & Roper 2019, p. 601). Since the intention of gamification is not always comprehensible for customers in business practice, it is important to ensure that no moral principles are violated. Recent studies also show that the formation of *digital ecosystems or communities* can be useful in building a brand, i.e. brand awareness, brand image and brand value (Scheer 2016, p. 281).

Conventional instruments from online marketing are also suited to increase customer loyalty and retention in the hotel industry. *Social media marketing, influencer marketing and booking platforms* are gaining in importance (Casaló et al. 2017; Conrady & Buck 2012). Facebook and Instagram enjoy the highest popularity among social media channels in the hotel industry (Oracle 2018). Particularly Instagram became important, because user engagement is higher than in other social medias due to emotional and activating photos (picture-superiority-effect, see Chen & Yuan 2018). Influencer Marketing like *Instagram Marketing* has become an important instrument of digital marketing for industries like tourism (Djafarova & Rushworth 2017).

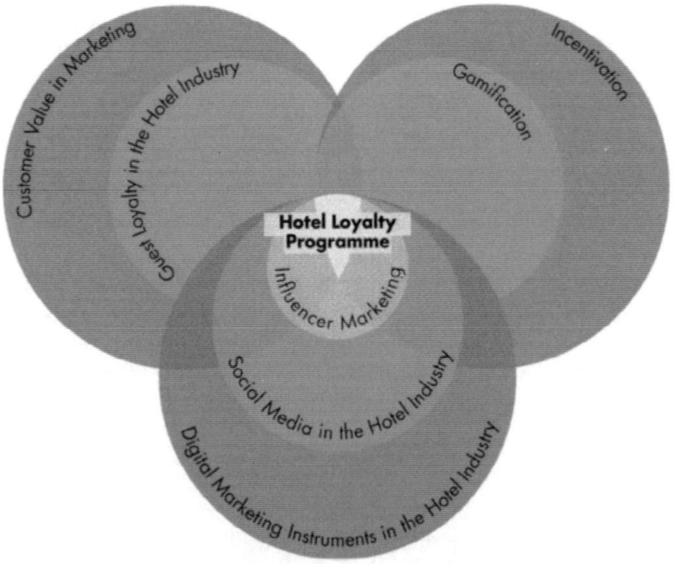

Figure 1. Theoretical Classification of this Paper

However, it does not matter how large the reach or the number of an influencer is. It is important that these are regarded as *trustworthy and authentic* by the guests (Gupta et al. 2017; Seiler & Kucza 2017).

Particularly young generations *trust more in influencers* than in conventional media and in advertising (De Veirman et al., 2017; Kohn 2016). Since social media usage is still growing, it is important to monitor them systematically and strategically. If a hotel knows its reputation on social media platforms and acts actively with its guests, this can be a competitive advantage, or an unique selling proposition (USP), respectively.

2.2 Needs and Motivation of Long-term Guests

In the methodical approach of the research project, the transcripts of the conducted interviews were evaluated by a topic analysis. An *inductive coding method* was chosen, in which following eight codes were developed.

The first code «**social media**» shows that the *(potential) guests are mainly active on Instagram*, which corresponds to literature and to the assessments of the experts.

Code 2 «**content**» and code 3 «**influenced action**» was found among potential guests. They indicate that they generate contributions in social media about their *spare time and reference to companies*. They state that they are influenced in their actions by content on social media and that they feel that their content also inspires and influences friends. This confirms the experts' statement that social media platforms are increasingly used as source of inspiration. Code 4 dealt with «**influencers**». The experts recommend that *targeted influencers and micro-influencers* should be used to reach potential guests. This opinion was confirmed by the target group.

In code 5 «**loyalty program**», guests, internal and external experts agreed that it is time to introduce a *new approach to the market*. The new program should be easy to use, ideally connected to various companies or partners and *approach the guest in a differentiated and personal way*. This should also be reflected in «**rewards**» (code 6). Guests indicate that they *prefer social incentives*. This assessment was also confirmed by the interviews of tourism experts. In addition, they recommend giving guests an *advance of trust through instant rewards and providing exclusive incentives* to improve the guest experience.

In terms of «**loyalty**» (code 7), potential guests want their expectations to be exceeded and *personal contact with them to be maintained*. For experts, loyalty is reflected in an added value for the business, which they specify in the form of a booking, although alternatives hotel offers would be cheaper.

The eighth and last code dealt with the «**community idea**». It turned out that potential guests *like to be part of a community* as long as they can extract personal added value. The experts are also aware of this, because in their opinion a community only works if it offers attractive content and exclusive advantages. From their point of view, networking with external partners, guests, local people and employees is a promising idea. This is also the opinion of the external experts: they see a community as an opportunity for a hotel to network locally and to offer guests exclusive advantages. However, the development of a community should not be underestimated.

3. DIGITAL LOYALTY PROGRAMS IN THE HOTEL INDUSTRY

3.1 Loyal Guest

In theory, a customer is described as **loyal** if he buys a *product or service more often* and is therefore economically valuable for a company. Customers who recommend a product to their environment, such as to friends or family, are also referred to be loyal.

In the hotel business one could go one step further. Hotel guests who *return to a hotel* thanks to economic incentives are often described as loyal. However, various studies have shown that this is not loyalty only on which a hotel should aim for in the long run. The hotel industry should focus on guests who return because of a *good experience* they have had with the hotel. A good customer experience often base on human factors such as friendly staff or an excellent service. More loyalty should be ascribed to these guests, as the financially incentivised ones will drop out as soon as competitors provides a better offer. This is also the opinion of the experts surveyed. They would describe a guest as loyal if he or she also booked a hotel *although the competitors make a better price*. Since not all guests can book the same hotel several times, the factor of word-of-mouth propaganda also plays an important role. In this case, however, it would be important that the guests talk positively about the brand after their visit and thus *recommend a hotel to friends or acquaintances actively or passively*. In their opinion, a guest can also be described as loyal if (s)he talks more positively about the hotel.

The experts of the analysed hotel group are also aware of this problem. In the experts point of view, there are different levels of loyalty: on the one hand, they see a guest as loyal when he returns to the hotel, but also when he extends his stay or recommends the hotel.

To sum up the findings, **three levels of loyalty** can be defined: The first is when a *guest returns* to a hotel again and again or extends his stay. Secondly, if he *recommends* the hotel to friends, family or to acquaintances in any way and thirdly, if he books the hotel, even if competitors makes *cheaper offers*. Depending on corporate objectives, these three levels of loyalty can and should be weighted differently.

3.2 Willingness of Guests to Invest into a Brand

If the interviewed (potential) guests are convinced of hotel and it's services, they are ready to invest in the hotel brand in following three areas.

- First, hotel guests are active on **social media** and regularly report on their travels, excursions, experiences with friends about interesting buildings, hotel rooms or objects and (digital) services. They like to link their contributions to *official company accounts or mark the location* where they are. They advertise a company, a location or a product to their friends without being paid for it. The interviewed guests all say that they do not expect to be paid, because they see social media as a *platform of inspiration* and for them it is enough to be inspired by contributions from their friends and followers for new services, places or products.
- Second, they have all indicated that they would like to recommend hotels or restaurants to their friends and family if they are completely satisfied with a **service** or were *positively surprised* during their hotel stay. This statement is also confirmed by the theory that customers recommend something on their own as soon as a company regularly exceeds their expectations. In order to know exactly what customer's expectations are, a company should understand its customers and regularly ask them about their expectations.
- The third point mentioned by guests is the **sense of community** and being part of a community. Everyone could imagine that they are involved in a community. Offering yoga lessons in a hotel in their place of residence, guiding guests through their hometown or passing on insider tips are possible examples.

In summary, loyal hotel guests are *willing to recommend* a hotel to their friends and acquaintances, report on it on their social media channels like Facebook or Instagram and/or they get involved in a community.

3.3 Guests Motivation for Recommendation

As mentioned above, the interviews with the guests and the theory show that they are prepared to recommend a brand as soon as their *expectations are exceeded*. It is not easy to define how these expectations can generally be met or exceeded, as this is a very individual view and each guest has different expectations based on past experiences or recommendations from friends. In the opinion of the experts, *hotel staff* plays an important role in the recommendation. For example, if the receptionist remembers in the evening that a guest had to leave early for a meeting and asks how things went in the evening, this can contribute a lot to the positive experience. Ideally, the hotel may be also provide this guest with a free drink or a spa voucher.

Other factors for exceeding expectations can be a rooftop bar, a new digital service, or a generally appealing location that looks good on Instagram. According to the experts, so-called **instagrammable moments**, i.e. subjects that are well suited for Instagram, should be generated by hotels and touristic organisations.

The interviewed guests also indicated that they recommend a brand if it offers *exclusive access to events or networks*. They also appreciate it when they can look behind the scenes of a hotel or when a hotel provides individualised welcome gifts.

Finally, guests are willing to recommend the brand as soon as it either offers them *attractive content* for their social media channels or in some way exceeds their expectations of a hotel.

3.4 Incentives from Hotels

The interviews with the internal experts of the hotel group clearly showed that hotels are willing to give social and monetary incentives to their guests. Launching a loyalty program, hotel groups want to be generous, even if there is often no fixed budget available. According to the respondents, most of the hotels are willing to pay monetary incentives such as *discounts*, develop an exclusive product line with an external partner, or they offer free cancellation. They could also imagine working with partners if they could make a more attractive offer available to the guests. So far, most hotels often have not yet considered this.

3.5 Guests' Expectations for their Loyalty

Based on the results of primary and secondary research, the answer to the question about guests' expectations can be divided into two following parts.

1. When it comes to loyalty, which is measured by **recommendations**, guests often do not expect anything. On the contrary, especially when it comes to content on social media channels, guests, experts and theory agree that caution must be exercised. As soon as it is known that guests are rewarded for contributions in their private profiles, these are quickly considered *more implausible and bought*, which can have negative effects on a brand.
2. When it comes to loyalty, which is measured by **trust**, for example when a guest often returns to a hotel, extends her/his stay or is part of a community, guests clearly expect *personal added value*. This can take the form of discounts, the possibility of free cancellation or invitations to exclusive events. According to experts, theory and potential guests interviewed, it is important that the guests see personal added value and that the incentive is either individually tailored or can be determined by the guest himself. Another aspect are *surprises*. The guests surveyed stated that they appreciated it most when they received something from the hotel that they had not expected. These can be small gifts in the room or discount codes tailored to them for third parties they receive during their stay.

Finally, it can be said that hotel guests often do not expect anything directly for their loyalty, but only become loyal if the experience is great, if the service is right, if the staff takes care about the individual needs of their guests and/or if their expectations during their stay are exceeded in some way. This can take the form of personalised monetary or social incentives.

3.6 Implementation of a Loyalty Program

The theory and interviews showed that loyalty programs should take into account various factors. It is important that the program is attractive for all of the guest. It may be worthwhile if a loyalty program is not defined or labelled as such, as loyalty programs are often stored in a drawer per se and the user tends to compare them.

One possibility would be to build a community. If one offers *exclusive advantages* to the members and binds them to the brand, these are ideally also on the side of the company in the case of negative reporting and defend it. For branding and marketing, a well-functioning community is also important. This would also bring a certain flexibility, if a hotel (group) want to integrate partners.

Potential customers as well as experts believe that future loyalty programs would be more attractive if they provided by *several brands*. If different, complemental companies cooperative, they can provide higher and more differentiated incentives. When it comes to incentives, it is important to divide them into monetary *and* social incentives, which should be preferred for sustainable loyalty. *Instant rewards* can be used to give customers an edge of trust on their first visit or to exceed their expectations. It is important that guests' expectations can be exceeded. However, according to the theory and interviews results this is not always easy. Hotels have to know and understand its guests and ask them for feedback continuously.

Moreover, it makes sense to integrate *gamification elements* into the loyalty program, as these motivate users and customers to be a part of it. For example, there might be different **statuses** that can be achieved and depending on the status, new, previously unknown incentives will be activated. It is important that incentives are personally attractive for the guest. An individualisation should be aimed at.

Finally, the program should be *easy to use*. This includes, among other things, a user-friendly and visually attractive user interface that is optimised for mobile devices as smartphones or tablets. It can be considered that customers can register directly with a social media profile. Online ratings and reviews written by customers can also be shared again or commented on, which is well received by potential and new guests. It is not decisive whether the contributions are negative or positive. A hotel should pay particular attention to *ratings and rewiews on booking platforms* like Trip Advisor, Booking.com, Hotels.com, eBookers.com, Expedia.com, etc.

According to the expert interviews, Instagram, Facebook and ratings on booking platforms are considered the most important sources of information and inspiration before booking. The experts also mention *LinkedIn* as a social media channel that will become increasingly important for companies in the future. The interviewed guests use LinkedIn primarily for professional purposes. Even though in academic research no study could be found describing a positive effect of LinkedIn in the hotel industry, the channel should not be ignored.

For a successful implementation of a (community-based) loyalty program it is important that hotels know what is reported and discussed about them in the social media and that they actively participate in the discourse. The program must be continuously adapted to the current needs of guests to be successful in the long term.

3.7 Benefits of a Loyalty Program for Customer Acquisition

Interviews with internal and external experts and theory show that a loyalty program can basically be used in **five ways to win customers**.

- Firstly, new customers can be won by *integrating third parties*. If a hotel joins forces with partners, their customers become aware of the hotel and ideally book it if required or recommend it to their community.
- Secondly, new customers can be acquired indirectly by *referring existing guests* to social media. If a guest is part of the loyalty program and thus receives an individual value added, she or he is likely to mention it on social media in form of a review or rating on his private social media channels. Informed or inspired by these platforms, new customers can be acquired. In this case, guests would act as *micro-influencers*.
- Thirdly, new guests can be won if an existing guest is completely satisfied with his stay and therefore *actively recommends* the hotel to others.
- Fourthly, an incentive could be created in the loyalty program if new guests are brought in. A new kind of *recommendation program should be combined with a loyalty program*. With this mechanism, the hotel would specifically seek to reward guests who acquire new guests. However, care must always be taken to ensure that the measure does not appear chummy or untrustworthy. The mechanism should be designed that loyal guests can be won and not the other ones, who only participate because of the incentive.
- Fifthly, a loyalty program can lead to new guests if it is well received and its *possibilities are so exclusive and appealing* that new guests become aware of it on their own. They will book a hotel so that they can also be part of this program or community.

3.8 Development of New Loyalty Programs

Based on the findings of the partial research questions, the main research question was "what kind of loyalty program can a hotel launch to maximise the loyalty of its guests?". From the interviews with potential guests and experts, it emerged that the guests are above all loyal and therefore recommend the brand to others when they are *addressed personally and individually*. Therefore, it is important to develop a loyalty program that rewards the guests individuality. In doing so, the loyalty program should contain a wide range of rewards so that members can either choose from them or be rewarded in a personalised way by the hotel with the help of collected data. As discussed above, it makes sense to work together with selected third-party partners in the loyalty program. When choosing a partner, it is important that the product or service is suitable for the hotel guest and that he or she regards it as added value.

When launching a new loyalty program, it should also be noted that it is not advertised as such, but that the community idea is in the foreground. The loyalty program should be based on the fact that everyone, whether the hotel, the guests or third party partners, derive added value from it and they are equal. No member should feel exploited or discriminated at any time. Members should be aware that their data will be collected and used for marketing purposes, but in turn they will be rewarded with exclusive incentives.

Furthermore, the incentives should be designed in such a way that they are also suitable (instagrammable) for social media contributions. If guests report positively about their stay, this also inspires new guests to book the hotel. Guests could then act as micro-influencers.

The program should also have a playful character so that it does not become unattractive, boring or forgotten at some point. The guests should remain motivated to be an *active part of the community* even after their stay in the hotel. It is important that the guests feel that they are part of the hotel community and that the associated loyalty program or incentives for the guests are of secondary importance.

To achieve this, personal contact is essential. It should be done absolutely without the fact that the program is only dealt with online. Exclusive offline events as well as employees who personally look after and advise the guests are indispensable for success or for winning loyal guests.

In summary, it can be said that hotels should come on to the market with a new loyalty program which is not perceived as such, so that no comparisons are made. Especially at the beginning, when a hotel is not yet too well known, credible third-party partners should be involved and the recommendation of the guests and community members should be put on.

3.9 Case Study *«Stay KooooK»*

Based on the knowledge from the research questions an implementation concept for «Stay KooooK» could be developed, which contains differentiated and practical approaches. In a first step, incentives were defined that «Stay KooooK» guests would like from a hotel. These were divided into the categories «Gastronomy», «Local Nightlife», «Co-Working Spaces», «Exclusive Products», «Beauty&Spa», «Sports», «Music», «Locomotion», «Exclusive Events», «Stay KooooK Incentives» and «Social Engagement». In each case, concrete partners for the first «Stay KooooK» in Bern (Switzerland) were proposed. In addition, three types of mechanism were developed a «KooooKer community». In the first type, the members are given incentives tailored to their status. In the second type, all incentives are visible to all community members and can be purchased with so-called «KooooK-credits». In the third type, the status achieved within the community is regarded as an incentive. Various incentives are distributed or raffled directly to all members.

4. CONCLUSION

Answering the main research question, it became clear that hotels should launch a future loyalty program, which is not defined as such, but focuses on the community idea. Each member of this community should receive an individual incentive and should not be exploited at any time. To ensure that the hotels can provide enough attractive incentives, they should cooperate with third-party partners. However, the focus when choosing a partner should clearly be on the needs of the guests. Ultimately, the main goal of a hotel community should be that its guests behave loyally and ideally bring new guests.

The goal of the program could be that it becomes a part of the everyday life of the community and does not fall into oblivion. This aspect can be helped with playful elements. Nevertheless, the focus should always be that the guests want to be part of this community, as membership offers them exclusive advantages. The personal contact should not be forgotten, exclusive events as well as personal guest support are at the top of the guests' wish list. The aim is to positively surprise the guests and exceed their expectations, because this mechanism ultimately leads to the desired word-of-mouth propaganda, which generates new guests.

Literature review and empirical research showed that customer value and guest loyalty have been a major issue in marketing for a long time. However, it was interesting to note that there is hard to find literature in the hotel industry and tourism. It seems that this is a field of research that enjoys great interest.

Nevertheless, few scientific studies could be found that investigated how a loyalty program in the hotel industry, or in tourism in general, should be designed in the future. Moreover, only limited literature on *long-term travellers* could be found. In order to close these gaps, it was the right approach to carry out qualitative research in addition to literature research.

Thanks to the survey of potential guests, internal experts of a hotel group as well as external experts from the hotel industry and social media marketing, new insights could be gained which were valuable for answering the research questions. The findings from the interviews partly confirmed previously researched theories, but at the same time introduced new perspectives. Topics such as incentives and gamification have also arisen, which have already been dealt with in secondary research. It was thus confirmed that a future loyalty program in the hotel industry must function across the board and combine disciplines from psychology and online marketing. Based on these new findings, an innovative concept for the first Stay KooooK Hotel in Switzerland was developed and will be implemented in business practice. Since new loyalty program and community concepts have to be tested in business practice, their success and the added value of the present research for practice can only be assumed and has to assessed at a later point. However, since all the experts surveyed showed huge interest in being informed about the results later on, it can be assumed that the research hit the nerve of time, discovered a research gap and partly contributed to closing it.

In summary, it can be said that a hotel must come onto the market with a new loyalty programme, which is not perceived as such, so that no comparison is made. Especially in the case of new brands, credible third-party partners should be consulted at the outset and the recommendation of guests and community members should be the key. However, this explorative, qualitative and practice-oriented research approach of the underlying project is not representative. Therefore, quantitative research should investigate the topics discussed in this paper, by survey a large number of marketing managers in the touristic sector. The different findings and hypotheses of this paper have to be tested on a quantitative level. In future, new and innovative models of loyalty programs of community and influencer marketing have to be developed.

REFERENCES

Casaló, L. V., Flavián, C., & Ibáñez-Sánchez, S. (2017). Antecedents of consumer intention to follow and recommend an Instagram account. In: *Online Information Review*, Vol. 41, Iss. 7, pp. 1046-1063.

Chen, L., Yuan, S. (2018): Influencer Marketing: How Message Value and Credibility Affect Consumer Trust of Branded Content on Social Media, In: *Journal of Interactive Advertising*, Vol. 19, Is. 1, pp. 58-73.

Conrady, R., Buck, M. (2012). *Trends and Issues in Global Tourism 2012*, Berlin, Springer.

De Veirman, M., Cauberghe, V., & Hudders, L. (2017). *Marketing through Instagram influencer: Impact of number of followers and product divergence on brand attitude*. Ghent University, Belgium.

Djafarova, E., Rushworth, C. (2017). Exploring the credibility of online celebrities' Instagram profiles in influencing the purchase decisions of young female users. In: *Computers in Human Behavior*, Vol. 68, pp. 1-7.

Fehr, E., Falk, A. (2002). Psychologica foundations of incentives. In: *European Economic Review*, Vol. 46, Is. 4-5, pp. 687-724.

Gupta, R., Kishor, N., Verma, D. (2017). Construction and Validation of five-dimensional celebrity endorsement scale: Introducing the PATER Model. In: *British Journal of Marketing Studies*, Vol. 5, Is. 4, pp. 15-35.

Lewis, M. (2004). The influence of loyalty programs and shortterm promotions on customer retention. In: *Journal of Marketing Research*, Vol. 41, August, pp. 281-292.

Melancon, J., Noble, S., Noble, C. (2011). Managing rewards to enhance relational worth. In: *Journal of the Academy of Marketing Science*, Vol., 39, Is. 3, pp. 341-362.

Oracle (2018). *The Loyalty Divide*. Redwood Shores, California, USA.

Peppers, D., Rogers, M. (2004). *Managing Customer Relationships: A Strategic Framework.* Hoboken, New Jersey.

Ryu, G., Feick, L. (2007). A Penny for Your Thoughts: Referral Reward Programs and Referral Likelihood. In: *Journal of Marketing* Vol. 71, Is. 1, pp. 84-94.

Tahal, R. (2014). Loyalty Programs in E-Commerce and their perception by the young adult internet population. *Central European Business Review* Vol.3, Is. 2, pp. 7-13.

Thorpe, A., Roper, S. (2019). The Ethics of Gamification in a Marketing Context. In: *Journal of Business Ethics*, Vol. 155, pp. 597-609.

Scheer, A. (2016). Value Driver of Digitalisation (in German). In: *Informatik Spektrum*; Vol. 39, Is. 4, pp. 275-289.

Seiler, R., Kucza, G. (2017). Source Credibility Model, Source Attractiveness Model and Match-up-Hypothesis – An Integrated Model. In: *Journal of International Scientific Publications*, Vol. 11, pp. 1-15.

TWTRENDS: THE TOPIC-GRAPH EXTRACTION FROM TWITTER TRENDS

Jun Iio
Faculty of Global Informatics, Chuo University
1-18 Ichigaya-tamachi, Shinjuku-ku, Tokyo 162-8478, Japan

ABSTRACT

Twitter provides a list of trending topics, a list of social trends or issues that users of the social networking services (SNS) will be interested in at a given time. However, they are presented as a list of key phrases making it challenging to identify or infer the message of the trending topics. In an attempt decipher the meaning and the structure hidden in the list of trending topics provided by Twitter, we developed a system to visualize topic maps according to the co-occurrence structure of typical tweets that mention the trending topics. This paper describes an overview of the system structure, the main logic to construct topic maps, and findings from its operation from the 1st of January 2019 to 30th of June 2019.

KEYWORDS

Twitter, Trending Topics, Co-Occurrence Network, Topic Map, Trends Visualization, Social Network Graph

1. INTRODUCTION

Social network services (SNS) are commonly used today, and they have become fundamental tools for daily communication online. Twitter is a microblogging service with more than 326 million active users. It has 134 million daily active users worldwide and 45 million monthly active users in Japan.

Twitter provides a list of trending topics in an area e.g. a city such as Tokyo, Paris, and London (Figure 1). Trending topics are highly dependent on an area as they are representative and/or are connected to social issues in the area. Additionally, the tweets are presented in the language which the users speak in their daily lives. If one is interested in the trends in Japan, trending topics are the listed in Japanese, and if one is interested in the trends in the US, they are listed in English.

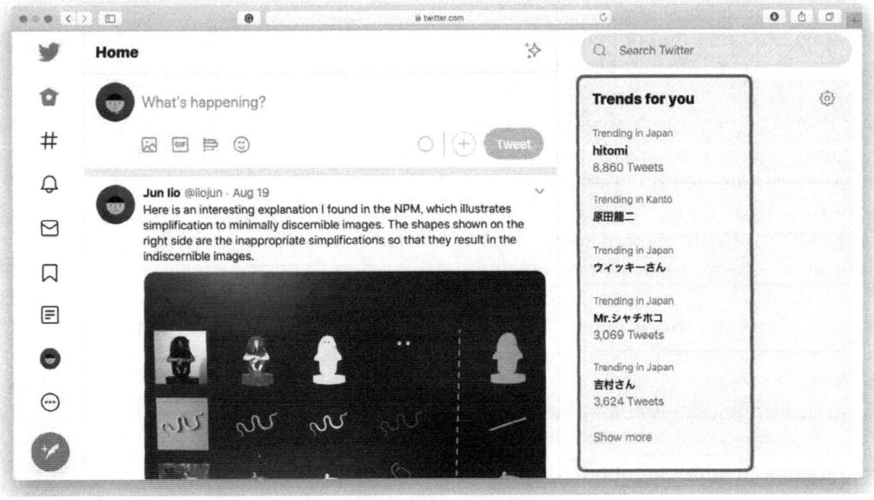

Figure 1. Twitter provides a list of the trending topics

The algorithm used by Twitter to select the trending topics is not known, however, the list of trending topics is derived from the most popular topics based on the number of users who submit tweets on the topic. This suggests that the list of trending topics shows several social phenomena and is a form of collective intelligence. The list of topics suggests to other users' topics to consider as interesting. However, they are sporadic, and this makes it difficult to select important topics and those which are not. Twitter only provides a list of key phrases and does elaborate the structure or relationship between the topics.

There are two kinds of trending topics i.e. one is a hashtag type topic phrase, and the other is non-hashtag type topic phrase. The hashtag type topic phrase has intentions of the user who creates it or the information of the providers. Twitter users who have interests in some issues use a specific hashtag to identify their tweets on that issue and to distinguish them from other topics. The non-hashtag type topics are spontaneously arising topics. In our study we excluded tweets with specific intentions by not including the hashtag type topics.

Analysis of the topics that are discussed on the SNS every day and how users of the SNS mention such issues in their tweets can reveal social trends. The aim of our study was to visualize topic structures and to construct trending-topic maps. Visualization would allow for us to easily capture the details and the information of the social trends generated by a large number of SNS users.

2. RELATED WORK

There are several studies on Twitter trends, especially on its application on citizen's attitude surveys of specific themes that are proposed by many researchers.

Lewis *et al.* analyzed a discussion on Twitter on the pros-and-cons of electronic cigarettes (Lewis *et al.* 2015). Bovet *et al.* examined the results of applying the Twitter analysis system they developed for the US presidential election in 2016 (Bovet *et al.* 2018). Lin *et al.* analyzed Twitter data to allow journalists to obtain news topics from social media and they conducted network analyses that provided network graphs comparable to what we are proposing in our study (Lin *et al.* 2016). Thus, there have been many studies that have applied Twitter's trend analysis to various themes.

Zubiaga *et al.* reported that Twitter had become an essential platform for socio-informatics researchers (Zubiaga *et al.* 2015). They defined a typology to classify a trending topic into four types: news, ongoing events, memes, and commemoratives and performed classification experiments using support vector machine classifiers. Dawar *et al.* also proposed a data-investigation tool for Twitter trends (Dawar *et al.* 2018), and their tool drew network graphs and is comparable to our proposed tool, although their diagram is a user-base network graph. Khandekar *et al.* (2017) and Wen and Marshall (2014) have also summarized the topics discussed on Twitter by using Twitter trends. However, the novelty of our study is not only in that it is visualization method but in that we also developed a system to provide visualized topics.

There are other approaches to disclosing social trends by analyzing Twitter trends. For example, Becker *et al.* (2011) used a standard machine-learning technique for their event classifier to distinguish between messages about real-world events and non-event messages. Several trending topics were shown in clusters identified by real-world events. Benhardus and Kalita proposed an algorithm to detect and identify trending topics from streaming data. Their approach applied a calculation based on a term frequency-inverse document frequency (tf-idf) analysis. Aiello *et al.* (2013) also discussed a method of detecting trends, using a set of tweets. In their case studies, they proposed an algorithm designed to extract trending topics from a massive set of tweets. On the other hand, our approach is based on the existing set of trending topics. Their results of previous studies can be used as input in the present study.

Guille and Favre proposed a novel method to detect events and provide visualizations of trending topics (Guille and Favre 2015). They proposed the mention-anomaly-based Event Detection (MABED) method, which detects events and also visualizes them. They conducted experiments on both English and French Twitter data and showed that several visualizations could provide insightful information. Giridhar and Abdelzaher (2017) reported an interesting finding in their work, which visualizes events extracted from SNS. Their system is unique because it analyzes both Twitter and Instagram simultaneously. It is a challenge to analyze social trends using multiple sources. Their method creates fusion models from location information, drawn from the Instagram application program interface (API) and detailed event information from Twitter API. Although these visualization methods are both interesting, they seem experimental. By contrast, our system is both practical and useful for real applications, such as marketing and cultural analysis.

3. THE METHOD OF OUR STUDY

The method of our study is simple and is described as follows:

1. collection of the lists of trending topics using Twitter trends API,
2. collection of tweets that mention the trending topics using Twitter standard search API, and
3. the development of a system and its use for co-occurrence network to show the structure of the trending topics.

This procedure was conducted every 20 minutes, and this was done daily. All data collected for a day was used to make a topic map from the set of all co-occurrence networks operated. The results were a visualization of the topic structure for the day, hidden in the list of topic sentences.

3.1 Preparation

Before implementing the system, we had to create a Twitter developers' program account which would give us the rights to access some of the APIs provided by Twitter. We registered ourselves as a developer for Twitter applications through their registration page[1], and we gave a short description of our information. Our request was assessed by Twitter, and when it was approved we were given access to the consumer API key (CK), the consumer API secret key (CS), the access token (AT), and the access token secret (AS), which are requested when a program accesses the server requesting for information from Twitter.

3.2 Trending Topics

Acquisition of the four essential codes allowed us to access several services from Twitter. Access to the Twitter trends API provides information on trends and also information on the region-specific trends. The "GET trends/available" command's response is a list of acceptable regions in a JavaScript Object Notation (JSON) form. The results of the trends APIs showed that there were twenty-two regions available in Japan.

We requested a list of the trending topics for the regions by sending the area-identifying information, in the form of "where on earth ID (WOEID)" as defined by Yahoo! and placed it in the parameters of the query in Twitter. The prototype system we developed in this study had one limitation on the system, which was for it to only collect the trends for the Twitter users living in the Tokyo metropolitan area (Figure 2). Note that the personal information (CK, CS, AT, and AS) is masked.

The system had other restrictions and options. The list of trending topics was updated every five minutes and accesses was restricted to 75 times every 15 minutes. The hashtag type trending topics were filtered out by adding the phrase "exclude=hashtag" to the query parameter.

Figure 2. The python script used to obtain the list of trending topics (left), and its result (right)

[1] https://developer.twitter.com

3.3 Tweets Mentioning the Trending Topics

After obtaining the list of trending topics, the system further filtered the tweets to sets of the listed issues. The tweets were obtained using the Twitter search API. There are three types of search APIs i.e. the standard, premium, and enterprise. The standard search API is available for free; however, the premium and enterprise search APIs are not free, and payment must be made for their use. In this study, we used the Standard search API as it is a free service, although it has some restrictions on retrieving tweets. The most significant limitation was that we could only access the tweets posted within a week. However, this did not impact this study because we were interested in the current topics. The standard search API also had a limited access and could only be accessed 180 times (in the case of user authentication base) or 450 times (in the case of app-authentication) every 15 minutes.

Under such restrictions, we collected a maximum of 100 tweets for each trending topic excluding retweets. We excluded retweets because they have identical sentences and were not suitable for word frequency or co-occurrence calculations. The retweets were filtered from the results by adding the phrase "exclude: retweets exclude:nativeretweets" to the query parameter.

3.4 Visualization of Trending Topics

The procedure of visualizing trending topics hides the calculation of the word frequency and the co-occurrence network. A morphological analysis was conducted on every tweet to allow for the calculation of word frequency and co-occurrence probabilities because all the words in sentence in Japanese are connected without any spacing characters except punctuations. The system filtered proper nouns from the set of words of each tweet. The word frequency and the co-occurrence network were calculated based on the proper noun sets.

The co-occurrence network illustrates the topic structure and the scope of co-occurrence in one tweet. The size and color of the node and the thickness of the link is dependent on the value of the word frequency and the co-occurrence probability, respectively. Note that only one-fourth of the links are shown in the graph to simplify the network graph.

An example of a co-occurrence network graph is given in Figure 3. The node "(Tabi (journey) salada)" has the largest word frequency and several links to other nodes. The link between "(Tabi (journey) salada)" and "(Milano)" has the largest value of co-occurrence probability, and the link is defined by the thickest line.

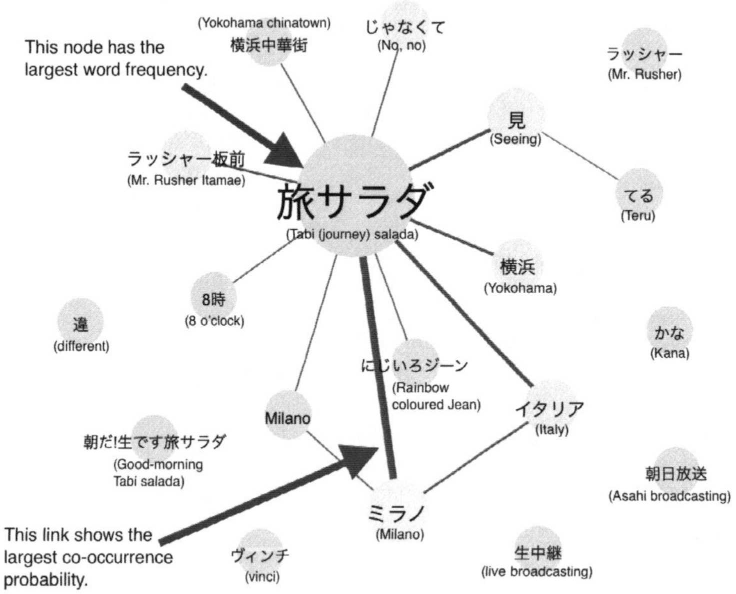

Figure 3. An example of the co-occurrence network graph

4. SYSTEM OVERVIEW

Based on the algorithm mentioned previously, the results show that the system we developed to retrieve trending topics on tweets was able to calculate word frequencies and co-occurrence networks, and the topic structure was visualization.

4.1 System Architecture

An overview of the system is given in Figure 4. The python script get_trends.py collected trending topics and tweets. It produced a Ruby script db/seeds.rb, which had the seeds to the database entries in the Ruby on Rails application. The system retrieves trending topics and tweets every 20 minutes. It analyzes the topic structure and stores the results in a database. The database stores the information on nodes and links as the co-occurrence network is not created on-demand dynamically.

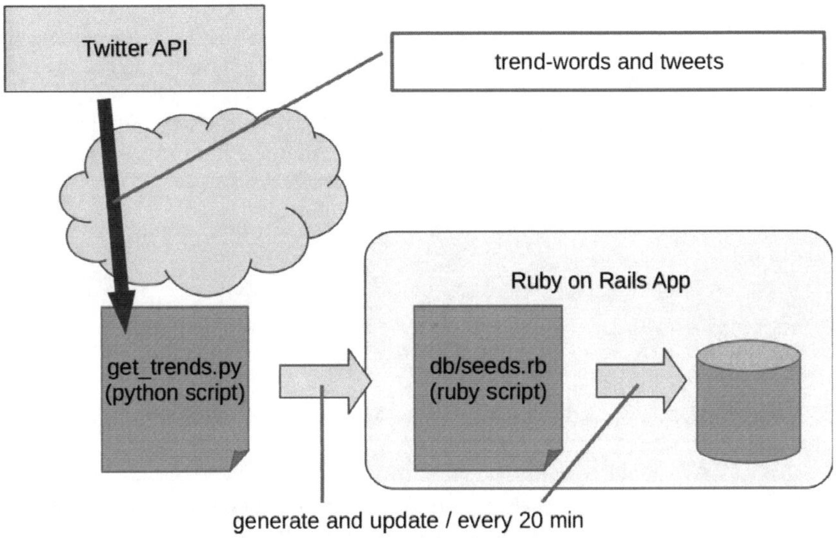

Figure 4. An overview of the system

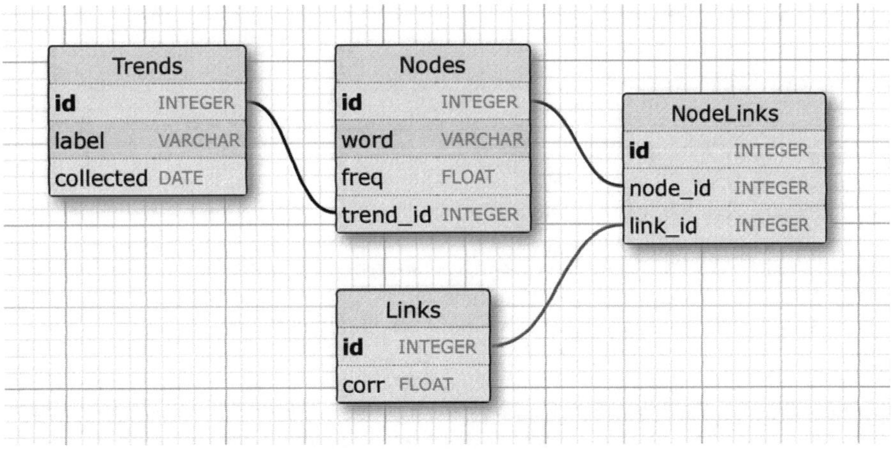

Figure 5. The schema of the database (which was drawn by WWW SQL designer[2])

[2] http://ondras.zarovi.cz/sql/demo/

The database schema had four tables and three references as shown in Figure 5. The database has four tables to represent the co-occurrence network graph. The table titled *Trends* had the list of trending topics, the tables titled *Nodes* and *Links* had the list of nodes and links shown in every co-occurrence network graph, and the table titled *NodeLinks* had the list of relations between the nodes and the links.

Presenting the network graphs was implemented using a web application framework called Ruby on Rails (RoR). The python script get_trends.py collecting trending topics and tweets did not access the database directly and it generated a Ruby script db/seeds.rb which stored the entries of the nodes and links. After the Ruby script was generated, the command "rails db:seed" was used and the data entries were stored in the database.

4.2 TWtrends: The Application for Topic Visualization

The implemented web system called TWtrends[3], was created based on Ruby as described previously. The application was deployed to the server and ran in the Apache web server. The application was run through the Phusion Passenger module (Phusion 2019).

The typical use-cases of the system are presented in Figure 6 and the index page that contains a list of the trending topics collected in a day is given on the left. All topics were clickable. When the users clicked any of the topic phrases, page transition occurred, and the co-occurrence network graph was presented (the middle of Figure 6). The network graph was drawn using D3.js (Zhu 2013) so as for them to be clickable and operable allowing for the modification of the shape of the figure. Additionally, the system had a keyword search function. The right part of Figure 6 shows the results of a search.

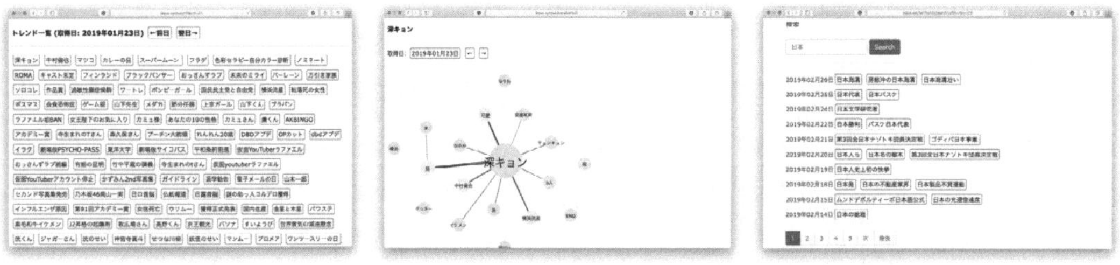

Figure 6. The screenshots of TWtrends: (Left) an index page, (Middle) showing the co-occurrence network graph, and (Right) a result of the keyword search

5. TOPIC MAP GRAPH

This section explains the second visualization based on the co-occurrence network graphs.

5.1 The Similarity of Topics

The system collects over 200 trending topics a day and a review of the topics showed that there were several relationships among some of the topics. The co-occurrence network graph of three topics is given in Figure 7. The graph on the left is for the topic *Aladdin*, the graph in middle id for the topic *Jasmine*, and the graph on the right is for the topic *Jafar*. Aladdin, Jasmine, and Jafar are names of characters of a Walt Disney film called *Aladdin*. These characters as topics were very popular among Twitter users on the 15th of June 2019, and they came up on Twitter's timeline as the trending topics in the Tokyo metropolitan area.

The three graphs are topologically comparable, and their similarities imply that there are several clusters hidden in the list of the trending topics. This suggests that these three topics arose from tweets mentioning the movie. Therefore, these three topics should be categorized into one cluster.

[3] The application 'TWtrends' is available at http://iiojun.xyz/twt/, and its source code is also available at https://github.com/iiojun/twt/

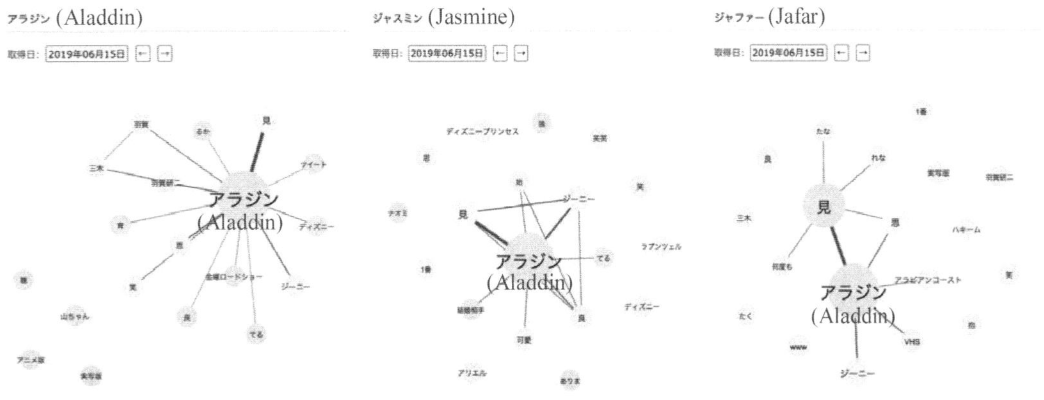

Figure 7. The co-occurrence network graphs on 'Aladdin' (Left), 'Jasmine' (Middle) and 'Jafar' (Right)

5.2 Topic Map Graph using Cosine Similarity

An example of the topic map graph, which was calculated on the 26th of January 2019 is given in Figure 8. On that day, the main topic was Ms. Naomi Osaka, a famous Japanese tennis player who won the women's trophy for the Australian Open, a tennis tournament. There was a big cluster with several topics on her win as shown in Figure 8.

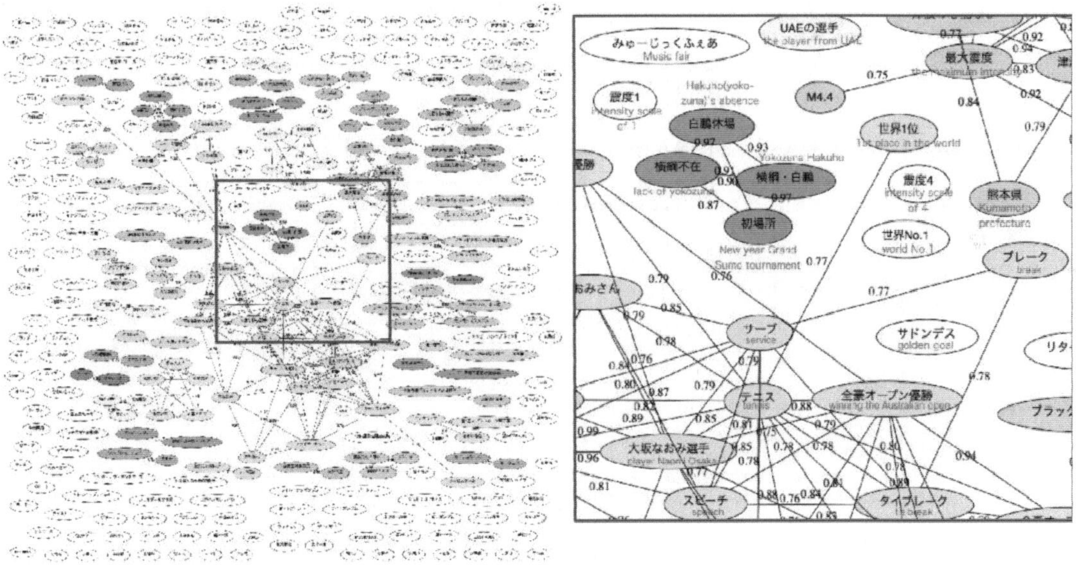

Figure 8. An example of the topic map graph calculated on the 26th of January 2019 (left). The magnified part of the topic-map graph with some English translations is illustrated (right)

Trending topics are associated with the co-occurrence network graphs. Using this relationship, we can build a massive word space which consists of all keywords appearing in the co-occurrence graphs in a day. A topic is considered as a point in the space. In such word spaces, the distance of the two topics can be calculated so that their similarity can be determined.

In this study, we used the cosine similarity as the measure of distance, e.g. if vector $\boldsymbol{a}$ is for topic A and the vector $\boldsymbol{b}$ is for the topic B, the cosine similarity between $\boldsymbol{a}$ and $\boldsymbol{b}$, which is denoted by sim(A, B), is calculated using the following formula:

$$\mathrm{sim}(A,B) = \frac{\boldsymbol{a} \cdot \boldsymbol{b}}{|\boldsymbol{a}||\boldsymbol{b}|}$$

We defined the threshold value as 0.75 and the nodes that had a similarity value more than the threshold were aggregated in one cluster. A topic map graph was drawn using GraphViz utilities (Ellison 2001) based on the results of the calculation. Figure 9 shows interim results of the calculation of similarities between each node, and a dot script for GraphVis created by the system based on the result of similarities calculations. After the generation of the dot script, an image of the topic map graph is rendered according to this code.

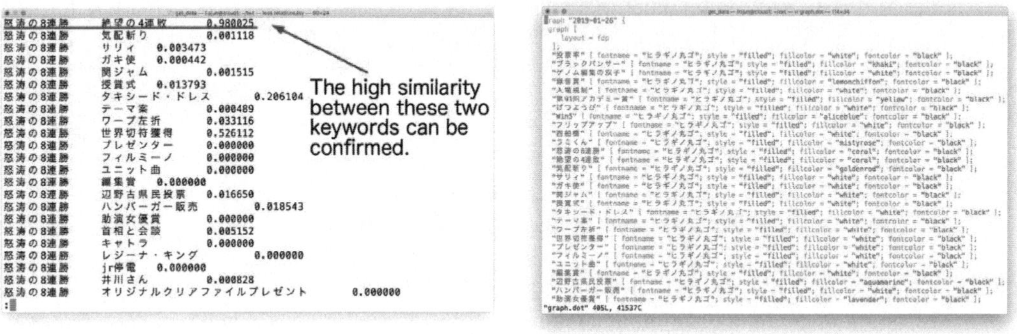

Figure 9. An example of the interim result of the calculation of similarities between each node (left), and a script ('dot script') for GraphViz created by the system (right)

5.3 A Distinguishing Social Trend Revealed by the System

The system was able to show the most popular topic of a day. The transition of the topic map from the 28th of April to 4th of May shown in Figure 10, and it shows that the topic maps on the 30th of April and the 1st of May had an unusual shape in comparison to the others.

We investigated the contents of the trending topics carefully, and the item "the last things in Heisei era" and similar issues were popular on the 30th of April. Similarly, we found that the topic "the first things in Reiwa era" and related matters were popular on the 1st of May. The results presented in Figure 10 showed that the changes in era from Heisei era to Reiwa era was a matter of considerable interest to the Japanese people.

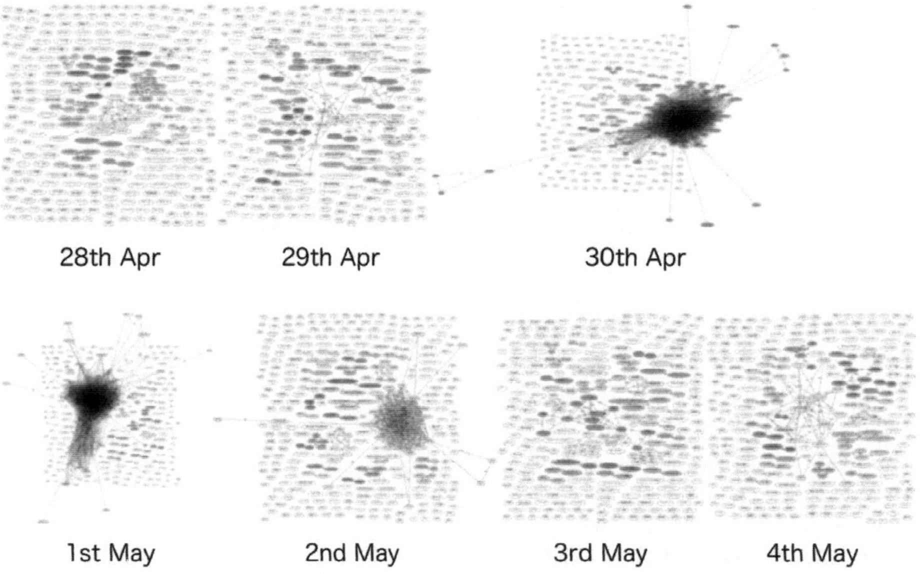

Figure 10. A typical example of the sequence of topic map graphs. These graphs were calculated every day from the 28th of April 2019 to the 4th of May 2019

6. CONCLUSIONS AND FUTURE WORK

In this study, we developed a system to visualize the structure of trending topics by calculating the word frequency and co-occurrence network. Trending topics were collected every 20 minutes, and the results of the calculation were stored in a database. The Visualization system was built based on the Ruby on Rails framework and the application was built using D3.js and Ajax.

The topic map graphs were constructed based on the word frequencies of the trending topics after calculating co-occurrence network graphs. The topic map graphs have several topic clusters, which were hidden in the list of topics. The analyses of the similarities in topics can show us relationships that allows us to know what topics are popular on SNSs.

The present paper also reports on a distinguishing example observed from the end of April to the beginning of May 2019. A historic event occurred in Japan that week: the change of an era, from Heisei to Reiwa. The magnitude of interest in that event among SNS users was shown in a sequence of topic map graphs, drawn by our system.

Although the current system is set up to process tweets written in Japanese, converting the system to enable it to process tweets in other languages will not be a difficult modification. The script code depends on language only to extract from the collected tweets a set of keywords, which constitute the candidate of the nodes in the co-occurrence network. As a small part of the process, this step can be easily modified. Our future work will involve making the system multilingual and evaluating it in other cultures overseas.

REFERENCES

Aiello, L. M., Petkos, G., Martin, C., Corney, D., Papadopoulos, S., Skraba, R., Goker, A., Kompatsiaris, Y., and Jaimes, A., 2013. Sensing trending topics in Twitter, *IEEE Transactions on Multimedia,* Vol. 15, No. 6, pp. 1268-1282. doi: 10.1109/AICCSA.2014.7073242

Becker, H., Naaman, M., and Gravano, L., 2011. Beyond Trending Topics: Real-World Event Identification on Twitter, *Proceedings of the Fifth International AAAI Conference on Weblogs and Social Media,* pp. 438-441.

Benhardus, J. and Kalita, J., 2013. Streaming trend detection in Twitter, *International Journal on Web Based Communities*, Vol. 9, No. 1, pp. 122-139.

Bovet, A., Morone, F., and Makse, H. A., 2018. Validation of Twitter opinion trends with national polling aggregates: Hillary Clinton vs Donald Trump, *Scientific Reports*, No. 8, Article Number: 8673.

Dawar, A., Purwar, A., Anand, N., and Singla. C., 2018. TweetRush: A tool for analysis of twitter data. *International Journal on Education and Management Engineering*, Vol. 8, No. 2, pp. 31-40, 2018. doi: 10.5815/ijeme.2018 .02.04

Ellson, J., Gansner, E., Koutsofios, L., North, S. C., and Woodhull, G., 2002. Graphviz— Open Source Graph Drawing Tools, *In: Mutzel P., Jünger M., Leipert S. (eds) Graph Drawing. GD 2001. Lecture Notes in Computer Science*, vol 2265. Springer, Berlin, Heidelberg.

Giridhar, P. and Abdelzaher, T., 2017. Visualization of Events Using Twitter and Instagram, *IEEE International Conference on Pervasive Computing and Communications Demonstrations,* Kona, HI, USA, pp. 82-84.

Khandekar, C., Daiya, R., Parekh, R., and Kelkar, K., 2017. TweetSum: Automated News Summarization of Twitter Trends, *International Journal of Computer Applications*, Vol. 165, No. 8, pp. 5-8.

Lewis, H. C., *et al.,* 2015. Social Listening: A Content Analysis of E-Cigarette Discussions on Twitter, *Journal of Medical Internet Research*, Vol. 17, No. 10, e243, doi:10.2196/jmir.4969

Lin, C.-Y., Li, T.-Y., and Chen. P., 2016. An information visualization system to assist news topics exploration with social media. *Proceedings of the 7th 2016 International Conference on Social Media & Society*, SMSociety '16, pp. 23:1-23:9. ACM, New York, NY, USA, doi: 10.1145/2930971.2930995

Phusion, 2019. *Passenger - Enterprise grade web app server for Ruby, Node.js, Python*, viewed 25 August 2019, https://www.phusionpassenger.com

Wen, D., and Marshall, G., 2014. Automatic Twitter Topic Sum-marization, *The 17th Intternational Conference on Computer Science and Engineering*, Chengdu, China. doi:10.1109/ CSE.2014.69

Zhu N. Q., 2013. *Data Visualization with D3.js Cookbock, Over 70 recipies to create dynamic data-driven visuzalization with D3.js*, Packt Publishing, Birmingham, UK.

Zubiaga, A., Spina, D., Martınez, R., and Fresno. V., 2015. Real-time classification of twitter trends. *Journal of the Association for Information Science and Technology*, Vol. 66, No. 3, pp. 462-473, 2015. doi: 10.1002/asi.23186

ON THE EXPLOITATION OF COLLABORATIVE ARGUMENTATION STRUCTURES FOR INDUCING REASONING BEHAVIOR

Nikos Karacapilidis[1] and Vassilis Tampakas[2]
[1]*IMIS Lab, MEAD, University of Patras, 26504 Rio Patras, Greece*
[2]*Electrical and Computer Engineering Department, University of Peloponnese, Greece*

ABSTRACT

Contemporary collaborative argumentation support systems provide limited or no support in analyzing and inducing their users' reasoning behavior. This article discusses the empowerment of such systems towards this direction through an innovative approach, which is based on the assessment of similar argumentation sequences. Representative cases where the proposed approach may be used to capture the users' behavior, improve their collaboration and increase the argumentation support system's awareness are examined.

KEYWORDS

Argumentation, Decision Making, Reasoning, Collaboration, IBIS

1. INTRODUCTION

Argumentation has been proven to be a very efficient process in cases where people attempt to resolve ill-defined problems and conflicting scenarios. The study of argumentation dates long before the "information age" and constitutes a cross-disciplinary research field. Scientists from different backgrounds such as linguistics, philosophy, education and recently from informatics and computer science have been actively involved in argumentation theory and related software systems.

Argumentation support systems are built on top of alternative argumentation models. Although each model serves a specific purpose, they all share some common characteristics: they define the types of argumentation objects and the actions that can be performed on them. Thus, once the system has adopted a model, every discourse is codified through and validated against it. Contemporary argumentation support systems usually impose sophisticated argumentation structures. However, they offer limited or no support in the analysis of the argumentation structure; they monitor the users' contributions in a passive way; provide limited feedback about the focus of the discussion and fail to assess or predict the evolution of an argumentative discourse.

As revealed from the argumentation related literature, individuals react to and understand the same input in different ways. For instance, people may overlook information that undermines their positions (the *confirmation bias* phenomenon (Jonas et al., 2001)) and show preference to supportive, rather than opposing (the *selective exposure* phenomenon (Kuhn, 1991)). Furthermore, newcomers have to face even more challenges, such as the examination of specific parts of a dialogue, the reconstruction of the discourse, and the identification of inconsistencies. Additionally, community leaders are facing the problem of keeping an overview of the developing discussions in order to intervene and retain the desired discourse objectives. For instance, there are cases where an argument might raise a new debate over a certain claim and users might be swept off to minor or irrelevant issues. We argue that such concerns are of major importance for maintaining a high quality argumentative discourse and that there appears to be limited system support with regards to these.

Motivated by similar initiatives that aim at organizing and understanding the enormous amount of user generated data, work reported in this paper focuses on the exploitation of argumentation structures for automatically inducing users' behavior in an argumentation context. The proposed approach enables the analysis of users' contributions in argumentation support systems and is based on the assessment of similar argumentation sequences.

The remainder of the paper is structured as follows. Section 2 provides a short introduction to the basic concepts and the history of argumentation support systems. Section 3 describes the mechanics of our approach in an intuitive and simple way. Section 4 presents and discusses representative examples about how this approach may be found useful. The last section concludes with some final remarks.

2. ARGUMENTATION SUPPORT SYSTEMS

The IBIS (Issue Based Information System (Kunz and Rittel, 1970)) has been one of the most influential systems that supports argumentation and group decision support. According to the IBIS approach, information units are classified as issues, positions or arguments. Users participating in a discussion can comment about problems or claims that are reflected in the corresponding visualized logical diagram. The aim of this activity is to support collective understanding and team-based reasoning. As a specific example, consider the instance of an argumentative discussion following the IBIS formalization shown in Figure 1. In this example, Reason!Able is used to chart an argumentative discussion taking place among several participants (van Gelder, 2003). Numerous arguments are proposed and linked to each other. The argumentation tree shown may constitute a refined, small part of the actual deliberation.

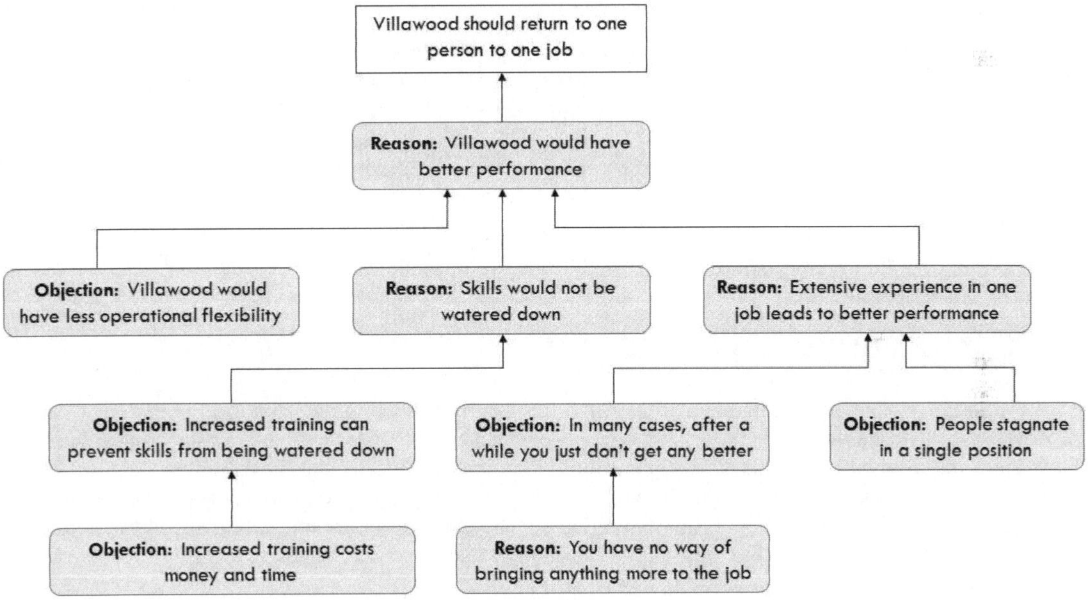

Figure 1. An instance of a partial argumentation tree, as visualized in Reason!Able (taken from (van Gelder, 2003)). The top node represents one conclusion (or claim) concerning the factory named Villawood, while the rest of the nodes are arguments clustered and linked to each other through support or opposition

A comprehensive review of existing argumentation support systems exceeds the scope of this paper. However, a short discussion about the evolution of the argumentation support systems follows. As shown in Table 1, systems that belong to the first generation were developed in the realms of hypertext systems. For instance, gIBIS (Conklin and Begeman, 1987) allow the visualization and interconnection of arguments. Nevertheless, the information units supported are mainly documented and no constraint imposed by the system exists. As a result of the above, the systems of this generation provide limited support for the correct representation of arguments. Contrary to the first generation, the second generation comprises systems where the identification of argumentation features is clear and noticeable. The emphasis is on the provision of knowledge management services, through the reuse of information and the employment of reasoning mechanisms (e.g. Hermes (Karacapilidis and Papadias, 2001), Belvedere (Suthers et al., 1995) and GeoMed (Karacapilidis et al., 1997)). As such, some of these systems are built to support learning activities (e.g. Reason!Able (van Gelder, 2003)). The third generation comprises systems that are deployed on the web and designed to support the collaborative production of arguments (e.g. PARMENIDES (http://cgi.csc.liv.ac.uk/~parmenides/), TruthMapping (http://www.truthmapping.com/), Cohere (http://cohere.open.ac.uk/) and CoPe_it! (Karacapilidis et al., 2009)). While they maintain the characteristics of those of the previous generation, they also provide mechanisms for administrating communities and allow the exploitation of existing resources through importing and exporting services.

Table 1. A classification of collaborative argumentation support systems

Argumentation support systems	**Characteristics**
First generation *(1987-1995)*	Emphasis on visualization aspects. Adoption of argumentation aspects, without a clear reference to specific model. Weak reuse of knowledge, no collaboration support.
Second generation *(1990-2007)*	Designed with regards to specific argumentation model. Appearance of mechanisms for reasoning and decision making support. Web applications. Partial collaboration support.
Third generation *(2003-today)*	Designed for collaboration and convenient reuse of system and web resources. Early provision for community support.

Despite the above developments, collaborative argumentation support systems continue to receive low user acceptance. As discussed in (Scheuer et al., 2010), the automatic analysis of single arguments with the intent to provide users with intelligent feedback enables active forms of support. Hence, it has strong potential in remedying the low acceptance of (and the low engagement of users with) existing argumentation support systems. In the majority of cases, this process concerns the construction of sound and syntactically valid arguments, which can then be analyzed to identify specific attributes that can be exploited by inference mechanisms, such as decision support algorithms. In line with the above, the approach proposed in the next section empowers argumentation support systems towards inducing the users' reasoning behavior.

3. THE PROPOSED APPROACH

An instance of an argumentation discourse exhibits a certain structure which allows one to draw conclusions about its state. For example, if one user is proposing an argument that receives low rating and at the same time there appear to be arguments attacking it with high rating, this means that the argument has most likely been defeated. Similar conclusions may be obtained by surveying the interrelation of arguments and not their content. Until now, these conclusions were left for the users of an argumentation support system, since the system was unable to capture and identify sequences of arguments that may express a certain attitude or behavior.

Our approach attempts to assess these structures by introducing the concept of Argumentation Sequence (AS), which can be simply described as "a set of arguments interrelated in a specific way". An example of different ASes is provided in Figure 2. The AS on the left may be interpreted as a sequence where the top argument is being under attack (only one argument supporting, which is under attack by two others), whereas the AS in the middle may indicate that the argument on top is being accepted (only one argument attacking, being under attack by two others). Similarly, the AS on the right may indicate that the root argument is of uncertain status. In fact, our approach aims at measuring the similarity among pairs of ASes. In order to achieve this, an innovative graph-based computational model has been introduced and described in detail in (Gkotsis and Karacapilidis, 2012). Our overall approach is based on the (commonly adopted in argumentative discourse and) following assumptions:

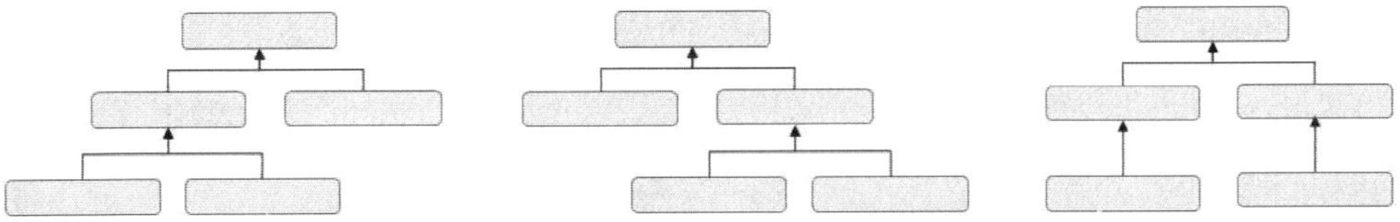

Figure 2. An example of three different Argumentation Sequences; while the size (5 arguments) and the depth of the sequences (until level 2) is the same, their interpretation in the argumentation context varies

- Similarly to the framework introduced by Dung (1995), the internal structure of arguments is not considered; each argument is an atomic entity.
- One or more attributes of the argument are exploited. An example of an attribute may be its rating, the name of the author or its publication date. The values of these attributes are used in order to introduce a fundamental distance function between different arguments (i.e. two arguments that have received exactly the same rating or belong to the same author have distance of value 0).
- Arguments are connected to each other in order to express explicitly (and exclusively) either agreement or disagreement.
- The discourse is structured and visualized as an argumentation tree. While there are cases where argumentation may be represented in other ways as well, the vast majority of the above systems adopt the tree-like representation of the information units (Freeman, 1991).

Our approach is influenced by similar graph and subgraph matching techniques but is tailored for the case of argumentation trees. The process of computing the similarity between two ASes includes the matching of vertices of one AS to those of the other by preserving their corresponding level. During this matching, we calculate the pairwise arguments' similarity for all levels. The matching must be such that the overall similarity measurement is maximized.

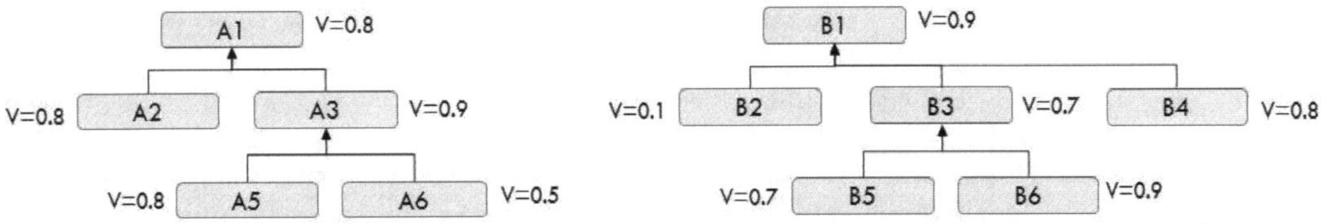

Figure 3. Two argumentation sequences with annotated rating

For instance, consider the two ASes shown in Figure 3. For each argument of the ASes, we presume that a rating submitted by the users exists, which is annotated. This rating is normalized on a scale from 0 to 1. Our algorithm for computing the similarity of the ASes results in the following arguments-vertices matching: {A1,B1},{A3,B3},{A2,B2},{A6,B5} and {A5,B6}. The final similarity score, which is normalized on a scale from 0 to 1, is 0.72. The partial similarity for the arguments of the second level (A2 and A3 versus B2, B3 and B4) is 0.28. This low value is due to the fact that arguments A3 and B3 were selected for matching, even though they are significantly different (A3 is opposing its parent argument and B3 is supporting it, both with high rating). The reason for this high cost matching is because it returns high matching for the arguments of the third level (A4, A5, B5, B6), thus maximizing the overall score.

In order to further exploit the above similarity measurement, the Boolean property of equivalence between ASes is used in order to classify two ASes as argumentatively equivalent. Essentially, this property introduces a threshold value as the minimum value of matching across each and every level of the ASes. For the example described above, the low similarity value for arguments of level 2 would have returned that the ASes are not equivalent. This threshold value is specified by the user. Unless the partial similarity score for all levels is higher than the threshold value, the two ASes are not considered argumentatively equivalent. The benefits of the above similarity measurement and the consequent concept of equivalence are discussed below.

4. INDUCING REASONING BEHAVIOR

Until now, we have argued about the need to reinforce argumentation models with intelligent processing mechanisms. For this reason, we have proposed the exploitation of argumentation sequences. We have also described intuitively (for details see (Gkotsis and Karacapilidis, 2012)) that it is possible to easily identify equivalent argumentation sequences. This section proposes specific cases where the adoption of the proposed approach may assist in Human Behavior Understanding (HBU), as defined in (Salah et al., 2010). As reported in the above work, HBU refers to "advanced pattern recognition techniques to automatically interpret complex behavioral patterns generated when humans interact with machines or with others". In this section, we sketch representative cases where our approach may be used to capture meaningful aspects of the users' behavior and consequently improve their collaboration by augmenting the awareness offered by an argumentation support system.

The first set of cases assumes that a predefined, meaningful set of argumentation sequences exists. The aim is to identify other sequences equivalent to the above ("situated" sequences). The predefined sequences may initially be system defined, but every user might choose to manually label more, or even exclude some. For instance, it is possible to include the ASes of Figure 2 and label them accordingly. More generally, a set of ASes that accounts the arguments' rating may be populated and labeled as "accepted arguments" and "defeated arguments". The results in favor of HBU may be one or more of the following:

- Fight selective exposure. Users are naturally inclined to ignore arguments or ideas they have already devalued. As reported in (Jonas et al., 2001), after making a decision, people prefer supporting instead of conflicting information. This bias may undermine the ability of users to identify weak points in their course of thinking. Spotting defeated arguments in a neutral, mechanical way will increase awareness for the users and will reduce the above bias. The result might be either the individual or the collective change of strategy regarding a debatable subject.
- Similarly to the above, automatic identification of interesting argumentation patterns may reduce confirmation bias. As reported in (Kuhn, 1991), people might overlook counter-arguments and may overvalue their initial predictions or estimations. Matching ASes against other labeled patterns of argumentation assists in bringing to surface parts of the discourse in an objective way and recommends reinstating specific arguments.
- More generally, the exploitation of arguments' rating may highlight information that the users overlook when examining the discourse. It will allow for increased introspection in the experienced users and will enable the more efficient survey, reconstruction and understanding of the argumentative discourse, especially for the newcomers. Administrators may be able to construct rich queries and efficiently search the discussions. Moreover, the above activities may be facilitated through notification mechanisms that are triggered every time an argumentation sequence matches a desired pattern.

The above cases are based on the existence of a collection of predefined, labeled ASes and allow the automatic identification of equivalent ASes as they are formed. Apart from the above, we believe that ASes may be subject to further exploitation through the mining and automatic discovery of emerging, otherwise unnoticeable patterns of communication. In order to achieve this, instead of the rating attribute, we consider the author or the publication date attributes. In this way, when a specific communication pattern based on users' identity reoccurs, the system will be able to report this information. For instance, if an attack relationship between arguments is repeating in a short period between two or more users, this behavior will be identified, without the need to exploit the rating attribute. More detailed ways on what kinds of unnoticed behaviors may be discovered are as follows:

- Users might be engaging in an endless, turn-based debate. In that case, the proposed approach will observe that a series of arguments by the same authors appears as ASes in the system, which will be recognized as an endless debate. In this case, the primary attribute to be exploited would be the author names. However, it is also possible to induce the same behavior by examining the time difference between different posts of arguments (i.e. short time interval between attacking arguments). In both cases, this user engagement will be spotted automatically.

- An a posteriori analysis of the discourse might return unnoticed patterns of behavior within the community. For example, it might be the case that some users might be colluding in order to mislead the discussion or repeatedly attack another user. In that case, several ASes containing the same group of people and replicating the same, aggressive behavior are discovered.
- Similarly to the above, a common problem in massive, public deliberation is the inflammation of the discourse with aggressive content and behavior. In this direction, general communication platforms, such as fora and other content management systems, may take measures against these users through banning or deleting their account. However, in the majority of the cases, these actions are either carried out manually or are based on simple rules. Thus, they are of limited application in an argumentation context. In our approach, the automatic identification of a specific behavior can trigger measures against this attitude.

Furthermore, it is worth noting that our approach can be particularly useful in specific applications of argumentation. The most common use of argumentation is in supporting learning. An argumentation support system powered by our model will help learners understand their behavior. Through the exploitation of ASes, the tutor is able to spot repeating reasoning behaviors. Similarly, learners are able to understand better how to confront argumentation by noticing the emerging interrelations of their contributions and ultimately improve their reasoning skills.

Another application of argumentation is found in discourse analysis and decision making support within organizations. For example, argumentation support systems such as Compendium (http://compendium.open.ac.uk/), which conforms to the IBIS approach, are built with the aim to capture organizational knowledge and complies with the principles of argumentation. A common case is when the same arguments may surface in different discussions and require further analysis. Our approach may be tailored in order to support the exploitation of existing resources with automated identification mechanisms.

The cases described above provide concrete examples of how a typical argumentation model may be further extended in order to uncover patterns of reasoning behavior. In all these cases, the main intention is to reveal and reduce behaviors related to user biases in rational and critical thinking. To achieve this, the complex but semantically rich structure of the Argumentation Sequence can be the central unit of the proposed computational model. Even though our approach adopts general concepts of IBIS like systems, it is worth discussing its limitations. First of all, the ASes must follow a tree structure, which is a common practice (as discussed earlier). Secondly, the assessment of argumentation structures can identify certain behavior, but is far from appearing as a semantically complete approach. While the exploitation of the proposed model accomplishes the annotation of some parts of an argumentative dialogue and highlights similarities with respect to previous discussions or predefined patterns, it cannot manage every case. Therefore, our approach can be viewed as a complementary, semi-automatic tool that adds awareness features in a broad category of argumentation support systems. Compared to related approaches, Belvedere's advisor (Paolucci et al., 1996) automatically assesses the validity of components of arguments either through its pairwise comparison of relations against an expert's diagram (consistency advisor), or through the rule-based, syntactic validation of diagrams against explicit conditions. The DOCE algorithm follows a machine learning approach in order to classify arbitrarily sized clusters of contributions (Mclaren et al., 2010). Our approach shares the same goals with DOCE, but introduces a more refined algorithm that manages to capture and discern structures, which would have been clustered equally in DOCE.

5. CONCLUSIONS

Argumentation is a form of informal reasoning. Even though it is supposed to be governed by rationalization, it remains an inherently complex process where humans often behave irrationally and unexpectedly. We have proposed an approach for assessing complex argumentation structures in order to identify meaningful reasoning patterns and accordingly induce the reasoning behavior of argumentation support systems' users. Our work does not intend to propose new ways of structuring and validating an argumentative discourse; instead, it aims at studying how to extend and exploit a widely adopted argumentation model (i.e. IBIS) for understanding and inducing human behavior. Through the provision of various cases, this paper is primarily arguing why such an approach is sensible and may contribute to both theoretical and practical aspects of argumentation.

REFERENCES

Conklin, J. and Begeman, M.L., 1987. gIBIS: A hypertext tool for team design deliberation. *Proceedings of the ACM Conference on Hypertext*, pp. 247-251, New York, NY, USA.

Dung, P.M., 1995. On the acceptability of arguments and its fundamental role in non-monotonic reasoning, logic programming and n-person games. *Artificial Intelligence*, Vol. 77, No. 2, pp. 321-357.

Freeman, J., 1991. *Dialectics and the macrostructure of arguments: a theory of argument structure*. Walter de Gruyter, Berlin/New York.

Gkotsis, G. and Karacapilidis, N. (2012). A computational model for the identification and assessment of structural similarities in argumentative discourses. *Journal of Intelligent Information Systems*, Vol. 39, No. 3, pp. 789-811.

Jonas, E. et al., 2001. Confirmation bias in sequential information search after preliminary decisions: An expansion of dissonance theoretical research on selective exposure to information. *Journal of Personality and Social Psychology*, Vol. 80, No. 4, pp. 557–571.

Karacapilidis, N. and Papadias, D., 2001. Computer supported argumentation and collaborative decision making: the Hermes system. *Information systems*, Vol. 26, No. 4, pp. 259-277.

Karacapilidis, N. et al., 2009. Tackling cognitively-complex collaboration with CoPe_it!. *International Journal of Web-Based Learning and Teaching Technologies*, Vol. 4, No. 3, pp. 22-38.

Karacapilidis, N. et al., 1997. Collaborative Environmental Planning with GeoMed. *European Journal of Operational Research*, Vol. 102, No. 2, pp. 335-346.

Kuhn, D., 1991. *The skills of argument*. Cambridge University Press, Cambridge, UK.

Kunz, W. and Rittel, H., 1970. Issues as Elements of Information Systems, Working Paper No. 131, Studiengruppe für Systemforschung, Heidelberg, Germany.

Mclaren, B.M. et al., 2010. Supporting collaborative learning and e-discussions using artificial intelligence techniques. *International Journal of Artificial Intelligence in Education*, Vol. 20, No. 1, pp. 1-46.

Paolucci, M. et al., 1996. Automated advice-giving strategies for scientific inquiry. *Proceedings of the Third International Conference on Intelligent Tutoring Systems*, Vol. 1086, pp. 372–381.

Salah, A. et al., 2010. Challenges of human behavior understanding. In: Salah, A.A. et al. (eds.) *Human Behavior Understanding,* LNCS, Vol. 6219, pp. 1–12, Springer, Heidelberg.

Scheuer, O. et al., 2010. Computer-supported argumentation: A review of the state of the art. *International Journal of Computer-Supported Collaborative Learning*, Vol. 5, No. 1, pp. 43-102.

Suthers, D. et al., 1995. Belvedere: Engaging students in critical discussion of science and public policy issues. *Proceedings of the 7th World Conference on Artificial Intelligence in Education*, Washington D.C, USA, pp. 266-273.

van Gelder, T.J., 2003. Enhancing deliberation through computer supported argument mapping. In: Kirschner, P.A. et al. (Eds.), *Visualizing argumentation: Software tools for collaborative and educational sense-making*, pp. 97-115, Springer-Verlag, London.

THE CHALLENGES OF DESIGNING THE INTERACTION DESIGN OF A COLLABORATIVE ART PROJECT

Jasmina Maric
The Swedish School of Library and Information Science, Borås, Sweden

ABSTRACT

While many of us researchers dream about the opportunity to design a collaborative art project that would connect our youth with big, mainstream cultural and educational institutions, we seldom analyse the challenges of such collaborations. This paper presents the most prevailing issues that arose during the user-centred, interdisciplinary interaction design (ID) of the collaborative digital art project. The design is made in collaboration with the young participants of the Meet the Ministry project run by the Dance Company of the Opera House (DCOH) in Gothenburg, and the members of The Swedish School of Library and Information Science Social Media Studies (TSLIS) research group. Using the research through design approach to augment the outreach of the collaborative digital art project, enhance youth engagement with the contemporary dance, and learn from the young participants, we analyse the implications introduced by inter-institutional and interdisciplinary collaboration. Finally, by looking at the results of this project, we claim that interdisciplinary collaborations are extremely risky because they are unpredictable in their cost, process, and outcome. Even though literature offers advice for successful interdisciplinary cooperation there are no guarantees that the risks can be fully avoided. Still, we argue that such collaborations are necessary and need to be continuously developed as they seem to be successful tools for interdisciplinary learning and bridging social capital acquisition. If nothing else, we should at least foster the practices of learning from our younger generations who seem to be interested in partnering with us in exploring communication and collaboration in digital art projects creation.

KEYWORDS

User-centred Design, Interaction Design, Social Innovation, Social Capital, Collaborative Art, Interdisciplinary Collaboration

1. INTRODUCTION

Our national research agendas often call for cooperation and interdisciplinary research between institutions giving special importance of using scientific results and methods outside of academia. Such a diverse collaborative undertake can result in new findings in the research itself (in this case, the capacity of collaborative digital storytelling to engage users and affect their bridging social capital), as well as offer new ideas on the design and practices of doing such research (in this case, the complexity of designing the process across disciplines and institutions). This paper epitomizes this kind of cooperation, and is based on the collaborative art project made between an art institution and academics.

1.1 Background

Meet the Ministry collaborative art project hosted by the DCOH[1] was aiming to create the knowledge about the reach-out and engagement of young audience (16-19 years) with the contemporary dance process. Through exploration of contemporary dance choreography creation for Ministry of Unresolved feelings show, delivered in a series of all-physical workshops, young participants are invited to engage in all-digital storytelling in order to share their impressions about the whole process.

[1] Dance Company webpage https://en.opera.se/om-oss/goteborgsoperans-danskompani/

The DCOH and TSLIS[2] have joined a solidarity effort, to collaborate and learn from that collaboration. Eventually, thanks to this interdisciplinary cooperation, the project that was envisioned as an offline participatory collaboration became the digital too.

2. THE RESEARCH THROUGH DESIGN

Since there is no one common definition of design (Franker and Racine, 2010), in this paper, design is considered an activity for planning and executing new actions, which might include deliverables as a by-product of the process (drawings, models, plans, or events). The core idea of the Meet the Ministry project is to learn from the young participants, users that are at the same time designers of the process. In other words, the methodological process is inspired by a human-centred Scandinavian participatory approach where design researchers collaborate with the people who are being served by design as co-creators in the process (Sanders, 2008).

During a series of meetings between the DCOH and TSLIS, the goals of the project are defined, as well as the necessary steps to arrive at the best possible results. The goals read as follows. Create the process in which we can learn from the young participants, creating knowledge; leave the process open so it can be re-designed or changed according to participants' needs; find ways to communicate with young participants and hear what young participants have to say; learn from the participants' feedback and reiterate the process design; provide the tools, materials, that will support better communication; and document the process and analyse results.

Young participants were recruited based on their motivation letters. They answered the surveys coupled with personal interviews, before the project started, and after the project was over. That way they were given a chance to evaluate the project, express their feelings, and ideas about the project. We also followed their participation through the whole process as well as the observation method.

In praxis each physical workshop with participants was followed by an evaluation meeting where all parties would discuss the results of the workshop and future moves. We can say that the design process was a set of ongoing iterations, comprising continuous analysis, feedback, and the designing of the next workshops.

In the next section we present the users that designed the process.

3. THE YOUNG PARTICIPANTS

Unlike the traditional notion of the *user*, a person who is using a specific software solution or service (Downing et al., 2000), in complex interdisciplinary collaborations it is not easy to define the *end-user*. The complexity comes from the fact that a person that is to *use* is at the same time is the person that *designs* the process. However, in this paper we look at the young participants as the *end-users* and *co-designers* of the ID. But how much do we really know about young people between 16 and 19 years old?

The young participants of this project are often characterized as having high digital literacy, multitasking skills, and the ability to operate fast. They are heavy users of smartphones, going online daily, with 24% of them reporting being online constantly (Flora, 2018). After Turkle (2015) argued that due to such heavy technological usage we lose the fabric that makes us human - the ability and interest to understand each other - many publications followed arguing that smartphones have ruined the life of millennials. According to that body of research millennials are not sleeping well, when learning they lack concentration, engagement and socialization (Karakas et al., 2015). However, according to a more recent publication younger millennials, or generation Z, seems not to be ruined at all (Flora, 2018).

In such high uncertainty, not really knowing who our youngest partners are, and how they like to do things, it was quite difficult to design the interactive process that could resonate with their needs. To start with, we have looked at 17 motivation letters from which we could learn more about their motivation to join the project, and we run the survey to get to know them better. Here is what we found out.

They all live in different parts of Gothenburg, but they frequently visit the city centre. The majority of them are native Swedish language speakers, and they are mostly interested in sports, performing arts, music, and reading. They are not interested in TV at all, while only one person expressed interest in computer games.

---

[2] The Swedish School of Library and Information Science webpage https://www.hb.se/en/The-Swedish-School-of-Library-and-Information-Science-SSLIS/

When asked to explain their motivation for participating to Meet the Ministry project, they use the following expressions: "inspiration", "learning more about the dance", "personal development through creation", "be more in Opera House", "meeting other people", "leaving my personal shell", etc. Finally, in majority they do not have any expectations to create something "beautiful", "cool", or maybe learn more about themselves and the others.

In order to understand up to what extent the participation in the collaborative art production project could positively affect bridging social capital, a series of questions addressed young participants' daily activities, and perception of their role in the community before the start of the Meet the Ministry project. The questions were designed in line with Williams' bridging social capital scale (Williams, 2006). Based on 12 answers (out of 17) one can argue that those who answered the survey are in majority outgoing persons, who like to cooperate with other people and are quite interested in what other people think or do. Furthermore, they expressed belief that the cooperation with the others brings new contacts and gives a feeling of being better connected to the outer world. It is clear that while explicitly saying they do not expect much, on an implicit level they have come to the Opera House expecting amazing experiences. This fact was an additional burden on the whole project, as well as on us who are designing according to participants' needs.

During the workshops with their digital storytelling mentors, TSLIS researchers and Göthenburgo (local NGO), young participants developed a strategic plan for Meet the Ministry project outreach (Table 1).

The complexity of this interinstitutional and interdisciplinary collaboration is presented in the following section.

4. CLASH OF WORLDS

When a high-end professional art production institution meets the academic institution in interinstitutional and interdisciplinary collaboration supported by new media technology, the traditional cliché of lonely, poor artists is completely changed. Not only that the creative process happens in a hive of ideas and people, this kind of collaboration also shifts boundaries of power, position, and identities between the collaborative participants and the knowledge domains (Shields and Spillane, 2018). Shifting traditional discipline boundaries and hierarchical power structures opens space for new collaborative structures and new ideas, but simultaneously and unexpectedly creates a powerful clash of two worlds.

Table 1. Digital outreach strategy developed by young participants

No	Type	Content	Video	Audio	Text	Quantity	Length
1	web series	- trailer - costume - Rehearsal Director - Choreography/er - improvisation - dance workshop	x	x		5-6	2-4,5 min
2	close-up	participants story on - why/how come I am in this project? - what did I get from it? - how should we do this in the future?	x	x		each participant	2 min
3	interviews	interview with the dancers, from a different point of view	x		x		
4	unresolved feelings	unresolved feelings are gathered in mail	x	x	x		
5	spontaneous reactions	post spontaneous reactions after each workshop with #motministeriet	x	x	x		#instagram
7	webpage on Opera.se	follow up of the process	x	x	x		

4.1 Time

Interdisciplinary research and collaboration projects often require additional resources, more time, infrastructure, and more effort (Briazu, 2017). Having in mind that this collaborative effort happened as a result of bottom-up interdisciplinary and inter institutional solidarity, without any additional budget, time became one of the most valuable resources.

A very important aspect is the time of employees who are employed or strongly tied to one cultural institution. Usually in creative visual arts the time of creative workers is at the centre of analysis, and the time of, for example, curators, art managers, public relations-support, is neglected. However, their employment and tasks have many features they share with creative workers, like self-exploitation, increase in personal responsibility, blurring the borders between work and personal life (Kuleva, 2018). In such climate finding enough time to plan the process of learning through design, run it, reflect on it, and improve it, is crucial for the overall success of the project.

It is quite hard to imagine how much time is needed to design the open process for collaboration, collaborative art creation, which will successfully meet the needs of all participants and serve as an open process for knowledge creation. The design of the frameworks for creative art practice, research, and learning, requires lots of time, bravery, and creativity. In the following text some time consuming aspects are listed.

4.2 Language

To begin with, the core idea of this project is the integrative communication over different boundaries, and knowledge creation. Therefore, it has been agreed to provide as many inputs as possible during the whole process. Still, when two strong, powerful institutions join the collaborative effort, their traditional disciplinary cages actually clash (Foucault, 1977). Contrary to Borgdorff's argument (2011) that during the interdisciplinary research collaboration working methods of separate disciplines remain intact, the experiences from this project show that the walls between the disciplines are porous. During the meetings it was quite common that people from one discipline wanted to penetrate into the other disciplines in order to understand the meaning, or to contribute, by changing or re-designing the events specified by the discipline. Thus, many discussions comprised of language balancing.

The *interaction space* for the DCOH members is usually physical space of the rehearsal room or the stage, whereas for the members of TSLIS that is the digital space delivered through user interfaces. For the young participants of this project the *space* can be a place where they have their bodies, while mentally and emotionally engaged somewhere else (Turkle, 2017). If *user interface* would pop-up in the conversation introduced by TSLIS team members, then translating it to the members of the DCOH was required so everybody on-board would be sure of the topic discussed. *Expressing feelings*, which is the main topic of this specific dance choreography, for DCOH is to communicate through body movements, while for TSLIS is expression through different digital forms (text, picture, video, and audio).

It was obvious that in order to arrive to a successful solution, all participants need to create, balance, and master the language of collaboration. There is no need to emphasize that young participants, whose participation was central to this project idea, needed the language that is disciplinary frigid, or in other words, free of disciplinary burden.

4.3 Going Digital – Power and Ownership

The same goes for understanding the "let's go digital" idea. Having in mind the ubiquitous nature of new media technology in the 21st century, all participants were and are frequent users of it. Still, the introduction the idea to augment the outreach of the Meet the Ministry project by going digital brought a lot of tensions. New technologies were always introducing changes to social and cultural reorganization, and that creates anxiety (Baym, 2015).

For TSLIS members, digital communication is a natural way of thinking and daily operating, while for members of the DCOH and other departments of the Opera House it represents completely the other domain and other set of issues. Many questions arose, from questioning the reasons for "going digital", over constant uncertainty over GDPR rules and regulations, to digital material ownership, and evaluation. Due to the obvious perception of the amazing power that digital information has, and speed by which it is shared, the ownership and power question came back on the main stage of this project. Albeit one of the crucial ideas of the project is to collaborate in the atmosphere of the flat power distribution, give power to participants, it was impossible to easily clear the road of traditional disciplinary approaches. While one department did everything to crush the walls wanting to escape the disciplinary, institutional cage, the other department would strongly hold traditional power blocking everything digital. The project was on hold.

Once that young participant finally got the chance to express their ideas on how they would like to communicate their impressions about the project through digital channels, they have easily come up with the digital communication strategy for outreach (Table 1). Still, two weeks before the premiere, there was only one web page with the photos and following text published online. Once the Opera House PR and communication department finally accepted publishing and advertising young participants' web series, the project immediately got another life and new energy.

4.4 Fears and Trust

Facing many conflicting situations that come with interdisciplinary collaborations (Briazu, 2017) it is not surprising that many fear such a project. Stepping into the unknown is not a comfortable professional arena. With so many unknowns in one project idea, like designing interaction for the unknown project participants, designing open ID process that can adapt to future participants' needs, create space for process design re-iteration, open new space for unknown participants' digital interaction, support collaborative art expression, etc., fear becomes an everyday companion.

For the members of TSLIS designing such ID that will eventually lead to social innovation is far from the professional comfort zone, where the ID design is designed for known users, and carefully controlled processes. On the other hand, for the Dance Company this project introduces much vulnerability, like opening the Opera House for outsiders who will transform to participants and collaborative art creators. In the situation when none of the collaborating parties had similar experience, many questions that tackle the acquisition of trust arose. Disciplinary walls are high. While scientist and researchers tend to be concrete and work with research results, statistics, explicit results, dancers work with body movements, imagination, are used to unpredictable situations and processes. Let alone that both disciplines, presented by digital immigrants (Prensky, 200) are to meet young participants, digital natives, and learn from them.

Once the young participants understood that the whole process is adaptable to change, that their voices are heard, and can influence the project - the trust is created. As the feeling of trust rose, the fears become weaker and fewer.

5. LESSONS LEARNED

Regardless of so many challenges introduced in this cooperation, one can surely argue that all participants learned a lot. At the moment of finishing this paper the project is over, together with several evaluations between the partners in the project. Due to the open dialogue that was characteristic for evaluation sessions we have arrived to a list of lessons learned. Here we will only briefly list them.

5.1 Young Participants

Through analysis of young participants' engagement, surveys and interviews, web series production[3] and finally by watching their presentation of the project at the Dance Festival 2019, we argue that for young participants this was rich and valuable experience. The great majority of young participants who answered the final survey, 7 of the 12 participants who finished the project, emphasized that the participation in the Meet the Ministry project was (1) really exciting, (2) they have learned a lot, and (3) they have made a lot of new contacts.

[3] Material produced during Meet the Ministry project: https://en.opera.se/om-oss/skapa/dans-med-skapa/mot-ministeriet/

They express positive feelings about being able to learn more about contemporary dance, but also experiment with video production. Even though they repeat they did not have any expectations from this project, in majority they were positively surprised. The participation in the workshops in the Opera House gave them a "*wow feeling*" and influenced their feeling of being closer to the Opera House. Almost all of them would participate in a similar project in the future, and would recommend such projects to their peers.

It is important not to forget that some of the young participants felt confused and would prefer better communication and organisation. Also, out of starting out with 17 participants, only 12 finished the project. Unfortunately, in the frame of this project it was not possible to go deeper in analysis about who are those that dropped out and the reason for it.

5.2 DCOH

With this project the Opera House not only sparked a new way of thinking about how to engage with the youngest audience, but also challenged many internal, traditional concepts. Acknowledging that the project has completely hit the target from one perspective - young participants have learned a lot about the contemporary dance form, the DCOH realised that there is a lot to be learned and accepted in order to be successful in outreach to the youngest. Here we briefly present identified challenges from different perspectives, (1) dancers', and (2) DCOH management.

(1) A majority of the dance professionals found the project frustrating and not clear enough, wishing they had a better understanding of the goals. Paired with the traditional lack of time which was also reported in this project, resulted in frustrating *"too many cooks"* and a *"reinvent the wheel"* atmosphere. Dancers report feeling good while doing workshops with the young participants but they wish the whole project was more structured and better organised. When asked if they would recommend such a project to their colleagues they were quite polarised.

(2) The management of DCOH and people who were responsible for the organisation of the project agree that the project was rich and valuable pilot, where they learned a lot about themselves and young participants. Pointing out that this project is perceived as extremely *"exclusive"* by engaging finally only 12 young people, they express ambition to continue exploring this model in the future aiming to increase the number of engaged young participants and improve the reachout. They list the following issues as the most important focus for future projects of this kind: strategic decisions on "*becoming digital*"; tighter and timely collaboration among internal departments; more time to prepare and plan; a need for better internal and external communication; improve the process and reiterate; and find ways to make a better usage of communication technology.

5.3 TSLIS

For us, researchers, this project was a very interesting way to learn too. Here again, we only briefly list the most important findings.

(1) The power of user-centred ID - When the user is also the designer of the ID we not only increase functionalities and project quality, we at the same time empower the user, the one who is to be affected by ID, by offering the opportunity to influence the design (Simonsen and Robertson, 2012; Kale, 2017). Still, we must not forget that such efforts are costly and require a lot of resources and time.

(2) Collaborative art projects seem to be successful tools for social innovation and interdisciplinary learning - On a social innovation level; collaborative art projects enable acquisition of bridging social capital. We should keep this important lesson in mind, and be more careful when we recruit participants, if, for example, we are to test such projects for social integration and empowerment. Furthermore, this project is a fine example of the power of experiential learning where project participants not only learned much about the contemporary dance, but at the same time learned new digital skills. In other words they learn 4Cs – creativity, communication, critical thinking, and collaboration, i.e. 21st century skills (Kivunja, 2015), through 5Es from real-life: experience, engagement, exploration, evaluation, and elaboration.

(3) Inter-institutional collaborations as the highways toward sustainability. Although we witness considerable focus on sustainability in science and politics, our society is continuously developing unsustainable paths. We agree with Abson and colleagues (2017) that one of the cornerstones for sustainable interventions is reconstruction of institutions, since they guide and restrict the actions. One of the most important lessons learned through this project collaboration is that interdisciplinary inter-institutional

collaboration augments social impact and learning. If we look at it from the perspective of the national governments who are traditional owners and funders of these institutions, it is easy to understand why and how inter-institutional collaboration leads to a more sustainable society.

6. CONCLUSION

We live in a world where our leading institutions claim that many of the complex problems society is currently facing demand innovative solutions that combine knowledge from different scientific disciplines (Van Rijnsoever and Hessels, 2011). However, we agree that interdisciplinary collaborations are extremely risky by being unpredictable in their outcome and the process (Kanakia, 2007). As Briazu argues (2017) even though the literature offers advice on principles for good interdisciplinary work (Nancarrow et al., 2013) there are still no guarantees that the risk and pitfalls can be fully avoided. One can only be brave and work hard hoping that benefits will outnumber the challenges.

Bearing in mind that interdisciplinary research has the potential to deepen knowledge in one's own discipline and to provide new insights and inspiration from other disciplines, we should continue developing interdisciplinary interinstitutional projects and learn from both the results and the process of creation. Most importantly, it seems that our youngest are interested in partnering up with us in exploring communication and collaboration in multidisciplinary interinstitutional settings. We should do nothing less than help them open as many doors as we can.

To conclude, we must say that there is a lot more to be done, be experienced and learn from, especially in the realm of digital storytelling as a tool for learning and bridging social capital acquisition. Therefore, this paper should be taken as a tool that will help the preparation and analysis of such complex and rich collaborations.

REFERENCES

Abson, D. J., Fischer, J., Leventon, J., Newig, J., Schomerus, T., Vilsmaier, U., ... & Lang, D. J. (2017). Leverage points for sustainability transformation. *Ambio*, *46*(1), 30-39.

Baym, N. K. (2015). *Personal connections in the digital age*. John Wiley & Sons.

Borgdorff, H. (2011). *The production of knowledge in artistic research*. na.

Briazu, R. A. (2017). The challenges and joys of interdisciplinary research: Insights from a psy-art collaboration. *Developmental Psychology Section*, 37.

Downing, D. A., Covington, M. A., & Covington, M. M. (2000). *Dictionary of computer and Internet terms*. Barron's Educational Series Inc..

Flora, C. (2018). Are Smartphones Really Destroying the Adolescent Brain?. Scientific American, 318(2), 30-37.

Frankel, L., & Racine, M. (2010). The complex field of research: For design, through design, and about design. In Proceedings of the *Design Research Society* (DRS) International Conference (No. 043).

Foucault, M. (1977). *Discipline and punish* (A. Sheridan, trans.). New York: Pantheon.

Kale, A. (2017). The Art of Social Connection: Exploring Former Refugee and Host Society Integration via a Collaborative, Participatory Painting Project in Wellington City.

Kanakia, R. (2007). Talk touts benefits of interdisciplinary approach, as well as some of its pitfalls. *Stanford News*. Retrieved 4 July 2019 from https://news.stanford.edu/news/2007/february7/barr-020707.html

Karakas, F., Manisaligil, A., & Sarigollu, E. (2015). Management learning at the speed of life: Designing reflective, creative, and collaborative spaces for millenials. *The International Journal of Management Education,* 13(3), 237-248.

Kivunja, C. (2015). Exploring the Pedagogical Meaning and Implications of the 4Cs "Super Skills" for the 21st

Century through Bruner's 5E Lenses of Knowledge Construction to Improve Pedagogies of the New Learning

Paradigm. Creative Education, 6(02), 224.

Kuleva, M. (2018). Cultural administrators as creative workers: the case of public and non-governmental cultural institutions in St. Petersburg. *Cultural Studies*, *32*(5), 727-746.

Nancarrow, S.A., Booth, A., Ariss, S. et al. (2013). Ten principles of good interdisciplinary team work. *Human Resources for Health,* 11(1), 19.

Prensky, M. (2001). Digital natives, digital immigrants part 1. *On the horizon*, 9(5), 1-6.

Sanders, L. (2008). An Evolving Map of Design Practice and Design Research. Interactions, 15(6), 13- 17.

Simonsen, J., & Robertson, T. (Eds.). (2012). *Routledge international handbook of participatory design*. Routledge.

Turkle, S. (2017). *Alone together: Why we expect more from technology and less from each other*. Hachette UK.

Turkle, S. (2015). Reclai*ming conversation: The power of talk in a digital age*. Penguin

Van Rijnsoever, F. J., & Hessels, L. K. (2011). Factors associated with disciplinary and interdisciplinary research collaboration. *Research policy*, 40(3), 463-472.

Williams, D. (2006). On and off the 'net: Scales for social capital in an online era. *Journal of Computer-Mediated Communication,* 11(2), article 11. Retrieved October 23, 2018 from http://jcmc.indiana.edu/vol11/issue2/williams.html

UNIVERSITY PROCESS OPTIMISATION THROUGH SMART CURRICULUM DESIGN AND BLOCKCHAIN-BASED STUDENT ACCREDITATION

Christos Kontzinos, Ourania Markaki, Panagiotis Kokkinakos, Vagelis Karakolis, Stavros Skalidakis and John Psarras
Decision Support Systems Lab National Technical University of Athens, Greece

ABSTRACT

The main goals of Higher Education Institutions (HEIs) are to develop the intellectual abilities of students as well as prepare them for entering the labor market. The connection between HEIs and the labor market is why the effectiveness and quality of the provided services of academic institutions tend to be evaluated in terms of the time it takes for their graduates to find employment. This paper presents work from the EU funded research project QualiChain that aims to transform and revolutionize the domain of public education as well as its interfaces with those of private education, the labor market, public and private organizations and society at large, drawing its added value proposition from the challenges currently faced in these domains. The ultimate goal of the project is the development of the QualiChain platform that will offer blockchain-enabled verification of education and other credentials as well as data analytics and decision support for process optimization. The platform will be validated via its implementation in four different pilot cases. The present paper focuses on the pilot of optimizing university operations through semantically enhanced data and advanced decision support algorithms that will be implemented in the National Technical University of Athens (NTUA).

KEYWORDS

Blockchain, Education, Labor Market, Verification, Curriculum Design, Student Accreditation

1. INTRODUCTION

When asked about the aim of Higher Education, most people would argue that its sole purpose is to meet the learning needs and aspirations of individuals through the development of their intellectual abilities and aptitudes throughout their lives. It is Higher Education after all that equips individuals to make the best use of their talents and the opportunities offered by society for self-fulfillment (South African Council on Higher Education 2013). However, in today's highly competitive environment, a major goal of higher education should be to address the development needs of society and provide the labor market with the ever-changing high-level competencies and expertise necessary for the growth and prosperity of a modern economy.

It is for that reason that the effectiveness of a country's tertiary education system is frequently assessed in terms of the respective unemployment rates, whereas the effectiveness and quality of the provided services of academic institutions themselves are accordingly and not unjustly evaluated in terms of the time it takes for their graduates to find employment. In spite of this informal correlation between education and the labor market though, the training curriculum of higher education institutions is often shaped with strictly academic criteria within an isolated environment and without thus taking into account the demands of the latter; not to mention that it is rarely modified, so as to incorporate recent developments particularly in technology-related fields, thereby ending up being obsolete and outdated. Another challenge that slows down the connection between academia and the labor market is the fact that education credentials are largely resisting the pull of technology often requiring paper documentation and time-consuming manual processes for their verification. This mainly has to do with the fact that higher education institutions (HEIs) keep student data in centralized databases and dedicated online systems that offer little or no interoperability.

As such, to have more efficient curriculum design and trustworthy student accreditation, fundamental changes are required in the way that HEIs operate. It can be surmised from the above that the main problem is the lack of suitable IT infrastructures that can lead to more efficient procedures by providing structure to university data as well as some degree of automation. Apart from existing IT systems and infrastructures, there are several innovative technologies that HEIs could take advantage of to develop trustworthy and efficient solutions. Particularly, blockchain technology, as a decentralized, permanent, unalterable store of information can help with the archiving and trust issues around academic credentials, whereas computational intelligence found in the technological domains of algorithmic techniques, data analytics, and semantic analysis may facilitate decision making and optimize work practices concerning administrative processes, course updates, etc.

Under these circumstances, this paper presents QualiChain, an EU funded project targeting the creation, piloting and evaluation of a distributed platform for storing, sharing and verifying academic and employment qualifications. To inspire trust in the projected platform, QualiChain will take advantage of blockchain's innate properties for decentralization, immutability and data protection. One of the project's target goals is to show that by combining various innovative technologies (semantic enrichment, data analytics, decision support algorithms, etc.) to develop tools and services on top of a trustworthy blockchain infrastructure can not only cover student accreditation but has the potential for wider university process optimization. To test and validate the projected platform in the field of education, QualiChain involves a pilot targeting student accreditation, curriculum design, and process optimization within the School of Electrical & Computer Engineering (ECE) of the National Technical University of Athens (NTUA). Along the above lines, the paper shall provide a comprehensive use case on how the aforementioned technologies may lead to university processes optimization and will discuss the added value and benefits generated for the stakeholders involved.

Section 1 introduces the scope of the present paper by presenting the current situation in Higher Education and explaining how blockchain and other innovative technologies can lead to more effective and secure solutions. Section 2 presents in greater detail the challenges faced by universities today as well as blockchain solutions that have been applied to address them. Section 3 introduces the QualiChain concept and describes the pilot use case to be applied in the ECE School of the NTUA. Finally, Section 4 concludes the paper and describes the future actions that will be taken to realize the project goals.

2. BACKGROUND

2.1 Current Challenges

Institutions of higher education are operating in an increasingly complex and competitive environment. They are under increasing pressure to respond to constant economic, political and social change such as growing student demands in certain disciplines, embedding workplace attributes to graduates and ensuring that the quality of learning programs is both nationally and globally relevant (Daniel 2015), especially in an era of rapid technological change. Furthermore, the increasing amounts of fraud and corruption around higher education degrees and credentials (Chapman and Lindner 2014; Mohamedbhai 2016) is shaking the trust in the education system. Consequently, various stakeholders (academia, private/public sector, public administration, etc.) are expecting HEIs to address the growing regulatory demands for transparency and accountability (Hazelkorn 2007).

In light of the aforementioned challenges, the slow digitization of the education sector is a major concern (Association of Universities in the Netherlands (VSNU) 2017). Even though existing IT infrastructures in universities support most of the logistic processes, such as timetabling courses and student administration, their databases are often hosted in centralized data centers inside the university, with restricted access to its IT professionals (Turkanovic et al. 2018). However, such data are reflective of how students learn (Koedinger, K. et al. 2008) and how HEIs operate and if analyzed, could generate knowledge that would help institutions respond effectively to changes happening within and outside them (Daniel 2015). Another shortcoming of current IT systems is that they seldom provide any usability and interoperability in education credential sharing. Such documents mainly exist in paper form and require extremely time-consuming processes for their verification. Hence, students can experience difficulties transferring to another HEI or applying for a job due to the inaccessibility and lack of standardization of their records. While there are different degrees of digitisation among HEIs and there are certainly universities with more modernized processes compared to others, current challenges arise from the lack of common ground between such institutions as well as their connections with the labor market. While, the remarks made throughout this document may seem more generalized than need be, the aim is to indicate the need for standardization of data and common processes in the sector.

2.2 BlockChain Potential for University Processes Optimization

To tackle the challenges described in the previous section fundamental changes are required in the way that HEIs operate. At the same time, innovative technologies uncover new possibilities for higher education and learning in general. Blockchain is one such technology that has been employed by several higher education institutions to design different solutions and approaches related to higher education. Specifically, the University of Nicosia, having a leading role in academia-oriented blockchain initiatives, was the first higher education institution to issue academic certificates whose authenticity can be verified through the Bitcoin blockchain (2017). Additionally, Sony Global Education has developed a blockchain for storing academic records, leveraging blockchain's secure properties to realize encrypted transmissions (2016). Sharples and Domingue (2016), drawing on their previous research into reputational management for educational systems, proposed a permanent distributed record of intellectual effort and associated reputational reward, based on the blockchain, that instantiates and democratizes educational reputation beyond the academic community. In more recent approaches, Rooksby and Kristiyan (2017) have implemented a blockchain system based on Ethereum for use by a university to store student grades and to provide a cryptocurrency. Moreover, Skiba (2017) took advantage of blockchain as a distributed ledger to allow students to own their credentials and in combination with new forms of digital credentials (badges, certification documents) make the job of checking and validating transcripts for courses attended in different universities/colleges easier by providing a more secure and trustworthy system that eliminates the middleman from the task of verifying transactions. Finally, Turkanovic (2018) proposed a global higher education credit platform, named EduCTX that is based on the concept of the European Credit Transfer and Accumulation System (ECTS), while Gräther (2018) developed the Blockchain for Education platform as a practical solution for issuing, validating and sharing of certificates.

3. QUALICHAIN APPROACH

QualiChain is a project that aspires to investigate and provide evidence on the transformative impact of disruptive technologies, such as blockchain, semantics, data analytics and gamification in the domain of public education, as well as the interfaces of the latter with the fields of private education, the labor market, and public sector administrative procedures. The concept and focus of the project lie more specifically in the design, implementation, piloting and thorough evaluation in terms of benefits, risks and other potential implications of the QualiChain technological solution, a distributed platform targeting the storage, service, and verification of academic and employment qualifications. At this point, attention has to be drawn to the fact that although originally inspired from the field of public education and the need to transform certificates' archiving and management, as well as to fight fraud around education awards, the QualiChain concept has practically a much larger scope, as its services transcend the mere validation of training certificates and bring forward solutions to major challenges of both public and private interest, such as those of lifelong learning, recruitment, mobility, better linking of education with the labor market, etc. thereby accommodating the needs of several stakeholders. The project consortium will pilot QualiChain's innovative combination of technologies in a set of four representative settings, to showcase the impact of the proposed solution on the full spectrum of potential stakeholders (education providers, public administrations selection procedures, HR-consulting for private companies, citizens as learners or employment seekers). In the following section, the pilot case that will have the QualiChain solution applied in the Electrical & Computer Engineering School (ECE) of the National Technical University of Athens (NTUA) will be described.

3.1 University Process Optimization Pilot Concept

In the light of addressing the challenges described in Section 2, this use case will apply the QualiChain technical solution in the ECE School of the NTUA. The first goal of the pilot will be to take advantage of the platform's blockchain for degree verification as well as for endorsing skills, awards, etc. that students receive during their attendance at the School via smart badges. Using smart badges as a means of enriching students' education profile is a novel idea that was introduced during the initial phases of the project in order to enrich the scope of this specific pilot case. On the other hand, NTUA, being the oldest academic institution for technical education in Greece, is committed to constantly being at the forefront of engineering developments and offering high-quality education services to its students. Moreover, the ECE School of the NTUA has many thematic fields that students can choose from, ranging from software development and computer sciences to energy efficiency and management. As such, this pilot use case will allow the consortium to test the QualiChain Consulting & Decision Support functionalities in an institution that a) has many different potential career possibilities for alumni that will allow targeting quite a big part of the job market and b) includes technology-related courses from different fields. Consequently, this pilot will leverage QualiChain data analytics and DSS functionalities in order to analyze the labor market requirements around the profession of the Electrical and Computer Engineer, as well as chart the School's current training curriculum and identify gaps and insufficiently addressed knowledge fields, thus providing guidance and decision support for the latter's amelioration in line with the labor market's requirements.

3.2 Stakeholders Involved

This particular pilot case revolves around three different groups of stakeholders of the NTUA; students, teachers and the ECE School as a whole. It should be mentioned that the ECE School, as a stakeholder includes various administrative and decision-making bodies such as the school's secretariat, committee, etc.

For this pilot, students of the ECE School were divided into two groups; undergraduate students and Ph.D. students. For undergraduate students, their main needs are finding and selecting the courses that present the most interest for them as well as improving their skills and knowledge so that they will be better prepared to enter the job market after completing their education. As of now, students cannot find specific courses, the curriculum of which also includes the teaching of general skills required in the labor market because the school's curriculum is not organized in such a way. Additionally, they do not have a personal profile where they can track their knowledge curve so they can make more informed decisions for their future. Finally, Ph.D. students have no way of getting recognized for any services they provide to the school such as teaching courses, grading exams, etc. and as such, their role and experiences gained working at the school cannot be validated. The involvement of PhD students in this specific pilot aims to showcase that they should also be considered as workers of a university whether that is as faculty, researchers or administrative personnel and as such their working experience in academia should be reflected in their professional profiles.

Concerning the added value that professors will receive from QualiChain, this revolves around the update of their courses to include the latest updates in the corresponding technological field and some general skills required by professions that are closely tied with their specific course. At the moment, professors rely exclusively on personal work and their perception to identify advancements/updates in the scientific domain addressed by a specific course. In special cases, they can consult domain professionals and/or employer representatives to identify relevant market requirements but the whole process is manual and time-consuming.

Finally, the main need of the ECE School is the optimization of its administrative processes and its role can be viewed as an amalgamation of the actions that professors and students of the school will be called to participate in. The end-goal for the school (represented by its committee), as it pertains to this pilot, is to modify the current curriculum in a way that will positively impact the skillset and career path of future graduates, improve its score in university rankings and enhance its prestige. At the moment, formal modifications of the curriculum have to follow very strict procedures and usually take place during meetings of the school's committee.

3.3 Innovations Applied

This pilot will take advantage of the platform's blockchain ledger for verification of skills and micro-accreditations (via smart badges) that students receive from participating in seminars, hackathons, special lectures, etc. that are organized under the scope of the school's activities. Additionally, the platform's blockchain will be used to recognize and validate the role of lecturers, Ph.D. students and other stakeholders of the school (apart from students and professors) for the services they may offer to the ECE School. The processes described in this sub-section were a late addition to this pilot in order to expand its scope and take full advantage of the projected platform's functionalities for improving university processes and enriching student profiles. The specifics of these processes can be seen in Figure 1 and will be explained below.

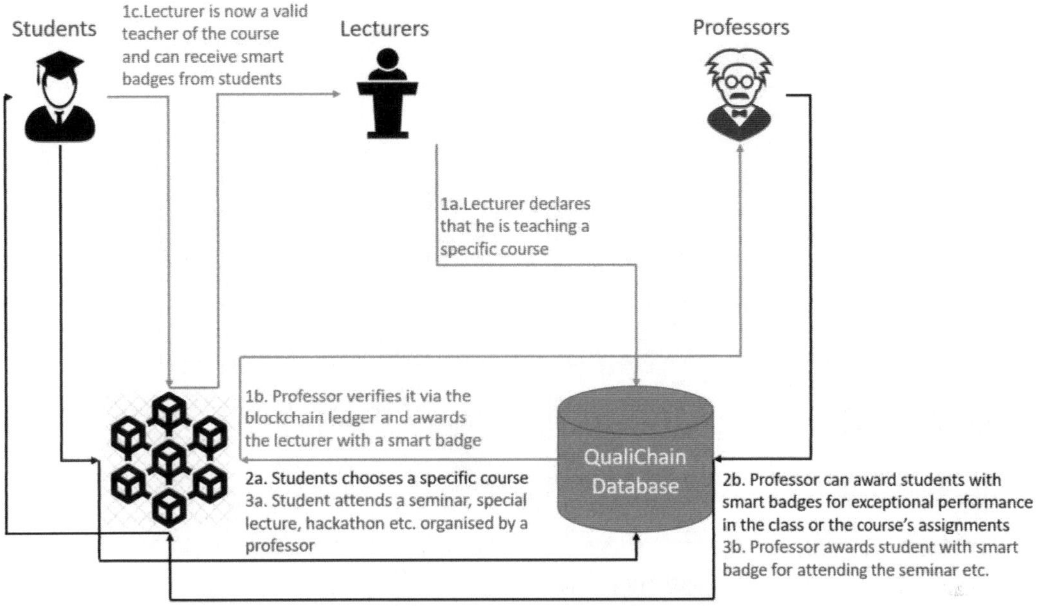

Figure 1. Smart badge endorsement

It can be observed from Figure 1 that smart badges will be mainly awarded from professors to undergraduate students. Given that some courses have group/personal assignments, professors of a course will be able to award smart badges to the students or groups of students that achieved the best results. Such results can include but are not limited to the most efficient algorithms in software-related courses, the best results in group assignments, etc. Moreover, students will be awarded smart badges for attending workshops, hackathons, seminars, special lectures and other activities that are not in the school's curriculum but are organized by the school and fall under the general scope of its activities. Such badges will usually be awarded and verified by the professor(s) that organize such activities and events.

On another note, many courses are being taught not only by the professors but also by lecturers (usually Ph.D. candidates) who are not being recognized their involvement with the course. QualiChain, through this pilot, proposes the following solution: the professor will first verify with a smart badge the lecturer's involvement in the course. During the course, students will be able to award lecturers with smart badges for being communicative, their way of teaching, etc. thus the lecturers of such academic institutions can also get recognized for their efforts and contributions and improve their profile in QualiChain as well.

3.4 Use Case Description

Having explained the role of smart badges in the context of this pilot, the next step was to design the overall process flow between this pilot's stakeholders. The outcome of this task is reflected in Figure 2 that shows the process that will be followed by the pilot's stakeholders. In addition, the figure and the accompanying methodology shows the interaction of the stakeholders with the platform's projected modules and as such will be used as input by the project's technical team to design the input and output flow of data from the platform, as well as design and develop the various modules and services. The main interactions take place between students, lecturers, professors, and the QualiChain platform and the final results stemming from these interactions will be used by the committee of the ECE School to update the curriculum.

The first step of the process will require students to create their profile on the platform. As such, they will use an Intelligent Profiling module that draws data from the platform's database (verified credentials, smart badges) and the web (labor market data, technological developments, etc.), creates the account and saves it in QualiChain. This step is integral to the rest of the procedure given that student data need to be stored in QualiChain in a structured way to be used as input for some of the analyses.

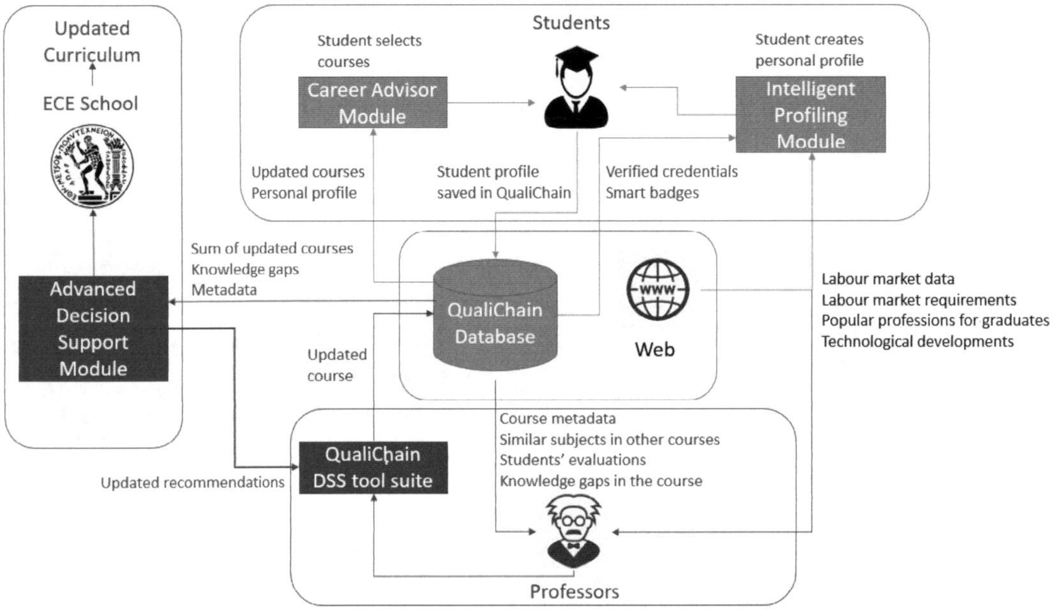

Figure 2. Process flow between stakeholders

The next step of the process requires professors to use the platform's Decision Support System (DSS) tool suite to update their course(s). As such, they will have to insert into the platform information about their course (course metadata). Moreover, past student evaluations that are usually collected with the end of the semester will be semantically enhanced and provided structure so they can be analyzed and assessed along with the rest of the course's data. For using such information as input in QualiChain, university data will be semantically enhanced in order to make the process of data entering by professors as automated as possible.

It should be mentioned that the QualiChain data analytics and DSS tool suite will draw data from QualiChain (student profiles, smart badges, course metadata, student's evaluations, similar subjects, etc.) and the web (labor market data, technological developments, etc.) and has the potential to produce various analyses. Such analyses can either be used by professors for course updates/modifications or by students for decision support on course selection.

When a professor uses the aforementioned services to update a course, the updated course is saved in QualiChain and the updated course description is then synchronized with the Advanced Decision Support Module that will provide updated suggestions for the other courses. Additionally, in case some of the knowledge gaps of the curriculum were addressed in this course, then the system will stop recommending the same changes for other courses. Students can then use the Career Advisor module that analyses the student's profile along with the updated course(s) descriptions to provide suggestions on course selection. Finally, the sum of updated courses, knowledge gaps, similar subjects taught in different courses is fed into the Advanced Decision Support module which in turn produces recommendations for a new curriculum for the entire school.

3.5 BlockChain Potential for University Processes Optimization

The use case presented in the previous sections, promises to have a positive impact on the ECE School and its students, professors and other personnel. On the one hand, students will possess a holistic personal profile where they can track their learning curve, set goals, receive personalized recommendations and validate their skills and certifications via smart badges. Moreover, the updated curriculum will include a more interesting pool of courses that can provide them with the necessary all-around skill set that is required from the labor market.

Professors of the school will be given a tool that will help them optimize the process of updating their courses. Besides, they will be able to recognize and validate the participation of lecturers and Ph.D. students in courses and other activities through Smart Badges Accreditation. Furthermore, the school's secretariat will avoid time-consuming processes for degree verification and other administrative issues, given that the pertinent documents will exist in QualiChain, secure and already verified. In the long term, all of the aforementioned can lead to an improved reputation for the school as a whole and less time for the employment of graduates.

In the pilot case presented here it is evident that blockchain is mainly useful for the purpose of smart-badge accreditation via a trustworthy and immutable infrastructure. However, that is the case because this pilot focuses on the school's internal processes. Using Blockchain for degree and skill verification can also strengthen the bond between universities (e.g. student transfers) as well as between academia and the labor market and create an ecosystem where pertinent stakeholders can perform everyday tasks more effectively. On the other hand, it can be stated that public and private organisations use their own information systems and will not be able to interact with QualiChain. However, QualiChain is a research project that recognizes the role that blockchain will play in shaping educational and administrative procedures in the future and as such the final solution is projected to be blockchain-agnostic so that it will be able to interact with as many other systems as possible. As such, the role of Blockchain, while being an integral part of this pilot as well, can be better assessed under the scope of QualiChain's projected offerings as a whole.

4. CONCLUSION

In this era of rapid digitization, the education sector is still searching for the appropriate level and appropriate methods of digitization. Consequently, student accreditations and documents are mostly used in paper form and their digital equivalents are not flexible enough to be integrated into labor market processes while university IT systems are in most cases inefficient and outdated. QualiChain, the project presented in this paper, recognizes these issues and plans to address them by developing an innovative platform that combines blockchain, semantics, data analytics and decision support algorithmic techniques among others. Furthermore, the pilot that will be applied in the ECE School of the NTUA aims to showcase the benefits of QualiChain in a real-life university environment as well as gather feedback that will be used to improve the platform.

At its current stage, the project has completed the initial research tasks and requirement elicitation stages. Future steps of the project include the elicitation of technical requirements, data gathering for the pilot cases and initiation of the platform development. Specifically, for the pilot presented in this paper, future work will assess the school's current curriculum to identify gaps between labor market needs and the skills developed in the current courses. Furthermore, the specification of the technical assets, such as the ontology that will be used to semantically enhance the school's data and the profiling model that will include all the information related to the user are already underway. Under that context, additional steps include selecting the appropriate data mining techniques and multi-criteria decision support algorithms that will be used on the platform's modules as well as the types of visualizations that will be provided to the users to facilitate a complete overview of the data that they investigate.

ACKNOWLEDGEMENT

This work has been co-funded by the European Union's Horizon 2020 research and innovation programme under the QualiChain project, Grant Agreement No 822404.

REFERENCES

Association of Universities in the Netherlands (VSNU) (2017): Digitisation in academic education. Our agenda for a future-proof range of degree programmes. Available online at https://www.vsnu.nl/files/documenten/VSNU%20Digitisation%20in%20academic%20education.pdf.

Chapman, David W.; Lindner, Samira (2014): Degrees of integrity. The threat of corruption in higher education. In Studies in Higher Education 41 (2), pp. 247–268. DOI: 10.1080/03075079.2014.927854 .

Daniel, Ben (2015): Big Data and analytics in higher education. Opportunities and challenges. In Br J Educ Technol 46 (5), pp. 904–920. DOI: 10.1111/bjet.12230 .

Gräther, Wolfgang et al. (2018): Blockchain for Education. Lifelong Learning Passport.

Hazelkorn, E. (2007): The impact of league tables and ranking systems on higher education decision making. In Higher Education Management and Policy 19 (2), pp. 1–24. DOI: 10.1787/17269822 .

Koedinger, K et al. (2008): An open repository and analysis tools for fine-grained, longitudinal learner data. In 1st International Conference on Educational Data Mining, Montreal, pp. 157–166.

Mohamedbhai, Goolam (2016): The Scourge of Fraud and Corruption in Higher Education. In IHE (84), p. 12. DOI: 10.6017/ihe.2016.84.9111 .

Rooksby, John; Kristiyan, DImitrov (2017): Trustless education? A blockchain system for university grades. In New Value Transactions: Understanding and Designing for Distributed Autonomous Organisations, Workshop at DIS.

Sharples, Mike; Domingue, John (2016): The Blockchain and Kudos. A Distributed System for Educational Record, Reputation and Reward. In Katrien Verbert, Mike Sharples, Tomaž Klobučar (Eds.): Adaptive and adaptable learning. 11th European Conference on Technology Enhanced Learning, EC-TEL 2016, Lyon, France, September 13-16, 2016, Proceedings / Katrien Verbert, Mike Sharples, Tomaž Klobučar (eds.), vol. 9891. Switzerland: Springer (LNCS sublibrary. SL 3, Information systems and applications, incl. Internet/Web, and HCI, 9891), pp. 490–496.

Skiba, Diane J. (2017): The Potential of Blockchain in Education and Health Care. In Nursing education perspectives 38 (4), pp. 220–221. DOI: 10.1097/01.NEP.0000000000000190 .

Sony Global Education (2016): Sony Global Education Develops Technology Using Blockchain for Open Sharing of Academic Proficiency and Progress Records. Available online at http://www.sony.net/SonyInfo/News/Press/201602/16-0222E/index.html.

South African Council on Higher Education (2013): The Aims of Higher Education. Pretoria - South Africa: Council on Higher Education (9). Available online at https://www.che.ac.za/sites/default/files/publications/kagisano9.pdf.

Turkanovic, Muhamed et al. (2018): EduCTX. A Blockchain-Based Higher Education Credit Platform. In IEEE Access 6, pp. 5112–5127. DOI: 10.1109/ACCESS.2018.2789929 .

University of Nicosia (2017): Academic Certificates on the Blockchain. Available online at http://digitalcurrency.unic.ac.cy/free-introductory-mooc/academic-certificates-on-the-blockchain/.

AN EXPLORATORY EMPIRICAL ANALYSIS OF THE QUALITY OF MOBILE HEALTH APPS

Aude Cabrera[1], Mayoni Ranasinghe[1,a] , Cedric Frossard[1], Nicolas Postel-Vinay[2,a] and Celia Boyer[1,b]

[a]*MD*

[b]*Dr*

[1]*Health On the Net Foundation, 2 chemin du Petit-Bel Air, 1225 Chêne-Bourg, Switzerland*

[2]*Unité d'hypertension artérielle. Hôpital Européen Georges Pompidou, 20, rue Leblanc 75015 Paris - France*

ABSTRACT

Introduction: Owning a smartphone is now almost a given, and with smartphone use comes the benefit of access to a large pool of apps on every topic conceivable, including health. So, it is not surprising that mHealth apps development is on the rise, as is the use of mHealth apps. However, unlike apps intended for other purposes, the use of mHealth apps carry, not only the advantage of improved health but also the burdens of potential misuse, misleading content and possible security breach of personal data. In this paper, we attempt to evaluate the possible hazards of some of the most popular mHealth apps in app stores from France.

Objectives: To (1) examine the top 10 most downloaded health apps in term of security and transparency of content (2) identify the trends of the most downloaded apps (3) to assess the applicability of the mHONcode guidelines to identify main issues on health apps (4) to describe the still main risks of health apps and (5) to propose basic rules to overcome them.

Results: As expected, the 10 apps displayed varying degrees of quality and trustworthiness or lack thereof. Only 20% of the apps disclose the editorial team and the funding source. 80% of the apps use tracking tools such as analytics, crash reporting without prior consent or before the consent. 2 out of 10 apps did not used a https web address for health content and advertisement display. One app activates the location functionality without any justification in the app.

Conclusion

As was the case for online health information more than 2 decades ago, the lack of uniformity of the trustworthiness of mHealth apps is worrying and could have some serious public health concerns. And just like the HONcode was required then, the mHONcode is required now to ensure the regulation of health apps, thus providing the end-user with trustworthy and quality tools to help in the management and maintenance of their healthcare.

KEYWORDS

Mobile Applications, mHealth, Certification, Quality, Code of Conduct

1. INTRODUCTION

Health On the Net Foundation (HON) is a non-governmental organization in special relation with WHO (World Health Organization). It is the oldest online health information standardizing body and was founded in 1995 in Geneva, Switzerland. The Health On the Net Code of Conduct (HONcode), a set of 8 principles used to standardize online health information has been in use for over 20 years, for health websites. The mHONcode is the new code of conduct of HON, with guidelines adapted to mobile health apps. Apps owners voluntarily request the mHONcode certification, then their application is evaluated on the one hand on reliability by a medical expert and on the other hand on safety by a member of our IT team. Before any evaluation, a contribution is requested, since the processes require between 3 and 5 days of work by experts. This does not in any way guarantee that the certification will be obtained, the application needs to be fully compliant to be certified.

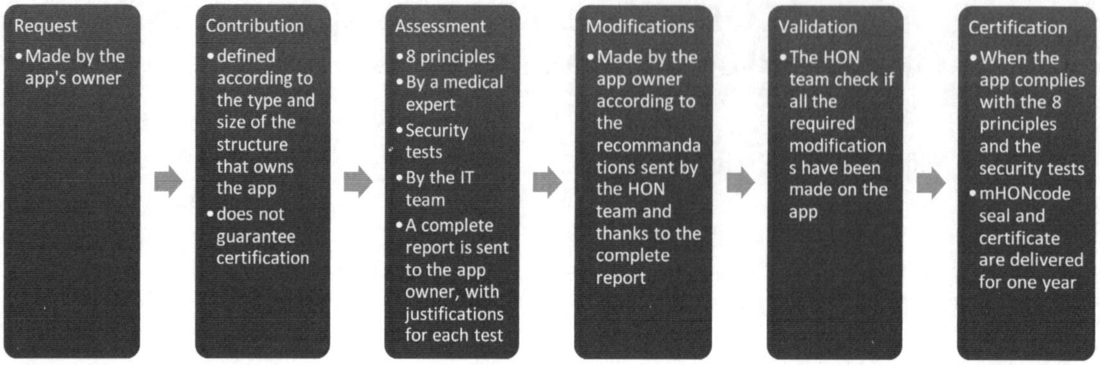

Figure 1. Process of the mHONcode certification

The former European Commissioner for Health Tonio Borg said in 2014 "mHealth has a great potential to empower citizens to manage their health and stay healthy longer, to trigger greater quality of care and comfort for patients, and to assist health professionals in their work. As such, exploring mHealth solutions can contribute to modern, efficient and sustainable health systems"[1]. Mr Borg's visionary comment was indeed true. However, as is the case with most things, there are always pros and cons. The pros are immense, with mHealth having the potential to greatly impact population health, but the cons are that there are no indicators to allow the public to discern trustworthy apps from the crowd.

So how popular are mHealth apps? Where do we stand today in 2019 in terms of mHealth adoption and usage? In 2017, 325,000 health apps were available in all major app stores (Google Play, Apple App, Windows Phone, Amazon App and Blackberry world), this equates to 3.7 billion of downloads (Research 2 Guidance, 2017). Between 2016 and 2017, 78,000 health apps were added to Google Play and Apple App stores (Research 2 Guidance, 2018). A systematic review conducted by McKay (2018) has shown the lack of one best practice approach to evaluate mobile health apps amongst the scientific community. In this huge market, how would the general public, without any medical knowledge or a health care provider recommending a health app, be able to gauge the trustworthiness, accuracy and security of an app to use or recommend? What are the criteria a mHealth app should fulfill to be available for download in the app stores? Are the security of health and personal data and the transparency of information considered a major issue to be considered in the mHealth arena? Are these issues taken seriously by mHealth developers and stakeholders commissioning the developments on their behalf?

Carroll et al. have shown that younger persons (18-44years) with a higher education (college graduate or higher) have a higher likelihood of adopting health apps than the ones aged 45-65+years. Furthermore, they highlighted the role of mobile phone health apps as a health promotion tool to change lifestyle behaviors (perform physical activity, change diet and lose weight). mHealth apps are in full expansion in the healthcare domain (Wellness. Education, Prevention, and Care) including in their use by the general public, however the regulation measures for these apps have not kept up.

The numbers are worrying: a study shows that 66% of the health apps certified as clinically safe by the UK NHS apps Library were in fact, sending identifying information over the internet without encryption and disclosure [Huckvale 2015 a]. Huckvale 2015 b, in another paper, demonstrates that 67% of the insulin dose calculator apps assessed provided inappropriate dosage recommendation. Plante in 2016 showed that a blood pressure measuring app produced false measurements, and this app had been downloaded 150,000 times. These are only a few examples. Wisniewski 2019 highlights that apps based on six diseases (depression, schizophrenia, addiction, hypertension, diabetes, and anxiety) provide questionable content or unsupported claims. Recent scientific publications have shown that sharing of user data is routine and yet far from transparent despite the introduction of the European Union General Data Protection Regulation (GDPR) in 2018, preventing the user from making an informed choice regarding the transmission of their data to third parties [Huckvale 2019 and Grundy 2019]. So, the ubiquity of smartphones, tablets, sensors and similar smart devices means that huge volumes of data concerning health and personal data are being harvested and processed without even the users' knowledge.

---

[1] http://europa.eu/rapid/press-release_IP-14-394_en.htm

Amid the massive choice available to the public along with the accompanying risks, no real, sustainable solution currently exists to help differentiate the trustworthy from the non-trustworthy. Additionally, knowing that 23% of the digital health marketers are non-healthcare professionals [Research 2 Guidance, 2017], how can users identify reliable applications?

2. OBJECTIVES

In this article, we observe the top 10 most downloaded health apps available on Google Play and Apple Stores in France to understand their offers and behaviors in terms of security and transparency of content. Through this first step, we categorize the most downloaded apps in France in terms of functionalities (Table 1). These 10 health apps are judged according to the mHONcode guidelines (Table 3) to identify the main issues on health apps. The idea is to understand if these guidelines are applicable to the commonly used health apps and how scalable it is to accommodate the growing number of apps, while considering the heterogeneity of the apps and the time spent on each of them. Based on the assessment, the main risks of the 10 health apps are identified and solutions are proposed to overcome them.

Given the increasing focus of data privacy breach or issues in the general press, apps making unsupported claims and the proliferation of health apps on the market, the understanding of these research questions is relevant and timely to guide healthcare providers, the public and stakeholders to improve health apps in terms of data privacy and content transparency and honesty.

3. METHODS

HON chose the 10 most downloaded free health apps in the two major stores Google Play & Apple with the limitation of the country in the URL of the stores being France, without discrimination of language, mission, functionalities and rating. None of these apps has voluntarily required the certification or been HONcode certified now. As we wanted to test if the GDPR[2] was adopted by apps after this new European regulation came into force across the European Union on 25th May 2018, we decided to opt and select the country France. The aim was then to have a representative sample of applications without any further sorting other than choosing the most downloaded applications by users, to obtain results that were limited but representative of the current market of mobile applications as in line with the other publications described below. As the top 10 apps is different for either the Apple Store or the Google Play Store, and also because this list changes from day to day, we selected the 10 most downloaded apps between the 2 stores, on May 24th 2019. We also reported the number and the score of ratings as users could base their choice on such criteria. All this information can be found in Tables 1 and 2.

Table 1. Positions, number of downloads for the 10 selected apps on May 24th, 2019, in France

Application	Versions	Owner	Category	Apple store's positions	GooglePlay store's positions	Downloads in the GooglePlay store
Doctolib	iOS 3.2.1 Android 3.1.9	Doctolib	Appointment booking	#1 Medical	#1 Medical	>1 million
Grossesse +	iOS 5.4 Android 5.2	Philips / Health & Parenting	Pregnancy	#2 Medical	#1 Parents	>10 million
Qare	iOS 1.7.65 Android 1.8.85	Qare SAS	Online consultation	#3 Medical	#2 Medical	>100 000
Staying Alive	iOS 6.1.3 Android 6.2.2	AEDMAP	Cartography	#4 Medical	#5 Medical	>500 000
Sauv Life	iOS 2.5.4 Android 2.3.4	Association S.A.U.V.	Cartography	#5 Medical	#7 Medical	>100 000

[2] https://ec.europa.eu/commission/priorities/justice-and-fundamental-rights/data-protection/

We Moms	iOS 2.14.17 Android 2.61.07	Globalia SAS	Forum	#6 Medical	#9 Parents	>500 000
Mon Ovulation	iOS 1.4.3 Android 2.7.1	Doctissimo / TF1 / Lagardère	Fertility	#7 Medical	#27 Medical	>500 000
Livi	iOS 3.0.6 Android 3.0.5	Digital Medical Supply France	Online Consultation	#8 Medical	#4 Medical	>100 000
Bébé +	iOS 1.9.4 Android 1.8.4	Philips / Health & Parenting	Baby's health	#9 Medical	#6 Parents	>500 000
Ma Grossess	iOS 2.6 Android 2.9.0	Doctissimo / TF1 / Lagardère	Pregnancy	#10 Medical	#12 Medical	>1 million

Table 2. Ratings and number of ratings for the 10 selected apps on May 24th, 2019

Application	Users's rating for GooglePlay	Numbers of rating For Google Play	User's rating For Apple Store	Numbers of rating for Apple Store
Doctolib	**4.8 / 5**	29 000	**4.8 / 5**	11 300
Grossesse +	**4.6 / 5**	384 000	**4.7 / 5**	5 800
Qare	**4.7 / 5**	567	**4.8 / 5**	2 000
Staying Alive	**4.1 / 5**	2 000	**4.2 / 5**	2
Sauv Life	**3.9 / 5**	786	**4.3 / 5**	297
We Moms	**4.6 / 5**	9 000	**4.7 / 5**	129
Mon Ovulation	**4.2 / 5**	4 000	**3.5 / 5**	6
Livi	**4.5 / 5**	877	**4.9 / 5**	2 700
Bébé +	**4.5 / 5**	29 000	**4.7 / 5**	1 300
Ma Grossesse	**4.3 / 5**	32 000	**4.3 / 5**	34

10 applications, French and English language-based health-related mobile apps were assessed by two senior expert members of the HON team, following the new guidelines for app certification: the mHONcode (Table 3). This new code of conduct also includes two security tests: an automated test for detection of weakness and vulnerabilities and a test about privacy & encryption which analyze the application's network, they can be found at the end of Table 3. Thus, 10 apps were manually checked by the IT team regarding the traffic of the data sent by apps on the Internet through differential traffic and network analysis. This allowed us to understand (1) the data sharing practice of the apps, how the personal data are transmitted (via a secure link SSL, and how the password and login are transmitted – encrypted or not) and (2) to which third parties personal data are sent with consent or not. These analyses have been done using Mitmproxy, a free open source interactive https proxy[3] allowing to be in between of the app transmission of data over the Internet and the phone. In addition, the Mobile App Security Test[4], free product by ImmuniWeb, has been used to scan the code. For Android the APK or the Google play link to upload the code was used, while for iOS an IPA archive was mandatory. This free product provides automated tests regarding six different test types: Static Application Security Testing (SAST); Dynamic Application Security Testing (DAST); Behavior Testing for malicious functionality and privacy; Software Composition Analysis; Mobile Application Outgoing Traffic and Mobile App External Communications. This product was selected as it provides a complete and easy to understand report and is free of charge, with an API or a web version. The results of these tests were analyzed by our team and major ones are reported in the results section. The 10 apps were downloaded to a HUAWEI P20 Android version 9.0.0, Android 8.1.0 and an iPhone 8 iOS version 12.2.

[3] https://mitmproxy.org/

[4] https://www.immuniweb.com/mobile/#about

Table 3. Presentation of the 8 principles of the mHONcode

Principles & Security Tests	Description	Examples of questions
1- Authority	Details about the editorial team, and the app team are clearly disclosed.	Are the name and qualifications of the editorial manager and the qualifications of writers provided? Who is in charge/responsible for the app?
2- Complementarity	Clear mention of the limitations of the app which does not replace the doctor-patient relationship.	Do you have a statement indicating that the information provided on the application is intended to encourage, not replace, direct relationships between the patient and health professionals?
3- Confidentiality	Statement explaining all legal requirements regarding the confidentiality of personal data.	Does the GPDR apply to your service? Is consent to data collection required for the use of the application? Are data transmitted to third parties?
4- Validity	App & all health and legal content have a 'last updated' date.	Does the medical, legal content and app have a last updated date?
5- Justifiability & Objectivity	Health information has references, is complete, and provided in an objective manner.	If app has services with formulae calculating dosage or health scores, are the references / scientific bases of these formulae given? If app has medical content, are the references given and medical information provided in an objective and balanced manner?
6- User's practice	The app is user friendly, its mission is clear, and the team is easily reachable.	What is the mission and audience of the application? Are there any instructions for use? Is a support contact address accessible or is it possible to leave a feedback?
7- Financial disclosure	All funding sources and paid services are identified and transparent.	What are the source(s) of funding? If the application needs an integrated purchase for its use, are there any general conditions available on this subject in the app? Is there a declaration of disclosure of links of interest for health professionals providing content or advice?
8- Advertisement policy	All ads are identified and clearly separated from the content.	If the application displays advertising, is it clearly identified as such and is there a viewable advertising policy on the application? If there aren't ads in the app, does a disclaimer indicate that there is none?

4. RESULTS

Various subjects were covered by the apps assessed: pregnancy, fertility, online consultation, cartography, baby's health, forum. The audience of these apps was the public. Regarding the new code of conduct and especially the 8 principles, the Table 4 shows for each application if it respects each principle. The symbol × means that the principle is not present in the app, while ✓ means that the principle is respected by the app, and **NA** means that the principle doesn't apply to the app. For some principles, we separated the results to be more precise, the signification of each initial is indicated below.

Table 4. Compliance with each principle for each application

Principles / Apps	**1 Authority**	**2 Complementarity**	**3 Confidentiality**		**4 Validity (Dates)**			**5 Justifiability Objectivity**		**6 User's practice**				**7 Financial disclosure**	**8 Advertisement policy**	
			Policy	*Consent*	*M*	*L*	*A*	*R*	*O*	*M*	*A*	*I*	*S*		*Policy*	*Identi-fication*
Doctolib	×	NA	×	×	NA	×	×	NA	NA	×	×	×	×	×	×	NA
Grossesse+	×	✓	✓	×	×	✓	×	×	✓	×	✓	✓	✓	×	×	×
Qare	✓	✓	✓	×	×	✓	×	NA	NA	✓	×	✓	✓	×	×	NA
Staying Alive	✓	✓	✓	×	NA	×	×	NA	NA	×	×	✓	✓	✓	✓	NA

Sauv Life	✗	NA	✓	✗	NA	✗	✗	NA	NA	✓	✓	✗	✗	✗	✗	NA
We Moms	✗	✓	✓	✓	✗	✓	✗	✗	✓	✓	✓	✓	✗	✗	✓	✓
Mon Ovulation	✗	✗	✗	✗	✗	✓	✗	✗	✓	✗	✓	✗	✓	✗	✗	✗
Livi	✗	✓	✓	✓	NA	✓	✗	NA	NA	✓	✓	✓	✓	✗	✗	NA
Bébé +	✗	✓	✓	✗	✗	✓	✗	✗	✓	✓	✓	✓	✓	✗	✗	✗
Ma Grossesse	✗	✗	✗	✗	✗	✓	✗	✗	✓	✗	✓	✗	✓	✗	✗	✗

Principle 4 Validity: M: Medical content / L: Legal content / A: Application
Principle 5 Justifiability & Objectivity: R: References / O: Objectivity
Principle 6 User's practice: MA: Mission & Audience / I: Instructions / S: Support

Regarding the automated code and privacy and encryption tests, 2 out of 10 apps are not using an https web address, a secure internet connection with SSL (Secure Socket Layer) for the transfer of health content, to access server type as content delivery network (to display images) as well as for displaying ads banners. The SSL certificate authenticate the identity of the organization delivering the service, ensure confidentiality and integrity of the content as information exchange cannot be intercepted and modified. So, personal data such as IP or health domain of interest could be intercepted by malwares.

One app is transmitting login and password information clearly displayed in the URL while the URL is using a secure protocol (HTTPS). The security whole in this case could be at the level of the storage of logs, where the login and password information are stored and potentially vulnerable to attacks.

Finally, 6 apps out of 10 use tracking such as analytics, crash reporting and others, transmitting personal data regarding to the GDPR without any prior consent of the user. 2 apps request prior consent but are already using tracking information before this explicit consent. Only 2 of the 10 apps required clear consent from the user at the time of first use, without clicking in the checkbox, users don't have access to any functionality of the application. 5 apps display a mention indicating that, by continuing to use the app, the user accepts the terms of conditions and confidentiality policy. Furthermore, 8 of the 10 assessed apps transmit data to third parties such as advertisement partners or tracking reporting or analytics tools.

During the analysis of the code via Immuniweb, we identified the following permission used by the apps such as camera (7 apps), microphone (4), location (7), phone (5), calendar (5), ssd storage or media storage (8), contact (1), Bluetooth (none but 4 apps declared in the code the need to use it), accelerometer (none but 5 apps declared in the code the need to use it). One app did ask the consent for using the location information, however this functionality was not used in the app so the demand of this usage was unjustified. Such behavior is infringing the GDPR.

8 out of 10 app declared the usage of above phone information in the code, without really using it. The habit of declaring the usage without using it, is not a good one as it is a potential security flaw for android versions above 6 Marshmallow used by 25% of android smartphone users[5].

In 90% of cases, the iOS and Android versions do not declare the same need of phone functionalities.

One app with the Android version was using the calendar of the phone without requesting permission, this has implied the crash of the app induced by Android OS as explicit permission was not granted.

5. DISCUSSION

After the assessment of the 10 most downloaded apps in France, we found major issues with the transparency, honesty and security of these apps.

Most of these apps didn't have any information about who is in charge/responsible for the app or the editorial team (Principle 1). Only 2/10 apps offering medical/health content mentioned the editorial process responsible, the authors or the process of information creation. None of the apps mentioned the sources of the health content nor the scientific background for the information (Principle 5). These apps are downloaded from 500,000 times to 10 million times; if the content is not verified, trustworthy, how can we not be alarmed by the major public health problem they are likely to represent?

Another issue presented in 2/10 apps is the missing statement that the health content or services on the app should not be used as a replacement of medical professional's advice. (Principle 2).

[5] https://developer.android.com/about/dashboards/

Additionally, particularly related to medical content but also legal content, is the date of the last update of the content (Principle 4). None of the 10 applications evaluated contained a creation date or last update of health information. This means that users' access health content, in most cases without references or authors, but also without knowing if it is still relevant. This creates a certain problem: the user bases his or her health decisions on potentially obsolete content. And yet it is well known that health and medical information is constantly and rapidly evolving.

Regarding the financial disclosure (Principle 7) only 1 of the 10 apps provided specific information on its funding.

Regarding advertising (Principle 8), 1 apps out of 10 displayed advertising inserts when used, but advertising policies on the subject are not well described and the ads in question are very poorly identified, or even very intrusive for one of the app.

Out of all, the 8 principles, the user experience (Principle 6) was the best represented for the 10 apps we evaluated. Most of them offer help, tutorials or a FAQ section to assist the user in using the application. 7 of them have easy access to a support address.

From a data privacy point of view, 8 out of 10 apps have a confidentiality policy specific to their app. 2/10 apps, with over one million downloads, with a service requiring registration of personal and identifiable information, did not have any reference to confidentiality or GDPR while having a very high rating score by the users.

In addition, the practice is different when examining the traffic of the data, 8 out of the 10 transmit personal data without prior consent or securely. This is a danger to users' data, users cannot be aware of such misuse. We could question if the developer team is aware of the good behaviour in terms of security and GDPR regulation. This is infringing the GDPR while these apps should strictly respect it unless penalties of 2% annual global turnover should apply. Probably this is due to the lack of policy enforcement and owner willingness.

The rating score given by end users is not reflecting the behaviour of the apps in term of transparency, ethics and security, in fact, it is even nearly the opposite. This was also identified by Wisniewski, which suggest the usage of the last update as a selection feature. In our case, this feature was only present. The issues identified in this article could be very easily corrected but concern the editorial process and the IT team developing the app.

6. LIMITATIONS

This study has limitations. The main one is that we only assessed 10 applications, the most downloaded in France. Nevertheless, these apps are representative of the common behavior of apps, as probably these apps have more potential to be in line with regulation such as the GDPR and good practice as all are owned by well-established organizations. So, the results presented, and the proportions should be read as indicators of the frequency of the behavior rather than definitive statistics.

HON is proposing new guidelines on mobile apps and have assessed these apps regarding these guidelines. This can be a bias; however, we equally assessed all the apps, by two senior HONcode experts.

The app behavior and services offered is sometimes based on the language of the phone which means that the service assessed differs so the review outcome can be different. This occurred on one application, LIVI, where when detected in English the service differed totally and required an address in UK, while when having a French version, even if we are in Switzerland, the service asked for the French security card or for online paid teleconsultation service.

Finally, with other studies analyzing the traffic of apps, this can only represent a snapshot at a given time.

7. CONCLUSION

mHealth is a huge market which provides users the opportunity to have better health and healthcare quality. Health apps support citizen's empowerment through self-management, health promotion, disease prevention, providing personalized health advice and care. However, the risks involved must be considered; the rapid development of the mHealth sector raises concerns about the potential risk of health functions apps providing transmission of health data, the capture of these data via sensors, self-diagnoses, disease management or diagnosis and appropriate processing of the data collected. Since mHealth solutions and devices can collect large quantities of personal information, including personal health information (e.g. data stored by the user on the device and data from different sensors, including location) and processes them.

The major difficulty for not only general users but also for health professionals who could recommend apps, is to discern trustworthy apps from the large pool of apps out there and our list assessment confirms this challenge.

Users, with this new technology in their hands, have direct access to medical and health information, with no need to take an appointment, straight from their pocket, which of course represents massive advancement in healthcare but also a real danger, if the displayed information is not reliable and if they believe that it can replace a consultation with a health professional.

As other studies, our study based on the 10 most downloaded mobile apps in France has shown clearly that mHealth apps, are sharing data which is far from transparent [Huckvale 2019 and Grundy 2019]. The non-respect of the 8 mHealth HONcode guidelines and issues in terms of privacy or security identified could be easily overcome with guidance to the developing team and decision from the owners of these apps. Given that there is no control, why would app developers decide to conform to strict editorial processes such as security, honesty and transparency which would cost more without short-term benefit in terms of number of downloads or ranking?

Although, even if only 10 apps were used in this study, it should be remembered that the 10 chosen were the most popular and thus, a representation of what the public downloads and uses.

mHealth apps are excellent ways to improve your health, in a fast, fun and accessible way, but only if they are reliable. Otherwise, which seems to be confirmed on this panel of apps, they represent a real public health danger, which can be overcome only with the commitment of the owners of these apps which the HON Foundation will try to address through its new code of conduct, the mHONcode.

ACKNOWLEDGEMENT

We thank the app owners who trust us and helped us finalize the HONcode principles.

REFERENCES

Boyer, C., & Geissbuhler, A. et al. 2007. Health on the Net Foundation: assessing the quality of health web pages all over the world. In *Medinfo 2007: Proceedings of the 12th World Congress on Health (Medical) Informatics; Building Sustainable Health Systems* (p. 1017).

Carroll, J. K., et al, 2017. Who uses mobile phone health apps and does use matter? A secondary data analytics approach. *Journal of medical Internet research*, *19*(4), e125.

Grundy, Q., Chiu, K., Held, F., Continella, A., Bero, L., & Holz, R. 2019. Data sharing practices of medicines related apps and the mobile ecosystem: traffic, content, and network analysis. *bmj*, *364*, l920.

Huckvale, K., et al, 2015 a. Unaddressed privacy risks in accredited health and wellness apps: a cross-sectional systematic assessment. *BMC medicine* Vol. 13: 214

Huckvale, K., Adomaviciute, S., et al, 2015 b. Smartphone apps for calculating insulin dose: a systematic assessment. *BMC medicine*, *13*(1), 106.

Huckvale, K., Torous, J., & Larsen, M. E. 2019. Assessment of the data sharing and privacy practices of smartphone apps for depression and smoking cessation. *JAMA network open*, *2*(4), e192542-e192542.

McKay, F. H., et al, 2018. Evaluating mobile phone applications for health behaviour change: a systematic review. *Journal of telemedicine and telecare*, *24*(1), pp. 22-30.

Plante, T. B., Urrea, B., et al, 2016. Validation of the instant blood pressure smartphone app. *JAMA internal medicine*, *176*(5), 700-702.

Ranasinghe, M., Cabrera, A., Postel-Vinay, N., & Boyer, C. 2018. Transparency and Quality of Health Apps: The HON Approach. *Studies in health technology and informatics*, *247*, 656-660.

Research 2 Guidance, 2017. *mHealth App Economics 2017/2018 Current Status and Future Trends in Mobile Health* Research2Guidance report. USA, pp 10. URL: https://research2guidance.com/product/mhealth-economics-2017-current-status-and-future-trends-in-mobile-health/ [Accessed May 2019]

Wisniewski, H., Liu, G., Henson, P., Vaidyam, A., Hajratalli, N. K., Onnela, J. P., & Torous, J. (2019). Understanding the quality, effectiveness and attributes of top-rated smartphone health apps. *Evidence-based mental health*, *22*(1), 4-9.

ANALYSING EGOVERNMENT RESEARCH: CURRENT AREAS AND DIMENSIONS

Demetrios Sarantis
United Nations University – Operating Unit on Policy-Driven Electronic Governance
Campus de Couros, Rua Vila Flor 166, 4810-445 Guimarães, Portugal

ABSTRACT

In recent years, there has been rapid growth in the volume of research output on the topic of eGovernment. The analysis of the literature reveals significant insights about the evolution of eGovernment research over time, the assessment of which serves as a basis for recommendations for future research on this global phenomenon. To understand this research better, the specific study has selected papers that contribute to the development of eGovernment research through conceptualizations and clarifications of the field, as well as by addressing significant issues and trends. Through reviewing those studies in eGovernment literature this paper categorises the outcomes and identifies three research areas and twenty dimensions in which the research community targets its efforts.

KEYWORDS

eGovernment, eGovernance, eGovernment Research, Dimensions, Areas, Domains

1. INTRODUCTION

The topic of eGovernment has arguably attained adequate autonomy to justify an investigation through specialised conferences, journals, books, MSc programs and through the new researchers it has attracted (Yıldız, 2012; Sarantis et al., 2019). eGovernment research takes place in a range of different types of institutions (Heeks, & Bailur, 2007). A recent study by the United Nations has shown that many emerging economies are making concrete steps to improve their eGovernment capacity (United Nations, 2016).

From the research side of the discourse there is no single dominant theme in eGovernment (Kankanhalli, Zuiderwijk, & Tayi, 2017). The field is as diverse as possible and eGovernment research has increasingly highlighted the complexities, interactions, and conflicts intrinsic to the public sector as pivotal for understanding eGovernment (Cordella, & Iannacci, 2010; Dawes, 2009). This fact highlights the difficulty in capturing a clear path of where the discipline is going, or what factors are driving and affecting research foci (Joseph, 2013).

Thus, there is a need to decompose and scrutinize existing literature to derive pathways in the published articles and develop a coherent and comprehensive research agenda to guide researchers in their pursuit for a better understanding of eGovernment. Because of this remarkable growth and importance of the field, we attempt, in this paper, to review the existing eGovernment research literature and draw conclusions from that reflection about current status and possible future directions. The structure of the paper is as follows. Next section introduces the research method applied while third section reviews identified relative literature. Then, the fourth section illustrates and analyses identified eGovernment research dimensions and sub dimensions. Finally, main conclusions are discussed in the last section.

2. RESEARCH METHOD

The exploratory research method applied in this study is based on tracking existing publications as a proxy for the research community's preferences and attribution of importance to different issues and topics within eGovernment field. This type of inductive approach has been chosen since authors consider that significant aspects and answers are already embedded in the current eGovernment literature.

To conduct this study, we decided to apply content analysis method and to focus on sources associated specifically with eGovernment, including those associated with existing research domains such as leading information systems (IS) or foremost public administration journals and conferences. The selected sources were those identified as the dominant and most cited eGovernment-specific research outlets after 2010. Ten papers were chosen that were subjected to analysis. We then proceeded to analyse and code identified research elements from all nine papers. The findings from this analysis are laid out below and are discussed in greater detail to fulfil the purpose of understanding the current standing of eGovernment research (Heeks, & Bailur, 2007). The content of the studies found as a result of this search effort are examined in detail to derive the key elements of eGovernment, which are presented below.

3. THE STATE OF THE FIELD OF EGOVERNMENT RESEARCH

Several studies have been conducted to explore eGovernment research agenda. The most recent and relevant identified in this review (Table 1) and they are analysed below.

Table 1. eGovernment Studies Analysed

#	Author	Title	Year
1	Estevez, Janowski	Electronic Governance for Sustainable Development - Conceptual framework and state of research	2013
2	Bélanger, Carter	Digitizing Government Interactions with Constituents: An Historical Review of E-Government Research in Information Systems	2012
3	Fonou et al	African E-Government Research Landscape	2014
4	Rana et al	Reflecting on e-government research: toward a taxonomy of theories and theoretical constructs	2011
5	Scholl, Scholl	Smart Governance: A Roadmap for Research and Practice	2014
6	Larsson, Grönlund	Future-oriented eGovernance: The sustainability concept in eGov research, and ways forward	2014
7	Ogonek	The Tale of e-Government: A Review of the Stories that Have Been Told So Far and What is Yet to Come	2017
8	Bolivar et al	Trends of e-Government Research. Contextualization and Research Opportunities	2010
9	Snead, Wright	E-government research in the United States	2014
10	Wirtz, Daiser	A meta-analysis of empirical e-government research and its future research implications	2016
11	Twizeyimana, Andersson	The public value of E-Government – A literature review	2019
12	Androutsopouloua et al	Transforming the communication between citizens and government through AI-guided chatbots	2019

In their study, **Estevez and Janowski** (Estevez, & Janowski, 2013) identify 5 eGovernment research dimensions, Government, Technology, Interaction, Customers and Society, analysing each one in specific elements. 78 research issues are identified in Government dimension (e.g. Alignment of strategies between central and local government, Infrastructure development, Providing broadband access). 24 research problems are identified in Technology dimension (e.g. Access in rural areas, Electronic channels for public service, Social media). 20 research problems are identified in Interaction dimension (e.g. Agreements between national-local governments, Governance of healthcare systems, Public computing centres). 19 research problems are identified in Customers dimension (e.g. Access for women, Affordable housing, Property value). 41 research problems are identified in Society dimension (e.g. Awareness of SD efforts, Hackathons for innovation, Participatory approach in developing a strategy for sustainability).

Bélanger and Carter (Bélanger, & Carter, 2012) analyse articles that refer to the eGovernment phenomenon in general. Assessed studies present benefits and challenges which may be easier to implement, since they do not have to be tethered to a particular agency. In addition, the results are not limited to the culture and processes of a specific government agency. However, with a generic concept, subjects may have diverse perceptions and experiences when providing responses to survey questions, which could confound the results.

Fonou & Rannyai (2014) used a qualitative technique based on online searches and literature reviews to address aspects of eGovernment development research in Africa. Amid several aspects, challenges and opportunities of eGovernment for African governments, is the most salient issue. This is aligned with the fact that most authors of eGovernment research focusing on Africa are interested in investigating the impact of the application of ICT in government (Nkomo, 2012; Agbele et al, 2012). Specific issues include Usage of ICTs in eGovernment implementation, Proposal of eGovernment strategies, Citizen roles and participation in eGovernment, Assessing state of eGovernment, Best Practices for eGovernment implementation, Analysis of eGovernment Readiness, Challenges and Opportunities of eGovernment, Implication of eGovernment on public policy, eGovernment initiatives undertaken, Accessibility of eGovernment services and Evaluation of Government web sites.

Rana et al., (2011) explore data that were collected from 779 research articles identified from the ISI Web of Knowledge database. The analysis of the various applications being used by the studies indicate that electronic government in general, is the most widely researched topic, followed by electronic government services. As far as specific electronic government applications are concerned, online tax filing system was researched maximum number of times. This is followed by information systems and technology, electronic filing, and broadband. Electronic or internet voting applications, website applications, internet services, information kiosks, electronic procurement, wireless technology and smartcard applications are also examined in several studies. Applications such as electronic learning, telephone channel integration, channel perception, electronic stamping, centralized customer service systems, electronic commerce, electronic tendering system, electronic complaint system, telecommunication, electronic channels, and virtual community are reviewed in few studies.

Scholl & Scholl (2014) present and discuss an agenda for research and practice, which advances the concept of smart, open, and participatory government of the 21st century. Topics discussed include: Governmental investments (Budgeting, controlling, evaluating), Electronic government and administrative modernization (eGovernment law, simplified and reliable administrative processes etc.), Security and Safety (standards with regard to data security, privacy etc.), Infrastructure Overhaul and Ubiquitous High-speed Connectivity (gigabit Internet etc.), Electric Mobility, Participation and Collaboration (Social media and social networking uses, active and individual involvement etc.), Open Data, Big Data, Transparency of data use, Effectiveness of participatory contribution, Open government, Transparency, and Accountability.

Larsson & Grönlund (2014) conduct a structured review of eGovernment literature investigating how various sustainability areas (social, economic, environmental and technical) are addressed. In Social category, the identify the following topics: Needs and participation, Politics and governance, Evaluation, Analysis and measurements, Values, goals and policies, Future uncertainty, Regulations, trust and security, Holistic view of organization and technology. In Economic category, they identify the following topics: Cooperation, Security & control, Feasible plan and model, Stakeholders & citizens, Alignment of social & technical planning aspects, Decision making and information. In Environmental category, they identify the following topics: Decision making and information, Infrastructure & energy, Environmental strategy, Environment as an important value for eGovernment. In Technical category, the identify the following topics: Standards and interoperability, Information preservation over generations, Holistic view, Technical infrastructure.

Ogonek's (2017) research main objective is to identify a set of topics that best represent the eGovernment research of recent years. The identified research topics range from current issues on how to increase the number of active eGovernment users by identifying the factors that lead to adoption and use of eGovernment to a more political perspective by analysing the political activity in social media to foster civic participation by direct communication through various social media products.

The first topic is eParticipation. This topic is predominantly concerned with the use of the internet and social media as communication means in electoral processes (eVoting) to foster the dialogue, engagement and active eParticipation of voters. The second topic deals with eGovernment adoption. The studies in this category identify factors that affect the acceptance and adoption of particular eGovernment services. Topic 3 is about the handling and management of governmental information. The fourth identified topic deals with eGovernment research. Topic 5, named Socio-economic Factors and Digital Divide, encompasses studies that examine the preconditions to implement eGovernment. The sixth topic adopts a rather technical perspective and describes the application of ICT systems and tools, as well as methodologies and ICT architecture for the support of eGovernment. Topic 7 examines eGovernment from an organizational point of view by addressing the implementation and management of eGovernment projects. Topic 8 embraces a policy perspective. It deals with public governance to foster openness and transparency, thus promoting the democratic process and participation by the proactive use of social media in eGovernment. Topic 9 deals with eGovernment websites. The tenth topic is about the provision of eGovernment services.

Bolivar et al., (2010) attempt to assist researchers in the development and direction of future analysis, identifying trends in terms of research and the methodology used. They identify the following research themes.

Technological innovation and modernization in public administration management: This theme focuses on the different changes in public administrations that allow greater transparency in the activities of government and public services. eGovernment programme/project evaluation and policy analysis: This topic studies the results of public programs evaluation related with initiatives of eGovernment and policies expansion of information technology. eParticipation and digital democracy: This theme searches emergent changes in the relationship between government and the citizen as result of eGovernment. eServices: This area discusses the transformation in the delivery of public sector services. Accountability, transparency and dissemination of information: This research theme discusses citizens' communication with governmental websites, achieving greater levels of disclosure of information to promote accountability of public managers online. Behaviour of citizens in relation to the applications of eGovernment: This topic focuses on user-centered study of the accessibility of eGovernment sites. eGovernment and personnel/human resources: This theme studies the experiences of designers of governmental Web pages; the acceptance of ICTs by public officials, as well as the challenges and efforts made by public administrations in the management of ICTs. Legislative architecture: This research focuses on administrative proceedings or any type of law that enables and encourages the adoption and implementation of eGovernment initiatives in public administrations. Intergovernmental relations: This research theme focuses on the political or institutional aspects of interagency relations between governmental units at the local, state, or national level. Digital divide and resistance barriers to eGovernment: This research item includes studies about obstacles presented by the different applications available to citizens, existing national programs to educate citizens to integrate ICTs in their daily lives, discovering its many benefits, as well as the evaluation of governmental websites to discover problems accessibility of these disabled by offering solutions. Organizational theory and behaviour: This theme researches models of innovation adoption that integrates the internal and external organizational factors, implementation factors exist in system of governance (organizational obstacles), application of business methods for the selection of investments of ICTs in the public administrations (financing challenges) as well as following the changes in the structures of public executive administrations.

Snead & Wright (2014) explore publications to assess research efforts specific to the U.S. eGovernment environment. Articles aggregated into the general governance perspective category essentially target issues that try to understand government actions and decisions. The study presents a breakdown of the governance perspective by 10 topic areas that best represent sample authors' described targets and situational context by government level.

The predominant governance topic area is citizen interaction, which includes how citizens engage and participate in governance and access government information. The next topic is agency eGovernment adoption where research focus is primarily on agency managers/personnel acceptance, skill level, and use of agency adopted or trial use of a type of technology. These are followed by: eGovernment model testing where researchers are either develop a model or test existing proposed models; technology adoption/management where the focus is on agency efforts to adopt and manage technology; and program roles/eGovernment engagement efforts or activities where the focus is on the roles and activities agencies assume to engage in eGovernment. The rest topics are Organizational change (Agency), eFinancial transactions (Agency–citizen/business), eContracting practices (Agency–government contractors), Technology acceptance (Society) and Business engagement/participation (Agency).

Wirtz & Daiser (2018) uncover 12 promising eGovernment research topics that carry innovative research potential. Adoption/drivers/development topic examines adoption, success factors, barriers, driver-related issues, as well as challenges with regards to eGovernment development and implementation. Acceptance/use/satisfaction topic deals with recognition and consent-based studies. Success/performance/value topic investigates the outcome of eGovernment usage. The next one, attitudes/trust studies the mindset or mental outlook, as well as the faith, that users and providers experience in relation to eGovernment. Socio-economic context group searches policy and participation issues and challenges that are related to society. The management aspects consider eGovernment from a strategic and organizational view, whereas human resource skills and development analyse personnel capacity and abilities. Information and data aspects deal with data quality and specification, as well as information requirements. Usability and complexity area explores eGovernment systems from a handling perspective. Culture-related domain examines the topic either from international or intra-group perspectives. Intergovernmental issues deal with eGovernment processes that engage multiple public sector organisations. Finally, autonomy and outsourcing area handles issues that have to do with institutional eGovernment sovereignty regarding services, processes and systems.

Twizeyimana & Andersson (2019) organize eGovernment research in six values: improved public services; improved administrative efficiency; open government capabilities; improved ethical behaviour and professionalism; improved trust and confidence in government; and improved social value and well-being.

Androutsopoulou et al. (2019) suggest that extensive research is required in the areas of artificial intelligence, natural language processing, machine learning and data mining technologies, in order to improve communication between government and citizens.

4. EGOVERNMENT RESEARCH AREAS AND DIMENSIONS

Based on aforementioned methodological approach and the review of the previous studies we classify the broader domain of eGovernment research into three areas and 20 specific research dimensions. Its dimension is characterised by specific research elements identified in literature review. The overarching areas identified both overlap and connect and in some cases even form parts of the other, but this is not visible in the table for practical reasons. The classification does not claim to be complete, but offers an approximate picture of the research field of eGovernment. Numbers inside brackets illustrate the source (Table 1) of identified research elements.

Table 2. Research Areas and Dimensions of Electronic Government

Government	Technology	Users
eGovernment Strategy-Policy	Electronic Services	Stakeholder Interaction
Organisation Role	Back Office Infrastructure	User Participation
eGovernment Framework	Data	User Needs
eGovernment Assessment	Social Media	User Role
eGovernment Legal Framework	Applications	Digital Inclusion
eGovernment Research Models	Trust and Security	Impact
	Channels	
	Interoperability	

A. Government

This research area explores the potential policies and related practices needed for the electronic government of the future (e.g. stages of digital transformation). It gives emphasis on the organizational level of analysis, since the interests are often focused on government agencies. Typical research questions include, "how should an appropriate strategy be developed and what should it comprise", "which are the proper ways to manage eGovernment projects". Several researchers have proposed models and frameworks for the successful development, monitoring and implementation of eGovernment. Research efforts provide insightful findings and actionable recommendations for government executives and managers, with several strategic areas focused on the use of information and communication technologies. It performs qualitative meta-analyses of eGovernment frameworks and adoption studies to develop unifying theories of eGovernment adoption. Various measurement frameworks are applied to assess public sector websites' security, usability, user satisfaction and design. Lessons that can be learned from developed countries that have successfully implemented eGovernment diversification and service delivery are discussed in several papers. The following are the proposed dimensions and the relative elements for Government research area.

eGovernment Strategy-Policy dimension includes the following research issues: eGovernance mission and goals (1), eGovernment strategies (3) (10), Implication of eGovernment on public policy (3), Growth-friendly consolidation (3), Politics and governance (6) (10), Values, goals and policies (6) (7) (11), Environmental strategy (6), eGovernment Programme (8) etc.

Organisation Role dimension includes the following research issues: Program roles (1) (9), eGovernment engagement and participation of the organisation (9). Organisation's operation (1) (11), Decision making and information (6), Holistic view of organization and technology (6) (12), Modernization in Public Administration Management (8), eGovernment and personnel (8), Human Resources (8) (10), eGovernment adoption (9) (10), Technology adoption and management (9) (10), Organizational change (9) (10), Institutional change (1).

eGovernment Framework dimension includes the following research issues: Best Practices for eGovernment implementation (3), Frameworks for implementing eGovernment (3), Models and feasible plan for implementation (3), Implementation and Management of eGovernment (7), Organizational Theory and Behaviour (8) (11).

eGovernment Assessment dimension includes the following research issues: Assessing state of eGovernment (3) (10), Analysis of eGovernment Readiness (3), Evaluation of Government web sites (3) (10), Evaluation analysis and measurement metrics and indicators (6), Project Evaluation and Policy Analysis (8).

eGovernment Legal Framework dimension includes the following research issues: eGovernment law (5), Regulations (6), Legislative Architecture (8).

eGovernment Research Models dimension includes the following research issues: Research method (7), research framework (7), research approach (7), research model (7), research model testing (9).

B. Technology

Technology is ingrained in almost every government activity today and it is perceived as an active part in transforming governance. This area studies issues like information infrastructure, which is a complex structure and involves conflict-prone matters. Information infrastructures include "hard" components (e.g. hardware and telecommunication backbones) as well as "soft" ones (e.g. applications, standards, information security, and information processes). For example, there is a need to agree on technical standards, interoperability rules at many layers and to develop and implement technology and train staff in numerous government agencies and companies to make this at all possible. Many research studies address the technical design of systems for successful implementation of eGovernment initiatives. Studies search the ways that technology and its elements affect the use and successful application of electronic services. eGovernment artefacts such as websites and eServices connecting government to its citizens are also frequently examined (Wray, & Van Olst, 2012). The following are the proposed dimensions and the relative elements for Technology research area.

Electronic Services dimension includes the following research issues: eGovernment initiatives undertaken, electronic government services (1) (3) (4) (7) (8) (11) (e.g. e-reverse auctions, GIS, online license renewal, mobile data services eFinancial transactions (9), eContracting practices (9)), Transaction types (1) (12) (integrated services, proactive services etc.).

Back Office Infrastructure dimension includes the following research issues: Back Office Equipment (1), Usage of ICTs in eGovernment implementation (3), Telecommunication Infrastructure (4), Public Sector Information systems and technology (4), Infrastructure Overhaul (5), Ubiquitous High-speed Connectivity (5), Electric Mobility (5), Infrastructure & energy (6), Technical infrastructure (6), IT and Systems Support for eGovernment (7), Technological Innovation (8).

Data dimension includes the following research issues: Public Data (1) (11), Open Data (5) (11), Big Data Provision (5), Information preservation over generations (6), Governmental Information Management (7) (10), eGovernment Websites (7).

Social Media dimension includes the following research issues: Social Media (1), Virtual community (4), Social media and social networking uses (5) (12), Digital Democracy (8).

Applications dimension includes the following research issues: Electronic government applications (1) (4) (7), Modular and adequate ICT support (5).

Trust and Security dimension includes the following research issues: Security and Safety (5), Trust and security (6), Security & control (6), Privacy (7), Security (7), Trust (1) (10) (11).

Channels dimension includes the following research issues: Channels (1), channel integration (4) (12), centralized customer service systems (4), Channel Strategy (1).

Interoperability dimension includes the following research issues: Interoperability (1), Standards and interoperability (6) (7).

C. Users

In this research area, individual user is placed in focus. Concepts of stakeholder interaction, user participation, user needs are met, with a view towards creating new perspectives for increasing citizen involvement in eGovernment and use of eGovernment services. Studies search how should eServices be developed from a citizen perspective, what is the contribution of the citizens in this development process and what are the current perspectives and in what way do they take citizens and businesses into consideration.

eGovernment researchers incorporate a variety of factors and contexts in their research. For example, culture might have a significant impact on eGovernment implementation success. Research theories emphasize the need for continuous interaction between government organizations and the private sector in implementing eGovernment (Dlodlo, Olwal, & Mvelase, 2012). The impact and implications of eGovernment initiatives on the structure and functioning of the public sector and the establishment of transformational change in the public sector are also discussed (Elkadi, & Abdelsalam, 2012). Finally, efforts to prevent corruption, suggesting eGovernment strategies that standardize and clarify procedures for delivery of government services are discussed in this area (Cloete, 2012). The following are the proposed dimensions and the relative elements for Users research area.

Stakeholder Interaction dimension includes the following research issues: Partnerships (1), Cooperation (6), Stakeholders & citizens (6), Intergovernmental Relations (8) (10)

User Participation dimension includes the following research issues: Participation (1), Citizen roles and participation in eGovernment (3) (12), Participation and Collaboration (5) (10), Needs and participation (6), eParticipation (8), eGovernment interaction-engagement (9), participation and access (9), community (7).

User Needs dimension includes the following research issues: Citizen information needs (1), individual information services (5), information (7), Service needs (1), development needs (10).

User Role dimension includes the following research issues: Producer roles (1), Consumer roles (1), Citizen roles and participation in eGovernment (3), electronic complaint system (4), Behaviour of Citizens in Relation to the applications of eGovernment (8).

Digital Inclusion dimension includes the following research issues: Accessibility (1), Accessibility of eGovernment services (3), Demography (1), Digital Inclusion (1), Role of libraries in eGovernment (3), electronic learning (4), Digital Divide and Resistance Barriers to eGovernment (8) (10), Social tension (1), Future uncertainty (6), Socio-economic Factors and Digital Divide (7) (11), Technology acceptance (Society) (9).

Impact dimension includes the following research issues: Public value (1) (10), showcasing the effects of contributions (5), Open Government (5), Transparency (5), Accountability (5), eGovernment Adoption Factors (7) (10), Public Governance and Open Government (7), Accountability, Transparency and Dissemination of Information (8), Benefits and challenges (2), Challenges and Opportunities of eGovernment (3).

5. CONCLUSIONS

eGovernment is a relatively new and multidisciplinary field and demands a variety of diverse research opportunities. Ultimately, the goal of research is to persist in spite of seemingly insurmountable boundaries and advance the field for the benefit of both researchers and practitioners (Dawes, 2009). This study can be seen as the initiation point for further studies to assess how the research in eGovernment area is evolving in terms of focal points. On the basis of this study, possible future research paths will be identified for eGovernment scholars to build on and extend its body of knowledge (Ogonek, 2017), looking at underlying perspectives and approaches to eGovernment research (Heeks, & Bailur, 2007).

The primary research question in this study focuses on research topics in the area of eGovernment. An exploration of what aspects are being explored can serve to extend the body of knowledge in the field. Insights from the past can provide direction and guidance to future studies in the field.

This study examined the field of eGovernment reviewing relative aspects at a specific point of time. A more comprehensive approach would include additional sources such as project deliverables, consulting studies, companies' reports etc. which will provide more detailed and practical insights. A future longitudinal study can be conducted to compare and contrast research practices and trends in the field of eGovernment. Further, a comparative interdisciplinary study can also be conducted to determine if patterns of research in the field of eGovernment converge with or diverge from other related disciplines, such as information systems, public administration, political and social sciences (Joseph, 2013). Additional efforts can provide an understanding of each topic area and identify research gaps, future research needs, and the development of long-term research goals and initiatives for topic areas. Overall, it is very likely that becoming more multi-disciplinary, comparative and multi-method will in the long run strengthen the theoretical capacity of eGovernment research (Yıldız, 2012). This assessment serves as the basis for a discussion of significant insights and trends related to this global phenomenon. Such insights and trends can be helpful in shaping future scholarly pursuits.

ACKNOWLEDGMENT

This paper is a result of the project "SmartEGOV: Harnessing EGOV for Smart Governance (Foundations, methods, Tools) / NORTE-01-0145-FEDER-000037", supported by Norte Portugal Regional Operational Programme (NORTE 2020), under the PORTUGAL 2020 Partnership Agreement, through the European Regional Development Fund (EFDR).

REFERENCES

Agbele, K. K., Azeez, N. A., Abidoye, A. P., Adesina, A. O., Venter, I. M., & Oyewole, A. S. (2012). Threats to e-government implementation in the civil service: Nigeria as a case study.

Androutsopoulou, A., Karacapilidis, N., Loukis, E., & Charalabidis, Y. (2019). Transforming the communication between citizens and government through AI-guided chatbots. Government Information Quarterly, 36(2), 358-367.

Bélanger, F., & Carter, L. (2012). Digitizing government interactions with constituents: an historical review of e-government research in information systems. Journal of the Association for information Systems, 13(5), 363.

Cloete, F. (2012). E-government lessons from South Africa 2001-2011: institutions, state of progress and measurement: Section II: Country perspectives on e-government emergence. The African Journal of information and communication, 2012(12), 128-142.

Cordella, A., & Iannacci, F. (2010). Information systems in the public sector: The e-Government enactment framework. The Journal of Strategic Information Systems, 19(1), 52-66.

Dawes, S. S. (2009). Governance in the digital age: A research and action framework for an uncertain future. Government Information Quarterly, 26(2), 257-264.

Dlodlo, N., Olwal, T., & Mvelase, P. (2012). The Internet of Things in bridging the gap in municipal service delivery in South Africa.

Elkadi, H. A., & Abdelsalam, H. M. (2012). e-Alexandria 2005-2010: a multi-perspective analysis: Section II: Country perspectives on e-government emergence. The African Journal of Information and Communication, 2012(12), 143-155.

Estevez, E., & Janowski, T. (2013). Electronic Governance for Sustainable Development—Conceptual framework and state of research. Government Information Quarterly, 30, S94-S109.

Fonou Dombeu, J. V., & Rannyai, N. (2014). African e-government research landscape. The African Journal of Information Systems, 6(3), 2.

Heeks, R., & Bailur, S. (2007). Analyzing e-government research: Perspectives, philosophies, theories, methods, and practice. Government information quarterly, 24(2), 243-265.

Joseph, R. C. (2013). A structured analysis of e-government studies: Trends and opportunities. Government Information Quarterly, 30(4), 435-440.

Kankanhalli, A., Zuiderwijk, A., & Tayi, G. K. (2017). Open innovation in the public sector: A research agenda.

Larsson, H., & Grönlund, Å. (2014). Future-oriented eGovernance: The sustainability concept in eGov research, and ways forward. Government Information Quarterly, 31(1), 137-149.

Nkomo, N. (2012). Implications of e-government on information delivery services. Department of Information studies, University of Zululand, South Africa.

Ogonek, N. (2017). The Tale of e-Government: A Review of the Stories that Have Been Told So Far and What is Yet to Come. In Proceedings of the 50th Hawaii International Conference on System Sciences.

Rana, N. P., Williams, M. D., Dwivedi, Y. K., & Williams, J. (2011). Reflecting on e-government research: Toward a taxonomy of theories and theoretical constructs. International Journal of Electronic Government Research (IJEGR), 7(4), 64-88.

Rodríguez Bolívar, M. P., Alcaide Muñoz, L., & López Hernández, A. M. (2010). Trends of e-government research: Contextualization and research opportunities.

Sarantis, D., Ben Dhaou, S., Alexopoulos, C., Ronzhyn, A., Viale Pereira, G., & Charalabidis, Y. (2019, May). The Evolving e-Governance Curriculum: A Worldwide mapping of Education Programs. In 12th International Conference on Theory and Practice of Electronic Governance (ICEGOV2019). ACM Press.

Scholl, H. J., & Scholl, M. (2014). Smart Governance: A Roadmap for Research and Practice. iConference. Proceedings, Berlin, March.

Snead, J. T., & Wright, E. (2014). E-government research in the United States. Government Information Quarterly, 31(1), 129-136.

Twizeyimana, J. D., & Andersson, A. (2019). The public value of E-Government–A literature review. Government Information Quarterly.

United Nations, (2016) government Survey 2016. Printed at the United Nations, New York, ISBN, pp.978-92.

Wirtz, B. W., & Daiser, P. (2018). A meta-analysis of empirical e-government research and its future research implications. International Review of Administrative Sciences, 84(1), 144-163.

Wray, C., & Van Olst, R. (2012). Enabling g-government in the Gauteng city-region: Section I: Themes and approaches to inform e-strategies. The African Journal of Information and Communication, 2012(12), 65-83.

Yıldız, M. (2012). Big questions of e-government research. Information Polity, 17(3, 4), 343-355.

5G EDGE NETWORK ACCELERATION FOR CROWD EVENTS

Alexandros Kostopoulos[1], Ioannis P. Chochliouros[1], Daniele Munaretto[2], Claus Keuker[3] and Ioannis Giannoulakis[4]
[1]*Hellenic Telecommunications Organization S.A. (OTE), Greece*
[2]*Athonet*
[3]*Smart Mobile Labs*
[4]*NCRS "Demokritos"*

ABSTRACT

The 5G ESSENCE Project investigates the concept of Edge cloud computing and Small Cell-as-a-Service (SCaaS). One of the selected use cases is called "5G edge network acceleration at stadium", which is focused on content distribution during crowd events. The paper describes the service VNFs and network services for 5G-based video production and video distribution into a football stadium.

KEYWORDS

5G, Cloud-enabled Small Cell (CESC), Network Functions Virtualization (NFV), Radio Resource Management (RRM)

1. INTRODUCTION

The 5G ESSENCE (5GESSENCE, 2017) effort "opens the door" to venue owners (e.g., municipalities, stadiums, site owners) and virtually anyone who manages a property and can install and run a local Small Cell (SC) network, to deploy a low cost infrastructure and to act as "neutral host network and service provider". Although probably none of such entities would offer static network coverage, many of them could foresee adequate chances for profits generated by exploiting the 5G ESSENCE concepts of multitenant small cells, able to provide wireless network coverage coupled with added-value services in close proximity to customers and visitors that belong to multiple network operators and vertical industries.

Broadcasters are looking for new ways to cover events, to offer exciting point-of-view perspectives to viewers on one hand, and to reduce production and delivery costs on the other. At the same time, network operators "target" to increase the usage of their networks and stadium owners have a strong interest in making the spectators' experience "as pleasant as possible", as well as increasing side-revenues through sponsor advertisement. The reception of live content from cameras located in the playing field, replays, and additional contextual information on mobile devices, is a strong use case for all the above actors. The main challenges even with 4G networks are the delay in the delivery of such content in the range of milliseconds rather than seconds, and the considerable strain imposed on the backhaul network. By deploying a 5G ESSENCE network, these challenges can be efficiently addressed.

In this paper, we focus on one of the selected use cases, which considers content distribution during crowd events. We describe the service VNFs and network services for 5G-based video production and video distribution into a football stadium. The paper is outlined as follows: Section 2 describes the considered use case. Section 3 presents the network functions for providing 5G services. Section 4 provides our testbed architecture overview. We conclude our remarks and present our future work in Section 5.

2. USE CASE DESCRIPTION

The 5G ESSENCE delivers benefits to media producers and mobile operators, enabling them to offer a highly interactive fan experience and to optimise operations by deploying key functionalities at the edge (i.e., evolved Multimedia Broadcast Multicast Services (eMBMS) together with multitenancy support from small cells). By leveraging the benefits of small cell virtualisation and radio resource abstraction, as well as by optimising network embedded cloud, it becomes possible to "ease" the coverage and capacity pressure on the multimedia infrastructure, and also to increase security since content will remain locally.

Furthermore, additional benefits for the operators and the venue owners arise such as: (i) *lower latency, due to shortening the data transmission path*, and; (ii) *increased backhaul capacity*, due to playing out the live feeds and replays locally that puts no additional strain on the backhaul network and upstream core network components. The 5G ESSENCE project will demonstrate a combined 5G-based video production and video distribution towards delivering benefits to both media producers and mobile operators, who will be able to offer enriched event experience to their subscribers. The production/distribution of locally generated content through the 5G ESSENCE platform, coupled with value-added services and rich user context, will enable secure, high-quality and resilient transmission, in real-time and with minimal latency.

In the context of the 5G ESSENCE infrastructure sharing support, each network operator will be in position to optimise his network usage, resulting in lower OPEX. Additionally, network operators will be able to rapidly deploy new services, to deliver directly to users higher Quality of Experience (QoE), and to offer "Content as-a-Service", increased bandwidth and storage solutions to content providers and venue owners. The content providers will also benefit from reduced latency and improved user QoE by positioning content on mobile edge and, in addition, they can offer augmented services by leveraging the network information. Finally, the stadium owner will obtain additional benefits by leveraging the deployed 5G ESSENCE infrastructure and its functionalities, by capitalising live content to spectators from many cameras, statistics, etc.

The scenario provides the logic for distributing the live video feeds received from the local production room to local spectators in a highly efficient manner. The municipal football stadium "Stavros Mavrothalassitis" will be covered with a cluster of multitenant, eMBMS enabled as CESCs (Cloud Enabled Small Cells) and, together with the CESCM and the Main DC, they can be connected to the core networks (CNs) of multiple telecom operators. The video content from cameras will be sent for processing locally at the Edge DC (similar to the proposed use case by ETSI MEC). Then the video streams will be broadcasted locally using the CESCs and spectators will be able to dynamically select between different streams offered. In this and in similar massive event scenarios, the data traffic will not impact the backhaul connection since it will be produced, processed and consumed locally. Figure 1 provides a high-level architecture of the 5G ESSENCE according. The specific components and the interfaces are described in more detail in (Chochliouros, 2017) and (Kostopoulos, 2018).

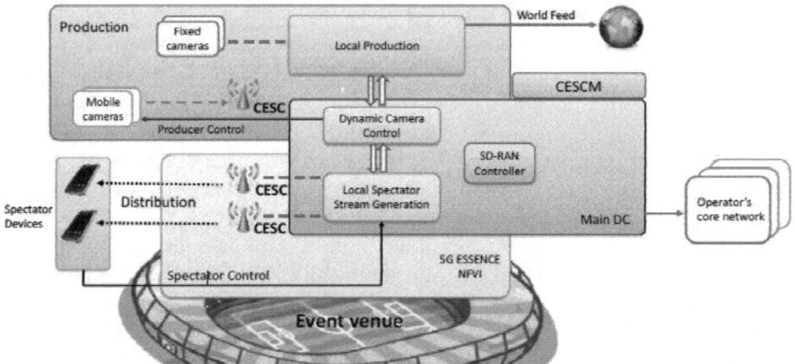

Figure 1. 5G edge network acceleration at stadium

3. NETWORK FUNCTIONS FOR 5G SERVICES

3.1 eMBMS Core

The eMBMS, is the simplest and most cost-effective way to deploy LTE Broadcast services to deliver video, software updates and other broadcast applications. The software solution can be: (i) *centralized* to connect to an existing MNO network, or; (ii) *distributed to specific locations* (e.g. in a stadium) to create localized LTE

Broadcast hotspots without affecting the existing network. The eMBMS solution includes the Mobility Management Entity (MME), MBMS Gateway (MBMS-GW) and Broadcast Multicast Service Center (BMSC). It can be deployed in conjunction with our distributed EPC, for best user experience, or as a standalone implementation.

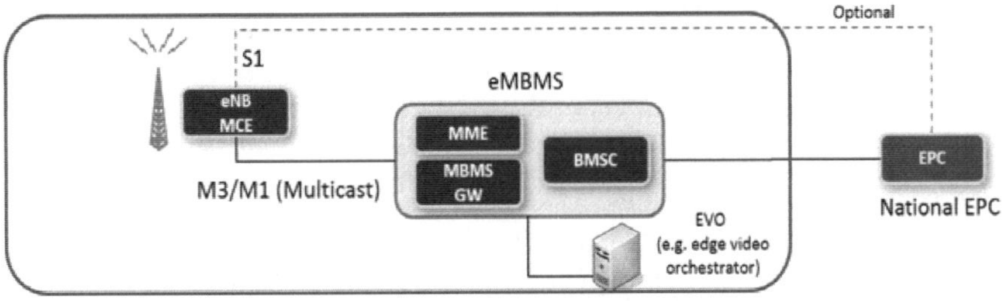

Figure 2. eMBMS core architecture

3.2 vEPC

The vEPC includes the HSS (Home Subscriber Server), P-GW (Packet Data Network Gateway), SGW (Serving Gateway), MME (Mobility Management Entity) and PCRF (Policy and Charging Rules Function). It comes with a fully web-based GUI for ease of configuration and management and extensive set of APIs for simple integration with mobile operator or enterprise OSS/BSS. It can be deployed either centralised or highly distributed on public cloud (e.g. AWS, Azure, Google, IBM, Oracle) or private cloud (e.g. telco cloud), enterprise data centres or on standard COTS servers running on Intel or ARM. Control Plane (CP) and User Plane (UP) functionalities can be distributed between central and edge-clouds or hardware nodes to enable hybrid-cloud, fog-computing or MEC type deployments.

3.3 Edge Video Orchestrator (EVO)

The deployment of the Edge Video Orchestrator service for the use case in stadium, consists of a single VNF. The VNF is running on the main DC. Its network address and ports are transparently seen by the entities that connect to it. The service is implemented with the help of the docker container technology running in a native network configuration within the VNF virtual machine (VM). The EVO VNF is connected to the BMSC. The EVO uses this entity to convey eMBMS traffic to the entities that are receiving the EVO's streams, called "stream-receivers". The entities that provide streams to the EVO, called as "stream-providers", are also connected to the EVO VNF.

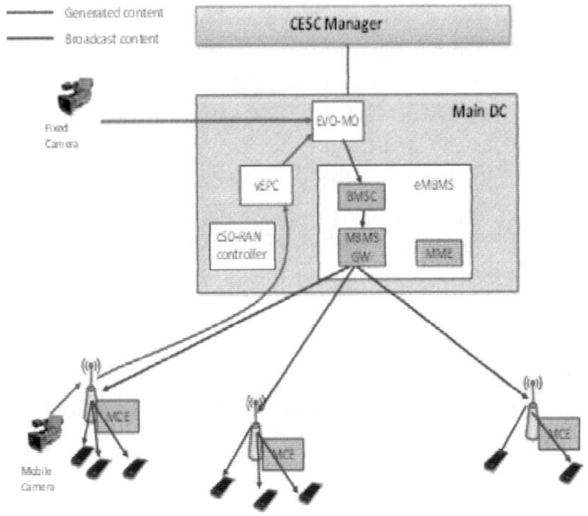

Figure 3. Overall service VNF placement

Considering a proper selection from the aforementioned facilities, the selected facility will be covered with a cluster of eMBMS enabled CESCs and, together with the Main DC, can be connected to the core networks of multiple telecom operators. The video content from cameras will be sent for processing locally at the Edge (similar to the proposed use case by ETSI MEC (5GIA, 2019), (ETSI, 2019), (ETSI, 2017a), (ETSI, 2017b), (ETSI, 2017c), (ETSI, 2017d). Then the video streams will be broadcasted locally by using the 3GPP eMBMS functionality. Spectators will be able to dynamically select among different offered broadcast streams. In this and in similar big event scenarios, massive data traffic will not affect -nor overload- the backhaul connection as it will be produced, processed and consumed just locally (i.e., the case of the 5G MEC scenario, aligned to the 5G 3GPP specifications (ETSI, 2017e), (3GPP, 2017a), (3GPP, 2017b), (DreamChip, 2019)).

3.3.1 Service Overview

The use case provides a set of services related to live video streaming. One of the "key" aspects is the lowest possible glass-to-glass latency of video streams. Glass-to-glass latency denotes the time needed for a scene in front of the camera glass to be detected, encoded, transmitted, decoded and rendered onto the display of the stream-receiver. This, in fact, increases the level immersion into the venue as it allows even distant observers to both see the original scene as well as additional videos of the same at the same instant in time.

The observer has a smart phone application which shows those additional video streams. The smartphone app allows the user to see a set of video streams in an overview-like layout. The number of video views in this mode is configurable within the application. The video views have a lower resolution and corresponding bitrate (SD resolution, around 0.8 Mbits/s bitrate) in order to limit the resource usage on the network and on the phone, itself. When touching one of the Multi View videos, an overlay showing stream name and current bitrate appears. On each of the video views, the actual stream to be shown can be chosen by the user. In parallel to switching to the full screen mode, the application stops the preview (SD) version of the stream and internally requests a high bitrate version of the same stream (HD view). Consequently, the user can watch the chosen camera perspective in high quality.

3.3.2 Service End-points

The Edge Video Orchestrator provides a REST API access its services. This REST API is used by the clients to seamlessly integrate with the system. Services offered by the EVO include, but are not limited to:

- Register new cameras;
- Query the list of streams available on the system;
- Request to receive a specified stream, or;
- Simulcast transmission of streams.

The next figure illustrates the overview of the system. Each connection to the EVO consists of two specific types of connections, as follows:

- **Control plane connection:** This connection is always implemented as a unicast connection. It carries control information or control requests that allow the EVO to manage the respective streaming operation. Typical content are authorization data or stream identification information.
- **User plane data:** Here, video and audio data are transmitted by using a connectionless protocol. Real-Time protocol (RTP) is used as a transport protocol. Additional protocol levels on top of RTP might be encryption or forward error correction (FEC) protocols.

Stream-providers typically may be active on the control plane and have several user plane streams, depending on the number of stream that the specific stream-provider announces. Regular encoders do announce the following elementary streams: high bitrate video stream, low bitrate video stream, and audio stream.

Devices integrated with the EVO system contain a software entity that communicates with the EVO with the help of the control plane and provide the correctly negotiated transport mechanisms. In order to have the sources/sinks of the streams not abstracted from the exact nature of the EVO interaction, the EVO Core SDK is introduced. The latter manages all EVO specific actions. The EVO Core SDK can be either directly used as a programming library or it can be embedded into a standalone application (throughout this document called Orchestrator Interactor – OCI). This approach eases the integration of new devices/ use cases into the EVO.

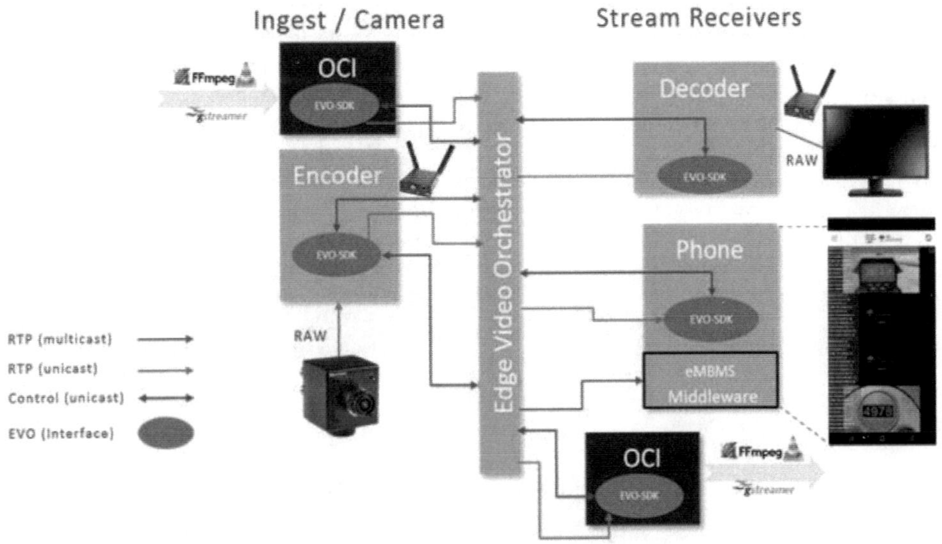

Figure 4. Overall system architecture

3.3.3 Client Types

For the planned use case several types of stream-providers and stream-receivers will be used, as described below.

Encoder types: Encoders of type "Dream Chip - Targa" will be used as stream providers for static cameras. Those encoders are integrated with the EVO system and natively support the EVO control plane interface. Targa transmitter is designed to enable TV broadcasts over LTE networks. This allows real-time video transmission into the cloud or any broadcast studio in the world with an incredibly low latency. Users can watch the content anywhere, anytime and with any device, whether it is mobile phone, tablet, laptop or PC. Targa transmitter is battery powered with a built-in rechargeable battery. It works without any cables to support easy mounting on humans, animals, vehicles or any special equipment. This transmitter has dedicated broadcasting functions and supports simultaneous dual video streaming, meaning one high resolution stream for the broadcast audience and one low resolution stream for preview of, for example, multiple camera views, both H.264 encoded. Additionally, Targa can store both streams on the local Flash Drive for remote playback, if the real-time transmission is interrupted due to unknown reasons.

Decoder types: Targa receiver is a compact video and audio decoder which is designed for TV broadcast applications. It is attached to LAN Networks using its Ethernet port. This receiver can decode SD and HD H.264 encoded elementary video streams and AAC audio streams. It features an integrated deinterlacer and scaler, which automatically upscales SD content to HD resolutions. The receiver supports professional video interfaces like HD-SDI and HDMI with integrated audio output. Additionally, it includes an analog audio output. When used in combination with a Targa transmitter, the receiver has several unique functions:

- *VPN-Tunnel*: The transmitter can connect to the receiver over an encrypted VPN tunnel for data security, and;
- *Audio Return Channel*: The receiver can record from analog audio input and stream it to the transmitter. This can, for example, be used by producers to give directions to the camera operators.

3.3.4 Transcoding Services

The EVO architecture foresees the transmission of two quality versions of a stream in order to manage wireless bandwidth usage in case of unicast transport. The encoding systems seamlessly integrated with the SML approach support this simulcasting already on the camera/encoder devices. However, in use case demonstration we will use an off-the-shelf 360° camera device and, therefore, the SD version of the stream has to be created elsewhere. For simplicity purposes, we chose to run the transcoding process on the EVO VNF itself. The transcoding process takes the original 360° video stream and forwards it to the normal EVO switching engine.

However, it also downscales the video of 3460x2560 to a low-resolution SD variant. It also reduces the bitrate from 8 Mbits/s (or higher) to 0.8 Mbits/s. The transcoder is connected to the EVO via an edge OCI process handling the EVO communication and protocols.

For this use case, we chose a transcoding process implemented in pure software. This simplifies the platform choice for the demonstration. In a real application it would be much more efficient to employ specific HW enabled encoding through graphic cards. This dramatically increases the capacity of the overall system and logically separates the CPU-intensive transcoding work from the network-centric EVO operation.

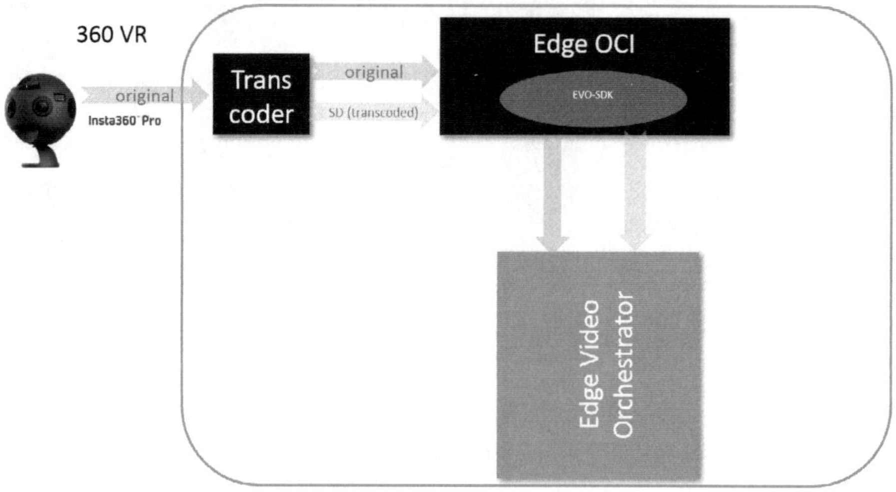

Figure 5. Transcoding for 360° video

3.3.5 Streaming to External Sources

The EVO-MO can also be configured to stream-to-stream receivers which do not support the EVO CP protocols natively. For example, the streams can be transcoded and transmuxed, such that *Facebook/YouTube* streaming servers can receive it.

3.3.6 Recording

The EVO system has the notion of "decoders"; those are virtual software entities or can be represented by hardware entities to which streams can be sent. Recording decoders are software entities which store the streams into .mp4 files. By this mechanism, all streams can be recorded for later playout or inspection.

3.3.7 Monitoring

The EVO system has several monitoring levels for performance verification. The provided figures help the operator to identify potential resource shortages, such as CPU or memory overload. This information is available by REST APIs and can be used in other management tools to visualize long-term trends or to be used in billing processes. In use cases with bigger number of users, this information is also used for load balancing between different EVO instances and/or to decide whether additional EVO instances need to be created. It is also possible to use this information for load management with the EVO instance itself. The EVO-MO supports to limit:

- The number of outgoing streams in order to limit the outgoing network occupancy, or;
- the number of users connected to an EVO instance. This is mostly used implicitly to limit the number of streams, but also to limit the control plane load on the EVO.

When a load limit is reached, new stream-receivers are rejected with an error code that the system capacity has reached.

4. TESTBED ARCHITECTURE OVERVIEW

The local video production and distribution through eMBMS will be ultimately performed in the Egaleo Stadium. However, the integrations, development and testing along the 5G ESSENCE project will be performed across testbeds made available by selected partners and connected among each other. The cloud testbed that will be used for the duration of the 5G ESSENCE, to enable this use case, consists of three different site deployments: the interconnected sites are located approximately 10-15 kilometres apart and their interconnection is based on microwave links. All three sites use a common base infrastructure, but each one has different features.

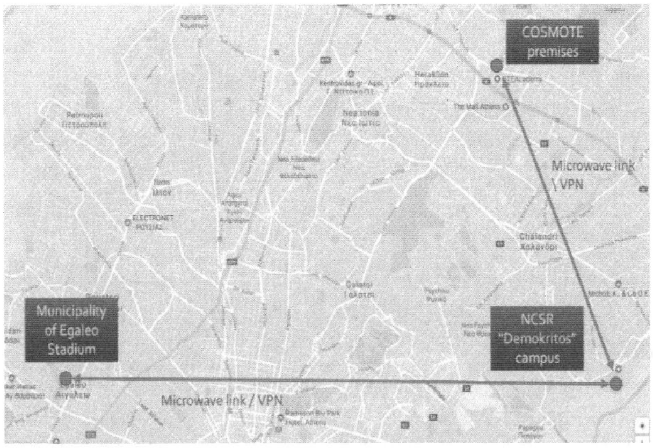

Figure 6. Map of the three testbed sites for the 5G ESSENCE pilot

The campus of *NCSR "Demokritos" (NCSRD)*, in north-east Athens, is a 150-acre area, combining indoor and outdoor environments, covered by five software-driven 5G wireless nodes and supported by an optical backbone. In particular, the experimental setup at the campus of NCSR "Demokritos" comprises five main parts: the core network; the backhaul network; the access network; mobile terminals connecting to the access network, and; distributed cloud deployments with computing, storage and networking resources.

The infrastructure provided by NCSRD consists of a macro-cell located at a high mast, covering a wider area, within the campus and three small cells that serve focused coverage areas. Both the macro-cell and small cells are purely software-defined (SD), in the sense that: (i) they are driven by fully reconfigurable and open SDR equipment, and; (ii) they also feature edge computing equipment ("light Data Centres") for hosting virtual appliances. All radio access points are connected to a core facility (currently based on LTE EPC) through dedicated fibre links. The testbed also features micro-servers integrated in each macro/small cell, according to the Cloud-Enabled Small Cell (CESC) concept. These micro-servers create a distributed Network Function Virtualisation Infrastructure (NFVI). In this manner, CESCs are both edge computing-capable and multitenant, enabling a small cell infrastructure to be shared among multiple tenants. Edge services deployed in the CESCs include several VNFs (vDPI, Security Appliance, Network Monitoring) as well as of virtualized appliances (Transcoder, Video analysis for object recognition).

The core functions (EPC) are also located on site. The EPCs from different vendors have been tested. The eNodeBs (Small Cells and Macro-Cell) are connected to the EPC over different types of backhaul links (fibre, RF, copper). User Equipments (UEs) of various types have been tested (mobile phones by various vendors, laptops equipped with appropriate dongles, software-defined UEs based on SDN platforms). All types of UEs have embedded USIMs, appropriate for authentication to the EPC. The testbed also hosts a core Cloud/SDN experimental platform for the experimentation needs of the 5G ESSENCE project. The cloud infrastructure is based on the OpenStack Cloud Operating System, comprising of 18 compute nodes and storage system supporting SAS (Serial Attached SCSI) and iSCSI (Internet Small Computer System Interface).

The NCSRD testbed also features SDN-enabled network devices, as well as legacy devices including firewalling and routing equipment. Finally, the NCSRD site connects to the Internet via the national NREN (GRNET), using a dedicated hardware firewall whose rules are fully customizable. VPN access is possible, via SSL and IPSec connections.

The *OTE building (OTEAcademy)*, to the north of the Maroussi-Athens city is a multi-functional complex, combining various indoor and outdoor usage scenarios. The testbed includes an OpenStack-based cloud infrastructure, consisting of 1 gateway, 5 controllers, 4 x86 + 2 ARM -based compute nodes, a VPN Server, switches/routers, while being interconnected to OTE's labs, providing thus additional capabilities for testing new technologies either for PoC or for field trials. The OTE testbed includes eight Nokia 4G/4G+/Wi-Fi small cells, a flexible end-to-end (E2E) IoT platform, as well as a broadband connection over GRNET [10], serving as backhaul link.

The *Egaleo stadium*, in west Athens, is going to be an actual "field" testbed, supporting a wide variety of real-life scenarios, ranging from massive MTC to flash crowd events. The Egaleo municipal stadium "Stavros Mavrothalassitis" is a football ground located in Egaleo, in the west of Athens. The stadium was built in 1966 and totally renovated in 2006. The stadium belongs to the Municipality of Egaleo (MoE) and its capacity is 8.217 (seated) spectators. The stadium is used by the football team of Egaleo (Egaleo FC). In addition to the football matches, the stadium is used for various events, such as music concerts. In general, the Egaleo municipal stadium is a modern stadium and has all the appropriate facilities and infrastructures. The infrastructure at the Egaleo municipal stadium aims at showcasing the value of 5G in big sports and/or cultural events. The access part of the infrastructure is based on three low-power cells, covering the entire stadium, integrated with local virtualization-capable IT resources, thus forming CESCs. The capability of the CESCs to be multi-tenant and to host edge services enable a new business model, under which the CESC infrastructure is owned by the stadium operator (rather than by MNOs), who, in turn, leases slices to MNOs, MVNOs and enterprise users. The stadium is connected to the main site of the testbed (NCSR "Demokritos"), where the core functions are expected to reside, with a backhaul point-to-point microwave link. A VPN over the Internet also exists, as a fall-back solution.

5. DISCUSSION

5G ESSENCE has focused on preparing an inventory of assets and resources which will be available during the integration and validation of the "5G Edge Network Acceleration at a Stadium" use case. Moreover, the preparation of the demonstration campaign has taken place. During this period, the *service VNFs* (i.e., hardware-accelerated video encoder/decoder, virtual Caching, transcoding, etc.) and *network services* for 5G-based video production and video distribution into a football stadium have been developed and fine-tuned, in order to "match" the stadium use case specific requirements. Also the setup, the demo configuration and the integration of 5G ESSENCE specific tools to the adjusted testbed that will be deployed at the football stadium have been finalized.

REFERENCES

3GPP TS 23.501 v15.0.0, "System Architecture for the 5G System; Stage 2 (Release 15)", December 2017.

3GPP TS 23.502 v15.0.0, "Procedures for the 5G System; Stage 2 (Release 15)", December 2017.

5G ESSENCE H2020 5G-PPP Project.

A. Kostopoulos, I. Chochliouros, I. Giannoulakis, A. Kourtis, E. Kafetzakis. "Small Cells-as-a-Service in 5G Networks". IEEE BMSB, June, 2018, Valencia, Spain.

Dream Chip website. Available at: https://www.dreamchip.de/home.html.

ETSI GS NFV-MAN 001 http://www.etsi.org/deliver/etsi_gs/NFV-MAN/001_099/001/01.01.01_60/gs_NFV-MAN001v010101p.pdf

ETSI Multi-access Edge Computing (MEC), http://www.etsi.org/technologies-clusters/technologies/multi-access-edge-computing

I. Chochliouros, A. Kostopoulos, I. Giannoulakis, A. Spiliopoulou, M. Belesioti, E. Sfakianakis, A. Kourtis, E. Kafetzakis. "Using Small Cells for Enhancing 5G Network Facilities". IEEE NFV-SDN NFVPN, Berlin, Germany, November, 2017.

Location API- GS MEC 013 http://www.etsi.org/deliver/etsi_gs/MEC/001_099/013/01.01.01_60/gs_MEC013v010101p.pdf

Mobile Edge Management; Part 2- GS MEC 010-2 http://www.etsi.org/deliver/etsi_gs/MEC/001_099/01002/01.01.01_60/gs_MEC01002v010101p.pdf

Mobile Edge Platform Application Enablement-GS MEC 011 http://www.etsi.org/deliver/etsi_gs/MEC/001_099/011/01.01.01_60/gs_MEC011v010101p.pdf

Radio Network Information API- GS MEC 012 http://www.etsi.org/deliver/etsi_gs/MEC/001_099/012/01.01.01_60/gs_MEC012v010101p.pdf

White papers from the 5G Infrastructure Association, available at https://5g-ppp.eu/white-papers/

OPEN GOVERNMENT PROPOSAL FOR TRANSPARENCY AND INFORMATION ACCESS IN COSTA RICA

Franchesca Rodriguez-Arias[1] and Roberto Cortes-Morales[2]
[1]*Master Program on Management for Information Technologies, Instituto Tecnológico de Costa Rica*
San José, Costa Rica
[2]*Graduate Department of Computing School, Instituto Tecnológico de Costa Rica*
Cartago, Costa Rica

ABSTRACT

This research deals with a public issue that affects many countries around the world, which is transparency. Therefore, an Open Government solution is proposed to face this problem. Through the multidimensional analysis, the current situation in Costa Rica can be assessed while best practices in Taiwan are identified to propose a roadmap that can be adopted in Costa Rica. Taiwan is one of the countries with the best open data index. Using comparative study case analysis, the research proposes how to implement Open Government in Costa Rica improving transparency and access to information offered by the State to general public.

KEYWORDS

Costa Rica, Taiwan, Open-government, Open-data, e-Government, Multidimensional Analysis

1. INTRODUCTION

The solution of public problems can be approached from a multidimensional analysis (Cortes-Morales, 2017), which aims to identify several key factors in potential solutions to be offered. In Digital Government solutions, this type of analysis allows us to cover not only the technological dimension, but also other factors that include the economic, political, administrative and social dimensions. Furthermore, it can identify actors, resources and variables for designing public policies that may provide solutions for specific problems generating public value. Through this analysis, the objective of this research is to propose an open government solution to improve transparency and access to information offered to citizens and other users of the public administration. Moreover, the proposal includes the creation of a knowledge repository intended to facilitate decision-making processes, not only for public managers, but also citizens and companies. The success of Taiwan in this domain has been taken as a reference for the multidimensional analysis to generate a proposal based on best practices that may solve issues related to transparency and information access in Costa Rica.

The article was organized as follows: in Section 2 the problem is contextualized. Section 3 contains the theoretical references that underlie the research. Section 4 defines the methodology used in this work. Section 5 develops the case analysis for the current situation of Costa Rica and presents a proposal based on Taiwan experience. Finally, conclusions of the research are presented in section 6.

2. PROBLEM CONTEXT

According to the results obtained by the Transparency Index of the Costa Rican Public Sector (ITSP) in 2018, the national average of transparency is of 34.55%, while access to information is 50.15% and open data availability just 21.20 %, as shown in Figure 1.

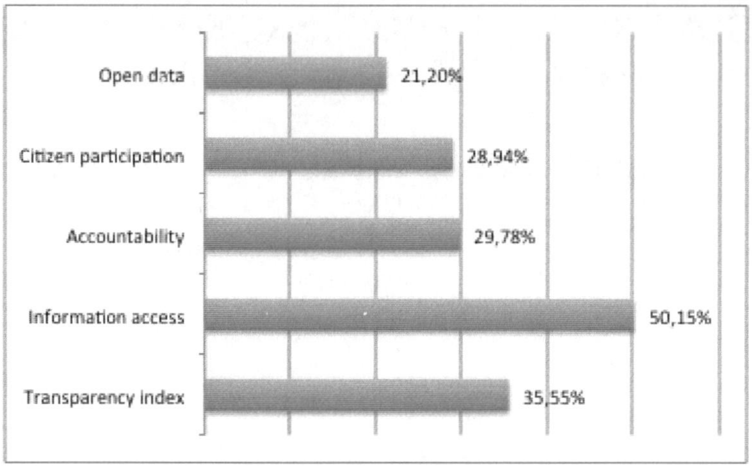

Figure 1. Transparency Index of Costa Rica's Public Sector (Costa Rica Citizen Defense Office, 2018)

The results shown in Figure 1 were obtained from the analysis of 254 Public Institutions. Considering that the transparency index of Costa Rica is 35%, it means that 166 institutions surveyed did not comply with the established parameters. An immediate conclusion is that an improvement in transparency offered by the institutions to citizens is required. Moreover, access to information is 50% representing that about 126 institutions do not provide access to information generated. Additionally, it is shown that just 21% of institutions under have an open data portal.

The survey was conducted analyzing information gathered from institution's web site. Thus, the issue corresponds in general in the way that the State provides public information to public.

Currently Costa Rica has an Open Government portal, however, it is outdated in most of the data it offers. This portal captures data coming from the different public institutions. Observing the results of the ITSP, it is concluded that the different Institutions do not provide the required data to the portal.

Additionally, Costa Rica has been making efforts to become a member of the Organization for Economic Cooperation and Development (OECD). Here is mandatory for Costa Rica to comply with OECD's requirement such as democracy, trust and progress. (OECD, 2018). Therefore, it is imperative to solve problems of openness and transparency to comply with the standards stipulated by this Organization.

3. THEORETICAL APPROACH

The research is based on the theoretical approaches of Digital Government, multidimensional analysis and Open Government. Digital Government refers to the use of technology and communications under modernization strategies to create public value. This includes government actors, non-governmental organizations, companies, citizen associations that support production and access to data, services and content, through interaction with the Government. (Pimiento, 2017)

In turn, Public Value is defined by (Moore & Khagram, 2004), as the means to establish a shared value in society, which allows resources to be invested to create a strategic triangle that provides legitimacy and operational capabilities for the implementation of public value.

Additionally (Pimiento, 2017), mentions some benefits offered by the implementation of digital government strategies, such as competitiveness, good governance, transparency, quality of service, innovation and empowerment.

Using Digital Government typologies proposed by (Fountain, 2001) described also in (UNPAN, 2010), the proposal focuses into the following ones: Government for Citizens (G2C) and Government to Business (G2B), because it looks to provide services to citizens and enterprises whom may have access to data and information efficiently. Also, Government to Government (G2G), taking into account that it allows communication between Institutions and the transfer of information in an efficient and up-to-date manner. Finally, Government for Knowledge (G4K) due to the proposal should provide a knowledge base for decision-making, and by having a collection of historical data, action can be taken on State acquisitions and also have a repository of good practices and lessons learned in different areas that can be applied into the different institutions. As can be noticed, the proposal is transversal to all class of digital government types.

Through the Multidimensional Analysis, an analysis is performed from the political, economic, administrative, social and technological dimensions. This allows a broader approach to the problem and the proposed solution. In this approach, we aim to find evidence in the different dimensions and identify actors to validate the feasibility of the proposal.

For actors' identification, we use the typology proposed in (Subirats et al., 2008): actors are individuals or groups defending a position regarding a public problem. Those actors can be categorized as public or private, and among those categories can be beneficiaries or objectives. In turn, those actors have veto power and support in decision-making (Cortés-Morales, 2017).

Open Data is defined as information displayed on the web in a tabular format of numbers, statistics, metrics, micro and macroeconomic data, geo-referenced or not, of all types of subject, without intellectual property restriction or control mechanisms in terms of access. In addition, it has three basic characteristics: accessible, interoperable and reusable. (Durán, 2013)

Under this open data concept, the Open Government and transparency policies are based. Therefore, Open Government can be defined as *"a new paradigm and model of relationship between governments, administrations and society: transparent, multidirectional, collaborative and oriented to the participation of citizens in both monitoring and public decision-making, from whose platform or action space it is possible to catalyze, articulate and create public value from and beyond the borders of the state bureaucracies"* (CEPAL, 2019).

In summary the research has used an approach where knowledge came from the perspectives above described such as digital government, multidimensional analysis, actors and public policies and open government.

4. METHODOLOGICAL APPROACH

Transparency in the State is a public problem. That's why we use a public policy approach (Subirats et al., 2008) where the definition of phases (problem identification, formulation, decision, among others) is important, both for academics or practitioners. In addition, public problems can be approached using multidimensional analysis where the definition of key factors in political, economic, social, administrative and technological dimensions looks to provide a scope for a solution focused not only on information technologies, but on generating public value identifying the challenges on those dimensions.

Using the comparative case study strategy (Yin, 2014), the multidimensional analysis allows the comparison of dimensions in different contexts, in order to obtain success factors and generate a proposal that can be adapted to the Costa Rican context from the experience of Taiwan. Here we have proposed to gather information that in turn has been mapped to the specific dimensions the could clarify the context of the success of Taiwan while is also used to compare Costa Rica's current characteristics and to project recommendations for a solution. For example, laws, decrees, actors' support and other political variables has been analyzed both at Costa Rica and Taiwan. Budgeting, funding in the economical dimensions also has been taken into account for both countries, and we have followed such logic in the remaining dimensions (administrative, technological and social). Combining the comparative case study research with the methodology of multidimensional analysis, we have deduced the strategy to overcome the weakness of Costa Rica's lack of transparency.

5. MODEL APPLICATION

5.1 Costa Rica's Case

5.1.1 Political Dimension

In this dimension, Costa Rica has created alliances with different agencies and open data programs and has developed a series of laws and decrees that are described below.

In January 2012, Costa Rica joins the multilateral initiative "Alliance for Open Government". In March 2014, the initiative for the "Promotion of Open Government in Public Institutions and Creation of the Open Government Intersectoral Commission" was established by resolution n ° 38276-RE-MIDEPLAN-MICITT.

In April 2017, the 40199-MP decree and government guideline nº 074-MP on "Opening Open Data" was published. The decree n ° 40199-MP indicates the way the Open Government will be implemented. The Ministry of the Presidency coordinates the Commission of Open Data. Furthermore, it mentions the creation of a Technical Secretary for the National Public Data Opening Policy, who is responsible for ensuring the execution of the policy, the action plans and the creation of instruments that lead to the availability and use of public open data. Moreover, it was established a progressive implementation where annual plans must be submitted to the Technical Secretariat. Finally, the decree establishes that, after two years, the implementation will be analyzed, and improvements or corrective actions will be carried out.

Following the typology mentioned on previous section, key actors from the described institutional framework can be identified:

Table 1. Costa Rica´s Actors' for Open Government Strategy

Type	Dependence or Origin	Actors
Public	National Commission for Open Government (CNGA)	Secretary of Communication Secretary of Finance and Treasury Secretary of Planning Secretary of Justice and Peace Ministry of Science, Technology and Telecommunications
	Technical Secretary of the CNGA	To be defined
Objective	Public institutions	Institutions that must keep the data open and updated
Beneficiaries	Costa Rican Union of Enterprises	President of the Enterprise Unions
	Costa Rica Intact	President of Intact Organization
	Association citizen center of studies for the open society (ACCESA)	President of ACCESA
	National Council of Public Universities	President of the Council
	Citizens	Enhanced interaction between the state and citizens is expected, as well as greater transparency and accessibility to data.
	Public institutions Private business	Both public and private organizations will have access to information

Some actors like "Costa Rica Intact" and National Council of Public Universities are included. Those Non-Government actors are intended for supporting the strategy for Open Government.

5.1.2 Economical Dimension

In this dimension, the Secretary of the Presidency coordinates the CNGA (who is the actor with the most confidence from the President); so, the project can be supported (hypothetically) with high support. However, since it involves several Public Institutions, each institution is required to allocate resources to support the initiative and looking to ensure that data is 100% up-to-date. No evidences (like budget or other actions) are clear in this support.

5.1.3 Social Dimension

In this dimension, Costa Rica it would be fixing a social problem from the perspectives of transparency, access, participation and accountability. It seeks to have more State / Citizen participation and obtain a transparent State with information constantly updated.

5.1.4 Administrative Dimension

In this dimension, the 3rd Plan of Action of the Alliance for Open Government is defined, which covers the period from November 2017 to August 2019. In it, social and sustainable development commitments are detailed for the institutions involved.

5.1.5 Technological Dimension

Currently, Costa Rica has an open government portal, which offers an API for information publishing. However, most of the information is outdated, revealing a lack of commitment in previous dimensions such as administrative and/or political. As part of the process of publishing information, validation of the data to be published must be carried out.

5.2 Taiwan's Open Government Case Reference

The Taiwan project for the implementation of an Open Government has allowed a greater relationship between the State and citizens, thus it is selected as a reference point for the case under study. In addition, Taiwan is selected for the similarity in territorial dimension it has with Costa Rica, this being considered a positive factor compared to other countries. In turn, both countries have laws that support the initiative of open data, transparency and access to information; Therefore, the strategy that Taiwan has implemented is seen as a success story, and can be a guide for Costa Rica.

The open data strategy in Taiwan is done by the publication of the Free Government Information Law, the Administrative Procedures Act and other legislations that were enacted and put into practice. The process of publishing the information was done gradually. (Tung-Mou, Jin, Hui-Ju, & Jing, 2013)

On the other hand, they have a value chain for the reuse of information and government data, that are composed of the following stages:

- Production and collection stage.
- The storage stages.
- The distribution stages.
- The adoption and value-added stage.
- The stage of marketing and providing service to end users.

As mentioned by Pin-Yu & Hsein-Lee (2018), Taiwan has been implementing its Open Data policy based on three principles and four strategies. The three principles are:

- Open data for public and Enterprise use.
- Free cost as a principle, charging as the exception.
- Automatic and systematic release and exchange of large volume of data.

The four strategies are:

- Proactive release of data and emphasis on people's welfare first, e.g., consumer data as priority.
- Drafting regulations for open data, e.g., Open Government Data Principles.
- Promotion of public use platform, e.g., the Open Data Platform.
- Demonstration, advocacy and promotion of services e.g. define scope for trial and encourage value addition and application.

In addition, according to Pin-Yu & Hsein-Lee (2018), since 2014 it has expanded to groups that work together with the Government in order to participate and cooperate to promotion of open data.

On the other hand, it is not only for public use. Government agencies also use open data produced by other agencies for the creation of networks and for cooperation purposes.

Some interesting facts about the implementation of Open Government in Taiwan are:

- Until September 15, 2017, the OGD platform has more than 30,090 data sets and 172 public application interfaces (APIs). Most of the datasets in the OGD platform are 3 stars, this means the data sets are available as machine-readable structured data plus a non-proprietary format.

- Open Knowledge International association has published global open data index 2016, showing that Taiwan topped the index for two consecutive years. Among the 15 key categories used to measure the state of open government data, Taiwan led 12 with 100 percent openness, such as land ownership, location and weather forecast, administrative boundaries, air quality, company register, draft legislation, election results, government budget, national maps, national statistics and procurement.
- NDC said the government would continue promoting OGD and releasing accurate and easy-to-use public data in a timely manner. The government will also collaborate with the private sector to ensure Taiwan continues to be an international reference point in this regard. (Pin-Yu & Hsein-Lee, 2018)

5.3 Proposed Solution for Costa Rica

According to the analysis carried out in the experience of Taiwan, a solution is proposed for Costa Rica that seeks to take advantage of previous efforts and try to achieve similar achievements to those of Taiwan. Having an updated Open Government platform, which currently exists in Costa Rica can be visualized as the "corner-stone" of the strategy. To do this, the proposal is described in four phases, this being a difference in how it was implemented in Taiwan, but it is adapting to the situation in Costa Rica.

- Phase 0: Consists of the period for the two years stipulated in transitory 4 of decree n ° 40199-MP to be fulfilled. At the end of this period the revision of the current state and the adjustments required for the continuity of the project will be made.
- Phase 1: This phase requires the creation of laws that establish deadlines for updating the data on the platform; this update will be made progressively. Moreover, responsible for each Institution will be defined to meet these deadlines. Each institution must have a compliance deadline that must be respected, and each institution must ensure the maintenance and updating of its information. In Costa Rica's context, such "law enforcement" increases the chances to implement the solution. Agreement on the Congress should be accomplished to obtain necessaries laws, thus, political leadership or to meet OECD's requirements has to be triggers on such strategy. Here we can notice the importance of political dimension and economic one (since resources and funding have to be granted on the law).
- Phase 2: Define Open Government strategies to raise awareness among citizens and institutions. To do this, they can take as a reference the ones used by Taiwan that would be, (1) Proactive release of data and emphases on people's welfare first, (2) Drafting regulations for open data, (3) Promotion of public use platform, and (4) Demonstration, advocacy and promotion of services. Social and political dimensions are important in this phase to encourage objectives of transparency.
- Phase 3: Define principles of open data, which strengthen the constant updating and publication of information. In this case, reference can be made to the success that Taiwan has had with its principles of, (1) Open data for public and Enterprise use, (2) Free in principle, charging as the exception, and (3) Automatic and systematic release and exchange of large volume of data. Here technological and economic dimensions are crucial. The first one in order to define particularities of data processing, transmission, storage among others factors. The second to define how services will be funded to provide a free access to people and enterprises.
- Phase 4: Establish a value chain in the use of data, adapted to Costa Rica that allows generating public value. Likewise, Taiwan experience is taken as a reference in this value chain, having the stages of (1) Production and collection stage, (2) The storage stage, (3) The distribution stage, (4) The adoption and value-added stage, and (5) The stage of marketing and providing service to end users. Beside the technological specifications of such value chain, an administrative structure should be implemented to manage such service.

With the development of these phases, it is intended that Costa Rica will have a platform with enough updated information to provide services as well as managerial knowledge of the situation of the country that allows them to facilitate decisions in a timely manner.

Finally, a configuration of actors both for sponsoring the project and to manage the implementation of the platform shall be defined. Formal actor's analysis as presented in (Cortes-Morales, 2017) is beyond the scope of this research. However, the support of important political actors like the Secretary of the Presidency should be a key factor on the development of the strategy. The list presented in Table 1 defines a set of actors that could be good enough (if committed) to successful support the policy.

6. CONCLUSION

This research has allowed, through multidimensional analysis, to analyze and identify the best practices of other countries worldwide, specifically Taiwan. It has been possible to clarify that beyond technological resources, political, economic, administrative and social factors must be taken into account, for the application of laws, decrees, strategies and regulations that allow offering citizens technological resources, easily accessible and that provide updated and reliable information. Therefore, the proposed solution expects the Costa Rica's State to improve its transparency indexes at the national level and thereby recover the confidence of citizens. Moreover, multidimensional analysis reminds us of the importance of not neglecting any factor to design an accurate solution that generates public value.

Costa Rica's efforts, although important, lack from a more robust policy in this area Taiwan with similar dimensions than Costa Rica, showed that good practices could be taken from each dimension to obtain and excel in the implementation of a platform of Open Government, a key factor for transparency.

Finally, this research as a case study doesn't look to generalize findings or conclusions. However, similar framework of analysis may be used on different political communities (national wide or local) to identify and/or suggest broad lines in solutions for similar issues.

REFERENCES

CEPAL. (04 de 2019). *Qué es Gobierno Abierto*. Obtenido de https://biblioguias.cepal.org/EstadoAbierto/concepto

Comisión Nacional de Gobierno Abierto. (2017 - 2019). Plan de Acción de la ALianza para un Gobierno Abierto .

Cortes-Morales, R., 2017. A comprehensive approach for e-govemment solutions. In CLEI, ed. *XLIII Latin American Conference on Informatics*. Cordoba, Argentina, 2017. CLEI.

Datos Abiertos. (s.f.). Obtenido de http://datosabiertos.presidencia.go.cr/home

Durán, O. (2013). Open Data O Datos Abiertos en Costa Rica. *UCR*.

Fountain, J. (2001). The Virtual State: Transforming American Government? . *National Civic Review*, 241-251.

Gurría, A. (s.f.). *Openness and Transparency - Pillars for Democracy, Trust and Progress*. Obtenido de OCDE: http://www.oecd.org/fr/etatsunis/opennessandtransparency-pillarsfordemocracytrustandprogress.htm

Hui-Ju, W., & Jin, L. (2010). Exploring Citizens' Intention to Use Government Websites in Taiwan: An Empirical Study. *iiWAS2010*.

La Defensoría de los Habitantes. (2018). *Índice de Transparencia del Sector Público Costarricense*. Obtenido de http://www.dhr.go.cr/Red_de_transparencia/indice_transparencia/resultados_itsp/2018/Resultados_ITSP_2018.pdf

La Gaceta. (2017). *Publicación de leyes*. Obtenido de https://www.imprentanacional.go.cr/pub/2017/05/12/ALCA102_12_05_2017.pdf

Moore, M., & Khagram, S. (2004). On Creating Public Value. *Corporate Social Responsability Initiative*.

OCDE. (2018). *Openness and Transparency - Pillars for Democracy, Trust and Progress*. Recuperado el 10 de June de 2019, de OCDE: http://www.oecd.org/fr/etatsunis/opennessandtransparency-pillarsfordemocracytrustandprogress.htm

Pimiento, J. (21 de 12 de 2017). *¿Qué es el Gobierno Digital?* Obtenido de https://goberna.org/que-es-gobierno-digital/

Pin-Yu, C., & Hsein-Lee, T. (2018). Open Data in Support of E-governance Evaluation: A Public Value Framework. *ICEGOV*.

Tung-Mou, Y., Jin, L., Hui-Ju, W., & Jing, S. (2013). Open Data Development and Value-Added Government Information: Case Studies of Taiwan E-Government. *ICEGOV*.

UNPAN. (2010). *United Nations e-Government Survey*. United Nations Public Administration Network. New York: United Nations.

SHORT PAPERS

BROWSERLESS WEB AUTOMATION FOR BLIND USERS

Ruslan R. Fayzrakhmanov and Andrey Kravchenko
Department of Computer Science, University of Oxford, UK

ABSTRACT

Navigating and performing different tasks on the Web can be frustrating for blind users. This is related to different aspects including a linear nature of navigation through the content, the issues of contemporary web pages not following accessibility guidelines, and limitations of assistive technologies trying to keep pace with a constantly changing web stack of technologies. Web automation tools help users to automate tasks and ease the navigation to a desired content. However, most of existing approaches are based on the web browser and, therefore, have some requirements on the hardware and software used, its performance. Furthermore, they have to take into account complex sequences of DOM events which reflect different changes and states on a web page, such as completion of the content loading or reaction on user actions. These non-trivial conglomerates of events often considerably reduce the robustness of web automation. In this paper we introduce a new approach, FastWrap4A, which can analyse user interactions and transpose the automation from the UI level directly to the level of data-focused interactions with web servers. This approach does not require a browser or an integrated web page rendering engine and can be executed on different devices.

KEYWORDS

Web Accessibility, Web Automation, Assistive Technology

1. INTRODUCTION

The Web is a huge information platform that provides vast opportunities for people by making it possible to effectively solve various tasks in business, education, science, and our everyday lives. However, these opportunities are not available for everybody. For example, people who are blind encounter a lot of problems surfing the Web. This is a direct result of the majority of web pages not following accessibility guidelines and standards, being oriented at sighted users, and not taking into account users who are blind. Moreover, web accessibility standards unfortunately always tend to be a step behind rapidly changing technologies and cannot cover various aspects of the web design and web navigation (Nogueira et al. 2019, Power et al. 2012).

There are two main directions for approaching the enhancement of web accessibility and usability: (1) by means of developing standards and guidelines which lead to the creation of more accessible content for specific groups of users and corresponding assistive technology that provides easier access to the accessible content; (2) by means of developing approaches and tools for making inaccessible content accessible (Fayzrakhmanov, 2013). Web automation is one of means to enhance accessibility of inaccessible websites. It is a technology that automates typical web browsing activities such as form filling and clicking links to reach the required content, by performing these actions on behalf of the user. Web automation is usually performed by manual invocation of a desired script, presented as a sequence of actions. A script can be written manually or automatically derived, for instance, with a technique such as programming by example (PBE).

Some representative examples of web automation systems are CoScripter (Leshed et al. 2008) (PBE-based system which enables users to record, play back, edit, and share generated scripts; the latter are both human- and machine-understandable), TrailBlazer (Bigham et al. 2009) (it assists blind users in performing certain web-based tasks while dynamically generating non-visual interface based on the database of scripts provided by CoScripter, and a relevant script is suggested to the user based on a provided short task description), Ubiquity (Erlewine 2009) (a multilingual textual interface for the Firefox browser enabling rapid information retrieval and task execution), CoCo (Lau et al. 2010) (framework which provides the user with necessary scripts with short textual commands and assists her with web tasks, utilising ActionShot and shared database of CoScripter), Ringer (Shaon et al. 2016) (a heuristic approach to browser-based PBE).

Most of known web automation systems are based on a web browser, the analysis of rendered web pages and mimicking user actions. Due to the complexity of contemporary web applications the use of the rendering engine is essential, since a web page can be constructed from different sources integrated via AJAX requests and transformed with comprehensive JavaScript code. The *rendering* typically consists of (a) parsing the web page and building a DOM tree, (b) applying CSS rules, fonts, and (c) executing JavaScript, which is usually the most computationally expensive part, often having wide-ranging effects on the page's DOM. The rendering can thus take up to 98% of the runtime with about 2% for actual data analysis and extraction (Furche et al., 2013). Another complicated problem of browser-based approaches is their robustness. They have to deal with the analysis of complex sequences of DOM events reflecting different states of a web page (e.g., load, DOMContentLoaded, unload, change, DOMNodeInserted) and handling different tabs opened after simulating user clicks. For example, OXPath implements non-trivial algorithms for handling complex cases related to changes on a web page caused by simulated user interaction and distinguishing them from those (irrelevant) changes related to updates in news or ads blocks.

In this paper, we present FastWrap4A, a best-effort solution to eliminate the web browser completely and provide the blind user with a more efficient and robust record-and-extract automation. Omitting the web browser gives us the possibility to directly interact with relevant web servers on the level of HTTP interactions, issuing only relevant HTTP requests. The goal of our invention is thus not related to the automation of user interactions with the user interface, but rather automation of the data access, making it robust and accessible. The core technology, FastWrap (Fayzrakhmanov et al. 2018), demonstrates its high robustness and performance. FastWrap scripts run, on average, in less than 7.14% of the runtime of the state-of-the-art web data extraction programs, using 1.77% of the HTTP calls, and 3.12% of the Web traffic. The scripts keep precision and recall equal to those of traditional web data extraction scripts (so-called wrappers).

FastWrap4A can generate parameterised automation scripts either in a PBE fashion with the use of a web browser extension FastWrap4A Listener or directly from the analysis of existing automation scripts, such as Ringer (Shaon et al. 2016). FastWrap4A Listener can be used by an experienced blind user or a sighted user to let FastWrap4A mine patterns within HTTP interactions and generate a script. This script models specific type of user tasks, be it checking the exchange rate for different *currencies* or train schedule for arbitrary *locations*. In this examples, *currencies* and *locations* are input parameters which are to be provided by the blind user while running the generated script. A direct generation of the FastWrap4A script is also possible by executing an existing script produced by another system. FastWrap4A can thus build its automation script either from HAR file or by listening to the HTTP request-response exchanges via the proxy server.

2. ARCHITECTURE AND APPROACH

FastWrap4A consists of two main modules: **FastWrap4A Listener** (a browser extension for Chrome for gathering HTTP interactions and the user input-output) and **FastWrap4A Engine** (a FastWrap-based technology for generating and running an automation script).

When the user surfs the Web, the *Listener* collects data-rich interactions between the client software and web servers along with entered data (e.g., via form filling) and the desired output. The input can be, for example, *departure-arrival locations* and *dates* in case of flight search or *location* in case of property search, while the output can be *available flights* or *properties* along with their prices. The Listener can be implemented as a proxy server, collecting all necessary HTTP interactions, or an extension for the web browser. In this paper we implemented FastWrap4A Listener realised as a browser extension as illustrated in Figure 1, which is compatible with popular screen readers, such as JAWS and NVDA. With the use of a preferable assistive technology and the FastWrap4A browser extension, the user can start a recording session navigating to a desired web page, entering data into web forms, performing interactions to navigate to a resulting page containing desired data. When the session is complete and desired data is labelled with the use of the browser extension, generated data-rich HTTP traces with input-output annotations are saved on the file system. Our study shows that usually three repetitions of the same interaction scenario with different input data are enough to construct a robust automation script.

Given a set of recorded HTTP traces (with input and output data), FastWrap4A *Engine* analyses them and generates a script which automates this scenario. The resulting script does not need a web browser and can be directly executed on any device, be it a PC or a mobile phone (Figure 1). It directly interacts with servers issuing only those HTTP requests which are related to obtaining desired data. To run a specific recorded scenario, it is enough to provide input data, usually the data entered in a web form, via an accessible web interface. Extracted data is returned as a table with ARIA annotations.

Figure 1. Software architecture for script generation and automation with FastWrap4A

Thus, through using our automation technology the user does not face the overhead related to web browser initialisation and rendering, which considerably increases the robustness and decrease the runtime of an automated scenario.

3. AUTOMATION WITH FASTWRAP4A

In this section, we introduce FastWrap4A Engine, our approach for automatically generating and executing HTTP scripts for web automation. A detailed description of the base approach with comprehensive evaluation is presented in (Fayzrakhmanov et al. 2018).

FastWrap4A Engine takes as input collected HTTP interactions (e.g., from the browser extension, web logs or an HAR file), along with input and output data, and produces as output a corresponding browserless HTTP script. The script extracts desired data by directly interacting with the website's servers and does not require loading and rendering the web page. Thus, it is more portable than existing automation technologies and also more robust.

The FastWrap4A Engine analyses the sequence of HTTP request-response exchanges (referred to as *HTTP traces*) between the client (i.e. a web browser or page rendering engine) and web servers. HTTP traces also include desired data labelled by the user (so-called *output records*). This data is used to identify *final HTTP interactions* with the desired output records in their responses. Furthermore, the provided records are used to generate *data selectors* to extract the data from the content and transform this data into a structured representation. If *input parameters* are necessary (e.g., for web form filling), HTTP traces also include these. Input and output parameters are used to correctly induce the output script and guarantee that the desired data is not overlooked. Automation of script creation is thus solely based on the direct analysis of these HTTP traces. This makes our approach applicable to a wide range of automation scenarios and avoids tying it to any particular system. Our pilot studies also show that it can be applied for transforming existing scripts such as Ringer and OXPath into considerably more efficient scripts, about 24 times faster (Fayzrakhmanov et al. 2018).

The overall FastWrap4A approach can be intuitively explained via the following two main phases.

Phase 1: Given a set of HTTP traces, identify final interactions carrying desired output data and model them as abstract final interactions. Generate data selectors and value transformers.

This step is illustrated in Figure 2. FastWrap4A iterates over all recorded HTTP interactions and detects those which contain the output data selected by the user within the web browser. These final interactions are clustered into sets of interactions according to the similarity of their HTTP response contents and HTTP requests. Each cluster is modelled by a so-called *abstract final interaction*. It, in turn, defines input parameters necessary to instantiate this class of interactions as well as *data selectors* to pull the desired user output data from the HTTP response and *value transformers* to convert extracted data into the necessary form. Both data selectors and value transformers mimic some typical data manipulation and transformation techniques implemented by the web page's JavaScript.

For output data and parameter value extraction from the HTTP response content, FastWrap4A can induce two types of data selectors: XPath for X/HTML documents and JSONPath for JSON(P). All data selectors can also select sub-structures (i.e., subtrees in the case of XPath and nested objects in the case of JSONPath)

To transform the extracted data into a parameter of a dependent HTTP request or the final output, the following value transformations are supported: (1) string manipulations, such as a subset, removal of double spaces, inserting a constant string, a character replacement; (2) URL encoding and decoding; (3) replacement of HTML escape symbols; (4) numerical manipulations such as changing the precision of real numbers. Our approach identifies the most specific transformation and can combine different transformations with each other, which we find quite useful in practice. For example, space-to-plus conversion followed by URL encoding or URL encoding followed by string concatenation.

(Recursive) Phase 2: Given an abstract interaction, identify other HTTP interactions within the set of HTTP traces containing data in their responses that are necessary to initialise the current abstract interaction. (*Instantiation is replacing parameters in an HTTP request of the abstract interaction with relevant data.)* Model discovered HTTP interactions as abstract interactions, set a corresponding dependency relation with data selectors and value transformers.

Repeat this step recursively until all dependencies are resolved.

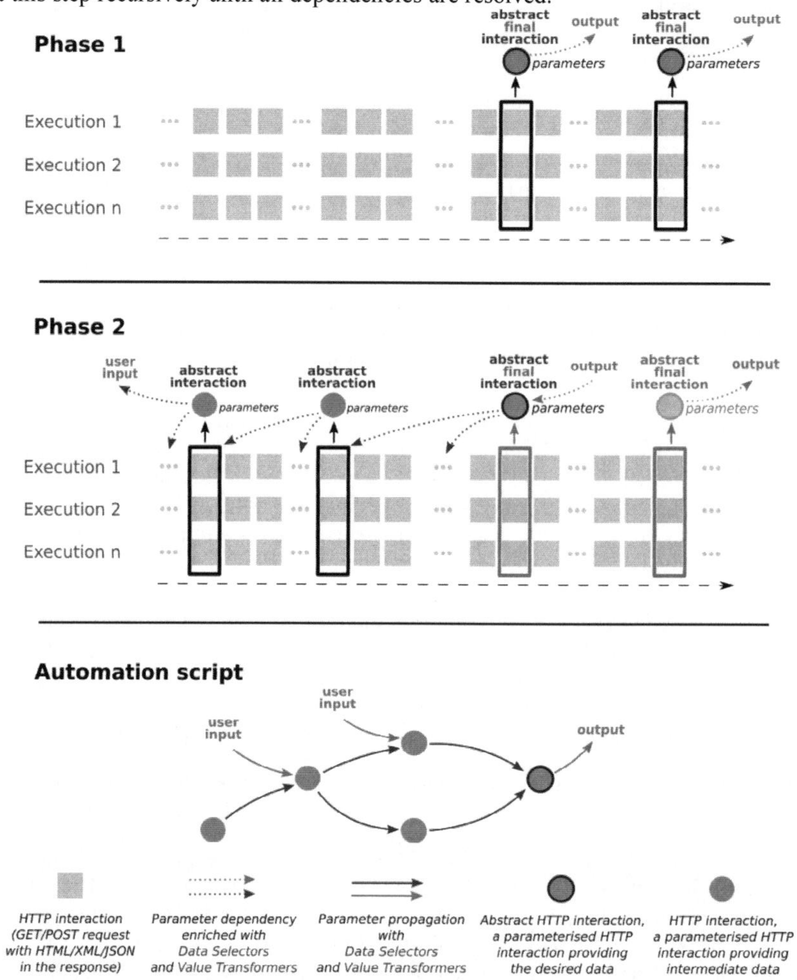

Figure 2. Two phases of automating script generation and schematic representation of the output script

This step is illustrated in Figure 2. Abstract (final) interactions can have input parameters which are propagated from HTTP responses of other interactions. Thus, in this step, FastWrap4A identifies HTTP interactions carrying the desired parameters, clusters those interactions, and generates abstract interactions for each formed cluster, similar to Phase 1. This phase has a recursive nature since a new-built abstract interaction can also have input parameters. During Phases 1 and 2 a graph is constructed, in which each node represents an abstract (final) interaction and arcs reflect the parameter propagation from HTTP interactions providing necessary data in their response to HTTP requests of dependent abstract interactions. Each arc is annotated with corresponding data selectors and data transformers. In case all dependencies are resolved a resulting web automation script is constructed as illustrated in Figure 2.

Automation is the execution of the generated script which requires the user to provide necessary input data, which she enters in the corresponding web form.

The script is executed in a recursive fashion navigating through the graph structure from the abstract final interaction to dependency-resolved interactions, which either require or do not require user input. An abstract interaction is instantiated and triggered in case all its dependent input parameters are instantiated via data selectors and value transformers.

4. CONCLUSION

We introduce FastWrap4A, a web automation tool, which can help blind users to automate their web tasks, be it checking flights, prices for flats, or weather forecasts. This approach does not require a web browser and can run on different devices, be it a PC or a mobile phone. Our approach can be used both for automating user interactions and converting existing databases of browser-dependant scripts into more efficient and lightweight automation scripts (e.g., OXPath or Ringer), which, in turn, can directly issue only relevant HTTP interactions providing the user efficiently with desired information in an accessible web content. We believe this novel approach and study can bring new technology and thoughts towards more advanced and robust web automation to blind users. Moreover, as future work we believe it is important to be able to automatically identify interesting information which could be relevant to the user, without requiring her to label the output data.

ACKNOWLEDGEMENT

This work is supported by the EPSRC programme grant EP/M025268/1 (VADA).

REFERENCES

Bigham, J. P. et al, 2009. TrailBlazer: Enabling Blind Users to Blaze Trails through the Web. *Proceedings of the 14th international conference on Intelligent user interfaces*, New York, USA, pp. 177–86.

Erlewine, M. Y., 2009. Ubiquity: Designing a Multilingual Natural Language Interface Features of a Natural Syntax. *SIGIR Workshop on Information Access in a Multilingual World*, Boston, USA, pp. 45–48.

Fayzrakhmanov, R. R. 2013. *Web Accessibility for the Blind Through Visual Representation Analysis*. Vienna University of Technology (PhD Thesis), Vienna, Austria.

Fayzrakhmanov, R. R. et al, 2018. Browserless Web Data Extraction: Challenges and Opportunities. *Proceedings of the 2018 World Wide Web Conference on World Wide Web (WWW'18)*. Lyon, France, pp. 1095–1104.

Furche, T. et al, 2013. OXPath: A language for scalable data extraction, automation, and crawling on the deep web. *VLDB Journal*, Vol. 22, No. 1, pp. 47–72.

Lau, T. et al, 2010. A conversational interface to web automation. *Proceedings of the 23nd annual ACM symposium on User interface software and technology*. New York, USA, pp. 229–238.

Leshed, G. et al, 2008. CoScripter: Automating & Sharing How-To Knowledge in the Enterprise. *Proceedings of the SIGCHI Conference on Human Factors in Computing Systems*, Florence, Italy, pp. 1719–1728.

Nogueira, T. C. et al. 2019. Comparing Sighted and Blind Users Task Performance in Responsive and Non-Responsive Web Design. *Knowledge and Information Systems*, Vol. 58, No. 2, pp. 319–39.

Power, C. et al. 2012. Guidelines are only half of the story: accessibility problems encountered by blind users on the Web. *Proceedings of the SIGCHI Conference on Human Factors in Computing Systems*, Austin, Texas, USA, pp. 433–442.

Shaon, B. et al, 2016. Ringer: web automation by demonstration. *Proceedings of the ACM International Conference on Object-Oriented Programming, Systems, Languages, and Applications*, Amsterdam, Netherlands, pp. 748-764.

GAMIFICATION STUDY: REVIEW AND RETRIEVAL

Olga Kononova[1] and Dmitry Prokudin[1,2]
[1]*St. Petersburg National Research University of Information Technologies, Mechanics and Optics (ITMO University) 197101, St. Petersburg, Russia*
[2]*St. Petersburg State University, 199034, St. Petersburg, Russia*

ABSTRACT

The digital transformations of the modern society often outstrip the processes of science transformation, forcing science to constantly improve both technologies and applied software. The phenomenon especially characterizes scientific studies in research areas such as the Digital Economy and the Smart City. In order to the urban environment becomes smarter, gamification technologies act as the motivational mechanisms, maintaining citizens' social activity and stimulating social growth. The purpose of the paper is an identification of development trends of gamification in the context of the sociocultural urban information space. Comparative analysis results of the publications' number, Russian scientific discourse about considered subject domains as well as its correspondence to the global trends are presented. The study has applied the synthetic method for the automated extraction and explication of contextual knowledge from an array of textual modality resources.

KEYWORDS

Context, Contextual Knowledge Explication, Full-Text and Multimodal Search, Gamification, Terminological Landscape

1. INTRODUCTION

In the relation to the implementation of Urban Development Projects, there is a number of main directions of interdisciplinary research areas. "Gamification in the social, scientific and educational subject domains" is one of these directions. The main topic of this direction is a gamification phenomenon which is the modern trend of technologies in social life. The purpose of the study presented in this paper is to identify the terminological landscape of gamification domain with usage of retrieval systems and semantic tools. A comparative analysis of the terminological landscape on the base of Synthetic Method presented by the authors [Kononova, Prokudin, 2018] has revealed the contexts of using gamification in the urban environment development and the modern city management. It has also highlighted promising proposals and practices on gamification using in the development of the city information space and formed the terminological base and thesaurus. Comparison of Russian with Global trends of gamification used in the development of the modern urban information environment has allowed focusing the attention of researchers on scientifically significant results. Synthetic Method proposed as an approach to the terminologically study and review has been successfully applied for the following interdisciplinary studies such as "Digital Economy: e-governance and smart technology" [Kononova, Prokudin, 2018], "Social parameters and reasons for getting involved in games" [Kononova at el., 2016], "Organization Scientific Research Activities" [Kononova, Liapin, 2016].

2. CONTEXTUAL KNOWLEDGE EXPLICATION

2.1 The Review of Gamification Studies

The terminological base forming has required the systematization of ideas in the area of study, extraction and application of contextual knowledge. The term 'gamification' was entered in business society and later in the scientific community in 2010. The use peak of this term was in 2016 and 2017. Researchers have now found many applications for digital gamification, linking gamification with solving social, public, cultural, and civil problems. Some of researchers believe that game mechanisms can stimulate e-participation and citizens' social behavior [Dorcec et al., 2019; Vanolo, 2018]. Although the academic debate on gamification is rather new, the scientific discourse has led to the understanding of using the possibility of gamification elements for urban development. No doubt, the global community recognizes the importance of gamification as a scientific phenomenon and conducting research in this area in order to learn how digital gamification can change our experience of the urban space using [Mueller et al., 2018]. The main directions of the modern research topics of the gamification phenomenon are presented in Table 1.

Table 1. Comparative review of gamification publications

Mechanisms	Spheres
	Education, Training
Motivation	L. Da Rocha Seixas, et al., 2016; L. Sera, et al., 2017; R. Landers, et al., 2017
	Business, Marketing,
Motivation	A. Shpakova, et al., 2016 O. El-Telbany, A. Elragal, 2017
Communication	A. Kampker, et al., 2014; A. Shpakova et al., 2016; L.F. Rodrigues et al., 2016; K. Huotari, J. Hamari, 2017
Communication/ Engagement	Ipeirotis, et al., 2014; Hamari, 2013, 2015; Y. Yang, et al., 2017
	Professional Communications, e-Government
Motivation	J.T. Harviainen, et al., 2019; T. Dargan, F. Evequoz, 2015
Engagement	M. Romano, et al., 2016; Agbozo E., Chepurov E. (2018); Hassan L., Hamari J. (2019)
	Health and Sport, Culture and Tourism
Motivation	Jones, et al., 2014; J. Hamari, J. Koivisto,2015
Communication/ Engagement	F. Xu, et al., 2017
Motivation/ Communication	N. P. Cechetti et al., 2019
	Urban Planning and Development, Civic Participation
Motivation	T. AlSkaif, et al., 2018
Engagement	T. AlSkaif, et al., 2018; R. Olszewski et al., 2017; M. R. Zica, et al., 2017; A. Vanolo, 2018; D. Johnson, et al., 2017; M. Romano et al., 2016
	Ecology
Motivation	S. Castellanos, 2016; T. AlSkaif, et al., 2018; D. Wemyss et al., 2019

Analysis of scientific publications has shown that gamification is used in the practice of managing urban areas: Transport, Utilities, Energy Saving, Waste Recycling, Ecology, and Urban Environment Preservation. Moreover, it is used in planning urban information spaces, implementing intelligent urban projects and producing "digital citizens". Gamification methods are also used in Education, Health, Culture, Tourism, e-Government, Civic e-Participation, Urban Cartography and Logistics, City Data Collection (IoT), and others. Both the media space and scientific literature have reflected this phenomenon.

Regardless of the application sphere, even when it comes to business, the authors of all publications write about gamification. They approach this issue first of all, as an instrument of motivation and self-organization, secondly, as support for social and professional communications, and, thirdly, as human-machine interactions (engagement, e-participation, e-involvement). It should be noted that selected spheres' combination presents modern city in all its diversity; selected gamification mechanisms (communication, motivation, engagement) correspond to Conceptualization of gamification [Huotari & Hamari, 2017] with its sequential addiction of affordances, psychological outcomes, behavioral outcomes.

2.2 Gamification in Russian and English Discourse

The theoretical basis of the study is discourse analysis, advanced content analysis with the subsequent explication of selected contexts (synthetic method), expert, and comparative analysis. The authors' automated technique of extraction and explication of contextual knowledge (a form of an interpretation of the texts and explication of meanings through contexts obtained as a result of search queries), using a hybrid query for the analysis of contexts from textual modality information resources, has been applied [Kononova, Prokudin, 2018].

In order to evaluate the dynamics of research interest to Gamification Technology, the study proposes a review of the corpus of Russian and Foreign scientific publications, as well as Russian media publications. Because of the synthetic method is independent of the instrumental environment for conducting research, the presentation language and the text format, the technique validation was performed for arrays of Russian and English scientific publications. The Russian web-based information systems libraries eLibrary (https://elibrary.ru/), T-Libra (http://77.234.221.107/bin/TauC.exe?DSN=tlibra), and multilingual web-based tool Voyant-Tools (https://voyant-tools.org/) has been used as the tools for search, explication, and analysis of contexts.

At this stage of the research, two corpuses of texts from Russian and English sources were searched and formed. The search has been carried out since 2010 and generally confirmed the findings of researchers who claimed that scientific papers on gamification appeared in the scientific discourse and in open sources in 2010. The results of the analysis of both textual corpuses in the given interval have shown the growing interest in the gamification. The first corpus contains the information resources from ScienceDirect, Web of Science и Scopus. There were 301 scientific publications found for the thematic query "gamification", selected in an expert manner on the relevance basis of the study subject domain. The dynamics of the scientific community interest (in the number of publications by year) to the topic of gamification demonstrates the following growth: 2011 – 5; 2012 – 11; 2013 – 20; 2014 – 25; 2015 – 45; 2016 – 47; 2017 – 61; 2018 – 56. Analysis of English text corpus has also allowed grouping the term-concepts corresponding with 'gamification' search queries. Firstly, 55 publications were selected from English text corpus for the period of 2015-2018. Then 18 papers relevant to topics of gamification in the city were selected from them by an expert method. The list of these term-concepts can become a part of the terminological core of subject domain in the future.

The results of the data analysis (Figure 1) have led to the following conclusions: the number of scientific publications on gamification in the world has been growing annually since 2010; the growth in the number of Russian scientific publications on this topic demonstrates two year delay. However, in general, the dynamics corresponds to global scientific trends; accessibility of Russian scientific publications for researchers is about a third of all Russian scientific publications; comparison of the data from Russian scientific publications and publications from Russian media allows concluding that the topic of gamification in the public discourse is illuminated to a lesser extent.

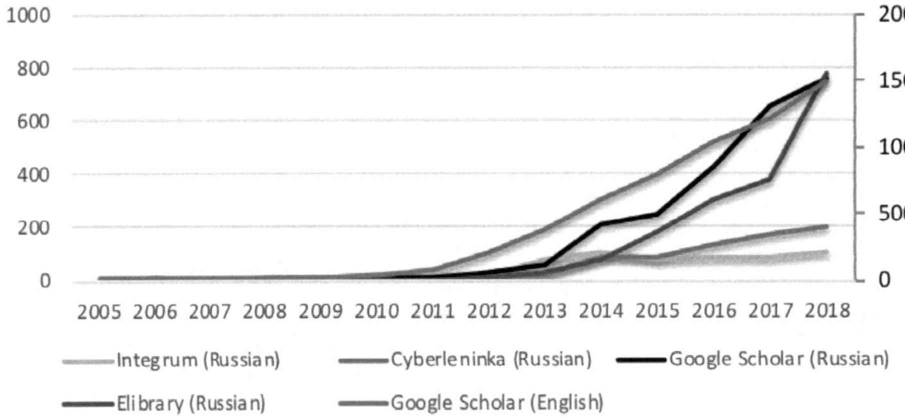

Figure 1. Dynamics of publication activity on the gamification for 2005-2018

Analysis of Russian text corpus has allowed gathering key words used from 2011 to 2018. There are some most common term-concepts: motivation, eLearning, education, game, game technology, gaming, personnel management, and others. Extra analysis of these terms' application will fill the terminological core of subject domain.

3. CONCLUSION

The study has formed the following conclusions: gamification as a direction of scientific research has begun to develop in the Russian scientific discourse since 2012. It indicates the influence of global trends in scientific research in the gamification domain in Russian studies. In Russian information space gamification forms more the scientific discourse than the extended public one. The main scopes of gamification in the Russian and global scale have been determined. Both Russian and Foreign researchers pay a lot of attention of gamification technologies in education. Russian scientific discourse discusses little the use of gamification in Urban Planning and e-Participation. In addition, the basic terms-concepts of the terminological core of the interdisciplinary research direction have been defined. Further development of the research will be focused on forming a thesaurus of the interdisciplinary research direction with Synthetic Method application and structured description of thematic contexts of textual modality (text corpus, document, document fragment – several paragraphs, paragraph) with the Dublin Core Metadata Element Set. The contextual knowledge description based on Dublin Core provides the usage of thesaurus for automated search and identification of contextual knowledge by search engines, open access to knowledge, the ability to use software that, along with the Dublin Core standard, is able to exchange automatically via the OAI-PMH protocol (for instance, DSpace, https://duraspace.org/dspace/), Eprints (https://www.eprints.org/uk/), OJS (https://pkp.sfu.ca/ojs/)).

ACKNOWLEDGEMENT

The reported study was funded by RFBR according to the research project "The integrated approach elaboration to the analysis of the terminological base of the developing interdisciplinary research in distributed network environment" № 18-011-00923, 2018-2020.

REFERENCES

Agbozo E., Chepurov E. (2018) Enhancing e-Participation via gamification of e-Government platforms: A possible solution to SubSaharan African e-Government initiatives // *CEUR Workshop Proceedings.* Vol. 2145. P. 83-86. http://ceur-ws.org/Vol-2145/p14.pdf

AlSkaif T., Lampropoulos I., Broek M. van den, Sark W.van (2018) Gamification-based framework for engagement of residential customers in energy applications // *Energy Research & Social Science.* Vol. 44. P. 187-195. DOI: 10.1016/j.erss.2018.04.043.

Barratt P. (2017) Healthy competition: A qualitative study investigating persuasive technologies and the gamification of cycling // *Health & Place.* Vol. 46. P. 328-336. DOI: 10.1016/j.healthplace.2016.09.009

Castellanos S. (2016) Delivering modal-shift incentives by using gamification and smartphones: A field study example in Bogota, Colombia // *Case studies on transport policy.* Vol. 4. №. 4. P. 269-278. DOI: 10.1016/j.cstp.2016.08.008

Cechetti N.P., Bellei E.A., Biduski D., Rodriguez J.P. (2019) Developing and im-plementing a gamification method to improve user engagement: A case study with an m-Health application for hypertension monitoring // *Telematics and Informatics.* Vol. 41. P. 126-138. DOI: 10.1016/j.tele.2019.04.007

Dargan T., Evequoz F. (2015) Designing engaging e-Government services by com-bining user-centered design and gamification: A use-case // *Proceedings of the 15th European Conference on eGovernment ECEG* 2015 University of Portsmouth, 70.

Da Rocha Seixas L., Sandro Gomes A., de Melo Filho I. (2016) Effectiveness of Gamification in the Engagement of Students // *Computers in Human Behavior.* Vol. 58. P. 48-63. DOI: 10.1016/j.chb.2015.11.021

Dias L.P.S., Barbosa J.L.V., Vianna H.D. (2018) Gamification and serious games in depression care: A systematic mapping study. // *Telematics and Informatics.* Vol. 35. P. 213–224. DOI: 10.1016/j.tele.2017.11.002

Dorcec L., Pevec D., Vdovic H., Babic J., Podobnik V. (2019) How do people value electric vehicle charging service? A gamified survey approach // *Journal of Cleaner Production.* Vol. 210. P. 887-897. DOI: 10.1016/j.jclepro.2018.11.032

El-Telbany O., Elragal A. (2017) Gamification of enterprise systems: A lifecycle approach // Procedia Computer Science. Vol. 121. P. 106-114. DOI: 10.1016/j.procs.2017.11.015

Hamari J., Koivisto J., Sarsa H. (2014) Does Gamification Work? — A Literature Review of Empirical Studies on Gamification // *Proceedings of the 2014 47th Hawaii International Conference on System Sciences (HICSS '14). IEEE Computer Society*, Washington, DC, USA. P. 3025-3034. DOI: 10.1109/HICSS.2014.377

Harviainen J. T., Hassan L. (2019) Governmental Service Gamification: Central Principles // *International Journal of Innovation in the Digital Economy (IJIDE)*. Vol. 10. № 3. P. 1-12. DOI: 10.4018/IJIDE.2019070101

Hassan L., Hamari J. (2019) Gamification of E-Participation: A Literature Review // *Proceedings of 52nd Hawaii International Conference on System Sciences (HICSS'52)*, At Maui HI, USA. P. 3077-3086.

Koivistoa J., Hamari J. (2019) The rise of motivational information systems: A review of gamification research // International Journal of Information Management 45. P. 191-210. https://doi.org/10.1016/j.ijinfomgt.2018.10.013

Johnson D., Horton E., Mulcahy R., Foth V. (2017) Gamification and serious games within the domain of domestic energy consumption: A systematic review // *Renewable and Sustainable Energy Reviews*. Vol. 73. P. 249–264. DOI: 10.1016/j.rser.2017.01.134

Jones B.A., Madden G.J., Wengreen H.J. (2014) The FIT Game: preliminary evalua-tion of a gamification approach to increasing fruit and vegetable consumption in school // *Prev Med.* Vol. 68. P. 76-79. DOI: 10.1016/j.ypmed.2014.04.015

Kononova O., Prokudin D. (2018) Synthetic Method in Interdisciplinary Termino-logical Landscape Research of Digital Economy // *SHS Web Conf.* Vol. 507. 01082. DOI: 10.1051/shsconf/20185001082

Kononova, O., Liapin S. (2016) Using the Contextual Search for the Organization Scientific Research Activities. Communications in Computer and Information Science. Vol. 674. P. 392-399. DOI: 10.1007/978-3-319-49700-6_38

Kononova, O., Sergeeva O., Orekh E., Kudriavtceva M. (2016) Towards Computer Game Research Area in Russia. Communications in Computer and Information Science. Vol. 674. P. 72-81. DOI: 10.1007/978-3-319-49700-6_9

Konstantakopoulos I.C., Barkan A.R., He S., Veeravalli T., Liu H., Spanos C. (2019) A deep learning and gamification approach to improving human-building in-teraction and energy efficiency in smart infrastructure // *Applied Energy*. Vol. 237. P. 810–821. DOI: 10.1016/j.apenergy.2018.12.065

Landers R., Bauer K., Callan R. (2017) Gamification of task performance with lead-erboards: A goal setting experiment // *Computers in Human Behavior*. Vol. 71. P. 508-515. DOI: 10.1016/j.chb.2015.08.008

Marcucci E., Gatta V., Le Pira V. (2018) Gamification design to foster stakeholder engagement and behavior change: An application to urban freight transport // *Transportation Research Part A: Policy and Practice*. Vol. 118. P. 119–132. DOI: 10.1016/j.tra.2018.08.028

Mueller C., Klein U., Hof A. (2018) An easy-to-use spatial simulation for urban planning in smaller municipalities // *Computers, Environment and Urban Systems*. Vol. 71. P. 109-119. DOI: 10.1016/j.compenvurbsys.2018.05.002

Olszewski R., Gnat M., Trojanowska H., Turek A., Wieladek A. (2017) Towards Social Fuzzy Geoparticipation Stimulated by Gamification and Augmented Reality // *13th International Conference on Natural Computation, Fuzzy Systems and Knowledge Discovery (ICNC-FSKD 2017)*. P. 1363-1370. DOI: 10.1109/FSKD.2017.8392965

Richter G., Raban D.R., Rafaeli S. (2015) Studying Gamification: The Effect of Re-wards and Incentives on Motivation // *Gamification in Education and Business. Springer, Cham.* P. 21-46. DOI 10.1007/978-3-319-10208-5_2

Rodrigues L.F., Carlos A.O., Costa J. (2016) Does ease-of-use contributes to the per-ception of enjoyment? A case of gamification in e-banking // *Computers in Human Behavior*. Vol. 61. P. 114-126. DOI:10.1016/j.chb.2016.03.015

Romano M., Onorati T., Aedo I., Diaz P. (2016) Designing mobile applications for emergency response: citizens acting as human sensors // *Sensors*. Vol. 16. № 3. 406. DOI: 10.3390/s16030406

Sera L, Wheeler E. (2017) Game on: The gamification of the pharmacy classroom // *Curr Pharm Teach Learn*. Vol. 9. №. 1. P. 155-159. DOI: 10.1016/j.cptl.2016.08.046

Shpakova A., Dörfler V., Macbryde J. (2016) The role (s) of gamification in knowledge management // *EURAM 2016: 16th Annual Conference of the European Academy of Management*. P. 1-40. https://strathprints.strath.ac.uk/56368/

Sardi L., Idri A., Fernandez-Aleman J.L. (2017) A systematic review of gamification in e-Health // *Journal of Biomedical Informatics*. Vol. 71. P. 31–48. DOI: 10.1016/j.jbi.2017.05.011

Vanolo A. (2018) Cities and the politics of Gamification // *Cities*. Vol. 74. P. 20-326. DOI: 10.1016/j.cities.2017.12.021

Wellington R. (2015) Context to Culture for Gamification // *HCI Requirements: Familiarity and Enculturement. Gamification in Education and Business*. Springer, Cham. P. 151-165. DOI 10.1007/978-3-319-10208-5_8

Wemyss D., Cellina F., Lobsiger-Kagi E., de Luca V., Castri R. (2019) Does it last? Long-term impacts of an appbased behavior change intervention on household electricity savings in Switzerland // *Energy Research & Social Science*. Vol. 47. P. 16–27. DOI: 10.1016/j.erss.2018.08.018

Xu F., Buhalis D., Weber J. (2017) Serious games and the gamification of tourism // *Tourism Management*. Vol. 60. P. 244-256. DOI: 10.1016/j.tourman.2016.11.020 \30

Yen B.T.H., Mulley C., Burke M. (2019) Gamification in transport interventions: Another way to improve travel behavioural change // *Cities*. Vol. 85. P. 140–149. DOI: 10.1016/j.cities.2018.09.002

SOCIOCULTURAL URBAN SPACE IN E-SOCIETY

Olga Kononova[1], Dmitry Prokudin[1,2] and Vitalina Karachay[1]
[1] *St. Petersburg National Research University of Information Technologies, Mechanics and Optics (ITMO University), 197101, St. Petersburg, Russia*
[2]*St. Petersburg State University, 199034, St. Petersburg, Russia*

ABSTRACT

The study focuses on the sociocultural aspects of urban development. Paper presents the complete deterministic concept of service oriented Sociocultural Information Urban Space (SIUS), considered as a logical development of the intercultural-communicational, technical-resource approaches and social machine concept in order to studying and understanding the features, possibilities, and base information flows of the Smart City sociocultural face. The SIUS idea helps to recognize or improve the data driving city concept because of smart technology use, so that greater range of digital services related to the sociocultural city facets can be provided to different stakeholders. The study includes exploring the interaction of pervasive processes of the urban space, specification of the SIUS architecture and concept. Based on principles and practices of the pervasive approach, the main mechanisms of citizens' involvement into the active creative development of the SIUS are identified. Moreover, the study discusses two application scenarios which demonstrate how pervasive processes of sustainable development and pervasive self-regulation mechanisms of SIUS can be used in order to consider the factual needs of citizens and decision-making.

KEYWORDS

Smart City, Social Machine, Smart Technology, Sociocultural Information Urban Space, e-Society

1. INTRODUCTION

Global urbanization has significantly increased over the past few centuries. The growth of the world's cities is ingrained in a culture of short-term economic benefit and often raging consumption and production practices that compromise the sustainability of the environment (World Cities Report, 2016). Modern urbanization process and urbanism have been basically conditioned by technological changes and by the organization of the city and society as a media-sphere (Wakabayashi, 2002). In this regard, the issue of description and feature characteristics determination of Sociocultural Information Urban Space (SIUS) and the study of motivation mechanisms identification for citizens' participation in the decision-making processes in urban development domain become relevant. The present research is aimed at identifying the mechanisms of citizens' involvement into Sociocultural Information Urban Space. The following tasks were specified in the paper: identify, study and classify the main SIUS subjects and objects and its interactions; based on the analysis of existing methods and approaches, including the investigation of the Sociocultural Information Urban Space of St. Petersburg, identify the main mechanisms of citizens' involvement into the active creative development of the SIUS. The authors propose a new concept of Sociocultural Information Urban Space, which is the evolutionary development of the existing conceptions. SIUS of the modern city is viewed in this paper as an interactive form of communication between the urban environment subjects. Our interests focus on the supplementation of existing interaction forms and types of actors within the framework of traditional social and cultural institutions, as well as on the development of the intellectual and creative activity of the people, both in real and virtual space. The study can be considered as a source of knowledge and facilitates the better urban design, making it more functioning and more sustainable; optimize the use of limited resources and make better decisions in the Smart City.

2. RELATED WORKS

It should be noted that the progress in ICT solutions enables not only the public and private sector, but also offers the potential for information urban space. In this regard, the essential research issue is increasing the citizen participation via efficient service provision and democracy instruments as key factor of the dynamic modern city promotion. Based on the overview of previous works, the following approaches to the information urban space were distinguished. In particular, the information environment can be viewed as the intercultural communication space, where the ICTs promote mutual recognition among peoples and their cultures (Drotianko and Yahodzinskyi, 2017). Technical (or resource) approach to the information environment defines it via the information, stored and circulating within this environment. Whereas, the sociocultural concepts of the information environment refer to the space of social communications and identify it as an integral part of the culture (Sokolova, 2002). According to the Belon et al. (2015), sociocultural space is a complex, dynamic construct that encompasses the community's social and cultural context that shapes beliefs, values, and practices, that may foster individual efforts to participate in physical activity. In the field of Human Computer Interaction (HCI), the sociocultural information space can be considered, focusing on studying the interactions and the relationships between humans and computers (Sharma and Mehta, 2016). Besides, the information space can be described as the environment where information is handled in order to navigate through the city (Masucci et al., 2014). The ecosystem approach (Ahlers et al., 2019) defines a large-scale smart city IT architecture that spans multiple actors in open and collaborative way, focused on the ICT aspect of the Smart City concept. This approach was designed to be open to additional stakeholders in and around a city, and to enable smart city evolution as an ongoing process. According Falco and Kleinhans (2018), the most important factor for innovative communication in the information space is understanding (at the management level) of the benefits that could be gained through advanced digital participatory platforms (DPPs) and social media in general. However, Barns (2018) argues that urban data platforms should aim to support the role of city governments in cultivating partnerships spanning public and private data custodians, citizens and software developers. This approach can better support more collaborative models of smart city governance ('smart cities 2.0'). Summarizing the overview of the related works, there are three main directions in the information urban space domain: technical/resource aspect, intercultural one, and social machine aspect (Table 1).

Table 1. Urban Space Approaches

Intercultural Communication Space	Technical-Resource Approach	A Social Machine
	Specific aspects:	
predetermination, weak human-dependent technology	sociotechnical, organizational sustainability	a social machine design is not a given, but a dialectic
	Authors and Opinions	
Belon et al., 2015	Masucci et al., 2014	Berners-Lee and Fischetti, 1999
a complex, dynamic construct that encompasses the community's social and cultural context	the information is handled in order to navigate through the city	humans and technology interacting and producing outputs or action, which would not be possible without both parties present
Drotianko and Yahodzinskyi, 2017	Ahvenniemi et al., 2017	Castronova, 2005
mutual recognition among peoples and their cultures	a process automation of data acquisition, storage, organization and analysis with the technologies	games and gamification: the players interact both with each other and with programmed machine features
Falco and Kleinhans, 2018	Yaxue Ma et al., 2018	Shadbolt et al., 2019
digital participatory platforms as a specific kind of collaborative social media	a forming of an urban data service system, covering the entire process of data collection, organization, analysis and management	there is no simple dividing line between the human and the technological (a particular function is performed by a person or a computer)

The social machine approaches take into account the social aspect, and, to our mind, look like the most constructive ones (Berners-Lee and Fischetti, 1999). Social machines are co-created by human participants and technological components (Shadbolt et al., 2019). They bring people together, using technology to enable communication and cooperation at scale. Castronova (2005) considers games and gamification as examples of social machines, as the players, possibly using avatars or alternative identities, interact both with each other and with programmed machine features in a synthetic environment. The concept of digital urban space (Ma et al., 2018) proposes to use urban big data sensed from urban Cyber-Physical-Social spaces by transformation into smart data to meet the needs of urban management and operation. This approach is a kind of pragmatic and utility, however, does not sufficiently take into account the concept of social machine. It should be noted that none of the concepts gives a complete picture of the complexity and features of the Sociocultural Information Urban Space. Moreover, most of the concepts do not include the methods and information models for citizen's engagement in its formation and mechanisms to motivate the citizens' participation in decision-making in urban development sphere. The given research is filling this gap, presenting complete deterministic concept of service oriented SIUS.

3. SOCIOCULTURAL INFORMATION URBAN SPACE DESIGN

In order to clarify the understanding of the structure and composition of the Information Urban Space in sociocultural aspect, three initial concepts, associated with information space, have been reviewed and compared: Social Machine, Intercultural Communication Space, Technical-Resource Approach. It has allowed suggesting a hybrid Sociocultural Information Urban Space (SIUS) approach.

Sociocultural Information Urban Space, in our opinion, is an evolutionary development of concepts, presented above (Kononova et al., 2019). It has unique features – the ability to self-organization and self-development that is the most important for the modern smart city sustainability. There are two scenarios for the investigation and the design such space at once: top-down design (purposeful planning' view which identifies initiatives of city authorities, government structures, and business) and bottom-up design (entropy' view which identifies personal and public initiatives).

The idea to focus on the city sociocultural development gets reflected in the case-study on the instance of the project 'The Smart City Saint Petersburg'. SIUS of the modern city is viewed in this paper as an interactive form of communication between the subjects of the urban space.

Designing of SIUS architecture is necessary to identify sustainable relationships between its objects and subjects that determines the cultural environment of the modern smart city formation and its sustainable development. Building the SIUS architecture will determine the main mechanisms of citizens' involvement into the sociocultural information urban space.

Based on the city construction (Ma et al., 2018), we propose specific approach to the Sociocultural Information Urban Space formation, represented as one of the components of Smart Living (Giffinger et al., 2010). There are following main components of the SIUS in the electronic network environment: Internet sites; service-oriented Internet portals; social network. Besides, the components are divided into several main levels: administrative, organization-oriented level, commercial, socially oriented level.

4. ST. PETERSBURG CASE

The sociocultural information urban space of St. Petersburg has been chosen as the base of the empirical study. It was determined by following issues: researchers are the St. Petersburg SIUS subjects and they are involved into the processes of interaction with it; St. Petersburg is the cultural capital of Russia, and therefore, its sociocultural information space is the most developed among all Russian cities. It pervasive, and contains all the diversity of Russian culture, and the development of information infrastructure allow to identify the main components of the information cultural space. It is worth to note, that the modern Smart City focuses not only on certain technology packages, but forms a new society; the city solving sociocultural problems defines a breakthrough into the future. One of the developed directions of activity within the framework of the Smart City is the "Smart Environment". In the concept of "The Smart City St. Petersburg" project the principles affected the challenges of smart urban environment and Saint Petersburg' Smart City Architecture were formulated. According to the Conception (2019), smart urban environment: provides the needs and expectations of all citizens in all situations of life; aggregates open data, services and tools for its use; improves the quality of information interaction of all participants in urban processes; creates wide opportunities for self-realization for all categories of residents.

The approach involves the development of all elements that determine the cultural and historical code of the city, that emphasizes the pervasive nature of the smart urban environment and the importance of the main features of SIUS, as stated above. In accordance with the proposed approach to the formation of the information cultural space of the city, various network information resources, which represent different levels of the developed architecture, were considered. The interconnected components were defined, and the flow of information was revealed with the help of the expert method. To illustrate the pilot study, the example of "Afisha" commercial project in SIUS structure is given below (Figure 1) (Kononova et al., 2019). The "Afisha" is one of the largest commercial projects for tickets sale for cultural, sports and other events in Russia. The information (tickets) suppliers are theaters, cinemas, concert halls, music clubs, exhibition halls, museums etc. The Afisha has several information projects, which are represented by separate sites on the Internet. Besides, the Afisha is presented in social networks. Information resources, associated with this commercial project, form a single information space, which implements the various functions of the proposed approach to SIUS formation.

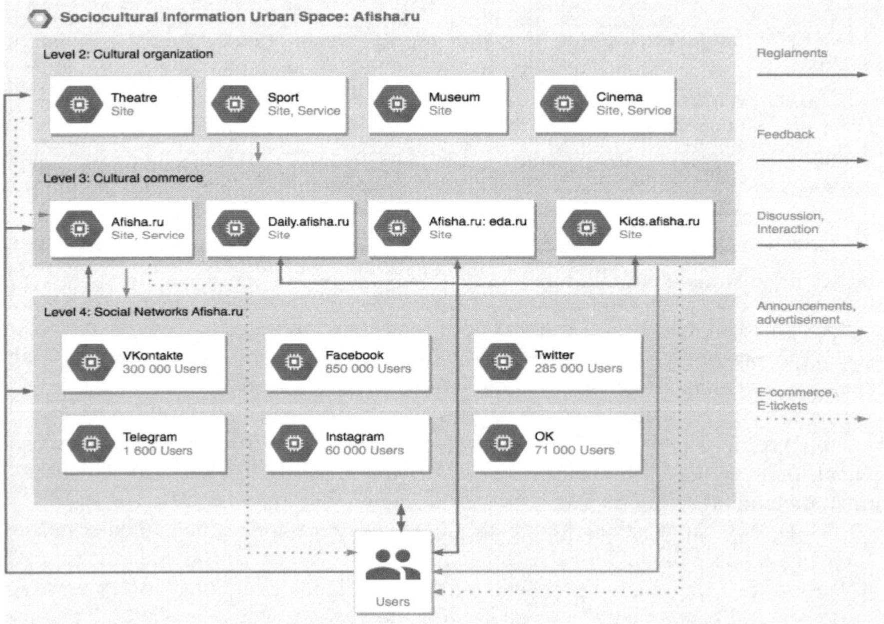

Figure 1. "Afisha" Commercial Project in SIUS Structure

5. CONCLUSION

In the result of the study the following items are concluded: the main subjects and objects of Sociocultural Information Urban Space (SIUS) and its interactions are identified; the main processes of SIUS are established; the Sociocultural Information Urban Space architecture has been developed, taking into account the pervasiveness peculiarities of the sociocultural space of the modern city; based on the analysis of Sociocultural Information Urban Space of St. Petersburg, various mechanisms of citizens' engagement into the active creative development of SIUS are revealed; It was found that the sustainable development of the modern information urban space is possible with maximum consideration of information flows: the sustainability is provided by information flows "from above" (formed by public and municipal authorities, cultural institutions and business); development is provided by information flows "from below" (people' initiatives and needs expressed in its activity in the SIUS); creative activity (Social Machines) and initiatives in SIUS should be supported by citizens presence and activity at all levels of architecture. The study can be considered as a source of knowledge and facilitates the better urban design, making it more functioning and more sustainable; optimize the use of limited resources and make better decisions in a Sociocultural Information Urban Space.

REFERENCES

Ahlers, D. et al, 2019. A Smart City Ecosystem Enabling Open Innovation. In: Lüke, K.-H., Eichler, G., Erfurth, C., Fahrnberger, G. *Innovations for Community Services.* 19th International Conference, I4CS 2019, Wolfsburg, Germany, June 24-26, Proceedings, pp. 109-122. DOI: https://link.springer.com/book/10.1007%2F978-3-030-22482-0.

Ahvenniemi, H. et al, 2017. What are the Differences Between Sustainable and Smart Cities? *Cities*, Vol. 60 (2017), pp. 234-245.

Barns, S., 2018. Smart Cities and Urban Data Platforms: Designing Interfaces for Smart Governance. *City, Culture and Society*, 12, pp. 5–12.

Belon, A. P. et al, 2015. Community Lenses Revealing the Role of Sociocultural Environment on Physical Activity. *In Am J Health Promot.* Vol. 30, No. 3, pp. e92–e100. DOI: 10.4278/ajhp.140428-QUAL-169.

Berners-Lee, T. and Fischetti, M., 1999. Weaving the Web: The Original Design and Ultimate Destiny of the World Wide Web by its inventor. Britain: Orion Business. ISBN 978-0-7528-2090-3.

Castronova E., 2005. *Synthetic Worlds: the Business and Culture of Online Games.* University of Chicago Press, Chicago.

Conception of St. Petersburg Development with the Help of 'Smart City' Technologies (Kontseptsia Razvitiya Sankt-Peterburga s Pomoshchyu Tekhnologiy 'Umnogo Goroda'), 2019. https://docs.wixstatic.com/ugd/548461_be60daeea6ca4768944e3af8344ba8b5.pdf.

Drotianko, L. and Yahodzinskyi, S., 2017. Information Environment as the Intercultural Communication Space. *MATEC Web Conf.*, Vol. 106. 01006. DOI: 10.1051/matecconf/201710601006.

Falco, E. and Kleinhans R., 2018. Beyond Technology: Identifying Local Government Challenges for Using Digital Platforms for Citizen Engagement. *International Journal of Information Management*, Vol. 40, pp. 17–20.

Giffinger, R. and Gudrun, H., 2010. Smart cities ranking: an effective instrument for the positioning of the cities? *Architecture City & Environment*, Vol. 6, No. 12, pp. 7-26.

Kartman, G, Sandnes, A., Smit, G., 2011. Creating Municipal ICT Architectures. A Reference Guide from Smart Cities. https://joinup.ec.europa.eu/document/eu-creating-municipal-ict-architectures-reference-guide-smart-cities.

Kononova O., Karachay V., Pilysova D., Prokudin D., 2019. Sociocultural Information Urban Space Construction. In Proceedings of the international conferences *ICT, Society and Human Beings 2019, Connected Smart Cities 2019 and Web Based Communities and Social Media 2019*, Porto, Portugal, July 17 - 19, 2019. Edited by Piet Kommers and Guo Chao Peng, IADIS Press, 2019. 456 p. Pp. 105-112. http://www.iadisportal.org/digital-library/sociocultural-information-urban-space-construction.

Ma, Y. et al., 2018. City profile: using smart data to create digital urban spaces. *ISPRS Ann. Photogramm. Remote Sens. Spatial Inf. Sci.*, Vol. IV-4/W7, pp. 75-82. DOI:10.5194/isprs-annals-IV-4-W7-75-2018.

Masucci, P. A. et al, 2014. Exploring the Evolution of London's Street Network in the Information Space: a Dual Approach. In Phys. Rev. E, Vol. 89, No. 1, 012805. DOI: 10.1103/PhysRevE.89.012805.

Narmeen, Z. B. and Jawwad, A. S., 2015. Smart City Architecture: Vision and Challenges. *In International Journal of Advanced Computer Science and Applications*, Vol. 6, No. 11, (2015), pp. 246-255. DOI: 10.14569/IJACSA.2015.061132.

Sharma, S. and Mehta, V., 2016. Socio-Cultural Context of Human Computer Interaction (HCI) in Online Shopping Environment. *In Apeejay-Journal of Management Sciences and Technology*, Vol. 4, No.1, pp. 26-36. https://apeejay.edu/aitsm/journal/docs/issue-oct-2016/ajmst040103.pdf.

Shadbolt, N., O'Hara, K., De Roure, D., Hall, W., 2019. *The Theory and Practice of Social Machines*. Springer Nature Switzerland AG, Switzerland. DOI: 10.1007/978-3-030-10889-2.

Sokolova, I. V., 2002. *Sotsialnaya Informatika (Social Informatics).* MGSU Publisher, Moscow, pp. 256.

Wakabayashi, M., 2002. Urban Space and Cyberspace: Urban Environment in the Age of Media and Information Technology. *International Journal of Japanese Sociology*. Vol. 11, No. 1, pp. 6-18. DOI: 10.1111/1475-6781.00014.

World Cities Report 2016. *Urbanization and Development: Emerging Futures.* United Nations Human Settlements Programme (UN-Habitat). http://wcr.unhabitat.org/wp-content/uploads/sites/16/2016/05/WCR-%20Full-Report-2016.pdf.

ONTOLOGY-DRIVEN SERVICE INTEGRATION INTO WEB APPLICATIONS: A DECLARATIVE APPROACH

Andreas Both[1], Didier Cherix[2] and Michael Martin[3]
[1]*Anhalt University of Applied Science; DATEV eG, Köthen, Germany; Nuremberg, Germany*
[2]*dokSAFE GmbH, Leipzig, Germany*
[3]*Institute for Applied Informatics (InfAI), Leipzig, Germany*

ABSTRACT

The majority of web applications nowadays are data-driven. However, that does not mean that all data is available while launching the respective application. While considering Web 2.0 applications, data is often fetched on-demand from remote web services, for example, after a location was provided, weather data could be fetched, and local news is loaded. This mashup approach is highly dynamical, i.e., based on the data input of the user, completely different execution paths might be performed. Currently, such workflows are implemented within the application logic requiring high development effort and maintenance of the implemented logic to prevent unintentional behavior.

In this paper, we present a novel approach to integrate web services dynamically, to decrease deployment and maintenance costs and to enable the next generation of interlinked data web applications to enables application architects to (re)define the data integration in a descriptive way in an ontology, validate the workflows and define logical requirements. However, our approach is not just a design method but also a method for ad hoc integration of new services. Our approach has a significant impact on the effort for generating and maintaining dynamic applications.

KEYWORDS

Service Composition, Web Service Integration, Web Application Engineering, Ontologies

1. INTRODUCTION

In the era of the web, an ecosystem of services has been established which provides various functionality to the web community. Nowadays, web applications are widely used and often driven by the data. Web applications take advantage of (a) data often provided by such services, (b) data which not exists while web applications are released, and (c) data which is not self-maintained and respective data structure could change during the lifecycle of the processing web application. Additionally, it can be observed that varying services are integrated having the same purpose but different preconditions before they can provide data. Hence, using web services provide several benefits and are legitimately used widely to develop web applications.

However, dynamically integrated services might lead to side effects because of many different application execution paths resulting in application workflows that can only be predicted and controlled by investing much time. While integrating services, the application logic needs to be updated or changed to prevent unwanted (or unsafe) situations (e.g., do not make functionality available without having the corresponding preconditions fulfilled). There would be a great benefit in providing a mechanism for auto-wiring web services as it will increase the efficiency and safety of the service integration dramatically. In particular, the manual investments (e.g., by application architects) for the service integration with relation to the given data structures can be replaced by an automatic configuration. In contrast to tool-centered approaches to integrate services, our approach is data-driven and provide solutions for most of the data integration challenges.

We provide a methodology based on the Web Ontology Language (OWL) to describe the data model of the web application and its service interfaces. Using this vocabulary application architects can define preconditions of service calls and resulting data flows of the application. As a consequence, (a) less source code has to be created (less time to market and decreased maintenance efforts) and (b) flexible configurations are available in a descriptive format (integration of new resp. modification of existing services at runtime) as well as (c) improved agile development processes will be enabled (coupling, rearrangement and reuse of software components). Hence, our approach has a major impact on the generation, extension and maintenance of web applications that are driven by data provided by external services.

2. RELATED WORK

A number of platform-specific frameworks emerged to assist ad hoc integration of functionalities into (web) applications, e.g., OSGi Service Platform[1]. Such frameworks ease development of modular and extensible applications, the control flow and integration logic still must be defined at design-time. In contrast, our approach enables emerging control-flows and specification of integration constraints at run-time.

In Web Engineering several methods have been proposed to componentize applications and, thus, make their development and evolution more efficient, e.g., WebComposition (Gellersen, 1997). Mashup platforms such as OMELETTE (Chudnovskyy, 2012) define coarse-grained components called widgets and enable ad hoc composition of applications by non-programmers. CRUISE (Pietschmann, 2011) operates with universal components such as data feeds, web services or UI widgets and applies Semantic Web technologies to perform run-time discovery and context-dependent adaptation of applications. However, this work focuses on data-driven components only and explores ways of their transparent integration into generic, also non-component-based applications. Hence, it is more general.

Intelligent integration of platform-independent modules has been discussed in the context of Semantic Web Services (SWS) aiming to enable automatic discovery, invocation and composition of distributed heterogeneous functionalities, e.g., OWL-S (Martin, 2004) and Minimal Service Model (Pedrinaci, 2010). Frameworks with automatic discovery and composition capabilities have been presented, e.g., proposing a method to semantically describe and compose web services, e.g. in (Rodriguez, 2015). However, the focus lies on application integration aspects and less on extensive capability modeling. Semantic technologies have been also applied to build generic web applications. Hera (Sluijs, 2010) enables the description of application structure and behavior using a set of semantic models and interpreted by a dedicated run-time engine. The presented approach also aims at defining business logic explicitly and in a declarative way. However, it doesn't require the whole application to be modelled semantically, but rather can be seamlessly integrated with in any environment and service type.

3. BACKGROUND

The Resource Description Framework (RDF)[2] is a general-purpose language for representing information in the web. On top of RDF the Web Ontology Language (OWL) is extending the vocabulary with more possibilities to describe relations between classes and properties. SPARQL is an RDF query language for adding, retrieving and changing RDF data. In the following the standardized Manchester syntax[3] is used to represent RDF data. Here, besides standard properties like `SubClassOf` and `rdf:label` we use just the following expressions, where `A` and `B` are resources and `prop` is a property (c.f., Listing 1).

`A prop: some B`: If `A` and `B` are resources, then the constraint hold iff there are instances available, s.t., it matches the expression `A prop: B`.	`A prop: max 0 B}`: If `A` and `B` are resources, then the constraint hold iff there is no data available matching the expression `A prop: B`.	`A EquivalentTo: B` (symmetric relation): If `A` and `B` are classes, then each instance of `A` is also an instance of `B`.

Listing 1. Used RDF expressions in Manchester syntax

For evaluation of constraints reasoners (reasoning engines) are used. They ensure that the defined rules are obeyed and highlight constraint violations (implementation depended). Here, we use only reasoners that follow the closed world assumptions, i.e., unless an atomic sentence is known to be true, it can be assumed to be false. In this paper we use the following (web) service definition: A call of a service `S` is defined by the signature `R S(P)`, where `R` is a struct of return values and `P` is a list of named parameters.

[1] https://www.osgi.org/developer/architecture/
[2] http://www.w3.org/TR/2004/REC-rdf-syntax-grammar-20040210/
[3] http://www.w3.org/TR/owl2-manchester-syntax/

4. PROBLEM DESCRIPTION AND GOALS

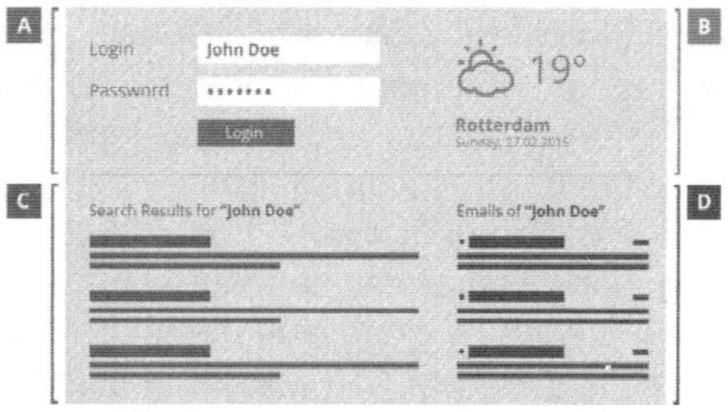


```
// service i2c: resolves an IP to a
Geolocation
(Point pos) i2c(Integer IP);
// service wea: returns weather data
for a given Geolocation
(Blob weather) wea(Point position);
// service pp: returns the personal
profile data of a user (protected
portal)
(String user, Blob emails, Blob
weather) pp(String user, String
password);
(String user, Blob emails, Blob
weather) pp(String accesstoken);
// service se: search engine provides
search results for a given query
string
(Blob searchresults) se(String
query);
```

Figure 1. Exemplary web portal and corresponding service signatures

Developing an application in the Web 2.0 era is very often driven by the integration of external services. In Figure 1 an application is described that allows to login (A) and shows thereafter the emails of the user (C). In addition, for the provided username a search is performed (D). The application also shows the weather of the user's location (B). All data is retrieved from external services that need to be integrated within the application. During the engineering process the application architect has to decide which functionality of external services has to be defined. E.g., `username` and `password` are used to identify the user and fetch the profile data of the user (it is also possible to login with an `accesstoken`), the `emails` of the user are part of the profile data, `weather` information is presented for the current user's location.

Application architects must capture all possible execution paths within the application. Therefore, we derive the following requirements: (R1) as application architect, I want to change the data flows of the application via configuration, and (R2) I want to integrate new services within the application via configuration, (R3) each service can be defined independently from the application including its constraints. Concluding, applications should integrate web services via a descriptive methodology.

5. APPROACH AND EXECUTION PROCESS

First the **creation of the application data model** *adm* needs to be performed while defining all available data types and data items while defining parameters, expected return values and the constraints.[4]

Class: n SubClassOf: gd:value some t, gd:value some gd:Thing DatatypeProperty: gd:value .	Prefix adm: <urn:example:current-application-data-model> Class: adm:IP SubClassOf: gd:Decimal SubClassOf: gd:Thing

Listing 2. General definition of a data type and the exemplary definition of the IP class

A data type[5] of the *adm* with the name `n` and the data type `t` is defined as in Listing 3. For example, a string data type can be defined with `n:=gd:String` and `t:=xsd:string`, making available a String data type within in the namespace `gd` and of type `String` of the `xsd` namespace which is also a subtype of

[4] A generalized exemplary implementation is shown in the online appendix using the services described in Figure 1 available at https://cutt.ly/CwTm75s.

[5] To be clear this definition of data type has nothing in common with RDF datatype.

`gd:Thing`.[6] Now, it is possible to define data items needed for the application as subtypes of the defined data types. A data item within the application data model *adm* with the name `n` and the data type `t` is defined as shown in Figure 1. The functionality shown there might be implemented using the corresponding services. The goal of the application is to provide the information to the user depending on the data that was made available. Data can be made available via user input (`username`) or by the client (`IP`).

(a) Class: n SubClassOf: t	(b) Class: adm:username SubClassOf: gd:String

Listing 3. General definition of a parameter and the exemplary definition of username

First, data items of the service are defined as resource. Data items of a service are made known by defining the label of each parameter. Additionally, for each field within the returned result the label is defined, too, as shown in Listing 4.

(a) Class: s:n Annotations: rdfs:label "n"	(a) Class pp:password Annotations: rdfs:label "password"

Listing 4. General definition of a return values and the exemplary definition of returning a password variable

Up to now the *adm* does not clarify whether the data item is a parameter of the service call or part of the result. It just defines the classes needed for the later data bindings. Hence, just the service data was defined.

Secondly, the preconditions of a service call have to be defined. In OWL syntax we use a type definition to represents that input parameters are necessary. A service is defined within the `gd` namespace and a relation called `hasParam` is defined to express the bound of a service instance to input parameters (see Listing 5).

(a) Class: gd:Service ObjectProperty: gd:hasParam Domain: gd:Service Range: gd:Thing	(b) Class se:constraint SubClassOf gd:Service EquivalentTo: (gd:hasParam some se:query) and (gd:hasParam max 0 se:searchresults)

Listing 5. General definition of the input of a service and the exemplary constraint of the searchengine service (se)

Now, it is possible to define the precondition for a service call. For a given service `s` (represented as namespace) a constraint is defined that demands that all mandatory parameter `p_i` are available and have at least one valid value assigned (in OWL: `some`) and at least one return value `r_j` was not computed yet (i.e., is not available). See the following listing for the general definition and an example (c.f., Listing 6).

(a) Class: s:constraint SubClassOf: gd:Service EquivalentTo: (gd:hasParam some p_1) and ... and (gd:hasParam some p_i) and ((gd:hasParam max 0 r_1) or ... or (gd:hasParam max 0 r_j))	(b) Class: pp:constraint SubClassOf: gd:Service EquivalentTo: (gd:hasParam some pp:username) AND (gd:hasParam some pp:password) AND (gd:hasParam max 0 pp:emails)

Listing 6. General definition of a service call precondition and the exemplary constraint of the pp service

Given these definitions of the services and their parameters, a formal representation of the service landscape was established within the constructed *adm*. Note that this representation is compatible with any kind of real-world service description. Hence, the requirement of composability is fulfilled.

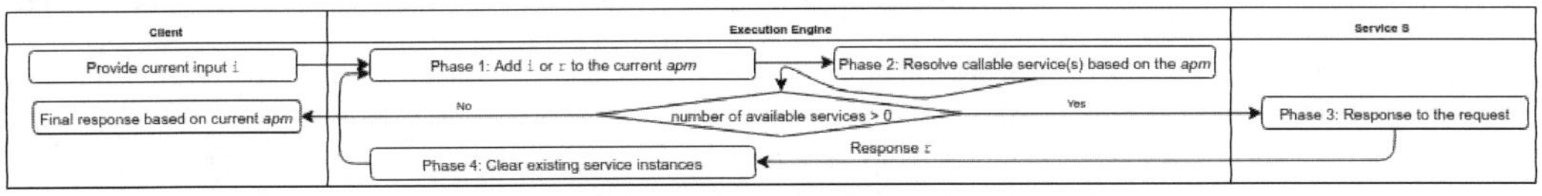

Figure 2. Execution process of automatic data integration

[6] Note: In the following the namespace `gd` is used for general definitions and the namespace `adm` for definitions of data items within the *apm*.

After creating the initial *adm* it is used in an **execution process** consisting of the phases (c.f., Figure 2): (1) data assignment, (2) constraint evaluation, (3) the execution of service calls, and (4) closing model cleanup. In **phase 1** (data assignment) the initial data application model *adm* is interpreted. Without any loss of generality, it is assumed that all data items of the *adm* are (defined but) not instantiated. To initialize a data flow, at least one data item of the *apm* must be instantiated. A new resource is inserted representing the value and making it available within the *apm*. Here, there is no constraint whether the data was assigned by a manual data input or any other interaction with the *adm*. In **phase 2** every constraint of the ontology is evaluated. This is done by just constructing a new service instances as the ontology will only allow to be instantiated if all corresponding constraints are obeyed. After this step the ontology contains instances of the type `gd:Service` that represent the services being enabled to be called. Thereafter all instances of services are available obeying the related preconditions. In **phase 3** the execution engine queries all service types (i.e., the services that can be called) via SPARQL. One service is chosen to be called (concurrent calls are possible but avoided in this paper for the sake of clarification). The required input parameters to call the chosen service are fetched from the ontology. The response of called service is stored in a temporal variable `r`. In **phase 4** all service instances are removed from the ontology. Thereafter, no service instances are available within the ontology. Now, the response data provided in `r` is used within phase 1 to establish a process loop.

6. CONCLUSION

Nowadays, many web applications are data-driven. In many cases, the data is not available completely within the application but needs to be fetched from remote services (often called mashup). Hence, integrating the data of web services is one of the main tasks for architects designing and developing industrial and academic web applications. However, it causes serious and increasing development effort using traditional methodologies where the application data flow logic is implemented (manually) in program code.

The main contribution our approach is the methodology of integrating services automatically. Our approach is capable of using the provided data within the application and to control the constraints in a descriptive way. In contrast to previous work, the application workflow is driven by configuration only. Additionally, it can be updated and extended at runtime and is not fixed to one type of web services.

The described process engine is independent from the actual service implementations and just driven by the ontology. This is a key feature of our method as it provides a formal description of the services and the process. The ontology is also the key asset on the way to control the application behavior. While using a standard vocabulary for describing the constraints, standard components (i.e., reasoners) can be used for validating the preconditions of service calls. Finally, the control of the application is actually in the hands of the application architect, leading to a consistent documentation, clear constraints and implementation of the data workflows leading to an application data model that can be extended and validated.

In the future, we will extend the data model by additional functionalities, e.g. time dependency, a data flow evaluation process (to prevent unreachable services) and integrating interfaces version (Arndt, 2018).

REFERENCES

Arndt, N. et al., 2018. Decentralized collaborative knowledge management using git. *Journal of Web Semantics*.

Chudnovskyy, O. et al., 2012. End-User-Oriented Telco Mashups: The OMELETTE Approach. *In WWW 2012 Companion Volume*, pages 235–238.

Gellersen, H.-W. et al., 1997. WebComposition: an object-oriented support system for the web engineering lifecycle. *Computer Networks and ISDN Systems*, 29(813):1429 – 1437.

Martin, D. et al., 2004. OWL-S: Semantic markup for web services. *W3C member submission*, 22:2007–04.

Pedrinaci, C. and Domingue, J., 2010. Toward the next wave of services: Linked services for the web of data. *J. of Universal Comp. Science*, 16(13):1694–1719.

Pietschmann, S. et al., 2011. Semantics-based discovery, selection and mediation for presentation-oriented mashups. *5th International Workshop on Web APIs and Service Mashups*, Mashups '11. ACM.

Rodriguez-Mier, P. et al., 2015. An Integrated Semantic Web Service Discovery and Composition Framework. *IEEE Transactions on Services Computing*, 9(4), pages 537–550.

DECENTRALIZING PRODUCTS CERTIFICATES USING BLOCKCHAIN TECHNOLOGY

Eduard Daoud and Martin Gaedke
Technische Universität Chemnitz, Germany

ABSTRACT

OECD wrote in their report 2016 that up to 5% of imports are counterfeited goods. The report estimated this damage at EUR 85 billion (OECD/EUIPO, 2016). The presence of counterfeit products on the European market is on the increase, therefore the intervention of inspection bodies and authorities alone is not sufficient, consumers can make their contribution and support this process. 2003 started the EU a program "Rapid Alert System" as an information platform to publish alerts about dangerous products in the market. Over 2 000 alerts published by the system yearly. Thus, allowing local authorities to screen their market and take appropriate action should the same product be found (Directorate-General for Justice and Consumers (European Commission), 2018). In this paper, we propose the foundations of a new system for decentralizing product certificate based on blockchain technology which close the gaps of the unilateral published digital certificate. The decentralizing of product certification by using blockchain technology empowers consumers by easily verifying a product certificate, at the same time enable certification bodies to issue and sharing a certificate in tamperproof ways. This could be one of the important steps in the direction to reduce counterfeiting. The goal of this paper is to create a new category of applications in which the end-user identifies counterfeit product certificates and contribute to the fight against product piracy.

KEYWORDS

Blockchain, Decentralization, Information Access, Certification Industry, Counterfeiting

1. INTRODUCTION AND THE CURRENT PROBLEM

The problem is that every certificate issuer publishes their certificate on their websites in a way which not easier to retrieve or check the validity of a certificate and interact with the certification marks. One of the possible solutions is to build a central database for all certificates from all certification bodies and inspection agencies as a single point of access but such a platform depends on the certification bodies in the first line which they are in a competitive relationship with each other, this reduces the willingness to implement such solutions much more important is the data inaccuracy and how easy to the fake certificate to go to the market.

Since its launch in 2003, the EU's Rapid Alert System has been providing EU member States with a network and communication tools to publicize counterfeit products. The system stabilizes at regular intervals, about 50 alerts are published each week on the European Commission's website, with slightly more than 2,000 alerts released each year. (Directorate-General for Justice and Consumers (European Commission), 2018).

The number of counterfeits reported products is extremely low in relation to the number of counterfeit products imported into the EU. OECD wrote in their report 2016 that up to 5% of imports are counterfeited goods. The report estimated this damage at EUR 85 billion (OECD/EUIPO, 2016). Currently, product certificate data are mainly stored separated by the deferent institutions, which hinders the easy information exchange and collaboration between consumer and these institutions. Data security and the competition situation on the market in the first line leads to the fact that the institutions don't share their data to create a single point of access, because the failure to secure the product provider/retailer (as regards the certificate) leads to legal and financial consequences for the institutions.

In the next section, we will introduce the principles of the Blockchain and headline the social value shortly, after introducing the principles of the approach, we examined and substantiated the software stack based on Ethereum Blockchain and other technical components to store and retrieve industry product certificate finally the challenges, conclusion and future works.

2. PRINCIPLES OF THE BLOCKCHAIN

A Blockchain is a distributed append-only store of transactions across computational nodes and structured as a linked list of blocks, each containing a set of transactions (Weber, et al., 2019). Blockchain was introduced as the technology behind Bitcoin (Nakamoto, 2008). The blockchain is generally categorized into two classes (Prusty, 2018):

Table 1. Categories of Blockchain (simplified)

Blockchain Category	Community	Example
Permissioned	proprietary networks	Group of banks
Permissionless	opensource networks	Anyone can access and use.

A Blockchain is a community topic as a distributed ledger every member of the community could validate any shared information collectively. Any digital assets could be recorded as an information entry. This entry is accessible, permanent, transparent and auditable. These characteristics enable the participants to understand everything at a certain point in time. Information is represented in entries blocks and stored at the end of the chain. The management of the entries and their distribution is the responsibility of blockchain protocol (consensus protocol). There is no central management, monitoring and trust instance in the Blockchain concept. (Grech & Camilleri, 2017).

To understand blockchain technology more we need to underline the term ledger. Ledgers are a list of sequential transactions with timestamp allowed each participant of the community at any time to determine the owner of an asset (Grech & Camilleri, 2017). Therefore, Blockchains are a linear sequence of blocks with a timestamp and linked internally cryptographically. There are some characteristics depend on the architecture of the Blockchain and the consensus protocol like immutability, security, validity and transparency.

Some Blockchains are established as a "distributed" network structure and facilitate peer-to-peer transactions across non-hierarchical nodes. Some blockchains, on the other hand, are to be categorized by their consensus protocol for the immutability of their ledgers. In order to understand and classify the impact of the blockchain on society, the topic of social principles of the blockchain should be explored and analyzed in the same way as technical principles. (Grech & Camilleri, 2017). Following the arguments in (Grech & Camilleri, 2017) in the educational environment and (Piscini, et al., 2016), in general, an attempt is to be made to propose some blockchain principles that represent social value propositions in the industrial environment like self-sovereignty and identity, trust, transparency and provenance, immutability and disintermediation.

After underlining of the principles for in this paper researched approach, we will not go into the details of the social principles. This is a topic for further leading research work. In order to understand the approach more deeply and after the introduction of the principle of Blockchain we shall lead to possible system architecture and its design to the creation of an industrial product and service certificate.

3. ARCHITECTURE DESIGN OF THE APPROACHED SYSTEM

Transactions, smart contract and digital signatures are generally the important records stored in a Blockchain. Transactions have two components digital currency and documentary part of ownership. Smart contracts are computer algorithm stored on a blockchain, describe an agreement between all participants in the Blockchain. Digital signatures are evidence that the statements have been issued by and to the named parties. Before we go deeper into the design of the system for managing industry product certificates, we need first to try to start defining industry certificates and shortly pointing out the demarcation line of the approach.

A certificate, in general, confirms a claim against standards. In the industrial environment, there are three areas for certification: certification of products and services or certification of management systems. A valid certificate can be issued if all financial and technical requirements are met (TÜV SÜD AG, 2019). In certain industries, certification is part of the legal requirements. In general, the certificates increase the credibility of the product or service and affect the expectations and decisions of the consumer. A certificate has essentially the following attributes, these are described in the following table:

Table 2. Certificate attributes

Attributes	Brief explanation
The claim	Statement/Declaration
An issuer	A company/third party that confirms the truth of the statement.
Evidence	The description of the test procedures with further clarification about the claim.
A recipient	The company/supplier or service provider that has submitted a claim for certification.
A certificate	Dataset of different metadata and parameters
A certification Mark	As a kind of image or textual representation to demonstrate compliance with certain standards.
A signature	A certificate contains a unique code for the product to validate and confirm its identity.

After shortly highlighting the topic certificate, the architecture of the system for managing product certificates should cover the involves three processes: issuing, sharing and retrieving. The new approached system should not cover certification in the education sector but only in the industrial area and in the same time it should be able to close the gap of current certificates systems between the consumer and certificate holder.

The current system in which most records are still issued as hybrid certificates (paper and digital) and there is no 'standard format' for certificates. The approached blockchain-based distributed system is based on a public Blockchain and allow a certificate issuer to signs a well-structured certificate and stores its hash within an Ethereum Blockchain transaction. Firstly, we need to go deeper on how is the method to issue a certificate in the Figure:

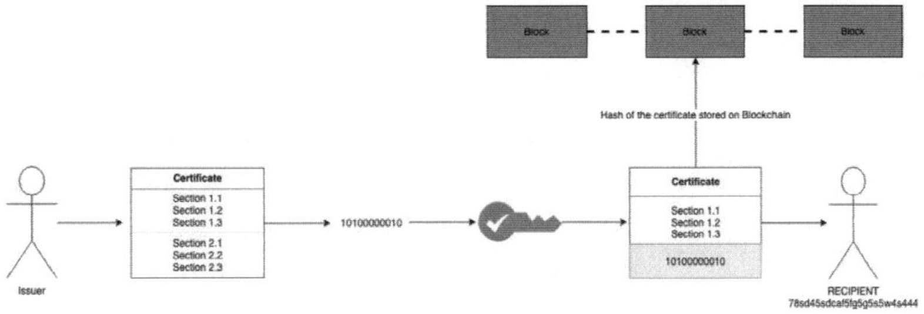

Figure 1. Issuing a certificate on Blockchain

As soon as the certification body creates a certificate in digital form, this file should be issued with some basic information like such as the name of the issuer and recipient and the issue date etc. The issuer shall then cryptographically sign the content of the certificate with a private key to which only the issuer has privileged access. The issuer of the certificate stores his signature in the certificate dataset. The cryptographic hashing the credentials information to allowed users to check the contents of the certificates against manipulation. In the end, the issuer uses his private key again to write the record in the blockchain.

The issuer makes the certificate available to the recipient (sharing), e.g. directly for accessing on his website. The important point in publishing and sharing the certificate is to ensure that every other internet user can access the certificate. The recipient can mention his digital certificates on his products or make them available on his website. Now, all basic requirements are fulfilled so that the end-consumer can simply check an issued certificate (retrieving). The system uses a permissionless (public) Blockchain for issuing certificates, this means that anyone connected to the network could validate and verify the certificate information with help of the smart contract address.

After introducing the three main processes of the approaches system: Issuing, sharing and retrieving of the certificate, the next figure addresses the high-level system component overview:

Figure 2. High level system overview

The high-level System overview provides an overview of the components which spat into frontend and backend as a main component. The frontend consists of different access clients. The backend based on a web server, a local Datastore and also runs a full Blockchain node (Ethereum). A more detailed view of the server architecture and using smart contract is provided in the next section.

4. SOFTWARE STACK BASED ON ETHEREUM BLOCKCHAIN

Ethereum provides a universal Blockchain combined with a Turing full programming language to enable the development and implementation of applications that make use of the Blockchain (Vitalik, 2014). Moreover, Hyperledger is also open-source technology which allows developers to set up their private network to advance cross-industry blockchain technologies (Grech & Camilleri, 2017).

We choose Ethereum Blockchain technology based on the following criteria. Transparent: Using Hyperledger is not possible, because the approached system should be a public blockchain network. Smart Contract: Allow using smart contracts to define some runnable code for negotiation and facilitation. To demonstrate the approach from the technical side we need to go deeper from the high-level overview to a software stack description of the two main components. The next figure explains the two main components:

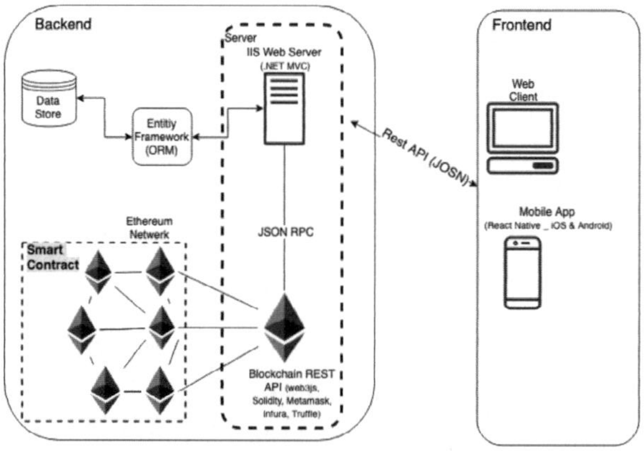

Figure 3. Technical architecture

The frontend is a public web application act as access clients (.NET MVC) communicate with a web server runs on IIS in the backend. The backend has also an internal JavaScript runtime environment (NodeJS). The two main components communicate with each other via the REST API (JSON) to handle user requests and interact with the Ethereum network. The web application framework is ASP.NET MVC an open-source framework, which implements the model-view-controller pattern. The webserver provides RESTful service endpoint. The most crucial part of the approach is the internal part (Backend) that interacts with the Ethereum network. The public web application handles user requests and interacts with NodeJS within IIS Web server to process these data that related to Ethereum network, such as: create a new smart contract, deploy it to Ethereum node, query data or search information.

Both parts are also connected to our internal management relational databases to make sure that these data have to be consistent. To interact with a smart contract, we use Nodejs to build our interaction part with the Blockchain network and Metamask to create and manage Blockchain wallet to connect to the network. To sign a smart contract, the system needs a tool like Truffle to sign the transaction. Importantly, data such as certificate information are not stored directly in the block of the Ethereum. Only the root node hashes of the transaction, state and receipt are stored directly in the blockchain to gain more experience and test how to store and retrieve certificate information from Ethereum Blockchain we started a new research process handle these two points separately.

In the following section, we discuss the challenges of our approach bevor we headline the summary and an outlook on our work.

5. CHALLENGES

From the analysis of the selected literature, a series of insights can be derived concerning the challenges of the approached blockchain-based distributed systems and its usability across a wide area of industry certification. However, like any other emerging technology, issues and challenges arise. One of the challenges in decentralizing of product certificates using blockchain technology is the integrity of data, followed by blockchain confidentiality and the willingness to share information.

Many companies include the data collected from the customer in their assessment of the value-added process to create new products and or services. Therefore, protecting privacy should be placed when considering how such records could be integrated into a Blockchain. Confidentiality involves the protection of data from unauthorized disclosure, either by direct retrieval or by indirect logical inference. Among others, issues such as third-party confidentiality violations are being scrutinized.

All changes in the Blockchain are to be acknowledged and stored audit-ably, that could be the best way to ensure the integrity of the data. This preserves the accuracy, consistency, and validity of the data throughout its lifecycle. Searchability, recoverability, traceability and connectivity of certificate data are some important properties provided by ensuring the integrity of data. The integrity of data should be comprehensively researched and some projects as Enigma in MIT (Zyskind, et al., 2015) could make a valuable contribution.

The willingness to share information from testing and inspections agencies is one of the no-technical challenges. By doing a small experimental project with real users and with one of the certification bodies could be a good start to demonstrate the long-term effects of the approach. In general, there are several of challenges and limitations of the blockchain technology these are comprehensively addressed in this paper (Casino, et al., 2019, pp. 55-81) like suitability of Blockchain, latency and scalability and blockchain adoption and interoperability. After highlighting the challenges, we headline a summary and an outlook on our work.

6. CONCLUSION AND FUTURE WORKS

This paper presents a new approach as platform architecture to decentralizing products certificates using blockchain technology. We evaluate the solution by using a Bitcoin Blockchain as a proof of concept focused on feasibility in this paper (Daoud, 2019) and found a lot of limitations.

The blockchain-based distributed approach used in core standard web technologies and Ethereum network. The conclusions we can define from the new approach are that the implementation of the system should be deeper researched, from the point of view of completely open blockchain or hybrid. The main focus is on which implementations have a positive impact on anti-counterfeiting of products and the adoption of blockchain-based certificates depends on how the consumer can easily and simply interact with the system.

In future work, we plan to explore and research more about using machine learning to classify certificate marks and logos of certification bodies to unleash the potential of blockchain-based certificate retrieving possibilities shortly we are intending to provide a better way of giving information, by scanning the products itself and using AI-based Image recognition. This would combine two state-of-the-art technologies, machine learning and blockchain, in one application. That will bring great convenience and a better experience for users.

However, we trust that the decentralizing of product certification by using blockchain technology will change the role and empower the consumer to drive the market for more transparency.

REFERENCES

Casino, F., Dasaklis, T. K. & Patsakis, C., 2019. A systematic literature review of blockchain-based applications. *Telematics and Informatics,* pp. 55-81.

Daoud, E., 2019. Decentralizing of Transparency: Using Blockchain to Reduce Counterfeiting. Utrecht, the Netherlands, IADIS Press, p. 8.

Directorate-General for Justice and Consumers (European Commission), 2018. *Results of the EU rapid alert system for dangerous non-food products,* Brussels: European Commission.

Elmasri, R. & Navathe , S. . B., 2015. *Fundamentals of Database Systems.* s.l.:Pearson.

Ethereum Foundation (Stiftung Ethereum), 2018. *Ethereum Project.* [Online] Available at: https://www.ethereum.org/ [Accessed 19 08 2019].

Gideon, G., 2017. *Blockchains vs Centalized databases.* [Online] Available at: https://www.multichain.com/blog/2016/03/blockchains-vs-centralized-databases/ [Accessed 19 01 2019].

Grech, A. & Camilleri, A. F., 2017. *Blockchain in Education,* European Union: European Union.

Nakamoto, S., 2008. *Bitcoin: A Peer-to-Peer Electronic Cash System.* [Online] Available at: https://bitcoin.org/bitcoin.pdf [Accessed 18 07 2019].

OECD/EUIPO, 2016. Trade in Counterfeit and Pirated Goods: Mapping the Economic Impact. Paris: OECD Publishing.

Peters, G. C. A. &. P. E. J. B. R., 2016. Opening discussion on banking sector risk exposures and vulnerabilities from Virtual currencies. *Journal of Banking Regulation,* Issue 4, p. 239–272.

Peters, G. W. & Panayi, E., 2015. Understanding modern banking ledgers through blockchain technologies. *Computers and Society (cs.CY); Cryptography and Security (cs.CR),* pp. 5-6.

Piscini, E., Guastella, J., Alex, R. & Nassim, T., 2016. *Deloitte University Press..* [Online] Available at: https://www2.deloitte.com/content/dam/Deloitte/uk/Documents/technology/deloitte-uk-tech-trends-2016-blockchain.pdf [Accessed 28 09 2019].

Prusty, N., 2018. Blockchain for Enterprise: : Build scalable blockchain applications with privacy, interoperability, and permissioned features. Birgmingham: s.n.

Redmond , E. & Wilson, J. R., 2012. Seven Databases in Seven Weeks: A Guide to Modern Databases and the NoSQL Movement. s.l.:North.

Remeur, C., 2017. *Market surveillance and product safety,* Bruessel: European Parliament.

Sirpa, P., Françoise, G. & Bart, S., n.d. *Member States should stop turning a blind eye to product safety,* s.l.: The Parliament Magazine.

TÜV SÜD AG, n.d. *Certificate Explorer.* [Online] Available at: https://www.tuev-sued.de/product-testing/certificates [Accessed 06 09 2019].

TÜV SÜD AG, n.d. *Misuse of quality marks.* [Online] Available at: https://www.tuev-sued.de/product-testing/_services/markets_and_competition/quality_and_test_marks/abuse_of_quality_marks [Accessed 12 08 2019].

Tabora, V., 2018. *Hacker Noon.* [Online] Available at: https://hackernoon.com/databases-and-blockchains-the-difference-is-in-their-purpose-and-design-56ba6335778b [Accessed 19 01 2019].

The Netherlands Court of Audit, 2017. *Products sold on the European market: unravelling the system of CE marking,* Netherlands: House of Representatives.

Vitalik, B., 2014. A next-generation smart contract and decentralized application platform. *Ethereum White Paper,* Volume 3, p. 37.

Vukolić, M., 2016. The quest for scalable blockchain fabric: Proof-of-work vs. BFT replication. Zurich, Springer Verlag.

Weber, I. et al., 2019. A Platform Architecture for Multi-Tenant Blockchain-Based Systems. *IEEE International Conference on Software Architecture (ICSA2019),* p. 10.

Zhao, J., Fan, S. &. Y. & J. , F. I., 2016. Overview of business innovations and research opportunities in blockchain and introduction to the special issue. *Financial Innovation,* 2(1), p. 28.

Zyskind, G., Nathan, O. & Pentland, A., 2015. Enigma: Decentralized Computation Platform with Guaranteed Privacy. *Cryptography and Security.*

DO NOT HATE THE PLAYERS THE DIGITAL ADVERTISING ECOSYSTEM AND ITS ACTORS

Valerio Stallone
Zurich University of Applied Sciences, Center for Digital Marketing
Stadthausstrasse 14, CH-8400 Winterthur, Switzerland

ABSTRACT

This paper presents a systematic review of the literature of 29 research articles, which used a visualization of the digital advertising ecosystem with a focus on online real-time advertising. This review aims to address a gap in the literature by identifying a standardization of digital advertising ecosystem visualization and explanation. Achieving this aim will bring together fragmented literature to serve as a foundation for research into digital advertising ecosystems and other related research. There are discrepancies, which imply different understandings of how the advertising ecosystem elements work and communicate. This work should minimize the risk of wrong conclusions in literature as well as in practice. The author therefore recommends a visualization; future researchers should challenge.

KEYWORDS

Digital Marketing, Display Advertising, Programmatic Advertising, Real-Time Bidding, Digital Advertising Ecosystem

1. INTRODUCTION

Visiting a website or opening a free app often results in a certain amount of frustration. This paper focuses on the advertising technology applications and players that build an ecosystem, which enables publishers to connect to advertisers. In the ecosystem that has evolved in literature, the author finds a setting of intermediaries who are taking part in an auction, which connects buyers and sellers of a unique, indivisible good: The impression (Feldman *et al.*, 2010). Stallone & Klaas have tried to keep up with the pace by modelling and analyzing different aspects of marketing technology adaptations (Stallone and Klaas, 2019). In their paper they have analyzed literature, which discussed at least two elements of the digital advertising ecosystem ("DAE") and dated 2015 or younger. By doing so, they were able to recommend a visualization of the DAE, which future researchers could have been relying upon for their studies. In this review, the author will enlarge the set of articles as well as presenting a new methodological approach to the literature review. In the last chapter, the author suggests an updated version of the standardization of the DAE visualization for scientific literature as well as for work in non-academic fields.

2. LITERATURE REVIEW

Attention is the resource advertisers and publisher depend upon: Muthukrishnan first stated this known concept in a digital framework in the end of the last decade (Muthukrishnan, 2009). Muthukrishnan also mentioned, that "the way of selling and buying ads on the Internet via an exchange (market) brings sellers (supply) and buyers (demand) together" (Muthukrishnan, 2009). The seller supplies inventory as well as human eyes, which the demand buys. This marketplace, the DAE, outgrew the simple exchange platform and added new elements to it: While keeping the supply, the demand, the market and the user side, researchers completed the DAE by the data side (Callejo, 2015; Yuan, 2015; Papadopoulos *et al.*, 2017; Wang, Zhang and Yuan, 2017). So-called data management platforms have emerged to help advertisers merge and manage data in large volumes in order to make better buying decisions (Nicholls, Malins and Horner, 2013).

3. RESEARCH METHOD

This review investigates the digital advertising ecosystem from a multidisciplinary perspective. The author selected peer-reviewed articles from four bibliographic databases (IEEE Xplore, Sage journals online, Science Direct & Google Scholar). The author considered peer-reviewed journals and conference proceedings based no their knowledge validity and their highest impact on the research field. To ensure the relevance of the articles in this study, the author used a combination of four keywords. Each of the selected articles is required to contain one of the following combinations of keywords at least in the abstract:

1. *digital advertising* AND *ecosystem*
2. *display advertising* AND *ecosystem*
3. *programmatic advertising* AND *ecosystem*
4. *real time bidding* AND *ecosystem*

After the first research round, the author found himself with a lack of content. This is why he enlarged the methodology by five combinations of keyword research and content analysis:

5. *ad exchange* AND containing a figure showing a visualization of an ecosystem
6. *data management platform* AND containing a figure showing a visualization of an ecosystem
7. *ad server* AND containing a figure showing a visualization of an ecosystem
8. *dsp*/*demand side platform* AND containing a figure showing a visualization of an ecosystem
9. *ssp*/*supply side platform* AND containing a figure showing a visualization of an ecosystem

The search of articles was limited to English & German speaking journals between 2013 & 2019. The rationale is to capture the latest change in investigating the digital advertising ecosystem. The first search generated 112 articles, which were further limited to those visualizing the digital advertising ecosystem. Finally, the author included 29 articles.

4. DESCRIPTIVE RESULTS

The author analyzed the reviewed literature on year of publication, theoretical framework and content differences.

4.1 Year of Publication

Table 1 shows that the highest number of publications between in 2017, which slightly declined in 2018. The trend is evident: Researchers obviously make use of a visualization of the DAE in their analyses, whereas the need is growing more and more.

Table 1. The overview of the reviewed papers

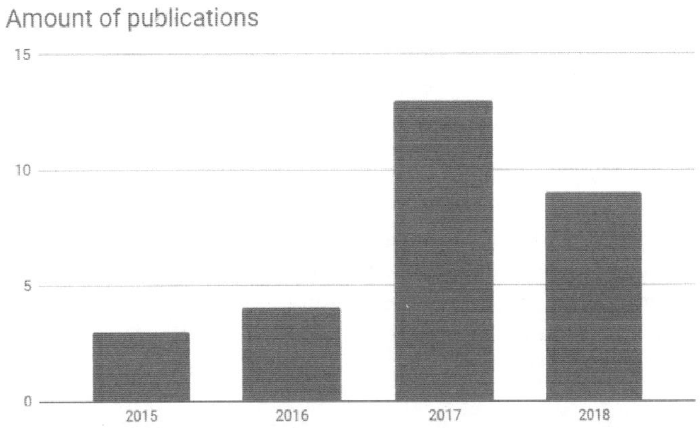

Year	2015	2016	2017	2018
Amount	3	4	13	9
Authors	(Callejo, 2015; Trofimov, Arsiriy and Arsiriy, 2015; Yuan, 2015)	(Chen *et al.*, 2016; Dwyer and Kanguri, 2016; Yamaguchi *et al.*, 2016; Zhou and Shariat, 2016)	(Chaudhuri, Bagherjeiran and Liu, 2017; Chen *et al.*, 2017; Sayedi *et al.*, 2017; Wang, Zhang and Yuan, 2017; Dwyer and Kanguri, 2017; Gardh and Amnäs, 2017; Högström and Wallin, 2017; Kumar, 2017; Niu *et al.*, 2017; Papadopoulos *et al.*, 2017; Qin, Yuan and Wang, 2017a, 2017b)	(Aksu *et al.*, 2018; Alaimo and Kallinikos, 2018; Arab *et al.*, 2018; Gupta and Mishra, 2018; Haider *et al.*, 2018; Iordanou *et al.*, 2018; Parssinen *et al.*, 2018; Qin, Yuan and Wang, 2018; Zhang, 2018)

This academic development reflects itself in the industry: Programmatic advertising has turned into a globally 200-billiondollars per annum business (Parssinen *et al.*, 2018) and has grown, since 2014, at a 40% year-on-year pace (Fisher, 2019).

4.2 Theoretical Framework

The DAE contains five different fields: demand side, supply side, market, data and the user (Wang, Zhang and Yuan, 2017). The advertisers represent the demand side: They bring in the monetary resources. The publishers represent the supply side: As stated above, they are responsible for the inventory as well as for the pair of eyes of the user. In the market, demand and supply meet to exchange the slot for money based on a second price auction (Zhang, 2018). Both, supply and demand side as well as third party actors, who enrich the information flow to make the user more transparent, create the data layer. The analysis of the literature – journals, book chapters, conference proceedings – controls for the presence of the five segments presented as well as the density of elements within those segments.

4.3 Content Differences

Visualizations of the digital advertising ecosystem vary from very simple versions with only three players (Alaimo and Kallinikos, 2018) to thirteen elements (Iordanou *et al.*, 2018). Research report the time component differently: From the advertising request due to the HTML request of a user on supply side to the delivery of the ad, their opinions differ. Starting at less than 100ms (Yuan, 2015; Chaudhuri, Bagherjeiran and Liu, 2017; Papadopoulos *et al.*, 2017; Parssinen *et al.*, 2018), to around 100ms (Callejo, 2015; Chen *et al.*, 2017; Niu *et al.*, 2017; Gupta and Mishra, 2018; Iordanou *et al.*, 2018), the opinions end at longer than 100ms (Dwyer and Kanguri, 2016, 2017; Kumar, 2017).

Visualizations in literature differ in elements mentioned. Some researchers even ignore entire categories the author described in this chapter. It leads to ignoring the data part (19 out of 29), to not mentioning the user (8 out of 29). Six out of twenty-nine publications do not contain neither the data, nor the user segment. Out of the nine articles published in 2018, four were complete containing all groups (2017: 3 out of 13; 2016: 0 out of 4; 2015: 1 out of 3). This positive trend reflects the knowledge enrichment in this field.

5. RESULTS

The author conducted a review of DAE visualizations in literature. This analysis focused on the mentioning of at least two key players within the ecosystem. The author therefore created an ecosystem visualization (see Figure 1) based on a "minimum viable version" of the literature review. It reflects the version of Stallone & Klaas with an important change: The user layer connects with the supplier and not with the demand side (Stallone and Klaas, 2019).

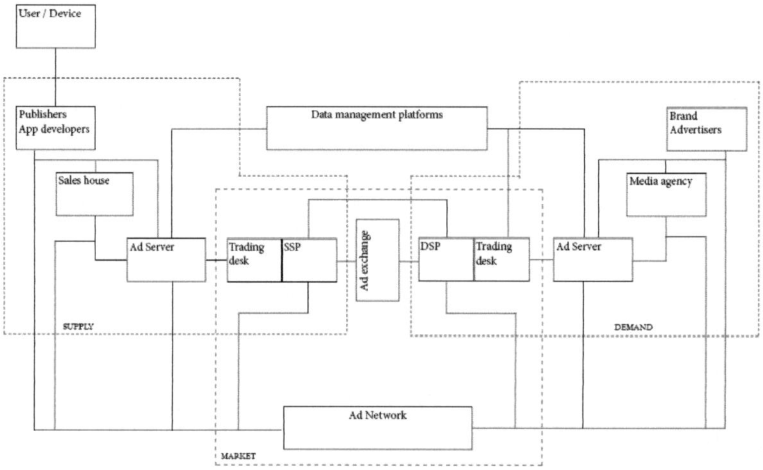

Figure 1. DAE according to the author

The five segments of the DAE are visible in Figure 1: User, Supply, Market, Demand and Data. On the supply side, the real-time bidding process starts when the user visits a publisher's website and then sends an advertising request to the Supply Side Platform. Publishers can also sell their advertising inventory through marketers. In addition to the supply side platform, there are other technical elements on the supply side such as the ad server or the trading desk. The demand side includes advertisers who often work with a media agency and who offer a demand side platform for advertising. As on the supply side, there are other technical elements on the demand side, such as ad servers and trading desks. The supply side and the demand side both use a data layer to target the advertising spaces. Therefore, there is a connection between the data layer and the ad servers of both sides. A central element in the ecosystem is the advertising exchange, which represents the market, where the trading of advertising inserts takes place.

6. CONCLUSION

The heterogeneity in the visualization itself is surprising: The fact that most of the papers did not represent the flow in its completeness reflects the lack of transparency of the ecosystem and its intermediaries. The rising trend in analyzing the field of programmatic advertising and of DAE shows the increasing interest of academia, which should reflect in a better understanding of the ecosystem and its functions. This paper presents a summarized version of the DAE, which scholars can use as a starting point for their analyses: By doing so and referring to it, they should be able to make sure to show all needed intermediaries involved in the DAE itself.

7. DISCUSSION

There is still a lot of work to do in this field. In this chapter, the author presents possible limitations as well as potential further research for scholars to focus on in future.

7.1 Limitations

The focus of this review was on the digital advertising ecosystem visualization and not on the visualization of the digital advertising conceptual flow. Furthermore, this review looked at literature coming from different fields of academia (e.g. marketing, information technology, game theory).

7.2 Further Research

Future research should focus on the following questions: Does the industry and academia accept the DAE in Figure 1? If not, which elements are gone missing? The author therefore suggests carrying an in-depth description and qualitative analysis of the various descriptions displayed in scientific and nonscientific visualizations based on this paper and move the discussion to the public eye. As Parssinen mentioned, "there needs to be a significant awareness campaign to support transformation toward a healthier online advertising ecosystem" (Parssinen *et al.*, 2018).

REFERENCES

Aksu, H. *et al.* (2018) 'Advertising in the IoT Era: Vision and Challenges', *IEEE Communications Magazine*, pp. 1–7. doi: 10.1109/MCOM.2017.1700871.

Alaimo, C. and Kallinikos, J. (2018) *Objects, Metrics and Practices: An Inquiry into Programmatic Advertising, IFIP Advances in Information and Communi- cation Technology*. San Francisco. Available at: https://www.researchgate.net/publication/327919972 (Accessed: 20 October 2018).

Arab, S. A. *et al.* (2018) 'Two-Layer Recommendation-Based Real Time Bidding (RTB)', in *2018 IEEE 27th International Conference on Enabling Technologies: Infrastructure for Collaborative Enterprises (WETICE)*. IEEE, pp. 91–94. doi: 10.1109/WETICE.2018.00024.

Callejo, P. (2015) *Master on Telematics Engineering Auditing Methodology to Asses the Quality of Online Display Advertising Campaigns*. Available at: http://eprints.networks.imdea.org/1483/1/TFM_Patricia_Callejo.pdf (Accessed: 20 October 2018).

Chaudhuri, S., Bagherjeiran, A. and Liu, J. (2017) 'Ranking and Calibrating Click-Attributed Purchases in Performance Display Advertising', in *Proceedings of the ADKDD'17*. doi: 10.1145/3124749.3124755.

Chen, G. *et al.* (2016) 'In-Depth Survey of Digital Advertising Technologies', *IEEE Communications Surveys & Tutorials*, 18(3), pp. 2124–2148. doi: 10.1109/COMST.2016.2519912.

Chen, Y. *et al.* (2017) 'Measuring Network Reputation in the Ad-Bidding Process', in *Detection of Intrusions and Malware, and Vulnerability Assessment*. Springer, Cham, pp. 388–409. doi: 10.1007/978-3-319-60876-1_18.

Dwyer, C. and Kanguri, A. (2016) 'Gone in 200 Milliseconds: The Challenge of Blocking Malvertising', *Student and Faculty Research Days*, (3). Available at: http://digitalcommons.pace.edu/sfresearchdayhttp://digitalcommons.pace.edu/sfresearchday/3 (Accessed: 20 October 2018).

Dwyer, C. and Kanguri, A. (2017) 'Malvertising - A Rising Threat To The Online Ecosystem', *Journal of Information Systems Applied Research*. Association of Information Technology Professionals, Education Special Interest Group, 10(3), pp. 29–37. Available at: http://jisar.org/2017-10/n3/JISARv10n3p29.html (Accessed: 20 October 2018).

Feldman, J. *et al.* (2010) 'Auctions with Intermediaries', in *EC '10 Proceedings of the 11th ACM conference on Electronic commerce*, pp. 23–32. doi: https://doi.org/10.1145/1807342.1807346.

Fisher, L. (2019) *US Programmatic Ad Spending Forecast 2019 - eMarketer Trends, Forecasts & Statistics, emarketer.com*. Available at: https://www.emarketer.com/content/us-programmatic-ad-spending-forecast-2019 (Accessed: 29 May 2019).

Gardh, M. and Amnäs, U. (2017) *Trading with digital ads*. KTH. Available at: https://pdfs.semanticscholar.org/53de/e01d71afffc5b7f0290da2c6e0c5502d6dc5.pdf (Accessed: 20 October 2018).

Gupta, S. and Mishra, A. (2018) 'Real Time Bidding With Comparative Study of Various User Responses Prediction Models', in *International Conference on Recent Innovations in Management, Engineering, Science and Technology*. Bareilly, p. 10. Available at: http://data.conferenceworld.in/IEEERAJSHREE/P493-502.pdf (Accessed: 29 October 2018).

Haider, C. M. R. *et al.* (2018) 'An ensemble learning based approach for impression fraud detection in mobile advertising', *Journal of Network and Computer Applications*, 112, pp. 126–141. doi: 10.1016/j.jnca.2018.02.021.

Högström, J. and Wallin, E. (2017) *Programmatic Advertising: A Quantitative Study of Consumer Attitudes Towards Highly Frequent Online Ads*. Halmstad University. Available at: http://www.diva-portal.org/smash/get/diva2:1106048/FULLTEXT01.pdf (Accessed: 29 October 2018).

Iordanou, C. *et al.* (2018) 'Tracing Cross Border Web Tracking', in *Internet Measurement Conference (IMC '18), October 31-November 2, 2018, Boston, MA, USA*. Boston: ACM, p. 14. doi: 10.1145/3278532.3278561.

Kumar, J. (2017) 'Timeout Analysis, Troubleshooting and Notification in Real Time Bidding Advertising System with Implementation', *Computer Science and Engineering*, 7(3), pp. 67–78. doi: 10.5923/j.computer.20170703.01.

Muthukrishnan, S. (2009) 'Ad Exchanges: Research Issues', in. Springer, Berlin, Heidelberg, pp. 1–12. doi: 10.1007/978-3-642-10841-9_1.

Nicholls, S., Malins, A. and Horner, M. (2013) *Real-Time Bidding in Online Advertising - The Death of the Mad Men*. Available at: http://printarchiv.absatzwirtschaft.de/pdf/Studie_Real_Time_Bidding_in_Online_Advertising.pdf (Accessed: 20 October 2018).

Niu, C. *et al.* (2017) 'ERA: Towards privacy preservation and verifiability for online ad exchanges', *Journal of Network and Computer Applications*, 98, pp. 1–10. doi: 10.1016/j.jnca.2017.08.012.

Papadopoulos, P. *et al.* (2017) 'If you are not paying for it, you are the product: How much do advertisers pay to reach you?', in *Proceedings of IMC '17, London, United Kingdom, November 1–3, 2017*. London, p. 15. doi: 10.1145/3131365.3131397.

Parssinen, M. *et al.* (2018) 'Is Blockchain Ready to Revolutionize Online Advertising?', *IEEE Access*, pp. 1–1. doi: 10.1109/ACCESS.2018.2872694.

Qin, R., Yuan, Y. and Wang, F.-Y. (2017a) 'Improving Auction Mechanisms for Online Real-Time Bidding Advertising with a Two-stage Resale Model', *IFAC-PapersOnLine*. Elsevier, 50(1), pp. 13575–13580. doi: 10.1016/J.IFACOL.2017.08.2372.

Qin, R., Yuan, Y. and Wang, F.-Y. (2017b) 'Optimizing the revenue for ad exchanges in header bidding advertising markets', in *2017 IEEE International Conference on Systems, Man, and Cybernetics (SMC)*. IEEE, pp. 432–437. doi: 10.1109/SMC.2017.8122643.

Qin, R., Yuan, Y. and Wang, F.-Y. (2018) 'A Pareto optimal mechanism for demand-side platforms in real time bidding advertising markets', *Information Sciences*. Elsevier, 469, pp. 119–140. doi: 10.1016/J.INS.2018.08.012.

Sayedi, A. *et al.* (2017) *Real-Time Bidding in Online Display Advertising*. Available at: https://papers.ssrn.com/sol3/papers.cfm?abstract_id=2916875 (Accessed: 29 October 2018).

Stallone, V. and Klaas, M. (2019) *The Digital Advertising Ecosystem Visualization - Literature Review*. Available at: http://www.iadisportal.org/digital-library/the-digital-advertising-ecosystem-visualization-— -literature-review (Accessed: 29 May 2019).

Trofimov, B. F., Arsiriy, E. A. and Arsiriy, A. V. (2015) 'User identification problems on DSP side in terms of advertising RTB auctions', in *2015 Information Technologies in Innovation Business Conference (ITIB)*. IEEE, pp. 97–100. doi: 10.1109/ITIB.2015.7355063.

Wang, J., Zhang, W. and Yuan, S. (2017) *Display Advertising with Real-Time Bidding (RTB) and Behavioural Targeting*. Boston: now publishers inc. Available at: https://arxiv.org/pdf/1610.03013.pdf (Accessed: 29 October 2018).

Yamaguchi, Y. *et al.* (2016) 'Web Advertising Recommender System Based On Estimating Users' Latent Interests', in *Proceedings of the 18th International Conference on Information Integration and Web-based Applications and Services*. Singapore, pp. 42–49. doi: 10.1145/3011141.3011180.

Yuan, S. (2015) *Supply Side Optimisation in Online Display Advertising*. University College London. Available at: http://discovery.ucl.ac.uk/1463229/1/ShuaiYuan-PhD-thesis.pdf (Accessed: 20 October 2018).

Zhang, Y. (2018) *Mathematical Approaches to Real Time Bidding Strategy (RTB) for Advertising Campaigns for Demand Side Platforms (DSP)*. NYU Shanghai. Available at: https://cdn.shanghai.nyu.edu/sites/default/files/zhang_yiyi_thesis_nyush_honors_2018.pdf (Accessed: 20 October 2018).

Zhou, B. and Shariat, S. (2016) 'Finding Needle in a Million Metrics: Anomaly Detection in a Large-scale Computational Advertising Platform', in *Proceeding of the 2nd International Workshop on Ad Targeting at Scale*. San Francisco. Available at: https://arxiv.org/pdf/1602.07057.pdf (Accessed: 20 October 2018).

NO AD BLOCKERS FOR OLD MEN? DEMOGRAPHIC EVIDENCE FOR AD BLOCKER USAGE FROM GERMANY

Valerio Stallone
Zurich University of Applied Sciences, Center for Digital Marketing
Stadthausstrasse 14, CH-8400 Winterthur, Switzerland

ABSTRACT

Web users are turning to ad blockers to avoid ads because they perceive them as an invasion of privacy, as annoying or as slackening their internet browsing experience. There has been significant research into factors driving ad blocker adoption. In this paper, the author will highlight significance correlation between ad blocker usage and age. The author conducted an online survey and built two groups, ad blocker users and non-users. When checking for significant differences in the demographic data, the author has found significant difference in the age of ad blocker users.

KEYWORDS

Ad Blocking, Online Advertising, Online Ads, Advertising Avoidance

1. INTRODUCTION

Attention is the currency, digital advertising is dealing with (Stourm & Bax, 2017). In the attempt of getting this crucial resource, different actors play a central role in the digital advertising ecosystem (Stallone & Klaas, 2019). This ecosystem highlights how digital advertising has become the vital source of revenue for the supply side containing the publishers, who are monetizing their web traffic (Brinson, Eastin, & Cicchirillo, 2018). To thwart the display of advertisement, numerous companies and organizations have focused on the development of systems (Post & Sekharan, 2015): In this paper, we will call them *ad blockers*.

The number of internet consumers adopting ad blocking has grown worldwide over the past five years and as the internet consumers become increasingly conscious of the possibility of ad blocking, even higher adoption rates must be expected globally (Tudoran, 2019).

This research contributes to the literature on online consumer behavior by highlighting demographic evidence of ad blocker usage. The author do so by analyzing a dataset from a German online survey and showing how the self-reported age correlates with the self-reported usage of ad blockers on desktop devices.

2. LITERATURE REVIEW

This review investigates the literature on ad blockers. The author selected peer-reviewed articles from four bibliographic databases (IEEE Xplore, Sage journals online, Science Direct & Google Scholar). The author considered peer-reviewed journals and conference proceedings based no their knowledge validity and their highest impact on the research field. To ensure the relevance of the articles in this study, the author used a combination of four keywords, contained at least in the abstract of the selected articles. The search of articles was limited to English & German speaking journals between 2007 & 2019. The rationale is to capture the latest change in investigating ad blockers.

1. *ad blocker*
2. *adblocker*
3. *ad blocking*
4. *adblocking*

2.1 Ad Blocker

In the *legal* field, academic literature tries to understand the implications of using ad blocker from the perspective of a whole country and/or from the publisher as an affected actor of the digital advertising ecosystem (Abrahamsen, 2017; Barbacovi, 2016; Lu, 2017; R. Miller, 2017; R. A. Miller, 2018).

Economic analyses show models on how the usage of ad blockers is affecting the players involved (Aseri, Dawande, Janakiraman, & Mookerjee, 2018; Bounie, Vallrie, & Quinn, 2017; Despotakis, Ravi, & Srinivasan, 2017; Jain, Czerwinski, Song, & He, 2010; Miklosik, Kuchta, & Zak, 2018; Ray, Ghasemkhani, & Kannan, 2017; Streitz & Tynan, 2016) with game theoretical approaches.

Scholars in the *technological* field research on how to develop either new ad blocking or anti ad blocking solutions (Backes, Bugiel, Styp-Rekowsky, & WiBfeld, 2017; Ikram & Kaafar, 2017a, 2017b; Jalba, Olteanu, & Draghici, 2016; Lashkari, Seo, Gil, & Ghorbani, 2017; Mughees, Qian, & Shafiq, 2017; Mughees, Qian, Shafiq, Dash, & Hui, 2016; Nithyanand et al., 2016; Tramèr, Dupré, Rusak, Pellegrino, & Boneh, 2018; Wills & Uzunoglu, 2016).

Researches in the *behavioral* field contains researches into the identification of factors influencing the usage of ad blockers. The most important factors leading the use of ad blocker are the needs for security/privacy, for avoiding further interruption online and for page loading speed (Boerman, Kruikemeier, & Zuiderveen Borgesius, 2018; Brinson et al., 2018; Mccoy, Everard, Polak, & Galletta, 2007; Redondo & Aznar, 2018; Zhao et al., 2017).

2.2 Age and Ad Blocker Usage

Young reported in his study, that "older individuals tended to report using ad blockers less [than younger individuals]" (Young, 2016). In another research it has been stated that there are no significant differences younger and older adults with respect to privacy concerns and privacy protective behaviors (Boerman et al., 2018)– both motivational factors for the usage of ad blockers as stated before. A significant difference was shown by Zhao et al., which stated that "people who are younger than 34 are more likely to use ad blockers" (Zhao et al., 2017). eMarketer states in its study of 2017 that "ad blocking continues to be far more prevalent among younger people" (eMarketer, 2017). Within their study, Despotakis et al. implied, by citing the PageFair and Adobe report that older non-ad blocker users would never use an ad blocker (Despotakis et al., 2017; PageFair & Adobe, 2015). Only the data of PageFair & Adobe could represent the reality, since every other research represented self-reported data on the usage of ad blocker.

3. RESEARCH METHOD

3.1 Data Collection

AdDefend designed a questionnaire, Appinio distributed the final questionnaire online to the Appinio panel members and managed the collection, monitoring, and processing of the data. AdDefend is an independent platform for ad block advertising that displays ads to users of ad blockers. That way, publishers remonetize their content with ads, advertisers have the opportunity to address this target group and users keep free access to their favorite content. Appinio is a German market research company.

Data for the study was collected with an online questionnaire targeted for Internet users from Germany. The survey resulted in 1511 valid responses. The questionnaire contained 22 questions about their internet consumption on desktop devices. The survey has been conducted during the second half of December 2018 to be sure to have a high density of ads shown to the participants due to the Christmas-related advertisement.

3.2 Participants

1761 panelists completed the questionnaire. 250 subjects were invalidated for having inconsistently and/or incompletely responded to the questions.

4. RESULTS

4.1 Descriptive Results

The final sample consisted of 1511 subjects (56% males and 44% females), with the following age distribution: 13% under 18 years of age, 34% aged between 18 and 24, 28% aged between 25 and 34, 15% aged between 35 and 44 and 9% above 45. Almost 48% of respondents reported to consume internet content multiple hours a day, 16% one hour a day, 16% multiple hours per week and almost 20% less than the above. Regarding ad blocker usage, 50% of the subjects were current users and 50% of the subjects were not current users.

4.2 Differences in Age

The author conducted first a t-test to explore any significant difference in age between the two groups of respondents. The author detected a significant result, which is shown in Table 1.

Table 1. Ad Blocker Use t-test

	Ad Blocker Use			
	Yes		**No**	
	Mean	**SD**	**Mean**	**SD**
Age	26.97	9.371	28.29	11.797

Ad blocker users are significantly younger ($p<0.05$), which is also stated in Table 2 with a correlation value of 0.062.

Table 2. Ad Blocker and age correlation

		Variables	
		Ad Blocker Use	Age
Ad Blocker Use	Correlation	1	-0.062*
	Significance (two-sided)		
	N	1511	1511
Age	Correlation		1
	Significance (two-sided)	-0.062*	
	N	1511	1511

$*p < 0.05$

These results do not differ from the ones presented by (Young, 2016). The following article shows a lower significance ($p < 0.05$ versus $p < .01$) as well as a lower β (-0.012 versus -0.093) than the mentioned one, which the Young identified running a simple binary regression explaining the fact of using an ad blocker by the age of the user (Young, 2016). The main difference though lies in the methodology: Whilst AdDefend surveyed exclusively about ad blocker usage, Young used data of YouGov for an annual report that "looks to map the changing ecology of news across countries" (Young, 2016). Another difference is, of course, the time stamp of the survey: YouGov's survey was taken in January 2015, AdDefend distributed it in December 2018 – almost four years.

5. DISCUSSION

5.1 Conclusion

This very first analysis of ad blocker use in Germany showed that there is almost no difference to other studies done in the United Kingdom and the United States. In this paper, the author highlighted the lack of thorough analysis of the influence of age on the usage of ad blockers. It confirms what has been found up until now in literature but shows a slight less intense correlation between the two variables, which can be due to cultural but also to simple sample differences.

5.2 Further Research

In this paper, the author showed the need for a thorough focus on the effects of age on ad blocker usage. To be able to identify the differences between younger and older users better, scholars should investigate the differences in motivational factors of ad blocker usage between the two groups: Are there the same significant differences within the sub-group of millennials and silver surfers? Besides the differences in age, the author suggests to move on with more analyses from other countries: Are there any differences from a cultural perspective? Ad blocker demographics should therefore remain a crucial focus in this field of academia.

REFERENCES

Abrahamsen, J. T. (2017). Ad Blockers, Convenience or Trespass: Click Here to Find out. *University of Illinois Journal of Law, Technology & Policy, 2017.* Retrieved from https://heinonline.org/HOL/Page?handle=hein.journals/jltp2017&id=499&div=&collection=

Aseri, M., Dawande, M., Janakiraman, G., & Mookerjee, V. (2018). Ad-Blockers: A Blessing or a Curse? *SSRN Electronic Journal.* https://doi.org/10.2139/ssrn.3299057

Backes, M., Bugiel, S., Styp-Rekowsky, P. von, & WiBfeld, M. (2017). Seamless In-App Ad Blocking on Stock Android. In *2017 IEEE Security and Privacy Workshops (SPW)* (pp. 163–168). IEEE. https://doi.org/10.1109/SPW.2017.24

Barbacovi, T. (2016). Blocking Ad Blockers. *John Marshall Review of Intellectual Property Law, 16.* Retrieved from https://heinonline.org/HOL/Page?handle=hein.journals/johnmars16&id=283&div=&collection=

Boerman, S. C., Kruikemeier, S., & Zuiderveen Borgesius, F. J. (2018). Exploring Motivations for Online Privacy Protection Behavior: Insights From Panel Data. *Communication Research,* 9365021880091. https://doi.org/10.1177/0093650218800915

Bounie, D., Vallrie, M., & Quinn, M. (2017). Do You See What I See? Ad Viewability and the Economics of Online Advertising. *SSRN Electronic Journal.* https://doi.org/10.2139/ssrn.2854265

Brinson, N. H., Eastin, M. S., & Cicchirillo, V. J. (2018). Reactance to Personalization: Understanding the Drivers Behind the Growth of Ad Blocking. *Journal of Interactive Advertising, 18*(2), 136–147. https://doi.org/10.1080/15252019.2018.1491350

Despotakis, S., Ravi, R., & Srinivasan, K. (2017). The Beneficial Effects of Ad Blockers. *SSRN Electronic Journal.* https://doi.org/10.2139/ssrn.3083119

eMarketer. (2017). eMarketer Scales Back Estimates of Ad Blocking in the US - eMarketer. Retrieved June 21, 2019, from https://www.emarketer.com/Article/eMarketer-Scales-Back-Estimates-of-Ad-Blocking-US/1015243

Ikram, M., & Kaafar, M. A. (2017a). *A First Look at Ad Blocking Apps on Google Play.* Retrieved from http://arxiv.org/abs/1709.02901

Ikram, M., & Kaafar, M. A. (2017b). A first look at mobile Ad-Blocking apps. In *2017 IEEE 16th International Symposium on Network Computing and Applications (NCA)* (pp. 1–8). IEEE. https://doi.org/10.1109/NCA.2017.8171376

Jain, K., Czerwinski, M., Song, Y., & He, L.-W. (2010). *Evaluating the Unaccounted Cost of Distraction of Display Ads to the Users.* Retrieved from http://seattletimes.nwsource.com/html/businesstechnology/

Jalba, I., Olteanu, A.-C., & Draghici, A. (2016). Customized ad blocking. In *2016 15th RoEduNet Conference: Networking in Education and Research* (pp. 1–5). IEEE. https://doi.org/10.1109/RoEduNet.2016.7753245

Lashkari, A. H., Seo, A., Gil, G. D., & Ghorbani, A. (2017). CIC-AB: Online ad blocker for browsers. In *2017 International Carnahan Conference on Security Technology (ICCST)* (pp. 1–7). IEEE. https://doi.org/10.1109/CCST.2017.8167846

Lu, B. (2017). The unique Chinese legal approach to online ad blocking: Is it in the right direction? *Computer Law & Security Review*, *33*(6), 786–801. https://doi.org/10.1016/J.CLSR.2017.05.012

Mccoy, S., Everard, A., Polak, P., & Galletta, D. F. (2007). *THE EFFECTS OF ONLINE ADVERTISING. COMMUNICATIONS OF THE ACM* (Vol. 50). Retrieved from http://delivery.acm.org/10.1145/1230000/1226740/p84-mccoy.pdf?ip=160.85.7.55&id=1226740&acc=ACTIVE SERVICE&key=FC66C24E42F07228.89BA465B3F8E8007.4D4702B0C3E38B35.4D4702B0C3E38B35&__acm__=1559306947_6eb4260fd60ab7f3e89ab5051f91906c

Miklosik, A., Kuchta, M., & Zak, S. (2018). Privacy Protection Versus Advertising Revenues: The Case of Content Publishers. *Connectist: Istanbul University Journal of Communication Sciences*, *54*, 117–140. https://doi.org/10.26650/CONNECTIST404711

Miller, R. (2017). Liberation, Not Extortion: The Fate of Internet Ad-Blocking in German and American Law. *SSRN Electronic Journal*. https://doi.org/10.2139/ssrn.3019254

Miller, R. A. (2018). The Legal Fate of Internet Ad-Blocking. *Boston University Journal of Science and Technology Law*, *24*. Retrieved from https://heinonline.org/HOL/Page?handle=hein.journals/jstl24&id=317&div=&collection=

Mughees, M. H., Qian, Z., & Shafiq, Z. (2017). Detecting Anti Ad-blockers in the Wild. *Proceedings on Privacy Enhancing Technologies*, *3*, 130–146. https://doi.org/10.1515/popets-2017-0032

Mughees, M. H., Qian, Z., Shafiq, Z., Dash, K., & Hui, P. (2016). A First Look at Ad-block Detection: A New Arms Race on the Web. https://doi.org/10.1145/1235

Nithyanand, R., Khattak, S., Javed, M., Vallina-Rodriguez, N., Falahrastegar, M., Powles, J. E., … Murdoch, S. J. (2016). Adblocking and Counter Blocking: A Slice of the Arms Race. In *6th USENIX Workshop on Free and Open Communications on the Internet (FOCI 2016)*. Retrieved from https://www.usenix.org/conference/foci16/workshop-program/presentation/nithyanand

PageFair, & Adobe. (2015). *The Cost of Ad Blocking: PageFair and Adobe 2015 Ad Blocking Report. PageFair and Adobe Ad Blocking Report*. Retrieved from http://downloads.pagefair.com/reports/2015_report-the_cost_of_ad_blocking.pdf

Post, E. L., & Sekharan, C. N. (2015). Comparative Study and Evaluation of Online Ad-Blockers. In *2015 2nd International Conference on Information Science and Security (ICISS)* (pp. 1–4). IEEE. https://doi.org/10.1109/ICISSEC.2015.7370988

Ray, A., Ghasemkhani, H., & Kannan, K. N. (2017). Ad-Blockers: Extortionists or Digital Age Robin Hoods? *SSRN Electronic Journal*. https://doi.org/10.2139/ssrn.2991805

Redondo, I., & Aznar, G. (2018). To use or not to use ad blockers? The roles of knowledge of ad blockers and attitude toward online advertising. *Telematics and Informatics*, *35*(6), 1607–1616. https://doi.org/10.1016/J.TELE.2018.04.008

Stallone, V., & Klaas, M. (2019). *The Digital Advertising Ecosystem Visualization - Literature Review*. Retrieved from http://www.iadisportal.org/digital-library/the-digital-advertising-ecosystem-visualization-- -literature-review

Stourm, V., & Bax, E. (2017). Incorporating hidden costs of annoying ads in display auctions. *International Journal of Research in Marketing*, *34*(3), 622–640. https://doi.org/10.1016/J.IJRESMAR.2017.02.002

Streitz, M., & Tynan, R. (2016). Are ad-blockers killing the media? Speigel Online's Matthias Streitz in a head-to-head debate with Privacy International's Richard Tynan. *Index on Censorship*, *45*(2), 78–80. https://doi.org/10.1177/0306422016657033

Tramèr, F., Dupré, P., Rusak, G., Pellegrino, G., & Boneh, D. (2018). Ad-versarial: Perceptual Ad-Blocking meets Adversarial Machine Learning. Retrieved from http://arxiv.org/abs/1811.03194

Tudoran, A. A. (2019). Why do internet consumers block ads? New evidence from consumer opinion mining and sentiment analysis. *Internet Research*, *29*(1), 144–166. https://doi.org/10.1108/IntR-06-2017-0221

Wills, C. E., & Uzunoglu, D. C. (2016). What Ad Blockers Are (and Are Not) Doing. In *2016 Fourth IEEE Workshop on Hot Topics in Web Systems and Technologies (HotWeb)* (pp. 72–77). IEEE. https://doi.org/10.1109/HotWeb.2016.21

Young, J. (2016). *MEET THE BLOCKERS: A QUANTITATIVE ANALYSIS OF AD BLOCKER USAGE*. Middle Tennessee State University. Retrieved from https://jewlscholar.mtsu.edu/bitstream/handle/mtsu/5033/Young_mtsu_0170N_10656.pdf?sequence=1&isAllowed=y

Zhao, S., Wang, C., Kalra, A., Vaks, L., Borcea, C., & Chen, Y. (2017). Ad Blocking and Counter-Ad Blocking: Analysis of Online Ad Blocker Usage. *AMCIS 2017 Proceedings*. Retrieved from https://aisel.aisnet.org/amcis2017/DataScience/Presentations/29

BEING WATCHED BY TV: SURVEILLANCE AT HOME

Ananda Mitra
Wake Forest University
Winston-Salem, NC 27106, USA

ABSTRACT

The Television (TV) that became a ubiquitous part of households in many parts of the World since World War II has been witnessing a significant transformation since the turn of the Twenty-First Century. Starting in the early 2000s, the TV has morphed in many ways such as in the size and quality of picture it delivers, the kind of content it can offer, and the multiple ways in which it can be used. Yet, in spite of these changes, it has been the case that the TV has remained a site to consume narratives. It is only in the past few years, with the advent of the "smart" TV has the tool been connected to the Internet and can gather information about the viewer in front of the TV instrument. In this essay I argue that the TV, originally the conduit for offering passive narratives to the audience, is transforming into a tool that can watch over the audience and construct a dynamic narrative of the audience, thus operating as tool for surveillance.

KEYWORDS

Surveillance, TV, Narrative, Panopticon

1. INTRODUCTION

Since the early days of TV in the developed countries of the West, the technology and the medium had been considered to be a passive device that was the conduit that brought information to the people who would watch the screen seeking anything from entertainment to education. TV has sometimes been called the "idiot tube," for the mesmerizing effect it would have on the watcher who could be distracted to catatonic inactivity just watching TV in a "mindless" way without having to bring any intellectual energy to the process of watching TV. This phenomenon was examined copiously by scholars from many disciplines and numerous theories were proposed and debated that examined the "effects" of watching TV as would be found in many introductory books on mass communication.

2. THE PASSIVE NARRATIVE

One important assumption that underpinned the emergent theories claimed that the audience of TV was a relatively passive and often disengaged person (see, e.g., early research by Klapper, 1960). This assumption was especially true for the programs of research that mimicked the natural scientific methods of research devising experiments and interventions with samples selected from the population to understand the effects of TV in numerical terms, as in the case of development of theories such as cultivation theory often considered to be a central tenet of understanding the effect of TV. Other researchers who subscribed to a more cultural anthropological, critical and cultural interpretations of the role of TV in everyday life sought answers in the ways the audience would talk about television, or through observational studies where the audience would be observed to see how they interacted with the narratives and discourses on television, as in the case of scholar originating in the Birmingham Center for Cultural Studies and offering the vast array of literature on the role of TV within popular culture starting with the work of scholars such as Hoggart (1957). In both approaches, however, there was the shared presumption of relative anonymity of the audience where any individual member of the audience was a part of a larger similar kind of people where the specific individual was unknown to those who created and circulated the content of TV.

This lack of information about a specific member of the audience was largely a factor of the way in which the TV technology worked from its inception to the time when the Internet became a part of everyday life for large groups of people. Traditional TV technology was designed to deliver a robust image and sound to the audience without the audience having to come to the place where the content was available as in the case of movies. The content distributors had little knowledge of who was watching the content, why they were watching the content or if the audience was liking the content. At the reception end of the process, TV technology was a "passive" tool that merely displayed the content on the screen. This status quo changed with the increasing adoption of the Internet in the public sphere.

With increasing home-based access to the digital network of global computers – the Internet – the interactive computer screen became a conduit to a larger virtual space with increasing libraries of data that the user could access. This data, often residing on computers all over the World, could be accessed by any of the computers using the computer screen. Even though the computer and the TV screen were beginning to look similar, their functions were constantly diverging with the TV screen becoming a site for narratives that the user could not control. The narratives of the TV screen were simply sent out to the user with the expectation that the user would subscribe to the narratives when the screen brought them home, indeed the users were expected to manage the everyday life practices of their lives to suit the demands of the TV screen if the users wanted to access the narratives on the TV screen. On the other hand, the narratives were within the control of the user on the computer screen. Here the user could build an unending narrative by accessing multiple data that were connected by hypertext to each other allowing the user to constantly explore and discover and construct the personalized narrative that the user sought and not what the TV institutions handed out.

The seduction of interactivity, coupled with the primacy of the computer screen over the TV screen led to the demand for a single-screen solution where the screens could be merged into one where the single screen would serve primarily as a conduit for interactions that would allow the user to construct their personalized narrative that would appear on this single converged screen. It is this demand for convergence that allowed the ubiquitous merged screen to become a site for collecting data about individuals.

3. THE INTERACTIVE NARRATIVE

The notion of convergence is particularly important in the context of the emergent screen in the private spaces occupied by individual members of the audience. The duality between computer screen as a site with the potential of creating an interactive narrative, such as writing a book, and the TV screen as a site of consuming narrative was increasingly being erased as a single converged screen was replacing the two where the single screen would converge the different functions into one site.

The new digital TV with access to the Internet built into the TV was becoming commonplace by the early 2000s and became nearly ubiquitous within five to six years, especially in the USA where all TV broadcast changed to digital broadcast on June 12, 2009 and nearly 97.5% of the American homes were ready for the mandatory transition. Within the next several years the transition to digital TV, the nearly ubiquitous availability of broadband connection to the Internet, and the emergence of content conglomerators, producers, and distributors that were distinct from the traditional media content providers offered new narratives to the audience. Thus, the dominance of corporations such as Netflix, Amazon, Hulu, YouTube and others less prominent institutions allowed for narratives to be converged on the now-interactive screen in the private home.

The popularity of the Internet, accompanied with the availability of content producers and distributors mentioned earlier, however, altered the way in which the viewer could interactively construct narratives. First, it became far simpler to shift the viewing time, an advantage that was already available through the more elaborate home-based recording technologies. The viewer now had the ability to seek and find narratives at any time the viewer wanted to consume narratives. Second, the narratives could be obtained from a multitude of sources where the viewer was no longer restricted to the traditional providers of narratives such as the TV channels. The increasing digitization of video (and audio) allowed for narratives to be obtained from sources that would never be considered providers of narratives, including non-institutional sources that could not have afforded to be in the public sphere before the availability of the Internet. In particular, is the example of the Worldwide video-sharing platform – YouTube. A viewer could now call upon narratives that were from individual composers of narratives who would never be found in the traditional media spaces. Third, the viewer could interact with multiple sources of narratives and create a customized "playlist" that specifically would be designed to meet the interest of the viewer and could be distinct from other viewers. Even though the viewer was still restricted to the narratives that were connected to the network, the choice was sufficiently large that a viewer could construct a very specific playlist to satisfy the "taste" of the viewer. Finally, all of the narratives, and the queries that create the conglomeration of narratives, could now be done through the interface of the TV screen which transformed from the passive screen to a site of interaction between narratives and the viewer.

The common theme for this transformation is the interactive power attributed to the viewer with the privilege of being able to search for the narratives based on the interests of the viewer. It is precisely this interactivity, now happening through the press of buttons on a TV remote control that transforms the relationship between the viewer and the TV screen which now serves as the gateway for the vast digital space where content is located. It is precisely the nature of the gateway that makes the TV screen the window into the World of the individual viewer who, while watching the narratives, is also being "watched" by the TV screen – in a process of surveillance as TVs were manufactured with listening devices and cameras where the TV could keep an "eye" on its surroundings.

4. WATCHED BY TV

The intimate connection between the maintenance of order and discipline becomes the central thesis of the academic examination of the process of surveillance when scholars such as Foucault (1979) begin to connect surveillance to power and discipline. Among the different ideas of surveillance that emerged as important was the notion of the Panopticon which claims that the powerful is constantly watching everything all the time (Bentham, 1995). The panopticon society was built around a strict definition of discipline and in the late 1800 and early 1900s the metaphor was principally used to describe the ways in which totalitarian nations and despots would want to constantly watch everything to maintain power and discipline (see, e.g., Bentham, 1962a, 1962b, 1995; Gandy, 1993; Lyon, 1994, 2003, 2006).

In some cases, however, there is the emergent interest in examining how the watchers could also include corporations and institutions that had a motive unrelated to discipline and power but more interested in understanding the "market" that the institution would be interested in serving (see, e.g., Manokha, 2018). This is especially true for the type of interactive technologies described in this essay. The advent of the technologies described earlier in this essay is, however, concerned with the corporate watching rather than the discipline- and power-based panopticon World that earlier scholars were concerned with. The TV in the house is now constantly watching and monitoring the individuals that use the TV not to stop sedition or to exercise power over the watched but to better understand the "taste" of the watched to ensure that the watcher can best deliver content to the watched that the watched is most likely to consume. In a transactional system where commodities would be sold for profit the process of TV watching the audience is to better commodify the audience who can then be sold to appropriate institutions as a part of a potential market. The process of watching is thus tied to creating the life story of the audience that the TV can obtain by "watching" the data that the individual generates. The panopticon TV in the living room is thus watching a set of different things that early surveillance studies have pointed towards, albeit no longer in the context of discipline and power. There are broadly two kinds of information that the watched offers to the watcher through the modern television – attitudes and behavior.

The information about the attitudes, interests, beliefs and tastes is offered by the specific discourse the watched offers to the different providers of information that bring content to the TV. Consider for instance the simple act of accessing a digital video service such as YouTube that can be accessed on a smartphone and then projected on the TV. In some cases, the TV itself would offer the option of connecting directly to a service such as YouTube. Indeed, it is estimated that nearly 80% of TVs in American homes would be connected to the Internet by 2019 and any TV that is connected to the Internet can potentially be accessing YouTube without the need for any other ancillary device . One of the key aspects of this connection is the ability of the person being watched search for specific kind of content that can be accessed by the TV and displayed on the screen. The person inscribes attitudes and preferences in the language of the search. There are ways in which such personalization of marketing messages can be turned off through the adjustment of specific settings on an application provided by a corporation. The matter becomes a little different on the TV where the very purpose of the tool, the TV, is to watch narratives, and in the environment of services such as YouTube the viewer must reveal interest information to customize what the person is watching or interested in watching. The process of using the TV to access narrative content is intimately connected with the process of revealing to the TV the watcher's interests, attitudes and beliefs.

This information is also connected with the disclosure of behavior patterns. Given that much of the consumption of the content is happening through the content providers such as YouTube, Hulu, Netflix and other Internet-based content delivery system, there is a constant record of what was watched, when it was watched, how it was paid for, and in some cases greater granular information related to the particular watcher in a multi-people home. The attitude and behavior data that such surveillance offers eventually becomes a narrative about the people who are being watched over. It is this narrative that becomes especially important in the new panopticon system produced by the modern TV.

5. THE STORY TO BE WATCHED

First, the narrative is cumulative. The TV is constantly watching and updating the narrative. Every time an individual interacts with the TV a new segment is being added to the narrative of the life of the person. The attitude and behavior data being collected by the TV is also constantly updated and the ongoing narrative of the life of a person is stored for future reference. This certainly has its advantages, where a viewer can, for instance, resume watching a show from where it was left off, offering the panopticon TV an opportunity to see how the "rhythm" of a person's life unfolds on a moment to moment basis. Similarly, because the TV knows the story of a person's life, it knows, through its applications, what the person may like to watch next with very well thought out suggestions being offered by the TV with respect to what entertainment the watched individual may be encouraged to watch. The TV watcher's life story is now known to the TV and the TV can gently help to shape that story to reinforce the elements of the story that have been prominent over time. Thus, a person who watched a few episodes of a science fiction, would be encouraged to watch other shows belonging to the same genre.

The longitudinally of the narrative is also connected with the way in which an attempt is constantly made by the different tools of surveillance, including the TV, to triangulate the data to create a narrative about the individual which would encompass all the data about the person. Current laws may make it a little difficult to correlate all the data sets, as in the case of privacy laws in the USA where the medical data of an individual is held sacrosanct and unavailable and generally unconnected with other narrative elements of a person's life. However, there is sufficient data about a person that can be available to the panopticon TV which would allow the TV to surveil the individual in a more precise manner and further help design the ongoing narrative of the person being watched. For instance, gadgets like the Alexa, which respond to voice commands, can be connected to the TV to control the TV with spoken words, as explained in a guide, "Once you link Quick Remote with your Roku device and Alexa, you can use voice commands to tell Quick Remote to navigate the Roku menu system and select any app to start playing." There are two important aspects that need to be noted in these instructions, first, it shows how to connect three different applications (Quick Remote, Roku and Alexa) to each other to have the convenience of sending voice commands to the panopticon TV. All these three systems are sharing the data with each other and thus creating a robust narrative about the person who is being watched.

The second important aspect pointed out in these, and numerous other such instructions, is that the user, or the watched, is offering the data to construct the narrative. There are no hidden cameras or stealthy sensors that are surreptitiously watching the person. On the other hand, the person chose to find the convenience of talking to the TV and thus voluntarily obtained the devices and the applications which help to create the dynamic narrative, that eventually makes the life of the person more comfortable. Indeed, this comfort is best maintained if the person's life story is fully known to the panopticon TV and its army of other devices that is constantly updating the narrative of the person and creating the zone of comfort for the person that eventually becomes comfort for the analog self where the digital narrative helps to predict what the analog self needs. Consider, for instance, the notion of Internet of Things (IoT) that hopes to convert information from and about every device that surrounds an individual to a centralized interconnected database about the person making the life story as complete as possible. When such projects come to fruition the surveillance, aided by the voluntary data offered by the individual, would transcend the TV. In that future, all devices, including the TV, would be geared to collating the most complete life story of the watched.

6. CONCLUSION

There are a few things worthy of note with respect to the way in which the TV has transformed into a tool for watching the watcher. First, this process has not been forced upon a population who had no option but to be watched. A small amount of knowledge about the ways in which the tools are watching us, can allow us to shut off the surveillance. None of these tools, including the TV, makes the data collection process a "required" activity to use the tool in its basic and rudimentary way. One can certainly watch television shows broadcast "over the air" without connecting the TV to the Internet. In a similar way, it is possible to use the Alexa speaker as only a portable speaker connected to a smartphone that has music stored in it.

However, as these examples show, when a user chooses to not connect the TV to the Internet, or Alexa to its manufacturer, and the smartphone to a data plan, the user is sacrificing the ability to use the tools to their full potential. Additionally, the user is sacrificing access to the numerous programming options offered through these tools. There is, therefore, a constant tension between the inclination to maintain a sense of privacy while watching TV and retaining the convenience of the TV making suggestions about what would be interesting to watch. If the TV is allowed to surveil, and it is connected with the other tools that surround the TV then it will eventually be able to create an increasingly complete life story of the person who uses the TV. This complete life story could become the way in which the TV constructs a mediated reality for the person who is being watched. As discussed earlier, this reality can become progressively myopic and an echo chamber within which the person would reside while the panopticon TV creates the comfortable media space for the person.

This future is increasingly realistic since the function of TV as the bearer of the programs offered "over the air" or even through the cable system that became common place in the 1980s is quickly shifting. In many parts of the World, there is the increasing tendency to "cut the cord" and get rid of the cable delivery of programming. Cable companies are increasingly facing a threat where the centrality of program delivery by cable is being replaced by program delivery via the Internet. Numerous companies such as Amazon, Roku, and Apple are offering accessories that could be connected to the TV and program would be delivered through the connection of the accessory to the Internet. Thus, a Roku "stick" can connect to the Internet and the programs would be offered by Roku in collaboration with other content aggregators such as Sling, YouTube, Hulu to name a few. In some cases, a complete ecosystem is produced by a company like Amazon that would offer the accessory for the TV, a household voice activated information retrieval system such as Alexa, and content through the vast store of content that Amazon owns. As the user is migrating to these options, the user is also required to share information through the conduit of the TV with all these different corporations that continue to watch the watcher. It is indeed a World of constant surveillance, whenever the TV is switched on.

REFERENCES

Bentham, J. (1995). The Panoptic Writings. London: Verzo.

Bentham, J. (1962a). Principles of Penal Law. In (John Bowring, Ed.), The Works of Jeremy Bentham: Volume I, 365-580. New York: Russell and Russell.

Bentham, J. (1962b). The Rationale of Evidence. In (John Bowring, Ed.), The Works of Jeremy Bentham: Volume I, 201-585. New York: Russell and Russell.

Fisher, W. R. (1984). Narration as Human Communication Paradigm: The Case of Public Moral Argument, Communication Monographs, 51, 1–22.

Foucault, M. (1979). Discipline and Punish: The Birth of the Prison. New York: Advantage Books.

Klapper, J.T. (1960). The effects of mass communications. Oxford, England: Free Press of Glencoe.

Kozloff, S. (1992). Narrative Theory and Television. In (R. Allen, Ed.) Channels of Discourse Reassembled. Chapel Hill: U of North Carolina Press.

Lyon, D. (1994). The Electronic Eye: The Rise of Surveillance Society. Minneapolis, MN: University of Minnesota Press.

Lyon, D. (2003). Surveillance as Social Sorting. New York: Routledge.

Lyon, D. (2006). Theorizing Surveillance: The Panopticon and Beyond. Devon: Willan.

Manokha, I. (2018). Surveillance, Panopticism, and Self-Discipline in the Digital Age. Surveillance & Society 16(2): 219-237.

Sherwell, P. and Barnett, L. (2013). Barack Obama 'approved tapping Angela Merkel's phone 3 years ago.' The Telegraph.

Thorburn, D. (1976). Television Melodrama. In (R. Adler, Ed.) Television as a Cultural Force, 77-94. New York: Praeger.

PRIVACY IN BRAZIL: ANALYSIS ON THE NEW LAW ON DATA PROTECTION

Eduardo Helfer de Farias and Gabriel Rached
Fluminense Federal University
Niterói/RJ, Brazil

ABSTRACT

Law nº 13.709/18 established a new legal basis on data protection in Brazil. Inspired by the General Data Protection Regulation of the European Union, this new legislation introduces new concepts, actors and tools to assure the enforceability of rights by the common citizen under Brazilian jurisdiction. However, the impacts this law may produce is still unclear and cannot be foreseen yet. This paper aims to introduce its key topics, discussing how the enforceability issues may arise, given the Brazilian legislation background. As final remarks, some possibilities for the next scenarios in Brazil are also taken into consideration.

KEYWORDS

Brazil, Data Protection, Privacy, LGPD

1. INTRODUCTION

Privacy is a right protected by Brazil's Federal Constitution of 1988 in its article 5, X, therefore, its especially protected by the public authorities of the country. In order to enforce this right given the current reality of data sharing, Brazilian National Congress approved on 14 August 2018 the law nº 13.709/18 (Câmara dos Deputados do Brasil, 2018), labelled "Data Protection General Law" ("LGPD" in Portuguese), which was inspired by the European GDPR (Cavalcante, 2018).

This paper will first present the legal aspects of the LGPD's "bill of rights" and then deal with practical issues regarding the enforceability of the law by those subjected to it.

2. BRAZILIAN DATA PROTECTION LAW: LEGAL ASPECTS

For the purpose of this paper, it shall be considered only the current status of the LGPD given the changes made by Law nº 13.853 of 8 July 2019, which is expected to come into force on 16 August 2020. For its understanding, its important to have in mind: (i) who is subjected to the law; (ii) what duties it imposes; (iii) who enforces the law; and (iv) the possible penalties of a violation of the law.

Art. 3 of the LGPD describes that anyone who (i) holds an establishment in Brazil; (ii) offer products or services to the Brazilian market; (iii) or register personal data of people currently in the country; shall be subjected to the law. Its relevant to note that to fall under the scope of the law it doesn't matter the nature of the person (natural person, company or government), the headquarters of the company, the physical location of the data, if it was collected online or offline, or even the nationality of the citizen. If one of these three criteria checks, there is a mandatory duty to follow the law (SILVA et al. 2019). The only exceptions to the scope – as for now – would be the ones described in art. 4 of the LGPD: private and non-economic goals; journalism and arts; public safety; national security; state security; or criminal investigation. There is a partial exception for academic purpose, which still requires the comply with art. 7 and 11 regarding the consent of the owner of the data for its processing, proper classification and guarantees against its misuse. Also, there is a conditional exception regarding data there is exclusively in traffic through the Brazilian borders, not being shared, collected or in any way processed within the country, except if the country to which the data is being sent have not a good standard of data protection.

For the purpose of the law, "establishment" can be any representation held within Brazilian borders, regardless if it is for business or not, physical or digital. Also, anyone doing trade with Brazilian market – even if itself is not within the country – shall be subject to the Brazilian law. As for data, there are three classifications for the concept in the art. 5: (i) personal data identifying or capable of identifying a natural person; (ii) sensible data regarding religion, political opinions, healthy, sexual life, genetics, race, among others; (iii) anonymous data over which technology is applied to make sure the person to whom it refers to cannot be identified given the current availability of technology. Important to that data regarding companies itself fall out of the scope of this law, given their protection under the intellectual property laws in Brazil.

Those subject to the LGPD should identify who, in their organization, is the "controller", person or company responsible for making decision about treatment of personal data; the "operator", person or company responsible for executing the orders of the controller; and the "commissionaire", responsible to be a channel of communication between the controller, the owners of the personal data and the Brazilian National Data Protection Agency ("ANPD" in Portuguese), still to be created.

Those who are dealing with the personal data – namely the controller and the operator – should perform duties to both the owners of the data and the ANPD. The main duty would be to get a consent of the data owners for a clear and specific purpose in the terms of art. 7, if the processing is not being due to mandatory reasons listed on the article. Once holding the personal data, the controller and the operator should still meet the demands of art. 18 upon request of the data's owners, namely: (i) confirmation of the existence of data; (ii) access to the data; (iii) correction of incomplete, wrong or outdated data; (iv) anonymization, block or termination of unnecessary or excessive or misused data; (v) portability of the data to another platform or company; (vi) termination of data, except if the company has to comply with regulatory measures, academic research or other cases of the law; (vii) information about with whom the controller shared the data; (viii) information about the possibility of denying consent and its consequences; (ix) enforce the revoke of consent by the data's owner. Upon the purpose for which the data was collected is reached or if so requested by the data's owner, the controller or operator should be able to delete the data in accordance with art. 16, unless the data is anonymized and kept for exclusive use of the controller or to meet some regulatory demands.

The ANPD has regulatory and police authority over personal data protection, being able to apply harsh penalties over those violating the law, may it be a 2% of the total revenue of the previous year or even 50 millions Brazilian reais. Besides, it may also determine the termination of the data stored, publicize the infraction or, in a less serious case, just give a notification. The ANPD may request the controller to handle reports about the consequences of his operations to the personal data held by him. These reports, in accordance with art. 38, should describe the data held, the methodology used to collect it, the safety measures and the analysis of the controller about possible risks.

After this brief overview of the law, the next chapter shall deal with the practical aspects of its enforceability.

3. TWO PRACTICAL ISSUES TO COMPLY WITH THE LGPD

In order to comply with the LGPD there will be two main practical issues to deal with: (i) possible conflicts of interpretation with the GDPR and other legislations; and (ii) the standard proceedings for collecting, managing and terminating personal data in accordance with the possible demands of the data's owner or ANPD.

The scope of application of the law will certainly have conflict with the GDPR, creating situations in which both laws are equally applied. It probably will not be something easily dealt with by the standard conflicts of laws proceedings, given the enforceability issue and the international way through which data flows. Despite the LGPD being inspired in the GDPR, there is no guarantee the country shall follow the interpretation of the GDPR in every case. To address this issue, the LGPD in its art. 33 prevents international data transfer if not to "countries with reasonable data protection standards". What are these "reasonable standards" is open to be defined by the ANPD in accordance with art. 34. This strategy points to Brazil's openness to a global regulation on the issue, as once expressed by former president Dilma Rousseff on her speech to the United Nations (Passarinho, 2013).

In order to meet the LGPD demands, the data treatment agents must (i) be sure to have the consent of the data's owner; (ii) be aware of the data they possess; (iii) who has access to the data; (iv) terminate the data, once the goal is reached or upon request of the data's owner; and (v) be able to provide full reports of the risks the data is exposed.

Given the objective responsibility of the law, the burden of proving the consent of the owner was well informed falls under the data treatment agents. On this issue, is important to specify what kind of data is being collected – in special if it falls under the sensitive data classification – and explain how, by whom and for which purpose the data will be used. The in-company management of data will imply a big cultural change. For example, many companies are not aware of the data they possess, where and how it is stored, let alone have a clear control of who has or should have access to this data. For example, in a draft of an appeal inside a law firm in favor of a client, documents holding sometimes very sensible data are shared in a chain of emails and forgotten there after the appeal is done. Usually, there is no policy for disposing of the data stored in those emails, even after the purpose is fulfilled or the business relation is terminated. The same goes for former employee's data, or for phone messages and calls, which might be forgotten in old digital or physical archives.

The advised preliminary safeguard measures would be: (i) the adoption of policy of work based on "as-need-to-know" basis, in order to avoid unauthorized access to data; (ii) the programmed anonymization or termination of data after its purpose is served or upon request; (iii) a dashboard capable of effectively receiving the demands of the data's owner or ANPD and quickly granting their request. Other measures might be adopted, case by case, depending on the business model and the evolution of technology.

4. CONCLUSION

The Data Protection Law in Brazil is one of the steps in the ongoing changing rules process on the digital world. More and more, the regulation of this market is moving from internet giants to the states. However, despite the technical quality of the writing of the law, it is still unclear if Brazil will take the necessary measures to enforce its rights. It's common in Latin America countries that public policies do not live up to the expectations rose by the laws, due to political, financial or technical contexts. Brazilians define such laws as "lei que não pega", meaning that, despite being formally approved, they will never really come into force.

Given that the issue is still on going and that the law has not came into force yet, it's not possible to make long term predictions. However, the key players to be observed in order to anticipate legal and technical problems regarding the personal data policy in Brazil would be: (i) the ANPD; and (ii) the internet giants.

It is unclear the modus operandi that shall be followed by the ANPD, but it is expected to follow the standard stablished by the GDPR. This tendency is even more visible given the emphasis given by the Brazilian law in international cooperation and international standards. On the other hand, the country has been going through a wave of nationalism and it is not clear if this might affect the future following up of foreign standards. The fact that the law was significantly changed twice before even coming into force reflects not just the controversy of the political spectrum, but also of the issue itself. The composition of the ANPD shall be decisive in observing how this institution will behave.

By the other side, the internet giants such as Google and Facebook have been adapting themselves to the policies of the GDPR and are likely to export these practices to Brazil and other countries. Smaller companies and those whose main business is not directly related to data management shall follow the standard of these two as a precaution, avoiding spending to much energy in something bigger players have already a policy for.

REFERENCES

Câmara dos Deputados do Brasil. Projeto de Lei nº 4.067/2012. Available in https://www.camara.leg.br/proposicoesWeb/fichadetramitacao?idProposicao=548066 . Date of access: 16 June 2019.

Cavalcante, Sóstenes, 2018. Report of the Project of Law nº 4.060/2012. Comissão de Ciência e Tecnologia, Comunicação e Informática da Câmara dos Deputados do Brasil. Brasília, Brasil, Available in https://www.camara.leg.br/proposicoesWeb/prop_mostrarintegra?codteor=1454623&filename=Tramitacao-PRL+1+CCTCI+%3D%3E+PL+4060/2012 . Date of access: 16 June of 2019.

Constituição Federal Da República Federativa Do Brasil de 1988. Available in http://www.planalto.gov.br/ccivil_03/constituicao/constituicao.htm. Date of access: 16 June 2019.

LGPD. Lei Brasileira Sobre Proteção De Dados Pessoais – Lei nº 13.709/18. Available at: http://www.planalto.gov.br/ccivil_03/_Ato2015-2018/2018/Lei/L13709.htm. Date of Access: 16 June 2019

Núcleo De Estudos e Pesquisas Do Senado Federal. Sumário executivo da medida provisória nº 869. Available at: https://www.congressonacional.leg.br/materias/medidas-provisorias/-/mpv/135062 Date of Access: 16 June 2019

Presidência da República do Brasil. Medida Provisória nº 869 de 2018. Available at: https://www.congressonacional.leg.br/materias/medidas-provisorias/-/mpv/135062. Data of Access: 16 June 2019

Passarinho, Natália. Dilma diz na ONU que espionagem fere a soberania e o direito internacional. Published at: http://g1.globo.com/mundo/noticia/2013/09/dilma-diz-na-onu-que-espionagem-fere-soberania-e-direito-internacional.html. Date of Access: 16 June 2019

Silva, Priscilla; Magrani, Eduardo; Affonso, Carlos; Viola, Mário. Introdução à lei brasileira de proteção de dados. Published at: https://mooc.escolavirtual.gov.br/course/view.php?id=3020. Data of Access: 16 June 2019

POSTERS

AN OPINION MINING MODEL BASED ON USER PREFERENCES

Manuela Angioni, Andrea Devola, Mario Locci and Franco Tuveri
Center for Research and Scientific Studies in Sardinia, Bld. 1, Piscina Manna, Pula, Cagliari, Italy

ABSTRACT

This paper proposes an Opinion Mining model, parameterized according to the reviewer profile. The work aims to highlight and resolve some issues resulting from previous activities in evaluating the goodness of the results obtained by the analysis of the reviews. A user profiling system provides the set of parameters to associate with the aspects and allows, working with the Opinion Mining system, to configure itself according to the user preferences.

KEYWORDS

Opinion Mining, Opinion Summarization, NLP, Semantic Categorization

1. INTRODUCTION

In a previous work (Angioni et al., 2016), we have proposed an ensemble of aspect-based Opinion Mining algorithms, using a lexicon-based approach, with a Matrix Factorization to improve the prediction of results in a recommendation system. In this context, we realized that it is necessary to adopt a user profiling system, applied to the user-related data, in order to avoid the differences expressed by the evaluators and the reviewers in the evaluation of the reviews and in the rating expressed. It is thus more likely that evaluators and reviewers having similar profiles express similar ratings about the same reviews. The user profiling system provides the set of parameters to associate with the aspects and it allows the Opinion Mining system to configure itself according to the user preferences. The analysis of the reviews has highlighted that users base their criticism on few aspects. In addition, different users focus on particular aspects rather than others. In our opinion, when a user is interested in a specific aspect spends more sentences to describe it. It is thus possible to capture the interest of a user by weighting their interests through the aspects he is talking about. The paper describes an Opinion Mining model, parameterized according to the user profile.

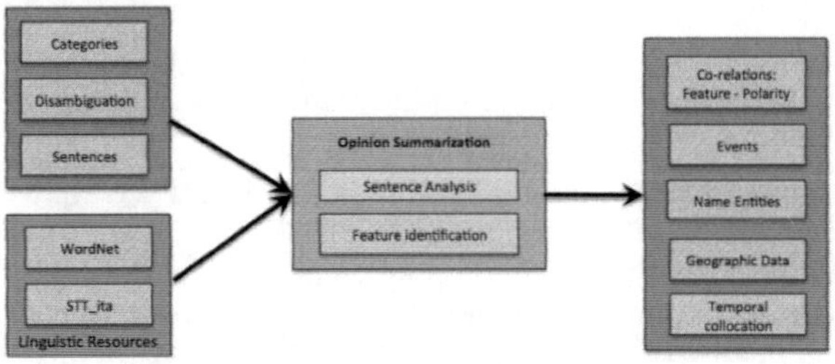

Figure 1. Opinion Summarization schema

The analysis of the reviews is illustrated in Figure 1, where are represented the linguistic resources, based on WordNet, used to perform the analysis and the text categorization, the semantic disambiguation and the analysis of sentences. In the Opinion Summarization phase the sentences are divided into subjective, usually expressing opinions, and objective. The identification of the features within the sentences allows associating the opinions to the aspects on which to focus the attention. A fundamental element is the features-polarity correlation, that allows evaluating the reviews. The Opinion Summarization phase is performed, through it, calculating the orientation, positive or negative, and referring it to the features or its attributes.

2. DATA ANALYSIS

To test the functionality of the Opinion Mining system, a demonstrator has been developed that, using reviews related to a collection of films, is able to extract contextual information and features from textual resources. Some filters facilitate the consultation of reviews by offering the user only those of real interest or to generate and represent summaries in an effective and more immediately readable format.

The data used for the demo are the result of the integration of the information extracted from two different datasets: the "Movies and TV" dataset (He and McAuley, 2016) (McAuley et al., 2015), provided by Amazon in "json" format, and a subset of the IMDb database (Internet Movie Database, available at https://www.imdb.com/interfaces/) to supplement the data extracted from the Amazon DB.

A new database was thus built from the integration of the two original datasets, containing, for each film a limited number of reviews selected on the basis of their length and referred to 6 film genres: Thriller, Horror, Comedy, SciFi, Western and Drama. From the analysis of the reviews of the films, 6 main aspects have been identified: Picture, Sound, Script, Awards, Director, Actor/Actress, with a set of key terms, called features, mostly used in order to describe each aspect. The features are the terms of the reviews referred to the six aspects above mentioned and extracted with a procedure already described in (Angioni and Tuveri, 2011). The features, mapped on the aspects, are inserted in a database table.

2.1 Semantic Analysis

The semantic analysis of the movie reviews is carried out through a linguistic approach that involves the use and the implementation of different tools and proceeds through different phases, as shown in Figure 2.

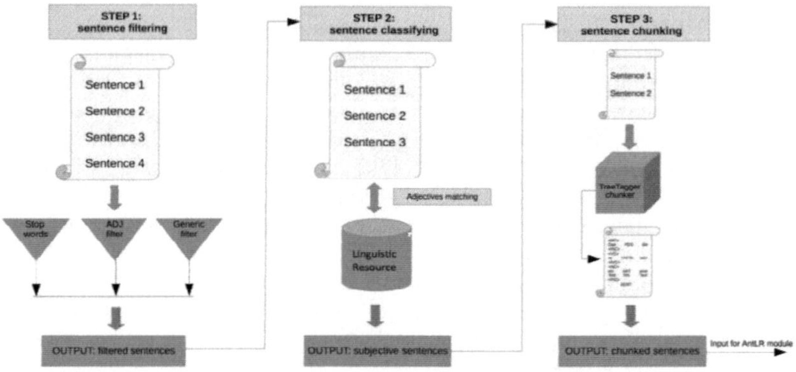

Figure 2. Text Analysis

2.1.1 Sentence Filtering

The sentence filtering is the first step of the analysis process of the reviews. It involves the identification of the sentences that compose a review. In this step the individual sentences are filtered, both through generic and specific filters, with the aim of searching for certain words or categories of words. As result, the portion of text to be analyzed is restricted due to the lower number of sentences to be analyzed.

The sentences are processed by several filters, some generic and some more specific, like the *adjective_filter*, named ADJ_filter, that allows the search for adjectives in each sentence received in input, or the *stopwords_filter*, for the identification of the stopwords. Purpose of those filters is to sift through the text of the sentence in search of certain words or categories of words, which will contribute to restrict the portion of text to be analyzed or the number of sentences to be considered. The ADJ_filter plays in this step a key role, as we'll see in the following step. The output, consisting of a small number of selected sentences, is used as input for the next phase of classification of the sentences.

2.1.2 Sentence Classifying

The sentences, selected in the Step 1, are now classified in order to distinguish between "subjective sentences", which express a personal opinion, and "objective sentences". The classification takes place through the following steps:

- given a sentence, to which the "adjective filter" was previously applied, it is verified that this adjective is included in the available linguistic resource;
- if the match occurs, the sentence can be selected, and cataloged as a sentence with polarity;
- if the match does not occur, the sentence is discarded.

At the end of this phase, only the subjective sentences will be selected and pass to the last step.

2.1.3 Sentence Chunking

In the Step 3, the Chunk Analysis module analyzes the subjective sentences of the reviews. The Chunker is able to associate the terms, identified as features, with its attributes, that are the adjectives and the adverbs having subjective value in the sentence. In this phase, the TreeTagger Chunker (TTC) (Schmid, 1994) has been used. The text processed by the chunker is provided, in form of chunks, to ANTLR (Another Tool for Language Recognition, available at https://www.antlr.org/), a parser generator that performs the chunk analysis. For this purpose a grammar, described by a number of rules, has been defined. The rules allow analyzing the chunks identifying adjectives, adverbs, and verbs in a number of combinations by a given pattern. By providing the system with the ability to syntactically and semantically analyze sentences written in natural language, it is possible to support the collection of subjective opinions relating to the aspects and the features that characterize a text. Then the polarity value relative to each adjective and adverb connected to the features is calculated, through the polarity values expressed in SentiWordNet (Baccianella et al., 2010). For each review, the polarity values will be calculated for each of the aspects considered. The overall assessment is made through the computation of a score, based on the relevance of each aspect and calculated according to the terms associated with them. The result is weighted according to the user preferences: the user profile will influence in this way the film proposed by the application.

3. CONCLUSION

The work presented in this paper will carry on mainly through the integration of the text analysis module, composed by the Chunk Analysis and the Feature Evaluation, with the parameterization of results based on user profiles. We are working on the integration of the software modules that will lead to a test phase and to the evaluation of the results.

REFERENCES

Angioni, M., Tuveri, F., 2011. A Semantic Approach to the Extraction of Feature Terms. *ICSOFT 2011, 6th International Conference on Software and Data Technologies*.

Angioni, M., Clemente, M.L., Tuveri, F., 2016. Improving Predictions with an Ensemble of Linguistic Approach and Matrix Factorization. *Web Information Systems and Technologies*, Springer Valérie Monfort, Karl-Heinz Krempels, Tim A. Majc, vol. 246, Lecture Notes in Business Information Processing, pp. 169-190.

Baccianella, S., Esuli, A., Sebastiani, F., 2010. SentiWordNet 3.0: An Enhanced Lexical Resource for Sentiment Analysis and Opinion Mining. In *Proceedings of LREC-10, 7th Conference on Language Resources and Evaluation.* Valletta, MT, pp. 2200-2204.

R. He, J. McAuley, 2016. Ups and downs: Modeling the visual evolution of fashion trends with one-class collaborative filtering. In *Proceedings of the 25th International Conference on World Wide Web (WWW '16).* pp. 507-517.

J. McAuley, C. Targett, J. Shi, A. van den Hengel, 2015. Image-based recommendations on styles and substitutes. *SIGIR*.

Schmid, H., 1994. Probabilistic Part-of-Speech Tagging Using Decision Trees. *Proceedings of International Conference on New Methods in Language Processing*. Manchester, UK.

Beck, K. and Ralph, J., 1994. Patterns Generates Architectures. *Proceedings of European Conference of Object-Oriented Programming.* Bologna, Italy, pp. 139-149.

INTERACTIVE AUDIO-TEXT GUIDE FOR MUSEUM ACCESSIBILITY

Gavino Paddeu, Andrea Devola, Andrea Ferrero and Antonio Pintori
Center for Research and Scientific Studies in Sardinia, Bld. 1, Piscina Manna, Pula, Cagliari, Italy

ABSTRACT

In this paper we discuss the basic architecture of a Web based information retrieval application using natural language question-answering system. The application is designed to improve the inclusiveness process. We focus on the production of audio-textual guides to make the exhibition experience accessible even by people with disabilities.

KEYWORDS

Interactive Audio Text Guide, Design for All, Museum Accessibility, Sensory Impairment, Natural Interaction, Edutainment

1. INTRODUCTION AND STATE OF THE ART

In this paper, we highlight the basic features to develop an inclusive Web-application for museum visitors. We have exploited the principle of universal design introduced by Dimitrova-Radojichikj, (2017) which improves the visiting experience for people with disabilities, e.g. blind and deaf people. Museums and art exhibitions are changing their look and feel: they are migrating from a traditionally based offer, which is a passive observation of art, to an immersive perception involving all the five senses. Artworks should be accessible to everyone. We found that the usual adopted mitigations, e.g. audio guides, tactile routes, guides in relief, description of artwork and information written in Braille, have obvious limitations: a traditional audio guide may not be beneficial for deaf people; some researchers have proposed specific solutions aimed at the visually impaired: Bliek, H. (2019) have shown a tactile approach by proposing a representation of a painting by 3D printing accompanied by an audio guide; Andreas Reichinger et al (October 2016) have proposed the possibility of exploring the work with the fingers, i.e. using a system based on recent low-cost depth cameras that operates directly on relief surfaces.

2. DESCRIPTION

The developed prototype improves the state-of-the-art by combining the use of a natural language conversational engine with an interactive tactile table to assist visually and hearing impaired people. The system interacts with the user in real-time: it is able to answer user's questions both in oral written form, while the user can explore the tactile-table (3D table in relief) representing the exposed artwork.

Our system is studied and developed for people with sensory impairments and it aims to combine the tactile experience with the sound and textual experiences in a single application, according to universal design (or design for All).

Figure 1 shows the overall of the system:

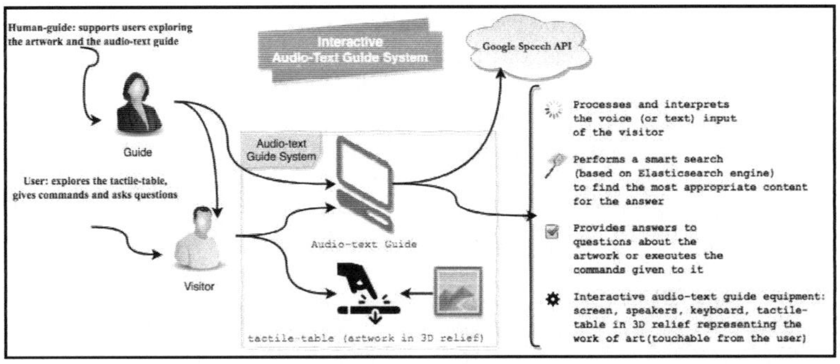

Figure 1. Audio-text guide System

The user can also explore the 3D table in relief: the system recognizes which portion is touched by means of tactile sensors inserted in the table; the audio-text guide gives a feedback customizing the content of the message based on the tactile exploration of the user, informing him or her (by voice or text) about which part of the artwork he is touching. The application supports the visually impaired (through oral exposure) as well as hearing impaired people (through the answers provided by text on screen): the user approaches the artwork with our system, equipped with video, keyboard, speakers and the tactile table. With his hands the user can touch the tactile board, which represents in 3D relief reproduction of the artwork. For the hearing impaired people the screen shows the text output of the audio-text guide and the keyboard allows the composition of questions.

The guide is also able to recognize simple oral and written commands: e.g., the current time, turn on or off the background music, or silencing the audio guide.

The Web application is developed in Javascript; it implements an audio-text guide, and it uses two main tools: the Google Speech API and Elasticsearch (it is also supported by some Node.js modules we have written).

3. CONVERSATIONAL ENGINE AND INTERACTIVE TACTILE-TABLE 3D

For the realization of our audio-text guide we have thought of a prototype of a conversational engine, resulting from the studies in the NLP field and related to Speech to Text and Text to Speech topics. It exploits the potential of Elasticsearch, with full-text capability, which has been specifically configured so that it can easily create a match between the question asked by the user and the contents of a database.

We used ElasticSearch queries, as shown in Figure 2. The list of questions (related to the artwork) and possible answers provided has been stored in JSON format. The adopted JSON format distinguishes between mandatory information that must be presented to the user and optional information that might be presented to the user. Moreover, with the appropriate use of the boost option it is possible to assign different weights to different parts of the text.

```
  query: {
     bool: {
        must: [
{
              bool: {
              should: [
              {match: {question: {query: text, boost: 2}}},
                                      {match: {answer: text}}
                                  ]}},
      {
      bool: {
         should: [
           {match: {title: "Pinacoteca"}},
           {match: {title: card}}
                            ]}}]}}
```

Figure 2. ElasticSearch query

As already mentioned, the prototype includes an interactive tactile 3D table (containing the artwork in relief) that recognizes which part of it is touched and then informs the user via audio/textual feedback.

The interactive touch table was produced in three main stages: 1) Image acquisition and processing of the artwork. 2) Transformation of the 2D image into a 3D representation and simplification of the details (keeping the peculiar characteristics indicated by art experts). 3) Creation of the tactile table using a 3D printer. Figure 3 shows an example of such a table and its processing:

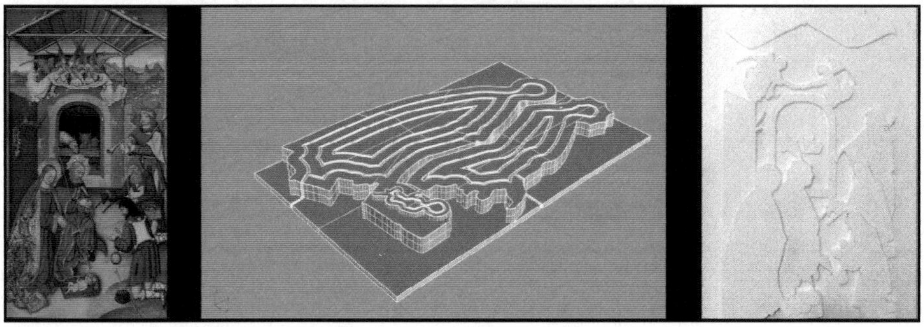

Figure 3. The artwork "Adorazione dei Pastori"; transformation into 3D representation; 3D printed table

4. TEST AND CONCLUSION

The prototype, being developed in collaboration with local and national museums and people with sensory disabilities, has been tested by fifteen people and partners of the project, by blind and able-bodied.
Each participant asked about twenty questions to the audio-text guide and we recorded every result.
First assessment gave a positive feedback showing 80% overall satisfaction.
We have planned a complete test to measure the benefits achieved with this work with a larger group of people.
The prototype will be available for testing during the conference, along with the poster for this article.

ACKNOWLEDGEMENT

This work is part of the Overtheview project, funded by POR FESR 2014/2020 funds, Priority Axis I "Scientific Research, Technological Development and Innovation".
Thanks to the "Polo Museale della Sardegna" and the "Pinacoteca Nazionale di Cagliari" for collaboration.

REFERENCES

Bliek, H. et al, 2019. *Making art accessible to visually impaired museum visitors*. Delft University of Technology, Delft, Netherlands.

Dimitrova-Radojichikj, D., 2017. Museums: Accessibility to visitors with visual impairment. Skopje, Republic of Macedonia, p. 2.

Elasticsearch, (https://www.elastic.co/).

Reichinger, A. et al, 2016. *A Concept for Re-useable Interactive Tactile Reliefs*. Wien, Austria.

DOCTORAL CONSORTIUM

IMPROVING E-CONSULTATION THROUGH DIGITAL CROWDSOURCING IN UGANDA: A QUANTITATIVE SURVEY

Elizabeth Asianzu
School of Computing and Informatics, College of Computing and Information Systems
Makerere University, Uganda

ABSTRACT

Information Communication Technology is identified by Uganda government as a key priority sector that will spur socio-economic transformation in the country. Unfortunately, ICT use for e-participation remains a challenge in Uganda. A pertinent issue with e-participation is e-consultation where citizens are expected to use ICT to access and participate in government programs. Despite government's efforts to increase ICT use by integrating it into its operations, minimal progress is recorded as e-consultation level remains low resulting in increase in corruption, lack of transparency and accountability. This study presents the prominent role of digital crowdsourcing in improving e-consultation in Uganda to be implemented using the ten-phase digital crowdsourcing implementation process with social media (Facebook) as a digital crowdsourcing tool. Using National Environmental Management Authority Facebook account to make an open call, randomly sampled participants will be availed self-administered, semi-structured, close-ended online questionnaires to identify the challenges and critical success factors for e-consultation. The participants will engage in the digital crowdsourcing process to address the problem of plastic waste pollution, a major eyesore globally. The major research outcome will be a consistent crowdsourcing implementation process that can be used to improve e-consultation in Uganda.

KEYWORDS

E-consultation, Challenges, Success Factors, Digital Crowdsourcing, Improvement

1. INTRODUCTION

Electronic consultation is viewed as the backbone and driver for electronic participation globally, (UN E-government Survey, 2016). E-participation is measured using e-information, e-consultation and e-democracy, (E-government Index, 2018). E-consultation is the engagement of citizens to contribute to and deliberate on public policies and services online (UN, 2018; E-government index, 2018; Sharma, 2014). It has globally grown from 73% in 2014 to 91% in 2016, (UN E-government Survey, 2016) with benefits in new policy decisions, regulation and development, (UN E-government Survey, 2016; Wakabi, 2016; Sharma, 2014). UN E-government Survey, (2016) articulates that while it is easier for governments to make progress in e-information stage by providing public information online, it is more challenging to engage in e-consultation and e-democracy yet they are very critical for e-participation.

Uganda suffers the same fate. While the country performs strongest in e-information at 73.5% resulting from government efforts to integrate Information Communication Technology (ICT) into its operations, there is minimal progress with e-consultation at 26.3% and zero implementation of e-decision making hence a decline in e-participation index from 0.4915 in 2016 to 0.36 in 2018, (E-government index, 2018). Further, Walugembe, (2018), Ipa, (2018) and Kugonza & Mukobi, (2015) emphasize the low citizen engagement by the government who sees it as secondary but not a priority thus presenting the urgent need for more investment in e-consultation, (UN E-government Survey, 2016). The current e-consultation strategies include use of websites, the Government-Citizen-Interaction-Center (GCIC) established in 2016, mobile apps, short messaging systems (SMS), social media (facebook and twitter) and putting up calls for public input into legislation, (E-government index, 2018; NDI, 2013).

These strategies present quite a number of challenges: the GCIC for e-consultation is still in its very early stages so its impact is not measured, only 19.5% of the Ministries, Departments and Agencies (MDA's) use SMS to collect queries/feedback/suggestions from the public, only 13% use mobile apps to offer services to citizens, (National IT Survey Report, 2018); government websites are irregularly updated, online information is not provided in reusable formats, websites suffer 'severe lack of information of public interest' and have several accessibility errors particularly to web browsers and special groups like people with disabilities (PWD's). Some government portals put up calls for input into legislation but 'the process lacks consistence' hence some laws are adopted without public input whereas for those with citizen inputs, they are often not adopted into policies/ laws. ICT use is majorly for government-to-government interaction but not government-citizen engagement, (E-government index, 2018; Wakabi, 2016). Further, the e-consultation tools used by government are 'one-way communication channels with queries and comments from citizens receiving no response,' (E-government Index, 2018), a poor type and quality of implementing participation where the tools cannot help citizens become drivers of change, (NDI, 2013). There is no implementation process from the social media guideline by National Information Technology Authority Uganda – NITA-U, (2019).

Uganda performs below the minimum e-consultation utilization level of 30% compared to other East African countries like Tanzania at 63% and below the global utilization level of 91%, (UN E-government survey, 2016). Consequently, there is increased corruption levels, bribery, lack of transparency and accountability by public officials where Uganda is ranked 149 out of 180 of the most corrupt countries in the world, (Transparency International Report, 2018). Further research is needed to examine the challenges of e-consultation, identify the critical success factors and propose a strategy to be implemented to address the problem of low e-consultation. This research contributes to filling these gaps and proposes digital crowdsourcing as a tool to improve e-consultation, (Haltofova, 2018) to be implemented using social media using the 11 step-process model for digital crowdsourcing implementation by Amrollahi (2016) to address the social problem of plastic waste pollution in Uganda.

Plastic waste pollution is a public concern and requires active participation of waste generators in the proper management of waste, (Kodwo et al, 2015). Globally, 79% of plastics is littered in the environment or accumulated in landfills, (Parker, 2017). In Uganda, plastic waste is the second largest part of solid waste at 37% to food remains at 38%. It affects Uganda's largest economy – agriculture which employs 75% of the population, (Edyegu 2018), generates 25% of Gross Domestic Product and accounts for 50% of all exports, (UBOS, 2017). 39,000 tons plastics are discarded in the environment annually due to poor waste disposal habits of the people, (Edyegu, 2018; Mukama et al, 2016) and lack of awareness on proper waste management, (World Bank Group 2017). As a result, 4,700 acres of agricultural land is becoming infertile annually, (Edyegu, 2018) leading to low average agricultural growth of only 2% annually which is below the desired level, (World Bank, 2018) and lower than the average annual GDP growth rate of 5.2% targeted under vision 2040 and 'far short of the 6% growth target for the agricultural sector set by African governments, (MAAIF Report 2016).

With the widespread rise in mobile networks and social media usage globally, (Créquit et al, 2018), the digital crowdsourcing tool can be used to address complex and dynamic societal challenges including plastic waste pollution problem that has adverse effects on agriculture, a major economy in most developing countries. Developing countries will benefit more as Srivastava & Mostafavi, (2018) state that in 'developing countries, crowdsourcing is still in its budding stage and not much research has been conducted there.' It can improve the e-participation index for the 39 countries that have low index of less than 0.25, 36 countries with middle index of 0.25-0.50 and 47 countries with high index of 0.50-0.75 (E-government Index, 2018) who perform very well in e-information stage but very poor in e-consultation.

2. CHALLENGES & SUCCESS FACTORS FOR E-CONSULTATION

Major e-consultation challenges in Uganda include curtailing of internet freedom using laws like Regulations on Interception of Communications Act, 2010; arrests and prosecution of some social media users who comment on matters they deem sensitive; absence of data protection and privacy laws, lack of access and affordability of ICT for the poor, rural and disadvantaged groups like women, PWDs and youth; failure to implement enabling laws and policies, (E-government Index, 2018). Fear of reprisals by citizens whose online presence is monitored by government, (Wakabi, 2016). High ICT and internet cost which remains a major hindrance to ICT access and use by citizens, lack of awareness of e-government services (National IT Survey Report, 2018).

Key factors that can increase citizen's uptake of e-consultation include privacy and security of citizens information, (Wakabi, 2016); equal public access and affordability of basic ICT knowledge and infrastructure; citizen trust in both the technology and government, (UN E-government Survey, 2016); age differences between the young and old; education levels; wealth difference between high and low income earners, (Jafarkarimi et al, 2014); citizen involvement in designing e-government services, (National IT survey report, 2018), enforcement of various ICT tools for e-consultation (E-government Index, 2018).

3. DIGITAL CROWDSOURCING FOR E-CONSULTATION

Digital crowdsourcing is the use of digital technologies to gather and organize contributions from a multitude of non-professional individuals in order to obtain innovative solutions or products, (Marzano & Lizut, 2017). It is a successful e-consultation tool, (Haltofova, 2018) that improves e-consultation by fostering participation and making citizens part of the solution, (Zambrano & Eymann 2014) resulting in transparency and accountability in governments, (Bott, Gigler and Gregor, 2014). The source of control between the organization and the online involved community differentiates digital crowdsourcing from other forms of online participatory culture and user-generated content activities like online problem-solving, (Brabham, 2013). Through the widespread usage of mobile networks and the rise of social media globally, digital crowdsourcing addresses complex global and dynamic challenges, (Créquit et al, 2018). In Uganda, mobile phones and the internet have become integrated into many people's professional, health, business and social lives with mobile phone ownership rate at 70.9%, (NITA, 2018). With 21, 648, 672 mobile internet subscribers in Uganda, (UCC, 2018), 2,600,000 Facebook subscribers, (Internet World Stats, 2019), digital crowdsourcing has the potential of improving e-consultation in Uganda with ready social media guidelines, however, the guideline lacks an implementation process.

The generic 11 step-process model for digital crowdsourcing implementation presented by Amrollahi (2016) will be adopted in this study excluding the granting award stage since this is not for rewarding the best solution but an outcome-based process. Social media is an important tool used for digital crowdsourcing, (Créquit et al, 2018) and Uganda recognizes it as 'part of the broader efforts to engage citizens' using Twitter and Facebook accounts to engage with its citizens (NITA-U, 2019).

4. RESEARCH METHODS

Deductive research approach, a close ally to the philosophy of positivism will be adopted, (Trochim 2006; Shahid, 2014) using quantitative methods, (Yilmaz, 2013 quotes Creswell, 1994); (Eyisi, 2016), cross-sectional descriptive survey (Yilmaz, 2013) using semi-structured, close-ended online questionnaire as the data collection tool tested for validity, (Muhammad et al, 2008) and reliability, (Lakshmi & Mohideen, 2013). Practical implementation of digital crowdsourcing to improve e-consultation will be achieved using the 11 step generic process by Amrollahi, (2016) as explained:

Conceptual design stage identifies tasks to be performed and these include identifying the challenges and critical success factors for e-consultation and addressing the problem of plastic waste pollution in Uganda under National Environment Authority Management Uganda, (NEMA). Participant selection stage: Facebook subscribers who are 2,600,000 (Internet World Stats, 2019) with 62.36% subscribers will be used as opposed to Twitter 9.97%, (Stats Counter, 2019). The technical design stage answers the question of how the digital crowdsourcing should be performed, either using an existing or a new designed platform. In this study, Facebook as an existing tool will be used. In the communication stage, NEMA's Facebook account https://www.facebook.com/NemaUg/, (NITA-U, 2019) will be used to invite as many facebook subscribers as possible through an open call, advertisement media and direct correspondence with subscribers on facebook to participate in the study. According to Morgan's table for sample size presented by The Research Advisors, (2010), for a population of 250,000 to 300,000,000, the sample size is 384 respondents at confidence of 95% and 5% margin of error. Therefore, a total of 384 respondents will be randomly selected from the population of 2,600,000 facebook subscribers who will respond to the call and be trained for the task. In the idea/task entry phase, the selected respondents will start to interact through the NEMA facebook account with regard to the specific tasks. In the monitoring phase, the researcher and team from NEMA responsible for managing the facebook account will coordinate the crowd, manage the time for posting tasks, response time and sanction inappropriate entries.

The idea/task revision stage will focus on management of errors from submissions while the submission of entries will be evaluated based on the criteria. Since the crowdsourcing is contribution-based and outcome-based, there will be no rewards to participants hence no granting award phase. In the process evaluation and documentation phase, lessons learnt from this digital crowdsourcing implementation will be documented; future practices will be arranged with plans to retain the participants based on the outcome of the process. In the implementation phase, results from the plastic waste pollution solutions will be presented, analyzed and implemented by the researcher through NEMA.

In conclusion, despite government efforts, e-consultation in Uganda remains low. However, e-consultation presents a huge opportunity for citizen participation in Uganda that will help address key challenges facing the economy. Digital crowdsourcing is expected to improve e-consultation given the high number of internet and facebook subscribers in Uganda. This can only be achieved with a favorable online environment that creates citizen trust in technology and government with properly and carefully implementing digital crowdsourcing using clearly set and realistic objectives and communicating them to all parties concerned.

REFERENCES

Amrollahi, A. (2016). A Process Model for Crowdsourcing: Insights from the Literature on Implementation, *Australasian Conference on Information Systems* https://www.researchgate.net/publication/303281353

Barazzetta, S. (2015). Plastic waste management in Africa: lessons from social enterprises, accessed on 1st September, 2018 thru https://www.researchgate.net/publication

Bott, M., Björn-Sören G. & Gregor, Y. (2014). The Role of Crowdsourcing for Better Governance in Fragile State Contexts. World Bank Publications. http://wbi.worldbank.org/

Brabham, C. D. (2013). Using Crowdsourcing in Government. IBM Center for the Business of Government. Accessed thru www.businessofgovernment.org

Créquit, P., Mansouri, P., Benchoufi, M., Vivot, A. & Ravaud, P. (2018). Mapping of Crowdsourcing in Health: Systematic Review, J Med Internet Res *2018; 20(5): e187 Vol 20, No 5*

Edyegu, D. (2018). Uganda Grapples with Plastic Pollution. American Media Institute, accessed on 15th October 2018 thru https://aminewswire.org/stories/3182/

E-government Index, (2018). State of open e-government index Uganda https://cipesa.org/?wpfb_dl=255

Eyisi, D. (2016). The Usefulness of Qualitative and Quantitative Approaches and Methods in Researching Problem-Solving Ability in Science Education Curriculum. *Journal of Education and Practice*, Vol.7, No.15, https://files.eric.ed.gov/fulltext/EJ1103224.

Haltofova, B. (2018). Using Crowdsourcing to Support Civic Engagement in Strategic Urban Development Planning: A Case Study of Ostrava, Czech Republic, *Journal of Competitiveness,* Vol. 10, Issue 1, pp. 85 - 103, June 2018. Internet World Stats, (2019). Internet Users Statistics for Africa, https://www.internetworldstats.com/stats1.htm

Ipa, (2018). Strengthening Local Political Accountability in Uganda. https://www.poverty-action.org/study/

Jafarkarimi, H., Sim, A., Saadatdoost, R. & Hee M.J. (2014). The Impact of ICT on Reinforcing Citizens' Role in Government Decision Making. *International Journal of Emerging Technology and Advanced Engineering* Website: www.ijetae.com, Volume 4, Issue 1

Kugonza, S. & Mukobi, R. (2015). Public participation in services delivery projects in Buikwe District Local Government Uganda. *Commonwealth Journal of Local Governance* https://epress.lib.uts.edu.au/journals/index.php/cjlg/

Kodwo, M., Kwasi O., Zsófia K., Bernard F., & Moses Y. M. (2015) Waste Management: Municipal solid waste characterization and quantification as a measure towards effective waste management in Ghana www.elsevier.com/locate/wasman pg15–27

Lakshmi, S & Mohideen, M., A. (2013). Issues in Reliability and Validity of Research. *International Journal of Management Research and Review* Ijmrr/ April 2013/ Volume 3/Issue 4/Article No-8/2752-2758, http://ijmrr.com/admin/upload_data/journal_S_Lakshmi__8apr13mrr.pdf

Marzano, G. & Lizut, J. (2017). Urban Crowdsourcing: Potential and Challenges. *Geographic Information Systems Conference and Exhibition.* https://www.researchgate.net/publication/

Ministry of Agriculture, Animal Industry and Fisheries (MAAIF), Report, (2016). Draft Agriculture Sector Strategic Plan 2015/16-2019/20. Accessed on 9th November 2018 thru http://npa.ug/wp-content/uploads/2016/

Mukama, T., Ndejjo R., Musoke, D., Musinguzi, G., Halage, A. A., Carpenter D. O. & Ssempebwa, J. C. (2016). Practices, Concerns, and Willingness to Participate in Solid Waste Management in Two Urban Slums in Central Uganda. Journal of Environmental and Public Health Volume 2016

Muhammad, B., Muhammad, T., A, and Muhammad, A. (2008). Reliability and Validity of Qualitative and Operational Research Paradigm, Vol. IV No.1, 35-45

National IT Survey Report, (2018). National IT Survey 2017/2018 Report. Accessed thruhttps://www.nita.go.ug/sites/default/files/publications/National%20IT%20Survey%April%2010th.pdf

National Information Technology Authority Uganda - NITA-U, (2019). Government of Uganda Social Media Guide, https://www.nita.go.ug/sites/default/files/pdf

National Information Technology Authority - NITA, (2018). National Information Technology Survey 2017/2018 Report, https://www.nita.go.ug/sites/default/files/

National Democratic Institute - NDI, (2013). Citizen Participation and Technology. Uganda Country Context: pg 41. https://www.ndi.org/sites/default/files/Citizen-Participation-and-Technology-an-NDI-Study.pdf

Parker, L. (2017). Here's How Much Plastic Trash is Littering the Earth, national geographic society, accessed on 1st

September, 2018 thru https://news.nationalgeographic.com

Shahid, N. K. (2014). Qualitative Research Method – Phenomenology. *Asian Social Science;* Vol. 10, No. 21. https://pdfs.semanticscholar.org/1478/abd02eb468f4639ee9af11c49c9322673957.pdf

Srivastava, P. & Mostafavi, A. (2018). Challenges and Opportunities of Crowdsourcing and Participatory Planning in Developing Infrastructure Systems of Smart Cities, Infrastructures 2018, 3, 51.

Stats Ccounter, (2019). Social Media Stats Uganda. http://gs.statcounter.com/social-media-stats/all/uganda

The Research Advisors, (2010). Sample Size Table. Accessed thruhttps://shodhganga.inflibnet.ac.in/bitstream/10603/154745/20/20_appendix%203.pdf

Transparency International Report, (2018). Uganda Corruption Index. https://www.transparency.org/country/UGA

Trochim, W., M., K. (2006). Web Center for Social Research Methods: Research Methods Knowledge Base http://www.socialresearchmethods.net/

Uganda Communications Commission - UCC, (2018). Post, Broadcasting and Telecommunications Market & Industry Q3 Report, https://www.ucc.co.ug/wp-content/uploads/2017/09/

Uganda Bureau of Statistics (UBOS) (2017). Health status and associated factors, accessed thru https://uganda.unfpa.org

United Nations - UN, (2018). Gearing E-Government to Build Resilient Societies: Preconditions and Enabling Environment.

Annexes, https://publicadministration.un.org/

United Nations (UN) E-government survey, (2018). E-government Development Index: Uganda. https://publicadministration.un.org/egovkb/en-us/

United Nations (UN) E-government Survey, (2016). E-government in support of sustainable development https://books.google.co.ug/books?id=HE88DwAAQBAJ&pg=PT153&lpg=PT153&dq=e-consultation+figures+

Wakabi, W. (2016): Motivating eParticipation in Authoritarian Countries. Örebro Studies in Informatics https://www.diva-portal.org/smash/get/diva2:902111/FULLTEXT04.pdf

Walugembe, D. R. (2018). Engage citizens for better policy implementation, health information scientist. https://www.monitor.co.ug/OpEd/Commentary/

World Bank Group, (2017). Inclusive Innovations: Business Models for Integrated Waste Management, accessed thru https://www.innovationpolicyplatform.org/system/files/4%20Integrated%20Waste%20Manangement.pdf

Yilmaz, K. (2013). Comparison of Quantitative and Qualitative Research Traditions: epistemological, theoretical and methodological differences. *European Journal of Education,* Vol. 48, No. 2, https://pdfs.semanticscholar.org/f4

Zambrano, R. & Eymann, S. (2014). Crowdsourcing and Human Development: The Role of Governments. *Proceedings of the 8th International Conference on Theory and Practice of Electronic Governance ACM,* https://dl.acm.org/citation.cfm?id=269122